Utopia/Dystopia

Publication in partnership with
the Shelby Cullom Davis Center
at Princeton University

Other Books in the Series

Utopia/Dystopia

CONDITIONS OF HISTORICAL POSSIBILITY

Michael D. Gordin, Helen Tilley,
and Gyan Prakash, Editors

Princeton University Press ▪ Princeton and Oxford

Published by Princeton University Press,
41 William Street, Princeton, New Jersey 08540
In the United Kingdom: Princeton University Press,
6 Oxford Street, Woodstock, Oxfordshire OX20 1TW
press.princeton.edu

Library of Congress Cataloging-in-Publication Data

Utopia/dystopia : conditions of historical possibility / Michael D. Gordin, Helen Tilley, and
Gyan Prakash, editors.
    p. cm.
  Includes bibliographical references and index.
  ISBN 978-0-691-14697-3 (hbk. : alk. paper)—ISBN 978-0-691-14698-0 (pbk. : alk. paper)
    1. Utopias—History. 2. Dystopias—History.   I. Gordin, Michael D.   II. Tilley, Helen,
1968–   III. Prakash, Gyan, 1952–
  HX806.U777 2010
   335′.02—dc22   2010010267

British Library Cataloging-in-Publication Data is available
This book has been composed in Electra
Book designed by Marcella Engel Roberts
Printed on acid-free paper ∞
Printed in the United States of America

10 9 8 7 6 5 4 3 2 1

Contents

Utopia/Dystopia

Introduction

Michael D. Gordin, Helen Tilley,
and Gyan Prakash

Utopia and Dystopia beyond Space and Time

Utopias and dystopias are histories of the present. Even before we begin to explain that sentence, some readers may feel a nagging concern, for the very term "utopia" often sounds a little shopworn. It carries with it the trappings of an elaborate thought experiment, a kind of parlor game for intellectuals who set themselves the task of designing a future society, a perfect society—following the pun on the name in Greek (no place, good place: imaginary yet positive). Projecting a better world into the future renders present-day problems more clearly. Because utopias tend to be the products of scholars and bookworms, it is not surprising that from the time of the concept's (or at least the term's) formal birth in the Renaissance, it has attracted quite a bit of academic attention. Much of this history is easily accessible, even second nature, to intellectual historians, and it traces the genealogy of ideal, planned societies as envisaged from Plato to science fiction. The appeal and the resonances are obvious and rather powerful: religious roots in paradise, political roots in socialism, economic roots in communes, and so on. Ever since Thomas More established the literary genre of utopia in his 1516 work of that title, much of historians' writing on the relevance of utopia has focused on disembodied intellectual traditions, interrogating utopia as term, concept, and genre.[1]

Dystopia, utopia's twentieth-century doppelgänger, also has difficulty escaping its literary fetters. Much like utopia, dystopia has found fruitful ground to blossom in the copious expanses of science fiction, but it has also flourished in political fiction (and especially in anti-Soviet fiction), as demonstrated by the ease with which the term is applied to George Orwell's *1984*, Evgenii Zamiatin's *We*, and Aldous Huxley's *Brave New World*.[2] Despite the name, dystopia is not simply the opposite of utopia. A true opposite of utopia would be a society that is either completely unplanned or is planned to be deliberately terrifying and awful. Dystopia, typically invoked, is neither of these things; rather, it is a utopia that has gone wrong, or a utopia that functions only for a particular segment of society. In a sense, despite their relatively recent literary and cinematic invention, dystopias resemble the actual societies historians encounter in their research: planned, but not planned all that well or justly.[3] One need not be a cynic to believe that something in the notion of dystopia would be attractive and useful for historians of all stripes.

Every utopia always comes with its implied dystopia—whether the dystopia of the status quo, which the utopia is engineered to address, or a dystopia found in the way this specific utopia corrupts itself in practice. Yet a dystopia does not have to be exactly a utopia inverted. In a universe subjected to increasing entropy, one finds that there are many more ways for planning to go wrong than to go right, more ways to generate dystopia than utopia. And, crucially, dystopia—precisely because it is so much more common—bears the aspect of lived *experience*. People perceive their environments as dystopic, and alas they do so with depressing frequency. Whereas utopia takes us into a future and serves to indict the present, dystopia places us directly in a dark and depressing reality, conjuring up a terrifying future if we do not recognize and treat its symptoms in the here and now.[4] Thus the dialectic between the two imaginaries, the dream and the nightmare, also beg for inclusion *together*, something that traditional *Begriffsgeschichte* (conceptual history) would not permit almost by definition. The chief way to differentiate the two phenomena is with an eye to results, since the impulse or desire for a better future is usually present in each.

We confront, therefore, something of a puzzle, almost mathematical in nature: the opposite of dystopia seems to be utopia, but the converse does not hold. There is rather a triangle here—a nexus between the perfectly planned and beneficial, the perfectly planned and unjust, and the perfectly unplanned. This volume explores the zone between these three points. It is a call to examine the historical location and conditions of utopia and dystopia not as terms or genres but as scholarly categories that promise great potential in reformulating the ways we conceptualize relationships between the past, present, and future. But what unites these three poles with each other? To our mind, the central concept that links them requires excavating the "conditions of possibility"—even the "conditions of imaginability"—behind localized historical moments, an excavation that demands direct engagement with *radical change*. After all, utopias and dystopias by definition seek to alter the social order on a fundamental, systemic level. They address root causes and offer revolutionary solutions. This is what makes them recognizable. By foregrounding radical change and by considering utopia and dystopia as linked phenomena, we are able to consider just how ideas, desires, constraints, and effects interact simultaneously. Utopia, dystopia, chaos: these are not just ways of imagining the future (or the past) but can also be understood as concrete practices through which historically situated actors seek to reimagine their present and transform it into a plausible future. This is clearly *not* the way most historians who have engaged with the notions of utopia and dystopia have approached the issue, and it is worth taking a moment to explore the difference.

Historical attention to utopia and dystopia has been strikingly one-sided and consists of dominant leitmotifs without a thorough explanation of the conceptual space opened up by these categories. To cite one clear peculiarity of the literature: there is very little scholarship attempting to treat both notions together as intimately related acts of imagination.[5] The core interest for many of those who have already written about utopia and dystopia emphasizes the intellectual coherence (or incoherence) of the idea of specially planned space(s) or chronicles the rise and fall of particular experiments in utopia – albeit experiments ranging in scale from Brook Farm in Nathaniel Hawthorne's New England to Mao's Great Proletarian Cultural Revolution. There is much to be learned in such an approach, and we believe that we now have a quite rich and detailed understanding of the genealogies of utopias (at least for the Western tradition) and profound analyses of the ideologies underlying them.[6] It would be superfluous to retread this ground, and we do not propose to do so here. The manifest goal of this volume of essays—selected from the two-year seminar at the Shelby Cullom Davis Center for Historical Studies at Princeton University titled "Utopia/Dystopia"—is to revitalize the concepts of utopia and dystopia by treating them not so much as *objects* of study, but as *historically grounded analytic categories* with which to understand how individuals and groups around the world have interpreted their present tense with an eye to the future.

Such an analytic venture might seem peculiar at the present moment, which could justly be characterized as "beyond utopia."[7] Indeed, there is a direct connection between the demise of totalizing theories of social change and reality, including Marxism and positivism, and intellectuals' diminished faith in grand schemes "to improve the human condition."[8] Certainly, after the heady discourse of the "New World Order" died down following the collapse of Soviet communism and the end of the cold war, and sober reflection ensued on the dystopic qualities of the twentieth century (midwifed by Hitler, Mao, Pol Pot, Nixon, Stalin, Pinochet, and a cast of millions), the present appeared (and to many still appears) to be a time that called utopia into question.[9] We are done with such dreaming, so this story goes, and now focus on the present with more modest ambitions, no longer attempting to imagine majestic paradises. Perhaps. Yet large-scale planning of utopian or dystopian futures—whether by the World Trade Organization or Al Qaeda—persists, despite the unfashionableness of utopian thought in Western academia (and probably not only Western). Coming to grips with the impulse historically offers an opportunity to explore how much has changed, and how much has remained the same, in our present that is supposed to exist "beyond utopia."

This is a tall order, and it requires readers to let go of their conventional understandings of two major categories thinkers have used to analyze utopia to date: *space* and *time*. When one hears the word "utopia," one usually thinks of a space—typically a city, but not necessarily so—that has been organized and mapped out geographically. (In Thomas More's case, it was an island—although even in this case, the island was deliberately constructed by eradicating the isthmus that connected King Utopus's realm to the mainland—and this topographical feature does persist in many literary utopias.) Probing the concept a little more deeply, however, one sees that it implies not only spatial layout and distance—often great geographic distance—but also *time*. Utopias tend to be places of the future or, as in some earlier instances of utopias *avant la lettre*—the Land of Cockaigne, Hesiod's Golden Age, and the Garden of Eden—the distant past. Utopias (and dystopias) thus come laden already with conceptual anchors that fix them to specific space-time coordinates. This was, and is, surely one of the features of utopia/dystopia that explains its striking *realism*, its lasting pull on the intellect. But it also unnecessarily constrains the uses to which the historian can put it.

In our effort to reclaim utopia and dystopia as analytic categories of historical inquiry, we place space and time in the background and think instead of these phenomena as markers for *conditions of possibility*, understood in Michel Foucault's sense.[10] We hope to examine utopias (and dystopias) not for what they tell us about an intellectual construct in assorted individuals' heads, but rather for what they reveal about a set of abiding concerns and cultural formations that *generated* both the desire for utopian transcendence and the specific form that utopia/dystopia took. As such, utopias are not to be seen as referring to an imagined place at some future time; instead, we are interested in how the historian can use variants of utopian thinking and action to explore the specificity of a time and a place. Utopian visions are never arbitrary. They always draw on the resources present in the ambient culture and develop them with specific ends in mind that are heavily structured by the present. Heavily, but not totally, for in each instance the specific utopias produce consequences that force a questioning of the original vision and that shape both its development and how individuals experience it. Marxism, for example, emerged as a utopian form of thinking, but it did so initially in England in the context of industrialization; how Karl Marx and Friedrich Engels imagined their future utopia reflected directly and unambiguously on contemporary cultural perceptions of Victorian Manchester.[11] What we focus on, therefore, is utopia as a *practice*, as a technique used by historical actors for understanding their particular contemporary circumstances—and thus a valuable lens for the historian.[12]

Today, long after the rise and decline of structuralism and even post-structuralism, it is interesting to find this approach openly stated (and subsequently stubbornly neglected) in the classic of early sociology of knowledge, Karl Mannheim's *Ideology and Utopia*. For Mannheim, neither of these title terms refers to something that can be expressed as a mere concatenation of words, a document that can be read from beginning to end and then filed away. Rather, both ideology and utopia are *impulses* drawn directly from the sociological setting of individuals. Mannheim thus eschewed characterizations of utopia as an articulation of a planned ideal society and instead redefined it as a socially located critical stance. In the process, he emphasized some of the dilemmas involved in articulating and acting upon visions of radical change that this volume interrogates:

> The concept of *utopian* thinking reflects the opposite discovery of the political struggle, namely that certain oppressed groups are intellectually so strongly interested in the destruction and transformation of a given condition of society that they unwittingly see only those elements in the situation which tend to negate it. Their thinking is incapable of correctly diagnosing an existing condition of society. They are not at all concerned with what really exists; rather in their thinking they already seek to change the situation that exists. Their thought is never a diagnosis of the situation; it can be used only as a direction for action. In the utopian mentality, the collective unconscious, guided by wishful representation and the will to action, hides certain aspects of reality. It turns its back on everything which would shake its belief or paralyse its desire to change things.[13]

Or, as he put it more pithily: "The innermost structure of the mentality of a group can never be as clearly grasped as when we attempt to understand its conception of time in the light of its hopes, yearnings, and purposes."[14] By exhuming the aspirations of historically located actors, this volume seeks to meet Mannheim's challenge to present a series of partial histories of utopia/dystopia that will illuminate the subjective positionings of historical agents. Tell me what you yearn for, and I will tell you who you are.

In this volume we propose that a return to the crucial insights of the early generation of sociologists of knowledge such as Mannheim, coupled with the attention to discourse and practice that exemplifies recent scholarship inflected by post-structuralism, can breathe some new life into and bring new perspectives to historians' analytic categories.[15] To reiterate: this volume is *not* an effort to recast the historiography of utopia (or dystopia); instead, it is an attempt to import those categories as useful tools to probe different historical situations. We suggest, therefore, that readers think of utopia and dystopia (at least for the space of this volume) as styles of imagination, as approaches to radical change, and not simply as assessments of ambitious plans for social engineering that have positive (utopic) or negative (dystopic) results. Since those results would form an anachronistic imposition on the course of historical development—those doing the hoping and the dreaming could not possibly have clairvoyant knowledge of the outcome—we have decided to organize these chapters not along the lines of a section on utopia followed by a section on dystopia because this would obscure the very historical analysis we hope to uncover. Instead, we have opted to divide the essays in terms of two other modes of analysis: *anima* and *artifice*. As with utopia and dystopia, these terms are not exactly opposites; nor do they exist strictly in a binary relation. They are categories to begin to tease apart conditions of possibility.

Part 1: Anima

The first theme, anima, has several different inflections, all relating to human existence and its constraints. On the one hand, we are playing deliberately with the concept of natural limits, both actual and conjectural, and on the other we are invoking ideas of spirit and vision, that is, those things that animate different societies (and theories). There is often, as might be expected, an intimate relationship between the two. Our conceptualization, in fact, draws explicitly on the work of critical theorists, historians of science, and scholars in environmental history.[16] Anima conjures up both nature—including the first and second nature of Marxists—and those indeterminate elements that make up life itself, the exploration of which unites scientists, artists, and philosophers.

Utopia and dystopia in practice tend to test the boundaries of reality: the former approaches an ideal but rarely reaches it—stopped by the real world—and the latter makes visible various breaking points and vulnerabilities. Think, for instance, of the utopian project of disease eradication. For at least two centuries, this goal has seemed increasingly within the realm of the possible, yet in objective terms it has been achieved only once, with smallpox.[17] But has it really? In the expected twist from hope to horror, public health officials, critics, and scaremongers now help us appreciate the prospect that the remaining stores of the smallpox virus could become a weapon of bioterrorism.[18] In its dystopian inflection, eradication draws attention to the very frailties not just of the human form but of our moral codes as well. Anima ought to capture this interplay between life, with all its unpredictability, and the social systems we construct upon this ever-changing world.

Fredric Jameson begins his chapter by emphasizing the extent to which certain utopian visions have gone out of fashion, namely a belief in bourgeois progress and a faith in large-scale solutions. Implicitly he also reminds us that human survival is hardly a certainty. Whether the scenario is abrupt annihilation or merely the gradual erosion of ecological and social conditions that sustain life, nowhere in the world does he see viable alternatives that could confront these threats with sufficient force. For his purposes then, utopian projects are useful because they allow us to interrogate our own thinking and help us to understand the frontiers—and cobwebs—of our own imaginations. They are thus a means to historicize the present so that we can begin to conceive of new possibilities for the future. Jameson's two examples—Wal-Mart and the politics of the multitude—attempt to confront what he sees as a central obstacle within present-day utopian thought: "The difficulties in thinking quantity positively." Wal-Mart, for all its egregious and reprehensible practices, which have parallels elsewhere, possesses a kind of unparalleled emergent power, precisely because it purchases, prices, and distributes its wares on such a phenomenal scale. To lose sight of this potential is to miss an opportunity to grapple fully with alternative structures of production and consumption. The concept of multitude, in turn, similarly enables Jameson to discuss overpopulation and collectivity (as opposed to individualism) without insisting on casting either in terms of an inevitable loss of self. Rather than offer dismal Malthusian images or stoke anxieties about social degradation, he chooses to consider how mass culture produces new forms of resistance, political participation, and cultural literacy.

We should perhaps not be so surprised to see some of these issues surfacing in Jennifer Wenzel's chapter on competing millennial movements in mid-nineteenth-century South Africa. This was a pivotal moment in colonial conquest, when contests over land were intensifying, a time when Europeans' faith in their civilizing mission approached its zenith. At the heart of Wenzel's analysis is the 1856–57 Xhosa cattle killing, an event prompted by a young Xhosa woman's prophetic vision that their culture could be renewed if only the Xhosa themselves were willing to sacrifice their material security. According to the prophecy, once Xhosa believers had killed their cattle, destroyed their grain, and improved their moral relations, the ancestors would step in to replenish their stocks and drive both Europeans and unbelievers to the coasts. Their utopian ambitions, in other words, were an attempt to address their unstable reality in the face of an external onslaught. Yet these dreams, as Wenzel is quick to point out, existed alongside equally elaborate aspirations among missionaries and administrators, who also sought to make Xhosa worlds anew. Indeed, the tools they marshaled—guns, printing presses, and plows—were in many ways embedded in a symbolic and cultural framework that undermined Xhosa cosmologies at every turn. What the colonizers envisaged was total transformation: faith, land, and the social order would be entirely redefined. The tragic irony of Wenzel's story is that both prophecies went unrealized; the ancestors never appeared, touching off famine and dispersal rather than regeneration, and the officials and missionaries failed to work their magic. Predictions of abundant new economies and mass conversions remained a distant hope.

In this volume, Wenzel invokes a poignant line from Walter Ong to signal the jarring changes that occurred as societies made the transition from oral to textual literacy: "We have to die to continue living." Dipesh Chakrabarty is preoccupied with an analogous dilemma about the ways in which records of the past are resurrected and preserved, especially in the decades preceding a nation's political independence. The only way to give India a living past, according to his key protagonist, Jadunath Sarkar, was to unearth its textual ruins. So far, so good. But Sarkar, as Chakrabarty suggests, was involved in his own death march, taking up the losing side in a utopian struggle over the fate of universal history—the desire, so to speak, to narrate the past scientifically. In this sense Wenzel and Chakrabarty are in dialogue trying to draw our attention to the unsettling incoherence that lurks within all histories when we substitute narrators, choose different documentary evidence, or even select which points in the plot to emphasize. Both also help us appreciate how ideology matters, and in Chakrabarty's case he does so by contextualizing the very debates over a public and private sphere on which the historical profession in general and Indian historiography in particular were founded.

If history takes center stage for the actors in Wenzel's and Chakrabarty's chapters, Luise White's chapter on Rhodesia's Unilateral Declaration of Independence (1965–79) charts its course to the margins. As minority rule, colonialism, and even theories of racial supremacy beat a global retreat of sorts, loyalists to the Rhodesian cause were so preoccupied with their dream of countering these trends, fighting off the chaos they thought would ensue under majority rule—the fear of the masses that Jameson invoked—that they managed to eclipse Rhodesia's historical specificity in the process. There was nothing terribly new in Rhodesia's incarnation as a racial state, since it had already achieved that status following the First World War. What was new was its leaders' willingness to secede from the British Empire in order to defend this arrangement and their vociferous pursuit of political legitimacy in the face of competing trends elsewhere. As whites clung to alleged racial standards and utopian imagery of working telephones—the stand-in for qualities and conditions that helped them to justify minority rule—they tended to construct Rhodesia in their imaginations in ways that transcended both place and time. This was accompanied, paradoxically, by their deracination and denationalization, a point White underscores when she details just how many supporters of the Rhodesian Front were recent immigrants. Such a racial utopia—some might say dystopia—was difficult to sustain at the level of the state.

Where White's chapter revolves around questions relating to the limits of racial politics, Timothy Mitchell's chapter focuses on energy politics and, as he puts it, "the limits of carbon democracy." Mitchell seeks to bridge a range of debates that are often kept separate; these relate to natural resources, social movements, democratic institutions, and the history of ideas. Rather than isolate oil-rich states, especially those in the Middle East, and speak of an "oil curse" to explain their lack of democracy, Mitchell wishes to turn the tables and ask instead whether democracies themselves have been "carbon based." To focus only on recent patterns and events misses the forest for the trees or, to use Mitchell's terms, overlooks the nodes of networks that made "buried sunshine" a catalyst for new kinds of political and economic formations in the modern world. By exploring when and how coal and oil became foundational to geopolitics, Mitchell is also able to shed light on why these energy forms could both sustain *and* inhibit democratic institutions in different times and places. Take coal, for example. Its methods of extraction and distribution, between roughly 1850 and 1920, inadvertently gave miners, and to a lesser extent railway and dockworkers, a considerable degree of power to disrupt its flow at precisely the time coal energy was becoming increasingly essential to emerging industrial economies. Miners' militancy and their successful strikes in this period helped to constitute the phenomenon we now call mass politics. The gradual transition to oil in the mid-twentieth century, by contrast, wrested some of that power away from workers; indeed, as Mitchell argues, this was a central incentive for corporate and state actors to support the shift to oil. Where coal tended to be consumed within the countries in which it was produced—shoring up a domestic power base—oil, because of its liquid form and light weight, was a far more transportable energy source. This enabled existing democracies to uphold and even increase participatory politics domestically while their representatives simultaneously eroded emergent political movements elsewhere, especially in the Middle East. More significant still, according to Mitchell, in the postwar decades of large-scale oil production, these same democracies promoted the myth that hydrocarbon energy was limitless, a utopian vision on which such iconic ideologies as Keynesian economics were built. Only when Middle Eastern states began to threaten these carbon democracies, in the early 1970s, did oil companies invoke the idea of environmental limits, which in turn helped them orchestrate changes in the way these resources were priced globally. Coming to terms with these realities in the present, the literal constraints that the architects of a "hydrocarbon utopia" often concealed, may help us envisage a future in which energy and politics combine to be more truly democratic.

Part 2: Artifice

Our second theme explores more of what is specifically modern and subjective about utopian/dystopian thinking and practice: its *artificial* quality. The chapters in part 1 place greater stress on life-forms and natural objects— populations, cattle, land, archives, races, and carbon-based energy—and those in part 2 emphasize the role of human manipulations and abstractions, the links between Homo faber and Homo cogito.[19] Here we are interested in the ways in which old themes—memories of lost worlds, if you will—are repackaged in the transition to modernity. In the process, many of these reorientations went right to the heart of human subjectivity. The hope of a general reorganization of the world proved to be deeply and intimately connected to a highly specific conjuncture. That conjuncture was framed by a series of conditions of possibility—colonialism, capitalism, socialism, and even technocratic optimism—that in turn prompted the imagination of a future that was not imposed by the sheer thrust forward of time, but was a possibility produced through the architecture of rationality, variously defined. Understanding the artifice of human consciousness helps us to appreciate the ways in which the Self has also been imbricated in utopian politics.[20]

One way to track the fine distinction between anima and artifice would be to examine two very different approaches to one of the hallmarks of modernity, imagined and real: energy. Where Timothy Mitchell describes the linkages between oil and (lack of) democracy that seemed to build organically and interdependently upon carbon-based coal economies, John Krige's chapter offers a penetrating analysis of one twentieth-century phenomenon that was quintessentially modern, utterly constructed, and truly never before seen in the world: the power released by the fissioning of the atomic nucleus. Nuclear power (and its dark cousin, the nuclear weapon) spawned utopian visions embedded in the technical infrastructure—as, indeed, had to happen, for there were few preexisting patterns to condition this new form of energy (unlike oil). But as Krige explains, not only did the frame of the U.S.-Soviet cold war suffuse these visions with a dystopic tinge, but so too did the anticipation of empire's end. Focusing on the 1955 Geneva conference under the auspices of the American-led Atoms for Peace initiative, Krige provides a detailed study of the utopian aspirations behind the civilian project of atomic power plants and, more concretely, of the "education of desire": how cultures and individuals were brought to realize the position of the nuclear in their nation-building projects. This is utopia in Mannheim's sense, and in ours: the nuclear was an artifice that enabled people to think through their present by imagining a utopian beyond. This was nowhere truer than in the rapidly decolonizing nations of the "global South," to whom the Americans pitched a nuclear future as a ready alternative to the Marxist utopia that beckoned from the then-unified Sino-Soviet bloc. By the end of Krige's chapter, we come to see the incipient dystopias of nuclear weapons proliferation, atomic reactor meltdowns, and neocolonial dependency rising on the horizon. Technical choices made by various developing nations—"educated" into desiring what the United States wanted them to desire—solidified into a present that fell far short of the aspirations initially voiced.

World War II, the trauma that the peaceful atom was supposed to heal, was preceded by its own epoch of utopian therapists. The central and eastern European cosmopolitans of the interwar years, as Marci Shore persuasively argues, sought a literary, linguistic, and artistic utopia to remedy the disastrous wounds of the Great War. But as the term "interwar" should alert us, an even more horrific, more dystopian clash between fascism and communism would rip asunder the Polish, Czech, Russian, and German intellectuals who truly imagined that utopia was around the corner. Indeed, to some extent it seemed already present in the optimistic creative ferment that followed in the wake of the Bolshevik Revolution of 1917, both within Russian borders and in the penumbras of the dissolved Romanov empire. The avant-garde that Shore describes took the time and place issues of utopia seriously, and they rejected place in favor of time: modernity was the moment, and although that took many forms (liberalism, Marxism, fascism, futurism, and Dadaism), the important point was to live this present fully. Phenomenologists, structuralists, and other universalists populate her *Mitteleuropa*, traveling between the urban nodes of Vienna, Petrograd, Warsaw, Berlin, Paris, and others, knitting together a new utopia that severed the links to a diseased past. Among these intellectuals we also find the seeds for the terror that would follow as Europe disintegrated once again in its most dystopian/utopian of centuries, and the tour of optimism sounds an elegiac minor chord, as the European present proved too difficult to transcend.

David Pinder's situationists and letterists grabbed the utopian artifice by the other horn and sought quite literally to reimagine place. Much more directly than the cosmopolitans or the nuclear engineers, these avant-garde artists of the post–World War II era constructed their utopias through *explicit* emphasis on the nature of the present. Pinder builds his narrative of their reflections on the transformative (and utopian) possibilities inherent in the here and now by starting where they did: at the street. The tension between the humdrum quotidian aspect of a stroll on the street and the intense futuristic dynamism of architectural modernism of the Le Corbusier variant found expression in the situationist vision of a completely open architecture of the future, one whose design imposed almost nothing to shape the desires of those imagined future inhabitants. Here, the goal of utopia was to use the present to conjure a future liberated of the context of that very present. The contradictions were deeply felt and hard to ignore. Just as Jane Jacobs and other urban thinkers emphasized the possibilities inherent in the street, the skepticism toward the conservatism of the everyday proved recalcitrant. The utopian street contained its intrinsic dystopia, as reflected in the collapse of the Situationist International, which Pinder chronicles. Yet, for all their intensity, these debates remained largely in the arena of the theoretical and analytical.

Not so in Igal Halfin's exploration of the discourse in the basements of the People's Commissariat for Internal Affairs (NKVD) in the Soviet Union amid the Stalinist purges of the late 1930s. The central problematic for Halfin is how the Communists brought before NKVD tribunals, knowing that they would be shot for crimes they did not commit, not only did not resist the secret police but even *confessed* to the invented accusations. Halfin's analysis draws from the transcripts of these confessions, which he embeds within the eschatological framework folded into Stalinist discourse and constitutive of it. Here, as in the other chapters in this section, in the artifice of the Communist Party's utopian vision of messianism, the obverse side of wrecking, sabotage, and constant internal suspicion was laid bare. Thus, Halfin steers clear of conventional and simplistic interpretations of the bloodshed as a realized dystopia, which equates the readiness of the confessions with the steady application of torture—external force generated false self-accusation, yet the internal was left untainted and somehow pure. Halfin's accused share the same discourse as their interrogators, and the depth and extravagance of the confessions emerged from something that transcended facile internal-external binaries. The Communist worldview confessed its own sins to itself—the accused truly *believed* themselves to be guilty, in a nontrivial sense. Both interrogator and interrogated were utopians forged in the same furnace. The artifice of utopian thought should not be understood as existing in some blueprint of a Grand Designer; rather, we need to recognize that the artifice forms no less than a natural part of the self-conception of those embedded within its discourse. The kingdom of Utopus lies within us.

Aditya Nigam's essay on the politics of the Dalit movement—once the so-called untouchables—brings us full circle back to the questions Jameson and Wenzel posed in the first section of this volume. Nigam points to the notions of time implied in utopia, noting that utopias are always displaced in time from the present, and explores the features of Dalit politics that he terms "heterotopic": reform projects that emphasize the here and now, the presentness of the desired vision. Given the pervasive discrimination and prejudice against Dalits in present-day India, their leaders have emphasized the use of status quo mechanisms, such as affirmative action and antidiscrimination laws, to gain employment in the public sector when the private sector excludes them. Nigam discusses the representations of Mayawati, an important Dalit and on-and-off chief minister of Uttar Pradesh, as well as a contemporary short story, to explore the ways in which Dalits have made efforts to construct a counterutopia that aggressively deploys the artifices of the present instead of developing an animated, organic mass movement akin to those explored in the previous section. The political results may be equivocal, but the aspiration is no less real. Nigam's account of Dalit politics, by building itself into current discourse rather than fashioning a counterdiscourse like the Stalinists, demonstrates that even when the actors do not explicitly invoke the dystopic present or a utopian future (or past), scrutiny of the categories can yield valuable insights concerning opportunities for actual transformation.

A Utopian Beyond

> He still had faith in his fantastic vision,
> but in moments of doubt
> he worried that he'd given the world only
> a new version of despair.
> —Adam Zagajewski, "Old Marx"

Faith, fantasy, despair, and desire pervade these essays; in fact, they are the stock-in-trade of utopian/dystopian practice. Are we to believe that such dreaming has outlived its purpose? Must we accept the "skepticism about the possibilities of change," the "cynical reason" that Jameson describes? If so many emancipatory promises have been betrayed and liberatory movements come undone, does that mean that none should be attempted or proposed again? Have we really reached a point beyond utopia?

However complicated these questions might appear, especially when situated against the grand sweep of human history, the answers are rather simple: no. Even as the utopias of communism and cosmopolitan peace stand indicted, the neoliberal utopia of the market creeps up on us, now under the ideologically driven notion of a Smithian human nature.[21] This also produces the dystopic vision of the "planet of slums," a Dickensian wasteland of urban poverty, exploitation, and violence.[22] Everywhere we turn, historical conditions continue to throw up utopias and dystopias as ways to shape, understand, and critique our contemporary world. Perhaps this helps to explain not just why interest in utopian historicity is on the rise, but also why scholars focusing on Asia, Latin America, and Africa have begun to explore its implications.[23] This book, in fact, explicitly raises questions about what it means to analyze conditions of possibility at the transnational and global levels, especially when so many of our concepts derive from Europe. Several of our contributors grapple explicitly with cross-cultural phenomena — orality and textuality, scientific epistemologies and other ways of knowing, empire and nationhood, and so on. Others bring to the fore circulations that have a global effect: production systems, weapons, energy. As Chakrabarty's chapter reminds us, however, there still remains theoretical work to be done to understand the universal and particular elements of any utopian or dystopian impulse.

To invoke the proverb marshaled by grassroots organizers the world over, "Without a vision, the people perish." Yet as the chapters that follow reveal, visions themselves are inherently dangerous, whatever their underlying motives. They involve risk, they usually rest upon faith, and they often require their progenitors to relinquish control. More to the point, they are imbued with their own fault lines: limits and critique accompany the projection of utopias and dystopias. Zagajewski's Marx, caught in a snapshot at the end of his life, was not wrong to doubt, but nor was he wrong to continue to believe.[24] To draw a direct historical lesson from this volume: no matter how chimerical utopias may appear, dystopias are no less vulnerable; they have their breaking points too. The following chapters underline these fractures, drawing attention to the historical conditions that bring utopias/dystopias into view and simultaneously conceal their limits and flaws.

The conceptual framework we have selected to analyze these dynamics — anima and artifice — intentionally addresses our twenty-first century collective consciousness, if we can speak of such a thing. Nowhere in the world is it now realistic to deny the need to take into account planetary life as we envisage a better future. Whatever shape our utopian dreams may take, they cannot ignore the constraints and opportunities posed by nonhuman nature. These limits are increasingly evident in the genre of environmental histories, which draw our attention to human dependency and vulnerability in the face of nature's agency.[25] But nor should we undervalue the all-too-human need for "fantastic visions," especially in a context of equally fantastic threats. A historical analysis of these visions—and of the conditions that produce them—exercises our imaginations and animates our understanding of how and why things change. It has the potential, in other words, to breathe new life into transformative politics.

When we wed anima to artifice, it becomes possible to develop tools that help us move beyond the limits of utopian/dystopian politics of past ages. Whereas anima forces us to take into account those things that sustain life— and even to reject the ethos that humans can live beyond limits—artifice requires us to strike a balance between our inner and outer realities. Not only does what we construct outside ourselves matter—as the histories of failed technocratic solutions can attest—but also the way we construct our very selves shapes our future possibilities. Whether we speak of an "education of desire," the politics of the street, emergent cosmopolitanism, or even false confessions, understanding the historical interplay between self and collective allows us to sharpen not just our hindsight but potentially also our foresight. Yes, we are toolmakers, and, yes, those tools can help us test the boundaries of reality, but unless we account for our inner natures as well, most artifices will crumble. These are among the conditions of possibility that our analysis has brought to light. Many others are also imaginable. Our goal is to open the question, not to nail it down and seal it up.

Notes

1. See, for example, the collected utopias from antiquity to the present gathered in *The Utopia Reader*, ed. Gregory Claeys and Lyman Tower Sargent (New York: New York University Press, 1999). On the literary traditions, see Gary Saul Morson, *Boundaries of Genre: Dostoevsky's Diary of a Writer and the Traditions of Literary Utopia* (Austin: University of Texas Press, 1981); and Peter Edgerly Firchow, *Modern Utopian Fictions from H. G. Wells to Iris Murdoch* (Washington, DC: Catholic University of America Press, 2007).

2. Fredric Jameson has recently taken this location within science fiction to unearth some new potentials for the concept of utopia (although less so for dystopia), and his perspective colors this essay in particular. See Fredric Jameson, *Archaeologies of the Future: The Desire Called Utopia and Other Science Fictions* (New York: Verso, 2005). To some extent this follows on the attention to the intellectually productive features of science fiction articulated, for example, in Donna J. Haraway's *Simians, Cyborgs, and Women: The Reinvention of Nature* (New York: Routledge, 1991), and *Modest_Witness@Second_Millenium.FemaleMan_Meets_OncoMouse: Feminism and Technoscience* (New York: Routledge, 1997). See also Felicity D. Scott, *Architecture or Techno-*

utopia: Politics after Modernism (Cambridge, MA: MIT Press, 2007), and Patrick Parrinder, ed., *Learning from Other Worlds: Estrangement, Cognition, and the Politics of Science Fiction and Utopia* (Durham: Duke University Press, 2001).

3. For two recent analyses of dystopia, see Thomas Moylan, *Scraps of the Untainted Sky: Science Fiction, Utopia, Dystopia* (Boulder: Westview Press, 2000); and Raffaella Baccolini and Tom Moylan, eds., *Dark Horizons: Science Fiction and the Dystopian Imagination* (New York: Routledge, 2003).

4. Fritz Lang's *Metropolis* (1927) is a classic example of the kind of dystopic imagination we describe here. The film places viewers directly in a mechanistic utopia gone mad and alerts us of the danger of apocalypse if we do not pay heed. Indeed, only total destruction, the film suggests, can provide a new beginning.

5. There are, as always, very valuable exceptions to a statement like this one. See, for example, Mark Featherstone, *Tocqueville's Virus: Utopia and Dystopia in Western Social and Political Thought* (New York: Routledge, 2008); Jaap Verheul, ed., *Dreams of Paradise, Visions of Apocalypse: Utopia and Dystopia in American Culture* (Amsterdam: VU University Press, 2004); and Everett Mendelsohn and Helga Nowotny, eds., *Nineteen Eighty-Four: Science between Utopia and Dystopia* (Dordrecht: Kluwer Academic Publishers, 1984).

6. For some more general treatments, see J. C. Davis, *Utopia and the Ideal Society: A Study of English Utopian Writing, 1516–1700* (Cambridge: Cambridge University Press, 1981); Ruth Levitas, *The Concept of Utopia* (New York: Philip Allan, 1990); Marina Leslie, *Renaissance Utopias and the Problem of History* (Ithaca, NY: Cornell University Press, 1999); Howard P. Segal, *Technology and Utopia* (Washington, DC: Society for the History of Technology, 2006); and Phillip E. Wegner, *Imaginary Communities: Utopia, the Nation, and the Spatial Histories of Modernity* (Berkeley: University of California Press, 2002).

7. Such a mood has even hit literary scholarship: Nicholas Spencer, *After Utopia: The Rise of Critical Space in Twentieth-Century American Fiction* (Lincoln: University of Nebraska Press, 2006).

8. James C. Scott, *Seeing Like a State: How Certain Schemes to Improve the Human Condition Have Failed* (New Haven: Yale University Press, 1998); Martin Jay, *Marxism and Totality: The Adventures of a Concept from Lukás to Habermas* (Berkeley: University of California Press, 1986); Vincent Geoghegan, *Utopianism and Marxism* (New York: Methuen, 1987); Richard Drayton, *Nature's Government: Science, Imperial Britain, and the "Improvement" of the World* (New Haven: Yale University Press, 2000); Tania Li, *The Will to Improve: Governmentality, Development, and the Practice of Politics* (Durham: Duke University Press, 2007). For an implicit rejoinder to at least some of these trends, see Paul Boghossian, *Fear of Knowledge: Against Relativism and Constructivism* (Oxford: Oxford University Press, 2007).

9. For a recent example, see Jack Lawrence Luzkow, *What's Left? Marxism, Utopianism, and the Revolt against History* (Lanham, MD: University Press of America, 2006).

10. This concept appears in many places in Foucault's writings, but perhaps most powerfully in his analysis of *epistemes* in *The Order of Things: An Archaeology of the Human Sciences* (New York: Vintage, 1994).

11. This is, in the end, one of the crucial insights of the chapters on Marx in the classic exploration of utopian socialism: Edmund Wilson, *To the Finland Station: A Study in the Writing and Acting of History* (Garden City, NY: Doubleday, 1940).

12. The notion of practice we deploy here derives mostly from the science-studies literature. For an introduction, see Stephen Turner, *The Social Theory of Practices: Tradition, Tacit Knowledge and Presuppositions* (London: Polity, 1994).

13. Karl Mannheim, *Ideology and Utopia: An Introduction to the Sociology of Knowledge*, trans. Louis Wirth and Edward Shils (San Diego: Harcourt Brace, 1991 [1929]), 40, emphasis in original. This point is further elaborated, in explicit contrast to the totemic intellectual style of analyzing utopias (and invoking Thomas More), on pp. 200–201.

14. Ibid., 209.

15. For an earlier expression, see Ernst Bloch, *The Spirit of Utopia*, trans. Anthony Nassar (Stanford: Stanford University Press, 2000 [1918]).

16. A few examples in critical theory include Frederick Engels's *Dialectics of Nature*, trans. and ed. Clemens Dutt with a preface by J.B.S. Haldane (New York: International Publishers, 1940 [1898]); Max Horkheimer and Theodor Adorno, *Dialectic of Enlightenment*, trans. John Cumming (New York: Herder and Herder, 1972); Alfred Schmidt, *The Concept of Nature in Marx*, trans. Ben Fowkes (London: N.L.B., 1971); William Leiss, *The Domination of Nature* (New York: Braziller, 1972); and Jay, *Marxism and Totality*. Historians of the life and environmental sciences explore related dimensions of our understanding of anima, as do those environmental and medical historians who consider nature's agency. These references are too numerous to list, but for a few early works see William McNeill, *Plagues and Peoples* (Garden City, NY: Anchor Press, 1976); Donald Worster, *Nature's Economy: The Roots of Ecology* (Cambridge: Cambridge University Press, 1977); and Alfred Crosby, *Ecological Imperialism: The Biological Expansion of Europe* (Cambridge: Cambridge University Press, 1986). More recently, historians of empire and science have taken up these themes as well, including Richard Grove, *Green Imperialism: Colonial Expansion, Tropical Island Edens, and the Origins of Environmentalism, 1600–1860* (Cambridge: Cambridge University Press, 1995).

17. Other diseases have been brought close to zero incidence, such as polio, but several thousand cases per year persist. See Harry Hull and Bruce Aylward, "Progress towards Global Polio Eradication," *Vaccine* 19 (2001): 4378–84.

18. Donald A. Henderson et al., "Smallpox as a Biological Weapon: Medical and Public Health Management," *Journal of the American Medical Association* 281, no. 22 (1999): 2127–37.

19. Although, again, there are several sources for our thinking here, we owe certain debts to intellectual historians concerned with technics and technology; a classic here would be Lewis Mumford's *Technics and Civilization* (New York: Harcourt, Brace, 1934).

20. This has become an increasingly popular theme; see Charles Taylor, *Sources of the Self: The Making of the Modern Identity* (Cambridge, MA: Harvard University Press, 1989).

21. See, for example, among many such recent titles, David Harvey, *A Brief History of Neoliberalism* (New York: Oxford University Press, 2007).

22. Mike Davis, *Planet of Slums* (New York: Verso, 2006).

23. Interest in utopian historicity can be seen, for instance, in literary works such as Tom Stoppard's trilogy *The Coast of Utopia* (London: Faber and Faber, 2002) and in academic analyses such as Eric Weitz's *A Century of Genocide: Utopias of Race and*

Nation (Princeton: Princeton University Press, 2003) and Jay Winter's *Dreams of Peace and Freedom: Utopian Moments in the Twentieth Century* (New Haven: Yale University Press, 2006). For regional breadth, we should note three contributions from the Utopia/Dystopia seminar series: Megan Vaughan, "Slavery in the Utopian Family: Mauritius in the Eighteenth Century"; Susanna Hecht, "Tropical Utopias: Practical and Political Imagination in the New World"; and Lauren Benton, "Empires of Exception: Heterotopia and Global Legal Geography." See also Jean-François Lejeune, ed., *Cruelty and Utopia: Cities and Landscapes of Latin America* (Princeton: Princeton Architectural Press, 2005); and Maurice Meisner, *Marxism, Maoism, Utopianism* (Madison: University of Wisconsin Press, 1982).

24. Adam Zagajewski, "Old Marx," *New Yorker*, 21 January 2008. This picture is interestingly related to the classic (and heavily contested) picture of Marx—and utopian socialism in general—in Wilson's *To the Finland Station*.

25. See, for example, the conjunction of urban planning and environmental constraints represented by the chapters in *The Nature of Cities*, ed. Andrew C. Isenberg (Rochester: University of Rochester Press, 2006). The vast (and growing) literature on environmental history speaks to these issues again and again.

PART ONE

ANIMA

1.

Fredric Jameson

Utopia as Method, or the Uses of the Future

We ordinarily think of utopia as a place, or if you like a nonplace that looks like a place. How can a place be a method? Such is the conundrum with which I wanted to confront you, and maybe it has an easy answer. If we think of historically new forms of space—historically new forms of the city, for example—they might well offer new models for urbanists and in that sense constitute a kind of method. The first freeways in Los Angeles, for example, project a new system of elevated express highways superimposed on an older system of surface streets. That new structural difference might be thought of as a philosophical concept in its own right, a new one, in terms of which you might want to rethink this or that older urban center, or better still, this or that as yet undeveloped Sun Belt agglomeration. For a time then, the Los Angeles concept is modern; whether it is utopian is another matter altogether, although Los Angeles has also been a utopia for many different kinds of people over the years. Here is Brecht on Hollywood:

> The village of Hollywood was planned according to the notion
> People in these parts have of heaven. In these parts
> They have come to the conclusion that God
> Requiring a heaven and a hell, didn't need to
> Plan two establishments but
> Just the one: heaven. It
> Serves the unprosperous, unsuccessful
> As hell.[1]

A true dialectic; a true unity of opposites! Will it be possible to untangle the negative from the positive in this particular utopia, which has perhaps also, like all the other utopias, never existed in the first place? Something like this will be our problem here, but we need to work through some further preliminaries before we get that far.

The hypothetical new kind of city that sets an example for the building or reorganization of other new kinds of cities to come is based on a conviction we may no longer be able to rely on, namely, the belief that progress is possible and that cities, for example, can be improved. What is utopian is then identified with this now-traditional and much criticized bourgeois idea of progress, and thus implicitly with teleology as such, with the grand narrative and the master plan, with the idea of a better future, a future not only dependent on our own will to bring it into being but also somehow inscribed in the very nature of things, waiting to be set free, lying in the deeper possibilities and potentialities of being, from which at length and with luck it may emerge. But does anyone believe in progress any longer? Even keeping to the realm of the spatial, which we have taken as an example, are the architects and urbanists still passionately at work on utopian cities? The utopian city was surely a staple of modernism; one thinks of everybody from Le Corbusier to Constant, from Rockefeller Center to the great Nazi or Soviet projects.[2] At a lower level, one thinks of urban renewal and of Robert Moses.[3] But modernism is over, and it is my impression that the postmodern city, west or east, north or south, does not encourage thoughts of progress or even improvement, let alone utopian visions of the older kind; and this for the very good reason that the postmodern city seems to be in permanent crisis and is to be thought of, if at all, as a catastrophe rather than an opportunity. As far as space is concerned, the rich are withdrawing ever more urgently into their gated communities and their fortified enclosures; the middle classes are tirelessly engaged in covering the last vestiges of nature with acres of identical development homes; and the poor, pouring in from the former countryside, swell the makeshift outskirts with a population explosion so irrepressible that in a few years none of the ten largest cities on the globe will include the familiar first-world metropolises any longer. Some of the great dystopias of the past—as in John Brunner's novels from the late 1960s and early 1970s[4]—centered on what was then the alleged nightmare of overpopulation; but that was a modernist nightmare, and what we confront today is perhaps not a dystopia either, but rather a certainty lived in a different way and with a properly postmodern ambivalence, which distinctly forecloses the possibility of progress or of solutions.

Indeed, it suffices to think of the four fundamental threats to the survival of the human race today—ecological catastrophe, worldwide poverty and famine, structural unemployment on a global scale, and the seemingly uncontrollable traffic in armaments of all kinds, including smart bombs and unmanned drones (in armaments, progress does apparently still exist!)—leaving pandemics, police states, race wars, and drugs out of the picture, for us to realize that in each of these areas no serious counterforce exists anywhere in the world, and certainly not in the United States, which is the cause of most of them.

Under these circumstances, the last gasp of a properly utopian vision, the last attempt at a utopian forecast of the future transfigured, was a rather perverse one: so-called free-market fundamentalism as it seized the moment of globalization to predict the rising of all boats and the wonder-working miraculous powers of worldwide unregulated global markets. But this utopia, drawing on the unconscious operations of Adam Smith's invisible hand, and in

sharp contrast to the hyperconsciousness of the utopian "intentional community," gambled everything on the unintentionality of its universal panacea, for
which any number of populations around the globe proved unwilling to wait.
Nor did this waning utopian effort recover much strength by shifting to a different code, from economics to politics, and rebaptizing the freedom of the
market as the freedom of democracy. To that degree, as a political slogan, the
banner of utopia has been passed to the critics and the enemies of free-market
globalization and has become the unifying rallying cry or "empty signifier"[5] of
all those varied new political forces who are trying to imagine how another
world might be possible.

Yet an empty signifier seems far enough away from the utopian visions with
which we are familiar from More and Plato on down, and this is probably the
right moment to say a word about the long book on utopias I have recently
published and of which this chapter is something of a reconsideration, if not
a supplement. What has tended to perplex readers of this book, *Archaeologies
of the Future*,[6] if not to annoy them, is not only the repeated insistence on the
form rather than the content of utopias—something that would, on the face of
it, scarcely be unusual in literary criticism, no matter how deplorable—but
also another thesis more likely to catch the unwary reader up short, namely
the repeated insistence that what is important in a utopia is not what can be
positively imagined and proposed, but rather what is not imaginable and not
conceivable. The utopia, I argue, is not a representation but an operation
calculated to disclose the limits of our own imagination of the future, the lines
beyond which we do not seem able to go in imagining changes in our own
society and world (except in the direction of dystopia and catastrophe). Is this
then a failure of imagination, or is it simply a fundamental skepticism about
the possibilities of change as such, no matter how attractive our visions of what
it would be desirable to change into? Do we not here touch on what has come
to be called cynical reason, rather than the impoverishment of our own sense
of the future or the waning of the utopian impulse itself? Cynical reason, as
the concept has evolved far beyond what Peter Sloterdijk named so many
years ago,[7] can be characterized as something like the inversion of political
apathy. It knows everything about our own society, everything that is wrong
with late capitalism, all the structural toxicities of the system, and yet it de-
clines indignation in a kind of impotent lucidity that may not even be bad
faith. It cannot be shocked or scandalized, as the privileged were able to at
earlier moments of the market system; nor is the deconcealment of this
system, its analysis and functional demonstration in the light of day, any longer effective in compelling critical reactions or motivations. We may say all
this in terms of ideology as well. If that word has fallen on hard times, it is
perhaps because in a sense there is no longer any false consciousness, no longer any need to disguise the workings of the system and its various programs in
terms of idealistic or altruistic rationalizations, so that the unmasking of those

rationalizations, the primordial gesture of debunking and of exposure, no longer seems necessary.

The waning of utopias is thus a conjuncture between all these developments: a weakening of historicity or of the sense of the future; a conviction that fundamental change is no longer possible, however desirable; and cynical reason as such. To this we might add that sheer power of excess money accumulated since the last great world war, which keeps the system in place everywhere, reinforcing its institutions and its armed forces. Or maybe we should adduce yet a different kind of factor, one of psychological conditioning—namely that omnipresent consumerism, having become an end in itself, is transforming the daily life of the advanced countries in such a way as to suggest that the utopianism of multiple desires and consumption is here already and needs no further supplement.

So much for the limits on our capacity to imagine utopia as such and for what it tells us about a present in which we can no longer envision that future. But it would clearly be wrong to say that today representational utopia has every-where disappeared. Another significant critique of my book suggested that I failed to do my duty as a utopian inasmuch as I omitted any mention of these surviving utopian visions that mostly center on the anti- or post-Communist conviction that small is beautiful, or even that growth is undesirable, that the self-organization of communities is the fundamental condition of utopian life, and that even with large-scale industry the first priority is self-management and cooperation; in other words, that what is essential in utopianism is not the ingenious economic scheme (the abolition of money, for example) so much as collectivity as such, the primacy of the social bond over the individualistic and the competitive impulses.

The great utopias of the 1960s and '70s tended to stage such visions in terms of race and gender; thus we have the unforgettable image of male breast-feeding in Marge Piercy's *Woman on the Edge of Time* (1976) and the ideal (in Ursula Le Guin) of the villages of the First Americans. Later on, at a different historical moment, in France, at the moment of the Socialist electoral victory of 1981, we have Jacques Attali's image of free collective tool shops, where anyone in the neighborhood can find the materials to repair, rebuild, and transform space, along with the periodic festivals that, as in Rousseau, reaffirm the collective project.[8] In our own time, meanwhile, with the resurgence of anarchism, a variety of vivid representations of workers' self-management restore the sense of class to these concerns, as in Avi Lewis and Naomi Klein's admirable film *The Take*, about the seizure of a factory in Argentina by workers who have been abandoned by their bankrupt owner. Such intermittent visions of the structural transformation of the shop floor have energized and revitalized political action from Marx's lectures on the Paris Commune all the way to the program of Yugoslavian autogestion and to soixante-huitard films such as Coup pour coup (Marin Karmitz, 1972); and they clearly persist in America yesterday and today.

It is not appropriate to raise practical political objections to these enclave utopias, which are always threatened by the hegemony of private business and monopoly all around them and are at the mercy of distribution as well, not to speak of the dominant legal system. I would rather speak of the genre of the revolutionary idyll; and indeed, in his *Some Versions of Pastoral* (1960), William Empson went a long way toward assimilating socialist realism in general to such a form, which, with its shepherds and shepherdesses and its rural peacefulness and fulfillment, seems to have died out everywhere in the literature of the bourgeois age. William Morris famously subtitled his great utopia "an epoch of rest"; and this is what, on an aesthetic level, the idyll or the pastoral promises as a genre: relief from the frenzied anxieties of the social world, a glimpse into a place of stillness and of transfigured human nature, of the transformations of social relations into what Brecht memorably called "friendliness." To that degree, what I've been calling representational utopias seem to take the form of the idyll or the pastoral, and assuredly we do need to recover the significance of these ancient genres and their value and usefulness in an age in which the very psyche and the unconscious have been thoroughly colonized by addictive frenzy and commotion, compulsiveness and frustration.

So I do see a place for the representational utopia, and even a political function for it. As I tried to argue in *Archaeologies*, these seemingly peaceful images are also, in and of themselves, violent ruptures with what is, breaks that destabilize our stereotypes of a future that is the same as our present, interventions that interrupt the reproduction of the system in habit and in ideological consent and that institute that fissure, however minimal and initially little more than a hairline fracture, through which another picture of the future and another system of temporality might emerge.

Yet I also want to project a different way of invoking that future and to propose a different function for the utopian; in a sense it is premised on the distinction I proposed at the very beginning of *Archaeologies* between the utopian program and the utopian impulse, between utopian planners and utopian interpreters, or between More or Fourier and Ernst Bloch. The utopian program, which aims at the realization of a utopia, can be as modest or as ambitious as one wants; it can range from a whole social revolution, on a national or even world scale, all the way down to the design of the uniquely utopian space of a building or garden. What all these have in common, however—besides the utopian transformation of reality—is that closure or enclave structure that all utopias seemingly must confront in one way or another. These utopian spaces are thus totalities, whatever their scale; they are symbolic of a world transformed, and as such they must posit limits, boundaries between the utopian and the nonutopian. It is with these limits and with this enclave structure that any serious critique of utopia will begin.

The interpretation of the utopian impulse, however, necessarily deals with fragments. It is not symbolic but allegorical; it does not correspond to a plan or to a utopian praxis; and it expresses utopian desire and invests it in a variety of unexpected and disguised, concealed, distorted ways. The utopian impulse, therefore, calls for a hermeneutic, for the detective work of a decipherment and a reading of utopian clues and traces in the landscape of the real; a theorization and interpretation of unconscious utopian investments in realities large or small, which may be far from utopian. The premise here is that the most noxious phenomena can serve as the repository and hiding place for all kinds of unsuspected wish fulfillments and utopian gratifications; indeed, I have often used the example of the humble aspirin as the unwitting bearer of the most extravagant longings for immortality and for the transfiguration of the body.

Marx

This kind of utopian analysis, however, may seem to foreground the subject and subjectivity and to risk transforming the utopian impulse into inconsequential projections that carry no historical weight and imply no practical consequences for the social world. This objection seems to be overstated to the degree to which human desire is constitutive of the collective project and of the historical construction of social formations, within the limits imposed by objective conditions of possibility. Still, it may be best to lay in place a view of those objective conditions before continuing and to outline a model of the objective possibilities of utopian social transformation against which interpretations in terms of some putative utopian impulse might be measured.

Indeed, we might well want to argue that the Marxian view of historical change combines both of these forms of utopian thinking, for it can be seen as a practical project as well as a space of the investment of unconscious forces. The old tension in Marxism between voluntarism and fatalism finds its origins here, in this twin or superimposed utopian perspective. A Marxist politics is a utopian project or program for transforming the world and replacing a capitalist mode of production with a radically different one.But it is also a conception of historical dynamics that posits that the whole new world is objectively in emergence all around us, without our necessarily perceiving it at once, so that alongside our conscious praxis and our strategies for producing change, we may take a more receptive and interpretive stance. In this stance, with the proper instruments and registering apparatus, we may detect the allegorical stirrings of a different state of things, the imperceptible and even immemorial ripenings of the seeds of time, the subliminal and subcutaneous eruptions of whole new forms of life and social relations.

At first Marx expressed this second model of temporality through the most banal of essential mysteries, which no longer carries much figural power for us. "No social order ever disappears," he wrote in 1859, "before all the productive forces for which there is room in it have been developed." So far, so good.

This observation was not sufficiently meditated upon in the 1980s and '90s. Marx goes on: "And new, higher relations of production never appear before the material conditions of their existence have matured in the womb of the old society."[9] Yet so far this is nothing but a metaphor, and childbirth is not necessarily the best figure of speech for the dynamics of the utopian impulse as Bloch described it, or for the allegories of utopian investment and the utopian libido, the hidden traces and signs of utopianism that lie in wait in the world abut us, like Rimbaud's flowers that secretly observe us as we pass by.

Meanwhile, we need to add that both Marx and Lenin wrote specifically utopian works, both of them based on the Paris Commune. Marx's lectures on the Commune ("The Civil War in France") are indeed something like a blueprint for a utopian democracy beyond the structures of bourgeois parliamentarianism. Lenin's *State and Revolution* then expands on this model of direct democracy, famously breaking off in August 1917 with the apologetic remark that it is more entertaining to make a revolution than to write about one. Both texts, however, deal with political rather than economic utopias, and it is clearly the latter that poses the greatest conceptual difficulties for us.

To be sure, the anarchist strain in Marx is not to be underestimated. When early in *Capital* he asks us "to imagine, for a change, an association [*Verein*] of free men, working with the means of production held in common, and expending their many different forms of labor-power in full self-awareness as one single social labor force,"[10] it is not clear whether this is not merely some expanded collective "Robinsonade," or Robinson Crusoe fantasy, or whether we are still not at the stage of petty commodity production, as in yeoman farming or the Germanic mode of production.

The decisive statement comes later on and will, as Marx puts it, "flirt with the Hegelian dialectic":

> The capitalist mode of appropriation, which springs from the capitalist mode of production, produces capitalist private property. This is the first negation of individual private property, as founded on the labor of its proprietor [a reference to the yeoman system I just mentioned]. But capitalist production begets, with the inexorability of a natural process, its own negation. This is the negation of the negation. It does not re-establish private property, but it does indeed establish individual property on the basis of the achievements of the capitalist era: namely cooperation of the possession in common of the land and the means of production produced by labor itself.[11]

Note that the metaphor of childbirth still persists in this passage, which describes "the centralization of the means of production and the socialization of labor"—in other words, what the Frankfurt School significantly called "Vergesellschaftung" (societalization) in a variety of contexts (and what Italian thinkers today, following the Marx of the *Grundrisse*, call "General Intellect").[12] Still, not only does the metaphor of pregnancy not go away, the child is actually born in this paragraph! The aforementioned centralization and socialization occur a few lines later in a famous peroration declared "incompatible with their capitalist integument" (in other words, the new infrastructure is becoming incompatible with the older superstructures): "This integument is burst asunder. The knell of capitalist private property sounds. The expropriators are expropriated." This is very much a figural climax, or the realization of several kinds of figures all at once (although not the ones we will shortly be concerned with). What is at stake in the account generally is, of course, the growth of monopoly; and it is monopoly that I perversely wish to identify as a utopian phenomenon. But before I do so, it seems appropriate to quote more of Marx's description of what Lenin will then theorize as capitalism's second (or "highest") stage, as it seems to me extraordinarily contemporary and powerfully relevant for our own third stage of capitalism, what we generally call globalization.

> This expropriation is accomplished through the action of the immanent laws of capitalist production itself, through the centralization of capitals. One capitalist always strikes down many others. Hand in hand with this centralization, or this expropriation of many capitalists by a few, other developments take place on an ever-increasing scale, such as the growth of the cooperative form of the labour process, the conscious technical application of science, the planned exploitation of the soil, the transformation of the means of labour into forms in which they can only be used in common, the economizing of all means of production by their use as the means of production of combined, socialized labour, the entanglement of all peoples in the net of the world market, and, with this, the growth of the international character of the capitalist regime. Along with the constant decrease in the number of capitalist magnates, who usurp and monopolize all the advantages of this process of transformation, the mass of misery, oppression, slavery, degradation and exploitation grows.[13]

It is then appropriate to prolong this standard Marxian picture of the transition from capitalism to socialism with Lenin's analyses, which omit the image of childbirth but insist even more vehemently on the ways in which the future society is "maturing within" the present one—in the form not only of the socialization of labor (combination, unionization, and so on) but above all of monopoly. Indeed, here we are at a certain watershed in radical or socialist thinking: where a progressive bourgeoisie seeks to deal with monopoly by breaking up the great corporations into smaller ones again, in order to permit the return of a healthier competition; and where anarchism denounces concentration as a figure for the state, which is to be destroyed at all costs and wherever its power appears. For Lenin the "withering away of the state" consists very specifically in the seizure of the monopolies and in their management by the producers themselves, which at one stroke does away not only with the managerial class but also with the political state and bureaucracy that run its affairs. Take, for example, the following passage on finance capital (also very relevant today):

> Capitalism has created an accounting *apparatus* in the shape of the banks, syndicates, postal services, consumers' societies, and office employees' unions. Without big banks socialism would be impossible. . . . The big banks are "state apparatus" which we need to bring about socialism, and which we take ready-made from capitalism; our task here is merely to lop off what capitalistically mutilates this excellent apparatus, to make it even bigger, even more democratic, even more comprehensive. Quantity will be transformed into quality. . . . We can "lay hold of" and "set in motion" this "state apparatus" (which is not fully a state apparatus under capitalism, but which will be so with us, under socialism) at one stroke, by a single decree.[14]

I have quoted these very representative passages at some length because their very defense of size and monopoly is shocking today, for those both on the Right and on the Left, for admirers of free markets as well as for those who believe that small is beautiful and that self-organization is the key to economic democracy. I often share these sympathies and do not particularly mean to take a position here, but I observe that in both cases—regulation and the breaking up of monopolies in the name of business competition on the one hand, and the return to smaller communities and collectivities on the other— we have to do with historical regression and the attempt to return to a past that no longer exists. But we apparently cannot think of an impending future of size, quantity, overpopulation, and the like, except in dystopian terms. Indeed, the difficulties in thinking quantity positively must be added to the list of obstacles facing utopian thought in our time.

Wal-Mart

This is the point at which I propose a model for utopian analysis that might be taken as a synthesis of these two subjective and objective approaches. I develop two examples of this kind of interpretation, which are what I want to identify not as the utopian method as such but at least as one possible method among others; these examples draw on history and theory respectively. My theoretical example is drawn from the now burgeoning field of manifestos for a politics of the "multitude"; my historical example, however, proposes a new institutional candidate for the function of utopian allegory, and that is the phenomenon called Wal-Mart. I trust that this proposal will be even more shocking than Lenin's celebration of monopoly, all the more so since information research tells us that an enormous percentage of Wal-Mart shoppers are sharply critical and even negative about this corporation (the critics also shop there).[15] Everyone knows the negative criticisms: a new Wal-Mart drives local businesses under and reduces the number of available jobs; Wal-Mart's jobs scarcely pay a living wage and offer no benefits or health insurance; the company is antiunion (except in China); it hires illegal immigrants and increasingly emphasizes part-time work; it drives American business abroad and promotes sweatshops and child labor outside the country; it is ruthless in its practices (which are mostly secret), exercises a reign of terror over its suppliers, destroys whole ecologies abroad and whole communities in the United States, locks its own employees in at night, and so on. The picture is unappetizing, and the prospects for the future—Wal-Mart is already the largest company, not only in the United States but also in the world!—are positively frightening and even, particularly if you have a bent for conspiracy theory, dystopian in the extreme. Here, rather than in the trusts and monopolies of Theodore Roosevelt's time, is the true embodiment of the Marxist-Leninist prophecy of concentration and the monopolistic tendency of late capitalism; yet as its commentators observe, the emergence of this entity—like a new virus or a new species—was not only unexpected but also theoretically unparalleled and resistant to current categories of economic, political, and social thinking: "Wal-Mart is something utterly new . . . carefully disguised as something ordinary, familiar, even prosaic. . . . Yes, Wal-Mart plays by the rules, but perhaps the most important part of the Wal-Mart effect is that the rules are antiquated. . . . At the moment, we are incapable as a society of understanding Wal-Mart because we haven't equipped ourselves to manage it."[16]

I must add the reminder that there is a type of thinking that can deal with this strange new phenomenon lucidly, at the same time that it explains why traditional thought is unable to do so, and that is the dialectic. Consider the following analysis: "That kind of dominance at both ends of the spectrum—dominance across a huge range of merchandise and dominance of geographical consumer markets—means that market capitalism is being strangled with the kind of slow inexorability of a boa constrictor."[17] And if this sounds like mere journalistic rhetoric, here is the observation of a CEO who flatly affirms of Wal-Mart: "They have killed free-market capitalism in America."[18] But what is this peculiar contradiction but the contemporary version of what Marx called the negation of the negation? Wal-Mart is not an aberration or an exception, but rather the purest expression of that dynamic of capitalism which devours itself, which abolishes the market by means of the market itself.

This dialectical character of the new reality Wal-Mart represents is also very much the source of the ambivalence universally felt about this business operation, whose capacity to reduce inflation and to hold down or even to lower prices and make life affordable for the poorest Americans is also the very source of their poverty and the prime mover in the dissolution of American industrial productivity and the irrevocable destruction of the American small town. This is the historically unique and dialectical dynamic of capitalism as a system, as Marx and Engels describe it in the *Manifesto* in pages that some have taken as a delirious celebration of the powers of the new mode of production and others as the ultimate moral judgment of it. But the dialectic is not moral in that sense, and what Marx and Engels identify is the simultaneity of "more and more colossal productive forces than all preceding generations together," along with the most destructive negativity ever unleashed ("all that is solid melts into air"). The dialectic is an injunction to think the negative and the positive together at one and the same time, in the unity of a single thought, where moralizing wants to have the luxury of condemning this evil without particularly imagining anything else in its place.

So Wal-Mart is celebrated as the ultimate in democracy as well as in efficiency: a streamlined organization that ruthlessly strips away all unnecessary frills and waste and that disciplines its bureaucracy, creating a class as admirable as the Prussian state or the great movement of *instituteurs* in late-nineteenth-century French lay education or even the dreams of a streamlined Soviet system. New desires are encouraged and satisfied as richly as the theoreticians of the 1960s (and Marx himself) predicted, and the problems of distribution are triumphantly addressed with all kinds of new technological innovations.

I enumerate a few of the latter: on the one (informational) hand, there is the evolution of the UPC, or the so-called bar code, one of what Hiromi Hosoya and Markus Schaeffer call "bit structures," which in general they define as "a new infrastructure in the city, providing unprecedented synchronization and organization in seeming formlessness. Bit structures reorganize the pattern of the city and allow its destabilization."[19] The bar code, meanwhile, "reverses the balance of power between retailer and distributor or manufacturer" via the introduction, in the early 1970s, of "a whole new generation of electronic cash registers," which were able to process the mass of information registered on the bar code, from inventory to customer preferences: a technological innovation pioneered, according to the oldest logic of capitalism, "as a remedy to a time of stagnation that forced competing manufacturers to cooperate."[20] The utopian features of the bar code project it as the equivalent, in the world of commodities, of the Internet among human subjects; and the reversal of dominance from production to distribution somewhat parallels the emergence of the ideologies of democracy in the social realm.

Yet on the side of the material object, there is another relevant development, as fundamental as this one but quite different from it, and that is the invention and emergence of containerization as a revolution in transport, whose multiple effects we cannot explore here.[21] This spatial innovation is similar to the response to demography and overpopulation in the social realm, and it leads us into a dialectic of quantity and quality. Indeed, these ends of the so-called supply chain demand a philosophical conceptualization and stand as the mediation between production and distribution and the virtual abolition of an opposition between distribution and consumption.

Meanwhile, the anarchy of capitalism and the market has been overcome and the necessities of life have been provided for an increasingly desperate and impoverished public, exploited by its government and its big businesses over whom it is scarcely able to exercise political control. Anyone who does not appreciate this historic originality of Wal-Mart and its strengths and accomplishments is really not up to the discussion; meanwhile—and I say this for the Left as well—there is an aesthetic appreciation to be demanded for this achievement, an appreciation of the type Brecht reserved for one of his favorite books, Gustavus Myers's *History of the Great American Fortunes*, which we might be willing to bestow on the manipulations and strategies of those archcriminals, the Russian oligarchs. But such admiration and positive judgment must be accompanied by the absolute condemnation that completes the dialectical ambivalence we bring to this historical phenomenon. Nor is Wal-Mart wholly oblivious to its own ambivalence; after avoiding journalists altogether for fear of letting damaging facts slip out, its publicity people have come to expect mixed feelings in which the harshest criticism is inevitably accompanied by celebratory concessions.[22]

I am tempted to add something about the ambivalence of the dialectic itself, particularly with respect to technological innovation. It is enough to recall the admiration of Lenin and Gramsci for Taylorism and Fordism to be perplexed by this weakness of revolutionaries for what is most exploitative and dehumanizing in the working life of capitalism. But this is precisely what is meant by the utopian here, namely that what is currently negative can also be imagined as positive in that immense changing of the valences that is the utopian future. And this is the way I want us to consider Wal-Mart, however briefly, as a thought experiment: not—after Lenin's crude but practical fashion—as an institution from which (after the revolution) we can "lop off what capitalistically mutilates this excellent apparatus," but rather as what Raymond Williams called the emergent, as opposed to the residual—the shape of a utopian future looming through the mist, which we must seize as an opportunity to exercise the utopian imagination more fully, rather than an occasion for moralizing judgments or regressive nostalgia.

I now address two further but extremely pertinent objections to this paradoxical affirmation, before moving on to a different utopian exercise. First, Wal-Mart may be a model of distribution, but it can scarcely be said to be a model of production in the strict sense, however much we might talk of the production of distribution and so on. This cuts to the very heart of our socioeconomic contradictions, one face of which is structural unemployment, the other the definitive outstripping (dating from 2003 in the United States) of "productive" employment by retailers. (Computerization and information would also have to be included in these new contradictory structures, and it is evident that Wal-Mart's special kind of success depends on computers and would have been impossible before them.) I look at this from the perspective of the dictatorship this retail company exercises over its productive suppliers (or "partners," as Wal-Mart likes to call them); it is a devastating power, in which the giant firm is able to force its suppliers to outsource, reduce the quality of materials and product, or even drive them out of business altogether. It is worth noting that this power could be exercised in exactly the opposite way by "using its enormous purchasing power," as Fishman suggests, "not just to raise the standard of living for its customers, but also for its suppliers"[23] (the example is the proposal that Wal-Mart impose ecological standards on the Chilean salmon fisheries it has created; one might imagine a similar positive dictatorship over working conditions and labor relations). It is a utopian suggestion, to the degree to which the valences of this power—from retail monopoly to the various producers—could be reversed without structural change.

But I also suggest—as at the end of Eisenstein's *Old and New* (1929, also known as *The General Line*), where the aviator and the peasant swap roles, the worker becoming an agriculturist and vice versa—that it seems possible for the new system to offer a chance to suppress this opposition altogether, this binary tension between production and distribution, which we do not seem to be able to think our way out of, and to imagine a wholly new set of categories: not to abandon production and the categories of class in favor of consumption or information, but rather to lift production into a new and more complex concept, about which we can no longer speculate here.

The other objection has to do with the profit motive. After all, the driving force of Wal-Mart is that it is a capitalist industry, and the failures of socialism all seemed to lie in the slackness encouraged by the command economy, in which corruption, favoritism, nepotism, or sheer research ignorance led to the scandals in which, famously, the basements of the GUM were filled with illimitable quantities of identical lampshades that no one wanted to buy. All that socialism seemed to be able to offer as a counterforce to the profit motive were the famous "moral incentives" Che invoked in Cuba, which require repeated mobilizations and exhausting campaigns to reinvigorate failing supplies of socialist enthusiasm.

Wal-Mart is also driven by moral incentives. The secret of its success is not profit but pricing, the shaving off of the final pennies, a policy fatal to any number of its suppliers. "Sam valued every penny," observes one of the founder's colleagues,[24] and it is a fateful sentence, for this imperative—"always low prices"—is driven by the most fundamental motive of all, the one Max Weber described as the Protestant ethic, a return to that thrift and obsessive frugality which characterized the first great moment of the system and which is recaptured (with or without its religious component) in the hagiography of Sam Walton and the heroic saga of his company. Perhaps, then, even the explanatory appeal to the profit motive is essentialist and pertains to an ideology of human nature that is part of the initial construction of capitalism. Marxism is not psychologically reductive in this way, and it asserts not determinism by greed or acquisitiveness but rather the determination by the system or mode of production, each of which produces and constructs its own historical version of human nature.

Virno

Let us describe with more precision the theory and practice of this new type of utopia that my account of Wal-Mart seems to presuppose. Indeed, the theoretical approaches to it are sometimes found in positions explicitly characterized as anti-utopian. This is the case with our next example, which will turn on the now well-known concept of the multitude, as developed (borrowing a term by Spinoza) by Michael Hardt and Antonio Negri in their books *Empire* and *Multitude*, respectively. It is worth noting that their specific denunciations of utopianism, although consistent with a good deal of post-structuralist doctrine, have the immediate political and historical reference of Stalinism and of the historic Communist Parties coming out of the Leninist tradition (despite the latter's own internal critique of utopianism from Lenin on). Here utopia is identified with slogans of historical inevitability and of "tomorrows that sing," the sacrifice of present generations for some future utopian state, and particularly with the party structure.

As for the concept of multitude, however flawed, it seems to constitute an attempt to substitute a new and more serviceable stand-in for older theorizations of collectivity and collective agents, such as those of "the people" (in populism) and of social class (in workerisms that excluded gender and race, and even sometimes the peasantry, from their narrow political definitions). Every new approach to collectivity is worth welcoming in an atomized and individualistic society (but I will come back to individualism in a moment). The older collective concepts were also clearly flawed in their own very different ways, at the same time that they expressed the social reality of the emergence of new forms of collective agents or subjects. But I am not particularly interested in entering the debate on "multitude" here, since it is essentially a methodological innovation I am trying to identify. To do so, however, I will draw not on the massive and complex books of Hardt and Negri, but rather on a briefer intervention in this discussion, a luminous exposition of some of the consequences of this new theoretical position (which by now is a new tradition) by one of the most remarkable philosophical minds of the era, the Italian philosopher Paolo Virno, who is still little known in the United States.

His book *Grammar of the Multitude* may be read as a series of notes on the changes the concept of multitude should be expected to bring to the phenomenology of everyday life in postmodernity (not his word) and indeed to our attitudes toward and evaluations of those changes. I will touch not on all of his themes and intentions here, but essentially on the book's revision of certain standard Heideggerian positions that are still very much with us today, in liberal as well as in conservative culture, and indeed in Western bourgeois daily life in general.

Heidegger called for a purgation of precisely those habits of bourgeois comfort by way of anxiety and the fear of death, and he saw modern life as dominated by inauthenticity and urban collectivity. You may also remember the four forms of degradation into which *Dasein's* daily life is alienated in the daily life of modernity, namely, "das Gerede, die Neugier, die Zweideutigkeit, und das Verfallen,"[25] or, as the translations of *Sein und Zeit* have it, "idle talk, curiosity, ambiguity, and falling" (or "falling prey"). It is essentially these categories, and the very concept of inauthenticity, that Virno has it in mind to revise (leaving Nazism and the later theories of technology out of it, as we will also do).

These diagnoses of "modernity" are not specific to Heidegger; they are part and parcel of a whole conservative and antimodernist ideology embraced by nonleftist intellectuals across the board in the 1920s, from T. S. Eliot to Ortega y Gasset, by traditionalists from China to America. This ideology expresses a horror of the new industrial city with its new working and white-collar classes, its mass culture and public sphere, its standardization and parliamentary systems; and it often implies a nostalgia for the older agriculturalist ways of life, as in the American "Fugitives," English yeoman farmers, or the Heideggerian "Feldweg." It is unnecessary to add that this ideology is informed by an abiding fear of socialism or communism, and that the corporatisms that dominate the political life of the 1930s, from Roosevelt's New Deal to Stalin's Five-Year Plans, from Nazism and Italian fascism to Fabian social democracy, are from this perspective to be seen as so many compromises with such traditionalism as it resists the so-called modernities of the age of so-called "mass man."

Those compromises have for the most part entered history (leaving contemporary social democracy in some disarray and in a situation in which free-market fundamentalism is so far the only serviceable new practical-political ideology); but the general social attitudes of the older conservative ideology I have just outlined (and of which Heidegger is only the most extraordinary philosophical theorist) are still largely with us and still intellectually and ideologically operative.

I return to the issue of representational utopias I raised earlier. Indeed, the standard way of dealing with the social anxieties that inform the old antimodernist ideology has been to accept it while assuring us that in whatever future "more perfect society," all of the negative features it enumerates will have been corrected. Thus, in these pastorals, there will be no social insecurity to generate anxiety (and even death will be postponed), idle gossip will presumably be replaced by a purified language and by genuine human relationships, morbid curiosity by a certain healthy distance from others as well as an enlightened awareness of our position in the social totality, "ambiguity" (by which Heidegger means the lies and propaganda of mass culture and the public sphere) will be cured by our more authentic relationships to the project and to work and action in general, and *Verfallenheit* (our "loss of self in the public dimension of the man," or the inauthenticity of "mass man") will be replaced by some more genuine individualism and a more authentic isolation of the self in its own existential concerns and commitments. Now these are all no doubt excellent and desirable developments, but it is not hard to see that they are also essentially reactive; that is, they constitute so many obedient replacements of the reigning negative terms by their positive opposites. But this very reactivity of the Heideggerian response tends to confirm the priority of the negative diagnosis in the first place.

It may also be confirmed by current dystopian visions in which the multidimensional fear of all those unknown others who constitute "society" beyond one's immediate circle of acquaintances is once again, under postmodern or globalized conditions, concentrated in the fear of multiplicity and overpopulation. Clearly an ancient tradition of satire from the Hebrew prophets onward rehearsed this horror of the collective other in the form of the denunciation of a sinful or fallen society, just as philosophical speculations such as Descartes' assimilation of the other to the automaton expressed the scandal in a different way from its theological version (the stream of soulless employees going to work across London Bridge in *The Waste Land*) or from journalistic "culture critiques" of alienation. The SF of the 1960s, particularly with John Brunner's classic tetralogy, gave nonideological expression to various figures of social crisis, dissolution, or degradation, while the image of soulless clones or brainwashed zombies expressed a more overt denunciation of the unreformable stupidity of the modern democratic masses. Yet even in these expressions of crisis, the symptoms (pollution, atomic war, urban crime, the "degradation" of mass culture, standardization, impoverishment, unemployment, the predominance of the service sector, and so on) remained differentiated, and each gave rise to a different kind of monitory representation. It is only in postmodernity and globalization, with the world population explosion, the desertion of the countryside, the growth of the megacity, global warming and ecological catastrophe, the proliferation of urban guerrilla warfare, the financial collapse of the welfare state, and the universal emergence of small group politics of all kinds that these phenomena have seemed to fold back into each other around the primary cause (if that is the right category to use) of the scandal of multiplicity and of what is generally referred to as overpopulation, or in other words, the definitive appearance of the Other in multiple forms and as sheer quantity or number. Predictably, the representational response to this crystallization has taken the twin positive and negative forms of a vision of the "sprawl" as a seemingly dystopian urbanization of enormous sectors of the older global landscape, or of a retreat into precisely those pastoral visions of smaller collectivities evoked above. Few have been those who, like Rem Koolhaas, with his embrace of a "culture of congestion"[26] and his projection of new and positive spaces within which overpopulation can joyously flourish, have seized on a strategy of changing the valences and of converting the gloomy indexes of the pessimistic diagnosis into vital promises of some newly emergent historical reality to be welcomed rather than lamented.

It is indeed just such a strategy that I want to find at work in *Grammar of the Multitude*, whose themes may now be briefly (and incompletely) passed in review. For the insecurities of both fear and anxiety (sharply differentiated in Heidegger), Virno substitutes a wholesale attack on bourgeois security as such, to which I will return, observing only that security is also a spatial concept (related to Heideggerian "dwelling") and posits some initial physical separation from one's neighbor, which is also ideologically interrelated with concepts of property (in that sense, only the rich are truly secure, in their gated communities and their carefully policed and patrolled estates, whose function lies in occulting and repressing the existential fact of collectivity). The operator of the transvaluation recommended here, from anxiety to affirmation, is the Kantian notion of the sublime, which incorporates fear within its very *jouissance*; yet the practical consequences of such a transformation will also transform the pathos of Heideggerian homelessness into the animation of Deleuzian nomadism, as we shall see.

Nomadism, however, would also seem to characterize contemporary labor, in a situation in which, as the economists solemnly warn us, no one should expect to hold down a single lifelong job (they do not generally add the increasingly obvious supplement, namely that many should not expect to hold down any job at all). Virno's discussion of contemporary labor, which undertakes to challenge and to dismantle the traditional Aristotelian distinction (revived by Hannah Arendt) between labor, politics, and philosophy, would also seem to aim at a utopian restructuring of the whole notion of alienation, as it has been degraded from Marx's early analysis of industrial labor into some all-purpose cultural characterization. The Hegelian notion of externalization, of which Marx's concept was both a critique and a restructuring, itself constituted a kind of utopian celebration of handicraft activity and production, no longer relevant in the industrial era.[27] Virno now proposes a notion of production as virtuosity, a concept that redeems the old 1960s ideal of an aesthetization of life, as well as resituating the even more contemporary denunciations of contemporary society in terms of the spectacle (Debord) and the simulacrum (Baudrillard).

We must first note the specificities of labor today, as Virno outlines them, drawing the ultimate conclusion from the movement of all modern philosophy from categories of substance to categories of process. Modern (or perhaps postmodern) work is a matter of process, an activity for which the end has become secondary and the production of an object a mere pretext, the process having become an end in itself. This is comparable to virtuosity in the aesthetic realm, and indeed here we meet an unexpected avatar of the old Left dream of an aesthetic disalienation of the world, from Schiller to Marcuse and the 1960s. Yet this one will have none of the saving graces of the older aestheticism; it will be a culture of minding the machines, a postwork culture, an activity of language sharing and linguistic cooperation. This move then also entails the resituating of labor—hitherto ambiguously differentiated from both private and public spheres (it is not private life, but its framework is still owned by the capitalist and not open to the public)—within some new space from which the opposition between private and public has disappeared, without the reduction of one to the other.

This last is now a "publicness without a public sphere,"[28] a transformation that in turn leads to a series of other utopian consequences. For one thing, so-called mass culture is transformed, becoming "an industry of the means of production" (61). Its clichés and commonplaces are now an enactment of collective sharing and participation, and they come to have the redemptive innocence of childhood repetition. Indeed, at this point, Virno sketches out what might be a theory of the cultural equivalent of that theory of general intellect, which, drawing on Marx's *Grundrisse*, has been so crucial to the way in which Italian philosophy has sought to disclose the profound socialization and collectivization of late-capitalist social life and work. In this context, then, where science and language have soaked into the everyday and permeated all the pores of our daily lives, making everyone an intellectual (as Gramsci famously put it), a henceforth globalized mass culture and omnipresent communication have a very different significance. The multitude has its own new kind of linguistic and cultural literacy everywhere on the globe: there are no prehistoric peoples, no premodern survivals; tribals listen to their portables and nomads watch their DVDs; in mountain villages without electricity, as well as in the most dismal refugee camps, the dispossessed follow current events and listen to the vacuous speeches of our president. Yet in that dedifferentiation of culture and politics that characterizes postmodernity, such "publicness without a public sphere" also grounds and prepares what Virno calls "the feasibility of a non-representational democracy" (79).

It is evident that within this extraordinary reversal of the traditional judgments on mass society and its "degradations," Heidegger's existential inauthenticities will also be transformed. To the existential philosopher's enumeration (idle talk or gossip, curiosity, ambiguity, and *Verfallenheit*) Virno adds two others—opportunism and cynicism, which have perhaps attracted more explicit and fulsome condemnation in recent times. It may be increasingly obvious that gossip, as in Proust, is preeminently the mark of a human age and of the preponderance of the human other over the former relations between human beings and nature. But curiosity—particularly in the classic form of voyeuristic envy that Saint Augustine analyzed so long ago—is also to be accorded its utopian transfiguration. Walter Benjamin's paradoxical defense of "distraction" may now be reread as the designation of a new type of perception within a world of habit and numb routine in Virno's formulation:

> The media trains the senses to consider the known as if it were unknown, to distinguish "an enormous and sudden margin of freedom" even in the most trite and repetitive aspects of daily life. At the same time, however, the media trains the senses also for the opposite task: to consider the unknown as if it were known, to become familiar with the unexpected and the surprising, to become accustomed to the lack of established habits. (93)

As for opportunism, very much in the spirit of Hegel's defense of utilitarianism, it marks the indispensable emergence of the tactical and strategic coup d'oeil, the capacity to size up and evaluate the situation, the makings of a new and intensified sense of orientation in this new world of the utopian masses: "Opportunism gains in value as an indispensable resource whenever the concrete labor process is permeated by a diffuse 'communicative action' and thus no longer identifies itself solely with mute 'instrumental action'" (86). As for cynicism, today at the very center of liberal political reflection, it clearly also develops a new and original stance with respect to the knowledge of the way in which our system functions, renouncing "any claim to a standard of judgement which shares the nature of a moral evaluation" (88) and thereby, according to Virno, repudiating the very principle of equivalency on which moral judgments are founded. Cynicism thereby abandons the universalism of equivalency (read: exchange value) for that new kind of multiplicity that traditionalists call relativism, but which is a new effect of the multitude rather than some inherited philosophical position. With these few remarks, Virno opens up the whole urgent problem of cynical reason for some original retheorization.

If "ambiguity" designates Heidegger's anxiety about the degradation of language in the modern world of mass culture and universal literacy, *Verfallenheit* characterizes the more general way in which, according to him, the inauthentic *Dasein* is abandoned to the collective order and "falls prey" to the "world" of others, in which it forgets itself and loses its individuality—that is, for Heidegger, its existential solitude and that isolation in which it can alone know its freedom, its "being-unto-death." This loss of self in the crowd, the submersion of individuality in the multitude, has been the central indictment counterrevolutionary ideology proposed since its invention, knowing its high points in grisly mob scenes in the French Revolution (and their analysis by LeBon and Freud as the overcoming of the rational ego by collective irrationality), as well as in deplorable outrages to private property in practically any large-scale revolt you can instance.

And this is also the way our bourgeois tradition has, from time relatively immemorial, observed the crowd or the mob—that is, from a safe distance and deploring the excesses and the way in which its subjects run to and fro aimlessly, shouting and gesticulating, released from the constraints of law and decency, and, as it were, under the spell of a kind of shamanistic possession. What Virno has to tell us about this is extremely timely. These inherited pictures and prejudices, he argues, suggest that our traditional view of what we like to call modernity (first-world bourgeois capitalism) presupposes our emergence as individuals from some inchoate preindividualistic mass, and our fear of being resubmerged into a postindividualistic "multitude" in which we will again lose everything we have painfully achieved as individual subjects. The multitude is, on the contrary, the very condition for individuation; it is alone in the multitude and the collective that we arrive at our true singularity as individuals. We must abandon the habit of thinking of a host of things—language, culture, literacy, the state, the nation—as goals to be achieved in some arduous yet beneficent process of modernization. On the contrary, they are long since all achieved, everyone is modern, and modernization has been over for some time. "Unity," Virno tells us, "is no longer something (the State, the sovereign), towards which things converge, as in the case of the people; rather it is taken for granted, as a background or a necessary precondition. The many must be thought of as the individualization of the universal, of the generic, of the shared experience" (25).

The premise of unity articulated here is, to be sure, based on that understanding of general intellect alluded to above: the recognition of an immense expansion of the cultural sphere in late capitalism or postmodernity, the generalization of knowledge (very much including science) in that end of nature and the natural, that tendential humanization of the world implicit in Marx's "universalization of wage labor" and the approach of a genuine world market. It also casts a different light on the politics of difference, which has a meaning after the totalizations of capitalism that it could not possibly have had in early capitalist (or precapitalist) thought and experience. Even the unification of groups in some great collective project must necessarily work differently after the consolidation of a system of nation-states from the way it did when the very construction of the nation, incomplete, was a heroic and a progressive process.

So much, then, for some of the constitutive features of this new world of the multitude, which we are to train ourselves to welcome as the first fresh stirrings of the very storm of utopia. The last-mentioned aspect of the multitude's curiosity, however—"the lack of established habits"—will bring us back to the second theme I wanted to explore in Virno's book, and that is the very opening remarks about security and shelter. Established habits are also a security and a shelter, and perhaps the most fundamental feature of the new situation from which that new thing, the multitude, emerges can be addressed in that way, as some new and utter absence of security and shelter, as some new homelessness no longer to be reminiscent of nostalgia or bourgeois comfort, with Heideggerian "dwelling" or the protection of the state—a new and permanent crisis situation in which we are all refugees, whether we know it or not. What we are calling the multitude, then, is the population of those refugee camps as they supplant the promise of suburbs and the mobility of freeways, which have become permanent traffic jams.

Virno associates two kinds of actions with this new multitude, whether utopian or not. The first is civil disobedience, the rejection of the state, to which we can oppose the self-organization of the camps and bidonvilles, which have fallen below the state's radar. The second is his version of Deleuzian nomadism, namely emigration, as the latter hovers above modern Italian history (in Gianni Amelio's great film *Lamerica* [1994], for example) but also reappears in the very last chapter of *Capital*, where the European laborers are seen to desert the old country for the American East Coast and in a few years to "desert the factory, moving West, towards free lands. Wage labor is seen as a transitory phase, rather than as a life sentence" (45). The camps, the frontier: such is the deeper unseen reality of the world of the multitude that Virno asks us to embrace in Nietzschean fashion, not as some forever recurring of the present, but as the eternal return of the future and of utopian possibilities to be celebrated as though we had chosen them in the first place.

Method

I need to clarify the "method" to which my title refers and to give a theoretical account of the rather peculiar and even perverse readings I have offered of my two illustrations. Just as I hasten to assure the reader that I do not mean to celebrate Wal-Mart, let alone to forecast the emergence of anything good and progressive from this astonishing new postmonopoly institution, so also my discussion of Paolo Virno is not to be taken as an endorsement of some putative new politics of "multitude" or even as a practical-political discussion—something he is perfectly capable of conducting in his own voice, and indeed which the final chapter of his *Grammar* (on which I have not touched) begins to lay out. To put it in a different and more accurate way, it does not matter what I think personally about the future of the Wal-Mart-type business operation or about the "politics of multitude"; I have been using both topics and both occasions to illustrate a method, about which it is now important to say that it is meant to be distinct from any of those outlined at the beginning of this chapter.

The hermeneutic I want to demonstrate is therefore not predictive; nor is it symptomological. It is not meant as a way to read the outlines of the future within the present, nor is it meant to identify the operations of collective wish fulfillment within the rather unpleasant phenomena (monopoly, overpopulation) that are its objects of examination. The latter approach—generally identified with Ernst Bloch's work—would have to take the opinions and ideologies, the ways of life and situations, of social groups far more seriously and empirically into consideration than this exercise has done. The former line of inquiry, that of practical politics and programs, and identified here with Marx and with Lenin, would have had to assess the concrete world situation in its economic and political objectivity, as well as in the balance of ideological forces, from a strategic perspective rather than from isolated data.

I consider the utopian "method" outlined here as neither a hermeneutic nor a political program, but rather something like the structural inversion of what Foucault, following Nietzsche, called the genealogy. By that he meant to distinguish his own (or perhaps even some more generalized post-structural or postmodern) method from either empirical history or the evolutionary narratives reconstructed by idealist historians. The genealogy was, in effect, to be understood as neither chronological nor narrative but rather a logical operation (taking "logic" in a Hegelian sense without being Hegelian about it). Genealogy, in other words, was meant to lay in place the various logical preconditions for the appearance of a given phenomenon, without in any way implying that they constituted the latter's causes, let alone the latter's antecedents or early stages. To be sure, inasmuch as those genealogical preconditions almost always took the form of earlier historical events, misunderstanding—and the assimilation of the new construction to any of the older historical approaches (chronology, causality, narrative, idealist continuity)—was always inevitable, and it could not be warded off by Raymond Roussel's immortal anecdote of the tourist who claimed to have discovered, under glass in a provincial museum, "the skull of Voltaire as a child."

So far, there is no term as useful for the construction of the future as *genealogy* for such a construction of the past; it is certainly not to be called *futurology*, and *utopology* will never mean much, I fear. The operation itself, however, consists in a prodigious effort to change the valences on phenomena that so far exist only in our own present and experimentally to declare positive things that are clearly negative in our own world, to affirm that dystopia is in reality utopia if examined more closely, to isolate specific features in our empirical present so as to read them as components of a different system. This is what we have seen Virno do when he borrowed an enumeration of what in Heidegger are clearly meant to be negative and highly critical features of modern society or modern actuality, staging each of these alleged symptoms of degradation as an occasion for celebration and as a promise of what he does not—but what we may—call an alternate utopian future.

This kind of prospective hermeneutic is a political act only in one specific sense: as a contribution to the reawakening of the imagination of possible and alternate futures, a reawakening of that historicity which our system—offering itself as the very end of history—necessarily represses and paralyzes. This is the sense in which utopology revives long-dormant parts of the mind, unused organs of political, historical, and social imagination that have virtually atrophied for lack of use, muscles of praxis we have long since ceased exercising, revolutionary gestures we have lost the habit of performing, even subliminally. Such a revival of futurity and of the positing of alternate futures is not a political program or even a political practice, but it is hard to see how any durable or effective political action could come into being without it.

Notes

1. *Poems, 1913–1956*, ed. John Willett and Ralph Manheim (New York: Methuen, 1976), 380.

2. For the canonical account, see Siegfried Giedion, *Space, Time and Architecture* (Cambridge, MA: Harvard University Press, 1967).

3. Robert Caro's biography of Moses, *The Powerbroker* (New York: Knopf, 1974), is an indispensable resource.

4. John Brunner, *Stand on Zanzibar* (1968), *The Jagged Edge* (1969), *The Sheep Look Up* (1972), and *The Shockwave Rider* (1975).

5. See Ernesto Laclau and Chantal Mouffe, *Hegemony and Socialist Strategy* (London: Verso, 1985).

6. Fredric Jameson, *Archaeologies of the Future* (London: Verso, 2005).

7. Peter Sloterdijk, *The Critique of Cynical Reason* (Minneapolis: University of Minnesota Press, 1987).

8. Jacques Attali, *Les trios mondes: Pour une théorie de l'après-crise* (Paris: Fayard, 1983).

9. Karl Marx, preface to *Contribution to a Critique of Political Economy*, in *Marx and Engels: Basic Writings on Politics and Philosophy*, ed. Lewis S. Feuer (New York: Doubleday, 1959), 44.

10. Karl Marx, *Capital: A Critique of Political Economy*, vol. 1 (Harmondsworth: Penguin, 1976), 171.

11. Ibid., 929.

12. Karl Marx, *Grundrisse* (London: Penguin, 1973), 706; see also Paolo Virno, "The Ambivalence of Disenchantment," in *Radical Thought in Italy*, ed. Paolo Virno and Michael Hardt (Minneapolis: Minnesota University Press, 1996), 20–24.

13. Ibid., 929.

14. V. I. Lenin, quoted in Neil Harding's *Leninism* (Durham: Duke University Press, 1996), 145–46; emphasis in the original.

15. Charles Fishman, *The Wal-Mart Effect* (New York: Penguin, 2006), 220.

16. Ibid., 221–22.

17. Ibid., 234.

18. Ibid., 233.

19. *The Harvard Design School Guide to Shopping*, ed. Chuihua Judy Chung, Jeffrey Inaba, Rem Koolhaas, and Sze Tsung Leon (Cologne: Taschen, 2001), 157. (This book is volume 2 of Koolhaas's monumental *Project on the City*. And on technological innovations, see also "The Physical Internet," *The Economist*, 17 June 2006; and Thomas Friedman, *The World Is Flat* (New York: Farrar, Straus and Giroux, 2005), especially 128–141.

20. Ibid., 158.

21. But see Marc Levinson, *The Box* (Princeton: Princeton University Press, 2006).

22. Fishman, *Wal-Mart Effect*, 145–46.

23. Ibid., 181.

24. Ibid., 30.

25. Heidegger, *Sein und Zeit*, paragraphs 35, 36, 37, 38.

26. Rem Koolhaas, *Delirious New York* (New York: Oxford University Press, 1978), 7; and see also, on city size, his *S, M, L, XL* (New York: Monacelli Press, 1995), 961–71.

27. Hegel's discussion of "die Sache selbst" (the matter at hand) is in *Phenomenology of Spirit*, trans. A. V. Miller (Oxford: Oxford University Press, 1977), 237–52.

28. Paolo Virno, *A Grammar of the Multitude* (Los Angeles: Semiotext(e), 2004), 40. From here on, page numbers from this source are given in the chapter.

2.

JENNIFER WENZEL

Literacy and Futurity: Millennial Dreaming on the Nineteenth-Century Southern African Frontier

Prologue

This chapter examines two kinds of millennial dreaming involving the Xhosa people of southern Africa's eastern Cape: a prophet-led movement known as the Xhosa cattle killing of 1856–57 and the Christian evangelization (and colonial subjugation) of the Xhosa during the same period. The cattle killing was the climax of nearly a decade of millenarian prophecies among the ama-Xhosa, whose livelihood and culture were centered around cattle, and who had been repeatedly dislocated for more than half a century as the border of the British Cape Colony pushed eastward in a series of frontier wars. The cattle-killing prophecy was delivered in 1856 to a young Xhosa woman by strange men who identified themselves as ancestors of the amaXhosa. Their message was disseminated by the young woman, Nongqawuse, and her uncle Mhlakaza. The prophecy promised the return of the ancestors if the amaXhosa would kill their cattle, abstain from agriculture, and destroy the grain stored in underground pits. The amaXhosa were to prepare new grain pits, strengthen their houses, refrain from witchcraft and sexual impurity, and await the return of the ancestors, who would bring with them herds of new cattle and piles of grain. The world would be renewed, and the Europeans and unbelievers would be driven into the sea. In widespread—yet by no means universal—compliance with the prophecy, approximately 400,000 cattle were killed in 1856–57. (Compounding this decimation of the herds, as many as 150,000 cattle had already died or been culled during an epidemic of bovine pleuro-pneumonia, or lung sickness, that had arrived in the Cape in 1853.) The ancestors and cattle failed to return on the final announced date in February 1857, and the human toll was devastating: approximately 40,000 people died of starvation, and 50,000 left their land to become laborers in the Cape Colony. Those who remained were forced into villages as the British seized more than 600,000 acres of land.[1]

In this chapter, I argue that we must understand Nongqawuse's millennial vision within the context of the competing millennial dream of Christian missionaries and colonial administrators to make of the Xhosa a new people. This Christian civilizing mission began among the amaXhosa not long before the cattle killing and accelerated as some of the starving survivors sought relief at Christian missions. One of the crucial engines of this project was literacy, and my aim here is to read the cattle killing in terms of the literary, ideological, and material consequences of the dissemination of literacy in southern Africa, a process contemporary with the cattle killing. By tracing the resonances between textuality and narrative, on the one hand, and the temporality of prophecy's articulation and dissemination, on the other, I show how the various plots into which the cattle killing has been written point toward the tensions between competing dreams of the future at work in the eastern Cape in the nineteenth century. Although these Xhosa and colonial visions of futurity have been read as diametrically opposed, I suggest that we might see each as providing mutually constitutive conditions of possibility for the other, in terms of both material constraint and repertoires of the imaginary. European authors of nineteenth-century historical accounts of the cattle killing treat the "magical" aspects of the prophecy in metaphorical terms that ultimately expose their own implication in the material predicament of the decimated Xhosa. In a historical context in which the dissemination of literacy was a key modality of colonial conquest—what Adam Ashforth has called "both a product of domination and form of domination"[2]—these texts' engagements with questions of representation, narrative structure, and metaphor invite us to rethink the relationship between literacy and the material realities of the aftermath of the cattle killing.

New People: Xhosa and European Visions of
Radical Change in the Eastern Cape

Nongqawuse's followers were not the only people dreaming of a different future in the 1850s. In *The Dead Will Arise: Nongqawuse and the Great Xhosa Cattle-Killing Movement of 1856–7* (1989), J. B. Peires writes that those who accepted the cattle-killing prophecy, as well as those who rejected it, were looking for change, the believers "hoping for the regeneration of an old world, and the [unbelievers] grasping eagerly at the new."[3] That is, in these competing utopian visions, Nongqawuse's believers awaited the restoration of autonomy, resources, land, and loved ones lost in nearly a century of colonial encroachment and armed conflict, and the unbelievers saw possibility in a nascent mercantile economy in which cattle and grain were commodities rather than communal resources to be distributed by chiefs. These two dreams of newness differed fundamentally in their understanding of historical change:

Nongqawuse's prophecy promised a radical *renewal* in which the ancestors would return as "new people,"[4] whereas the colonial vision imagined a world and a people radically *transformed*. While believers and unbelievers disagreed most urgently over whether to kill cattle, their divergent utopias involved far deeper questions. The unbelievers' embrace of innovation, as opposed to the believers' hopes for renovation, was informed by (although not identical with) the hopes of Christian missionaries and colonial administrators to make of the amaXhosa a new people.

The missionary project of religious conversion is the most obvious of these imagined transformations in southern Africa, part of the nineteenth-century global dispersal of European and American Christian evangelicals who saw their work of spreading the gospel as redeeming the sin of slavery (particularly in the British case), creating a kingdom of God on earth, and even hastening the fulfillment of biblical prophecies of the millennium and the end of days.[5] For this reason I refer to the European civilizing mission as a millennial dream: missionaries did see their work in spreading the gospel to all the nations within the framework of Christian eschatology, whereas colonial administrators imagined a wholesale transformation of people and land, the creation of "new men" shaped by European values. As early as 1827, the missionary and government agent William Ritchie Thomson described a series of changes already under way at the Glasgow Missionary Society's (GMS) Tyhume station, at that time near the colonial frontier:

> Where formerly a wilderness of long grass was, and the soil never turned up since the Flood, we have now growing many of the necessaries, and even some of the luxuries of life. A neat little village has been formed, inhabited by those who a little while ago roamed the world at large, as wild and savage as their old neighbors, the lions and tigers of the forest. They imitate us in all things—even in their dress; and now beads and baubles have fallen in the market, and old clothes are in demand. . . . If you except the black faces, a stranger would almost think he had dropped into a little Scotch village.[6]

Thomson describes a process that resembles what John Krige, in chapter 6, calls an "education of desire," yet Thomson's account of a complete transformation of Xhosa desire at Tyhume significantly overstates the eagerness of most of the amaXhosa to take up a new economy, new clothes, new houses, and a new god.

In 1855 Colonel John Maclean, the chief commissioner of British Kaffraria, described a far more wary process of selective appropriation:

> The [Xhosa,] contented like the North American Indian with his barbarous state, and apathetic as to improvement, has in addition to these other characteristics, that he clings tenaciously to his old customs and habits, is proud of his race, which he considers pure and superior to others, is therefore

eminently national, is suspicious, and holds aloof from others; and while considering the white man as a means of obtaining certain articles which the despised industry of the latter supplies would yet prefer their absence. . . . They cling to the native chieftainship as to a power which . . . represents them and their race.[7]

Maclean describes the situation facing Sir George Grey, governor of the Cape Colony from 1854 to 1861. Beginning in 1795, a series of frontier wars between Europeans and the amaXhosa had pushed the colonial frontier eastward, resulting in successive evictions of the amaXhosa from lands where generations of ancestors were buried. By the mid-1850s, the amaXhosa inhabited territory on both sides of the Kei River, which served as the eastern boundary of British Kaffraria, a military colony directly east of the Cape Colony, established in 1847. Grey had direct authority (unmediated by a local elected body) over British Kaffraria, which was ruled under martial law through a network of military commissioners and magistrates settled with Xhosa chiefs of the Ngqika and Ndlambe clans. On the eastern side of the Kei River, the Gcaleka Xhosa chief Sarhili ruled over independent Xhosaland, and his authority as king (or paramount chief) of all the amaXhosa was recognized by chiefs on both sides of the Kei, that is, both those under British military occupation and those in unconquered territory. This political geography complicated the British response to Nongqawuse's prophecy, which was articulated in Sarhili's territory just across the Kei from British Kaffraria but soon spread among the amaXhosa within the military colony as well; British commissioners could exert pressure over the chiefs with whom they were resident, but they had almost no influence—save the not insignificant threat of invasion—over the chiefs in the Transkei.

Grey's project, even before the cattle killing, amounted to an antinational colonialism, a response to the resolute autonomy of the "eminently national" Xhosa that Maclean described earlier. Grey aimed to transform the chiefs in British Kaffraria into paid agents of the colonial administration and to replace the Xhosa pastoral economy with wage labor on European farms and other enterprises. To consolidate his control over British Kaffraria, Grey looked forward to the arrival of "new people" there: not the Xhosa ancestors whom the adherents of the cattle-killing prophecy expected, but rather British settlers whose influence would purportedly civilize the amaXhosa by capturing their labor.[8] "If we leave the natives beyond our border ignorant barbarians," Grey told the Cape parliament, "they must always remain a race of troublesome marauders." In stirring rhetoric that camouflaged the brutality of his policies, Grey urged rather that the colony "use our time of strength . . . to instruct and civilize—to change inveterate enemies into friends . . . destroyers of our stock into consumers of our goods and producers for our markets."[9] The role of missionaries in this process was to "help build up a whole system of new ideas, new needs and desires, new allegiances, new authorities, and a new morality, all leading to an *acceptance* of the new civilization by the Africans," as one twentieth-century critic of missionaries' colonial complicity has written.[10] In other words, more than one millennial dream was at work in the eastern Cape in the 1850s, and these visions of futurity—politically polarized yet powerfully resonant with one another in their repertoires of imagining—help us to understand the complex ideological fault lines of this colonial moment. Grey once described the vision articulated in the cattle-killing prophecy as "a kind of Kaffir paradise," but he had his own utopian plans for British Kaffraria.[11] For those who embraced the civilizing mission, according to Grey, "a day of hope had already dawned."[12]

The catastrophic end of Nongqawuse's dream in 1857 only furthered Grey's own vision; he wrote, "I think . . . that I see my way clearly out of all this trouble, and that instead of nothing but dangers resulting from the Kaffirs having during the excitement killed their cattle and made away with their food, we can draw very great permanent advantages from the circumstance, which may be made a stepping stone for the future [European] settlement of the country."[13] Grey's labor and resettlement policies after the failure of the prophecy made good his words: famine drew the Xhosa survivors into the missions, which were pressured to succor them only until they were strong enough to be sent into the colony under labor contracts. For those Xhosa people who earlier had joined mission communities and embraced at least some aspects of the colonial dream of "civilization," rather than having Grey's version of it forced on them in the aftermath of the cattle killing, the disillusionment would come a half century later with the foundation of postcolonial South Africa as a segregationist state:

> The African elite who readily assimilated missionary education in the hope of joining the millenarian society implicit in the promise of civilisation and Christianity, and who looked eagerly to the fulfillment of grand humanitarian ideals associated with the name of Victoria and formulated in the face of settler colonialism and Boer hostility, were ultimately betrayed as the "liberal" Cape Colony was drawn in to the first version of South Africa in 1910.[14]

Both the believers and the unbelievers in the cattle killing can be seen, then, as adherents of unrealized prophecies. "Loners and prophets, filled with delusions, fantasies, ambiguities, and otherworldliness" because they ignored the stark realities around them: so historian David Chanaiwa has described *not* Nongqawuse's followers, but rather the mission-educated elite who had rejected the cattle-killing prophecy.[15]

Nongqawuse's prophecy and the colonial project of civilization were competing millennial visions of a world remade. But the conventional terms in English—the "cattle killing," the "Xhosa national suicide"—for what is known in isiXhosa as the "Nongqawuse" focus attention on destruction and thereby obscure the other expectant preparations that the believers undertook. The prophecy called not only for killing cattle, discarding grain, and halting agriculture, but also for actions whose consequences would be *rejuvenating*; preparing new cattle kraals, grain pits, and homesteads and abjuring witchcraft and sexual misdemeanors would make way for the emergence of ancestors and superior cattle and grain from underground riverine caverns, in a reenactment of the creation in Xhosa cosmology. The Xhosa had long believed that if they could find uHlanga, the site of the original emergence, they could obtain new cattle; Nongqawuse claimed to have access to the site and to waiting herds and armies, ready to expel the invaders and restore the land.[16] In this aspect, then, the prophecy envisioned an iteration of the original creation. The emphasis of the colonial dream, on the other hand, was on the innovative, unprecedented aspects of millennialism. In other words, the Xhosa prophecy and the European civilizing mission can be roughly distinguished in terms of temporality, a recursive vision of renewal as compared with a unidirectional, linear vision of progress. But it would be a mistake to conceive of the cattle killing merely as a reactionary movement, imagined in some putative premodern, non-Western oceanic time. Fundamental elements of the prophecy were without precedent before the 1850s, and the realization of the prophecy would have been a radically new departure in the history of the amaXhosa, not simply a turning back of the clock.

The European project worked through technologies of transformation: guns that gave lethal motion to inert bits of lead, turning people to corpses; scripts and printing presses that gave visual, permanent, and reproducible form to spoken words; plows and irrigation furrows that helped turn agricultural surplus to money. Missionaries were the exponents of both literacy and new agricultural methods; "the construction of the irrigation furrow became the *sine qua non* of mission stations, for very good agricultural and evangelical reasons," writes Donovan Williams, historian of South African missions and biographer of the first ordained Xhosa missionary, Tiyo Soga.[17] Using water to draw communities to the Word, missionaries ultimately depended for their safety on the weapons of colonial armies and commandos.[18]

These technologies of transformation drove the civilizing mission; the printing press, which could reproduce grammars and dictionaries of African languages and subsequent translations of biblical and other religious texts, was particularly important to missionaries. Carrying a small press with him from Scotland, Reverend John Ross arrived at the Tyhume mission station in the eastern Cape on 16 December 1823 and joined his new colleague, John Bennie. In a 20 December letter, Bennie wrote to Dr. John Love, secretary of the Glasgow Missionary Society, "On the 17th, we got our Press in order; on the 18th the alphabet was set up; and yesterday we threw off 50 copies. . . . Through your instrumentality a new era has commenced in the history of the

Kaffer nation."[19] Bennie later described his work enumerating an isiXhosa vocabulary as "reducing to form and rule this language which hitherto floated in the wind."[20] The Tyhume station and its press were destroyed in the frontier war of 1834–35. A new station, named for Dr. Love, was built in 1838 at a nearby site. Thus the Lovedale Mission Press, among the oldest and most prolific mission presses in southern Africa, traces its origins to those four days in 1823. Scholars who discuss the history of Lovedale cite Bennie's words almost ritualistically, but none comments upon how he evokes the momentousness of this "new era" by describing its diligent, day-by-day creation in terms that echo the opening of Genesis, the emergence of human order from divine (or savage) chaos.

For the missionaries' immediate audience, the relationships among these technologies of transformation and the logic of the Christian resurrection or that of the colonial economy were no more nor less self-evident than Nongqawuse's idea of destroying wealth to renew the land.[21] Ntsikana, one of the earliest Christian converts, is remembered as having urged his followers to embrace the Bible brought by the "nation who comes from overseas," but to reject its other gift, the "round button with no holes in it [money], for as soon as you take it you will be scattered like a flock of sheep and lose your nation."[22] Several of Ntsikana's followers heeded his command and went to the missions; one of these men, Soga (a councillor of the chief Ngqika), was the first person to adopt plowing and irrigation at the GMS Tyhume mission station in the 1830s. Yet as Soga was to discover, the Bible and the button without a hole were not easily separated.

Nineteenth-century European missionaries among the amaXhosa understood Christianity in broadly civilizational, rather than narrowly doctrinal, terms, so that conversion was as much about everyday modes of living as about matters of faith.[23] GMS missionary Robert Niven reveals the agricultural idiom underlying the entire mission endeavor when he argues, "The gospel plough will speed the faster that it is accompanied by the *school* plough and the *land* plough."[24] Shortly after the frontier war of 1834–35, Soga asked C. L. Stretch, a military officer and the resident agent among the Ngqika Xhosa, for cattle to replace those lost in the recent war. In an 1835 diary entry, Stretch writes that he told Soga, "You have both oxen and cows in your beautiful Chumie land, and if you will take the trouble to dig them out of the field you will be relieved from begging." Soga no more believed Stretch's claim that herds of cattle waited under his fields than he would Nongqawuse's similar claim two decades later, but Stretch explained to him that by growing and selling vegetables, Soga could earn money to buy the cattle.[25]

The logic of the commodity could seem as magical as that of a resurrection; Ntsikana rightly regarded the transition to a monetized economy as a black magic that would break the nation. For the amaXhosa, cattle were a special kind of commodity, a singular locus of value: their ownership rested with chiefs and elders (and ultimately with the ancestors), and their circulation created networks of patronage and filiation that made social relationships visible, rather than obscuring them.[26] Cattle resist commodity fetishization, and their "auratic" aspect—"beyond the purview of the coin"—exceeds secular calculations of value; the use and exchange of cattle link people with the ancestors.[27] The commodity, Marx tells us, is a "very strange thing," with its "metaphysical subtleties and theological niceties,"[28] and some Xhosa converts found the value of literacy even more mysterious than the value of cattle may seem in Marxian analysis. Since literacy "does not literally make cows," missionary Niven wrote, "so the wanting it, [the amaXhosa] conclude, cannot be any great loss."[29] Finding apprentices for the press was particularly difficult, Lovedale principal James Stewart observed: "Every native can understand the value of being able to make a table, or a chair, or to repair a waggon [sic]. With printing, however, it was a different matter,—Kaffir experience not showing how a man could make a living by arranging small bits of lead in rows. By patience and much persuasion one apprentice was got."[30]

Stewart's agricultural image of typesetting, the orderly planting of lead yielding life, reverses the more common association between lead type and lead bullets, the "ink as well as blood" through which the British established in the eastern Cape a "powerful new order of representation" that was "backed by greater military and social power."[31] The literal interchangeability of these two forms of lead is evident in an oft-cited anecdote: during the seventh frontier war of 1846–47, when the Lovedale mission was abandoned and its denizens retreated to the safety of military forts, "the types of the printing-press were converted into bullets, and pages of the sacred books into wadding, for the guns of the Dutch Boers."[32] Not surprisingly, then, guns and books—specifically the Bible—have been yoked in the Xhosa imaginary. The contemporary *imbongi* (oral praise poet) David Livingstone Yali-Manisi draws upon a centuries-old trope of books turning into guns:

> The day the missionaries arrived
> They carried a Bible in front,
> But they had a breechload slung behind.[33]

Scholar Jeff Opland wonders whether the very survival of Xhosa oral poetry as a living tradition can be attributed to this long-standing suspicion of the "technology of writing."[34]

The first Xhosa convert ordained as a minister was Tiyo Soga, a son of "old" Soga, follower of Ntsikana and a skeptic of Stretch's claims. Tiyo Soga returned to Africa from his study and ordination in Scotland in July 1857, a few months after the new cattle and ancestors had failed to emerge as prophesied. Tiyo Soga took up work as a missionary among the Gcaleka people of the

Xhosa king Sarhili, where he encountered an uneasy understanding of the transformative and pacifying effect (in the notorious colonial sense) of "*the Word*," as Sarhili's people called it: "Missionaries are the emissaries of Government, to act upon the minds and feelings of the people, with an instrument which they call "*the Word*," and . . . those who become affected by the Word, and exchange Kafir customs for those of the white men, become subjects of the English Government. Thus white men plan to get a footing in their country, which they afterwards take altogether. These are the views of not a few of Kreli's people."[35]

This interpretation of the power of literacy appears in the biography of Tiyo Soga, composed by fellow GMS missionary John Aitken Chalmers. Although Chalmers might have wished to challenge this belief in the complicity of Christianity and conquest (which casts in a rather different light what Lovedale Press founder John Bennie had referred to as "instrumentality"), he did believe in the transformative potential of the Christian text. Religious conversion is figured in his biography as a process of textual transformation, and in exemplary cases like that of Tiyo Soga, as a process of transformative textualization; the full title of the biography is *Tiyo Soga: A Page of South African Mission Work*.

Tiyo Soga's tenuous position is evident in the pages of Chalmers's biography; the conviction of Sarhili's people that missionaries acted as colonial agents (which in fact was colonial policy until 1830) implicates Tiyo Soga's own vocation,[36] and he is also constructed by his fellow missionary as a "Model Kafir," evidence of the beneficent success of missionary endeavor. Negotiating this liminal position, Tiyo Soga drew on the power associated with writing when, at the laying of the foundation stone for his new church at Mgwali in 1861, he solemnly "read out, and held up for the people to see, two inscriptions on separate sheets of vellum paper, one in English and the other in Caffre," which were subsequently buried in a lead box under the foundation stone.[37]

Tiyo Soga's burial of text in the foundation of his church, like the convoluted association of books and guns in the Xhosa imaginary, reconfigures the association between literacy and death that Walter Ong made in *Orality and Literacy: The Technologizing of the Word*. Imagining the ambivalence of "persons rooted in primary orality," who desire the "vast complex of powers" associated with literacy yet fear to lose what is "deeply loved in the earlier oral world," Ong concludes that "we have to die to continue living."[38] But it is not only the individual or cultural transition to literate consciousness that is figured in terms of death; the Christian doctrine of the resurrection also deeply informs Ong's understanding of the text itself. The written or printed word is a dead thing nonetheless available to "being resurrected into limitless living contexts by a potentially infinite number of living readers."[39] Tiyo Soga literalizes this notion when he buries texts to inaugurate the life of his church. Dead men cannot speak (except through prophets); in literate and print cultures, however, their words can rise again.

Literacy, then, can be imagined as the *afterlife* of orality. If reading re-animates dead text, so too must inscribing old texts in new "limitless living contexts"—through citation, allusion, and other modes of appropriation and invocation—make the past live within the present. In this infinite potential for reanimation, textuality is intertextuality. The notion of afterlife connotes the ineffable commingling of essential continuity, substantial transformation, and spatiotemporal displacement and return that are implicit in a resurrection. Dying to live is also the paradoxical, millennial logic of the cattle killing, and what the Xhosa examples of literacy as death make explicit, in the link be-tween mission-sponsored literacy and British military supremacy, is that the sense of loss or rupture in the transition to literacy that Ong figures as death occurs within a context of coercion, if not quite at gunpoint. Furthermore, the traffic between orality and literacy in the nineteenth-century Xhosa context is more multivalent than Ong's eschatological imagery implies: dead texts re-main available to reanimation and transfiguration in oral modes as well. The relationship between orality and literacy in the colonial context is not a zero-sum game in which literacy makes steady advances over and against orality. Given the conjunction of formal education and Christian proselytization in the missions, it is important to remember that the oral transmission of Chris-tian ideas and images in African languages was just as important for the dissemination of Christianity and "civilization" as the printing of dictionaries, grammars, and biblical translations, which greatly facilitated this oral ex-change.[40] In other words, although I find Ong's evocative figurations of the transition from orality to literacy compelling and uniquely apposite to the dy-namics of the cattle killing, I want to set his metaphors in motion against the historical context of the British colonial conquest of southern Africa, in which the technology of literacy was a crucial modality.[41]

Mhala, the only Xhosa chief charged with treason in the aftermath of the cattle killing, understood very well both the transfigurational quality and the historical implications of writing and print during his testimony at his court martial: "I have nothing further to say but *I wish this recorded* and await what is in the heart of the court and beg them to remember that words do not per-ish, that though I may die [you had better judge me truly] that nothing here-after may arise to disturb you. People die of sickness, and are killed in war; my words seem few but they are long enough."[42] Not literate himself but con-scious of speaking into the juridical record, Mhala seizes upon the perma-nence of print, and its capacity to enable posthumous speech, as his only re-course against the representational machinery of the colonial state.

Ong labels the capacity of print to preserve and reanimate speech its "vatic quality": "Like the oracle or the prophet, the book relays an utterance from a source, the one who really 'said' or wrote the book."[43] This anthropomorphic trope of the book as secondhand speech effectively blurs Ong's distinction between orality and literacy, enabling a comparison between the mobility of words in each mode that depends upon thinking about authorship in terms of prophecy, as a form of divinity that speaks through the book. In "speaking" another's words, the book is a medium, as the prophet is an inspired bearer of suprahuman utterance. In contemporary literary theory, the author may be figured more as dead (and without hope of resurrection) than as divine; however, theorizing literacy in terms of prophecy and what I call the afterlives of textuality is particularly evocative in the context of the cattle killing, where the dissemination of textuality, and the textualization of the colonized other, are processes enmeshed within the project of colonial transformation against which the Xhosa prophecies were articulated.

The Peripeties of the Cattle Killing

In his 1877 biography of Tiyo Soga, fellow GMS missionary J. A. Chalmers interrupts his narrative with a chapter-long interlude, "The Cattle Killing Delusion," in which Tiyo Soga does not appear until the final paragraph.[44] He was in Scotland completing his studies during the events of 1856–57 and returned to Africa, newly ordained, on 2 July 1857, a few months after the failure of the cattle-killing prophecy. Near the beginning of this digressive chapter, we read of the articulation of the prophecy by Mhlakaza, Nongqawuse's uncle, who "preached to the Kafirs a *new gospel*, which was none other than a resurrection from the dead."[45] We read of the anticipated transformations, the unsteady dissemination of the prophecy in British Kaffraria and the Transkei, the perplexed colonial machinations to stop it, and the ultimate disappointment and desperation of a starving people nobly relieved through the Christian charity of the colonial administration and the missionaries.

Not content with the implicit rejoinder of the "injunction of Scripture" to the catastrophe of the Xhosa "new gospel," Chalmers, in his final paragraph, narrates the return of Tiyo Soga to African shores and his discovery that "those to whom he had come to preach the Gospel were a dispersed nation, utterly destroyed by their own folly." However personally devastating it was to Soga to find his people in such a state, Chalmers identifies as good news the prospect that "the nation that clung with such tenacity to a lie, and demolished its dearest idols in that belief, and so readily yielded up present possessions in the hope of future good, has surely the capacity of being taught to trust in Him who is the resurrection and the life. Tiyo Soga resolved . . . to teach his countrymen that there is a resurrection, in which all will participate, who look to Jesus."[46] Chalmers finds hope for Christian missions in the apparent Xhosa capacity for faith and their susceptibility to sacrificial logic. He juxtaposes the resurrections heralded by false and true Xhosa evangelists, the exceptionally deluded Mhlakaza and the exceptionally pious Tiyo Soga.[47] Christianity is the corrective to the Xhosa "gospel"; a people easily converted to error should be even more amenable to the Truth delivered by a prophet in his own land.

The arrival of Tiyo Soga, bearing another gospel to the Xhosa, functions as a link back to the narrative thread of Chalmers's interrupted biography, but the neatness of the chapter's structure points to a broader issue in the historiography of the cattle killing: how do colonial sources make sense of the ends of the movement in constructing the endings of their narratives, that is, how does narrative structure reflect a sense of historical teleology? The uneven parallelism of Mhlakaza and Tiyo Soga in Chalmers's biography implies that the civilizing mission might turn the apparent historical tragedy of the cattle killing into another narrative mode, in which Tiyo Soga will be the hero. I invoke the crucial insight of Hayden White—that the narrative impulse of historiography tends toward constructions of particular kinds of plots familiar to readers of literature—because Chalmers's framing of his cattle-killing narrative is only one example among many of the extravagantly literary aspects of historical accounts of the cattle killing.

White demonstrates how a narrativized history emanates a sense of naturalness, as if "the world [could] speak itself and speak itself as a story."[48] If literacy is the afterlife of orality, then written narratives mask and naturalize this transposition by projecting a speaking, storytelling world. In the context of purportedly nonfictional narratives of the cattle killing written by missionaries, colonial administrators, and early historians, however, what is remarkable is not their naturalness, but rather the insistence with which they call attention to their literariness. Although emplotted in a variety of ways, many of these narratives open with some variation on "once upon a time." This temptation to construe the cattle killing as story (and as a story heard, rather than read) is particularly striking when an account of the cattle killing is embedded within a broader, and more sober, discussion of missionary endeavor or Cape history.

Perhaps the best example of this tendency to construct the cattle killing as a literary set piece is to be found in the oeuvre of George McCall Theal, who began his voluminous output in southern African historiography while he was a teacher and printer at the Lovedale mission.[49] The cattle-killing account in Theal's *Compendium of the History and Geography of South Africa* (first published in 1874) begins, "One morning in May, 1856, a girl named NONGQAUSE, daughter of a councillor of SARILI, went to draw water from a little stream that flowed past her home."[50] The subjective narrative perspective in this early work by Theal is explicitly that of a Christian colonial observer in the Cape Colony in the 1860s and 1870s; he structures his history around moral themes of progress against "ignorance, superstition, and indolence."[51] Theal's later work *History of South Africa from 1795 to 1872* uses a radically different historiographical approach, offering an ostensibly objective political history structured more by chronology than by theme or individual chief,[52] but his account of the cattle killing appears nearly unchanged.[53] Theal's fabulous narration of the cattle killing is thus even more striking when it appears in his later, more sober scholarly history.

Theal's account is not unique in its figurative language or the descriptive energy invested in depicting the prophecy's anticipated transformations. Theal borrows biblical similes to describe the projected appearance of cattle "like stars of the sky in multitude. Enormous skin sacks were being made ready to contain the milk shortly to be like water in plenty."[54] Beyond sketching the wonders of the anticipated resurrections, other sources enumerate, with remarkable sympathy, the strange perceptions already afoot: "Wonderful reports were constantly in circulation. Armies were seen reviewing on the sea, others sailing in umbrellas; thousands of cattle were heard knocking their horns together and bellowing in caverns, impatient to rise, only waiting until all their fellows who still walked the earth were slain; dead men, years in the grave, had been seen, who sent pathetic appeals to their kindred not to delay their coming back to life by refusing to obey the prophet."[55]

This passage appears in Chalmers's biography of Tiyo Soga, but it was written by the wife of Charles Pacalt Brownlee, the commissioner of the Ngqika Xhosa in British Kaffraria at the time of the cattle killing.[56] The passive voice of Mrs. Brownlee's verbs allows her to heighten the impression of wondrous portents seen and heard while making her own sense of their credibility grammatically irrelevant and thus ideologically invisible.

These sympathetic, extended depictions of the expected transformations and the wonderful phenomena that bolstered the believers' faith are remarkable precisely because their authors could not have given them credence, either ideologically or temporally, since they were all written after the prophecy's failure. They differ substantially from the account of Wesleyan missionary William C. Holden, author of *The Past and Future of the Kaffir Races* (1866). Holden devotes almost no descriptive attention to the prophecy itself, which he castigates as a "gigantic piece of jugglery" orchestrated by chiefs who manipulated "the deluded superstitious masses [who] believed these wild unnatural announcements."[57] Holden does not suppress his contempt, which he would have to have done in order to give a reader any sense of how the prophecy might have appealed to the imagination.[58] In their descriptions of the promised resurrection, Theal and Brownlee are also more exuberant than Xhosa writers.

J. Henderson Soga, the son of Tiyo Soga, spares only four sentences in his *Ama-Xosa: Life and Customs* for a description of the prophecy. The relative asceticism of Soga's account is matched in his abrupt treatment of the aftermath: "Needless to say none of these wonders came to pass."[59] Soga's matter-of-fact narration of both expectations and actualities helps to explain Theal's and Brownlee's descriptive interest in the wonders promised to the Xhosa, which transfix a reader with a vision of the anticipated transformations. Soga actively undercuts his readers' potential enchantment by the prophecy, whereas writers such as Theal, Brownlee, and Chalmers build up descriptions of the expectations to heighten the effect of the disappointment.

The differences among the accounts are evident in their treatment of portentous movements of the sun and moon. Holden explains why a full red moon failed to rise in January 1857 as an anticipated sign of imminent resurrection: "The God who made the moon, had given no direction to the pale lamp of night to bestow her sanction on this gross superstition; and, therefore, she neither rose blood red, nor, when she changed, exhibited any extraordinary phenomena." Holden assumes that the movements of feminine heavenly bodies do indeed manifest signs of divine will, but that of the Christian god rather than Xhosa "spirits."[60] Chalmers, by contrast, notes that "the full moon rose blood-red," an encouraging sign to the believers that spurred the final acts of destruction.[61] What is more significant than the factual discrepancy between the two missionaries' statements about the moon is the vehemence with which Holden rejects any connection between the Xhosa prophecy and natural phenomena, compared with the fatal causal logic in which the fulfillment of minor predictions buttressed faith in the ultimate "marvellous transformation."[62] Holden implies that the Xhosa erred not in looking to the sky but in failing to recognize it as a creation of *his* god. In stark contrast to Holden, Theal and Mrs. Brownlee read the sky as a figure of human consciousness and find in the constancy of its diurnal rhythms an ironic foil for human error and disillusion. After depicting the anticipated wonders on which the Xhosa believers had staked their future, Theal writes that "the dawn of doubt had never entered their thoughts till the dawn of the fatal day."[63] Mrs. Brownlee links the "usual darkness" of an ordinary sunset with "the black darkness of a bitter disappointment in the hearts of thousands."[64] This pathetic rendering imbues the sky with meaning within the terms of Xhosa prophecy, even while registering its failure.

Another aspect of the prophecy that receives tropological attention is the anticipated return of the dead ancestors. They do not appear, and yet they do when the aftermath is figured as a reversal of the prophecy. The spectacle of widespread famine included "emaciated living skeletons passing from house to house," as Dr. John Fitzgerald of the King William's Town Native Hospital wrote to Chief Commissioner John Maclean.[65] "Living skeleton" seems almost a clinical diagnosis, as it recurs in Fitzgerald's correspondence in mid-1857. Mrs. Brownlee makes the reversal of expectations even more explicit, and the pathos of her account derives from the connections she draws among anticipated, actual, and figural appearances of the dead. Early in her account she links proleptically the innumerable, uneaten carcasses of slain cattle to a moment "later on [when] it was the carcases [*sic*] of men and women, young men and maidens, children and infants, that strewed the way-side."[66] She describes the starving masses in search of relief as a reversal of the prophecy's promise that the dead would rise: "As these spectres came in crowds and crawled along, one might have imagined that the prophet's prediction had come to pass, and that the dead had indeed risen from their graves."[67] Mrs. Brownlee captures the reader's imagination by framing the cattle killing as dependent upon, and productive of, human imaginings.

This investment in imagination aims to convey the enormity of physical suffering; Mrs. Brownlee allows the reader to sympathize with the expectant amaXhosa in order to heighten the affective response when the prophecy is figurally fulfilled—through reversal—in the appearance of the living dead.[68] In other words, the extravagance of Mrs. Brownlee's metaphors offers some sense of the stark reality of material devastation. In contrast to J. Henderson Soga, many of the colonial writers deem that it is *not* "needless to say" that the expectations were not fulfilled. Having framed their depictions of the antici-pated wonders as fairy tales that occurred "once upon a time," the authors must jolt enchanted readers into a generic recognition that history is not a fairy tale. The effect of these accounts depends upon the shock of reversal after readers temporarily suspend their disbelief in the prophecy, and whatever meaning is to be found in the cattle killing in these accounts is to be found in peripety, in the ironic pairings of before and after, of imagination and actual-ity. For Mrs. Brownlee, "sad horror" is the explicit effect of this reversal;[69] in recollecting the events in which her family had played a part two decades earlier, Mrs. Brownlee relives the pity and fear that Aristotle saw as the pre-cipitates of a tragic plot structured around *anagnorisis* (recognition) and *perip-eteia* (reversal). Although writers like Theal and Chalmers inscribe the cattle killing into plots of redemption rather than tragedy, the effect of peripety in each of these accounts depends upon an analogy between a reader's seduction and disillusion and that of the Xhosa believers; readers know objectively that the cattle-killing prophecy will not succeed, but the pathos of these accounts works toward the suspension of this historical knowledge. What is so remark-able about these accounts, in other words, is that they generate some measure of narrative surprise about the failure of a prophecy that their readers would not have expected to succeed.

The significance of reversal in these cattle-killing narratives explains why Holden devotes almost no rhetorical attention to the prophecy itself; he as-sumes that his readers *cannot* be seduced because "enlightened Christian na-tions" have left such things as witchcraft behind.[70] Now it is their duty to free others from its thrall: the cattle killing epitomizes the pervasive "vile supersti-tion" among the "Kaffir races" and thus "make[s] a loud and long appeal, not only to Missionary and philanthropic societies, for help, but also to *humanity*, to colonial governors and governments and magistrates . . . that these en-thralled nations may soon be liberated, and the privileges of civil and religious liberty succeed the reign of terror and death."[71] Holden misses or ignores the fact that the cattle-killing movement was directed *against* witchcraft. He is able to represent the expansion of colonial control as an act of liberation by figuring Xhosa witchcraft as a tool used to "enchain the national mind, and establish . . . undisputed empire over their souls."[72] The stakes of the contest between the empire of witchcraft and the "liberating" colonial government are so high that Holden seems immune to the cattle-killing prophecy's appeal to the imagination. If only in this aspect, Holden's account is surprisingly similar to that of J. Henderson Soga: a people whose ancestors suffered in the aftermath of the prophecy's failure, and whose subjugation to the colony was thereby consolidated, hardly need to be told that the expected phenomena did not occur.

The gravity that I read in Holden's account should not imply a corresponding levity in the accounts that offer a more protracted exposition of what Aristotle called the "tying" and "untying" of plots of the cattle killing; I do not mean to imply that Brownlee, Chalmers, and Theal are merely spinning a good yarn. The dynamism of peripety in their accounts also implicates their sustained interest in the elements of the prophecy that involve Europeans. The resurrection would inaugurate a "golden era of liberty,"[73] because the whites would meet a variety of catastrophic fates: metamorphosis into "frogs, mice and ants";[74] the sky falling and crushing them;[75] and, most spectacularly, being "driven into the sea" (together with Xhosa unbelievers) either by a "mighty wind" or by armies of the resurrected Xhosa ancestors.[76] Contemporary Europeans who recorded their thoughts seemed to have little doubt about the motive behind the movement. Amid the convoluted articulations of the prophecy, which varied in space and time, the singular image of being driven into the sea certainly captured the imagination of anxious settlers. The consensus in these accounts is that the cattle killing is, at least in part, anticolonial, directed at the destruction of whites and of colonial rule.

The chiefs' plot thesis—articulated in Grey's official correspondence during the events of 1856–57 and dominating colonial accounts long after—held that the cattle killing was a scheme by the Xhosa chiefs to drive their desperate people to war against the colony.[77] Both Grey and Charles Brownlee recognized the obvious logical problem with the chiefs' plot thesis; in Brownlee's words, "a starving people are not in a position to undertake an aggressive warfare."[78] Although no recent historians credit the chiefs' plot thesis, they have disagreed significantly about the extent to which this millenarian movement was an anticolonial movement, directed not merely against the *effects* of colonial presence but against the colonists themselves.[79] In the late nineteenth and early twentieth centuries, however, the chiefs' plot thesis dominated colonial historiography. George McCall Theal took the chiefs' plot thesis so completely for granted that he was unable to recognize it as hypothesis rather than fact; he refers to the seeming failure of the amaXhosa to storm the colony after the prophecy was not realized as a tactical "blunder, such as a child would hardly have made," rather than consider that this fact might undermine the chiefs' plot thesis.[80] The tenacity of the chiefs' plot thesis in the account of the cattle killing that appears nearly unrevised in Theal's successive historiographical endeavors reveals that another, implicit reversal is at work in the recurrent strategy of juxtaposing spectacular expectations with spectacular suffering. The Europeans would not have expected the Xhosa ancestors to appear bearing cattle and grain, but they may well have feared being "driven to the sea," however literally or metaphorically; this much-feared war against the colony, a war that never happened, would seem a "rational" explanation for Xhosa motivations, however ill-advised it was as a military strategy. Far from being driven into the sea, however, the Europeans remained to write these accounts; it is the Xhosa who are dead, starving, and driven out of British Kaffraria and into the Cape Colony as laborers.[81] Yet the very permanence of the European presence means that the image of being "driven into the sea" survived into the apartheid era as a quintessential icon of white anxiety in South Africa.

The narrative closure of these accounts belies an ideological thrust that, despite hiding in plain sight, is no less powerful than the one in Holden's polemic. Chalmers shifts from Mrs. Brownlee's depiction of the scene of suffering to his own account of acts of Christian charity, through which "the very nation, whose destruction was secretly sought by this perfidious tragedy, became the savior of many thousands of Kafirs." According to Chalmers, the epitome of this selflessness is Mrs. Brownlee, who not only worked alongside her husband at famine relief despite having lost several family members by blood and marriage to Xhosa "butcher[y]," but also took up a "graphic pen [and] narrated this tale of sorrow."[82] Chalmers here lays bare the narrative perspective that constitutes the peripeties of the cattle killing in colonial historiography: the European, Christian survivor of an anticolonial plot, surrounded by a sea of dying Xhosa people, responds not only with material acts of compassion but also with compassionate acts of textual composition. Chalmers's praise for Mrs. Brownlee gives way immediately to his narration of the arrival of Tiyo Soga, his "page" of South African mission work.[83] Later writers, who did not directly take part in the relief work, nonetheless stress the selflessness of those who aided the famished amaXhosa so soon after fearing that an attack on the colony was imminent.[84] At the end of the cattle killing, colonial individuals and institutions remained to give succor. Implicit in this narrative topos is the glimmer of a possibility, from a colonial perspective, that the teleological end of the cattle killing was precisely this opportunity to demonstrate the necessity of a European presence in the Cape: the Xhosa had been devastated so that they could be relieved of their suffering (as well as their autonomy and their land).[85] Having detailed the demise of the chiefs' authority and the capture of land and labor in the aftermath of the cattle killing, Grey remarked in March 1857, "However much Her Majesty's Government may deplore the sufferings which necessarily attend the crisis through which this country is passing, they may rest assured that ultimately the most beneficial consequences will follow from what is now taking place. All that is necessary is, that every exertion should be made to improve, to the utmost, the present occasion."[86]

As Grey's remarks imply, however, this topos of providential suffering and relief is precisely that—a rhetorical figure, whose relationship to actual colonial policy is inverted, even perverted. That is, although authors repeatedly lavished detail on the European charitable endeavors, they did so in English (or German) and sometimes decades after the fact. During the actual relief effort, Chief Commissioner Maclean was very concerned not to publicize, among the amaXhosa, the European relief efforts, particularly those which did not match his stringent Victorian understanding of "true charity," relief only for those willing to indenture themselves in the colony: "If the idea once gain ground that Relief is afforded in King W[illiams] Town to the starving who seek it—no amount of accommodation or funds will be sufficient for those who crowd in for Relief."[87] The spectacle of European charity toward the formerly hostile Xhosa nation has a radically different valence, depending on the projected audience for such images.

Brushed against the grain in this way, to invoke Walter Benjamin, the most sympathetic emplotment of the cattle killing is also an act of domination that is all the more insidious for being bathed in the warm light of compassion.[88] The more sympathetic accounts are thus not so different from Holden's Manichaean argument for European colonial liberation of the "Kaffir race" from the empire of evil. I mean not to assert an ideological uniformity among the authors of these accounts, but rather to call attention to them as documents produced out of a history of conquest and conversion.[89] My concern is not so much with their composition by individual writers who can be counted among the victors, but rather with what Benjamin refers to as their modes of cultural transmission: the very technologies of representation themselves at stake in the competing millennial dream in the eastern Cape in the nineteenth century. The accounts that I have been calling "sympathetic" are extravagantly literary, in the sense that they intimate, however paradoxically, a desire to fashion a narrative that creates the illusion of storytelling, of orality in its textual afterlife.

At the level of form, these accounts foster a presumed identification with the subjects of the story as members of an oral culture. Theal concludes the opening of his description of the prophecy by writing, "Such is the tale which the Kaffirs told each other, of the manner in which MHLAKAZA and NONGQAUSE became acquainted with the secrets of the spirit world."[90] Theal takes his fabrication of the illusion of storytelling so far as to put his narrative into the mouths of Xhosa survivors as "the tale [they] told each other." Here

anima meets artifice: Theal's invented scenario dramatizes a process of prophetic transmediation across the oral-literate divide, yet the scene paradoxically buttresses the authority and hegemony of his colonial historiography by
describing it as a Xhosa tale, by cloaking literacy in the mantle of orality.
Theal ultimately privileges the truth claims of written history over the wild
and dangerous imaginings of oral "tales": it is Nongqawuse's prophecy that
Theal frames as a fantastic "tale [the amaXhosa] told each other," set within
his authoritative, written narrative of the event and its all-too-real aftermath.

Epilogue

Tiyo Soga turned to the Bible to discern portents of the future survival of the
amaXhosa. These colonial authors, conversely, found in Xhosa prophecy and
its aftermath signs of the rightness of their own presence and endeavor. The
cattle killing departed from previous Xhosa responses to colonialism in not
immediately engaging guns and assegais, and the technologies of the book
were a crucial means through which missionaries, administrators, and historians managed the immediate afterlife of the event, by framing its meaning
within a teleological narrative of colonial beneficence. The passage from orality to literacy was an important part of this teleology, yet, as we have seen,
orality retains a complex and contradictory appeal within these narratives, not
merely in their actual, textual form, but also in the content of the form, in
Hayden White's phrase. Authors such as Chalmers, Frances Brownlee, and
Theal inhabit literate traditions with particular conventions and expectations
for structuring narrative and dramatic plots. By imagining the cattle killing as
a story of recognition and reversal, these colonial authors append their own
redemptive denouement to the tragedy of the cattle killing: they link the failure of the prophecy to the enduring necessity of colonial presence, and they
inscribe their narratives within the enduring medium of print. These accounts
of the cattle killing thus manifest what Hayden White identifies as one of the
effects of a narrativized history, "a coherence that allows us to see 'the end' in
every beginning."[91] This perspicacity of narrative is analogous to a capacity to
read the future. "All plots have something in common with prophecy, for they
must appear to educe from the prime matter of the situation the forms of a
future," writes Frank Kermode in *The Sense of an Ending*.[92] Kermode reminds
us of the importance of peripeteia for Aristotle, and he argues that the "more
daring the peripeteia," the more a fiction, "by upsetting the ordinary balance
of our naive expectations, is finding something out for us, something *real*."[93]

The relationship between the structures of narrative fiction and the *"real"*
in Kermode's examination of apocalyptic thinking characterizes the fundamental tension regarding the reversals of the cattle killing: any epistemological work of "finding out" that the cattle-killing prophecy might be made to do

is undermined by the extremity of its adherents' disappointment. This extremity of suffering—as measured in the deaths of tens of thousands of people, the dislocation of many more, the loss of land and livelihood, the crumbling of autonomy, and the enduring conditions of colonial subjugation and postcolonial poverty—is too easily contained in written narratives, evacuated of its materiality when it is opposed and equated to the fantastic excesses of the anticipated transformations. The technology of literacy, in other words, is a site where anima and artifice collide: visionary impulses and material limits associated with the cattle killing become legible and productive in historically specific ways in the written archive, both in the nineteenth-century eastern Cape and in the afterlives of the event. These tensions not only impel my consideration of the cattle killing but also implicate my own project within the epistemological and technological legacies of the intersections between literacy and this event in Xhosa history. My challenge is to seek to understand the recurrent fascination with the cattle killing's spectacles of hope and failure and the utopian (and dystopian) uses to which such fascination has been put—a task that involves analyzing and deploying within my own argument the imaginative appeal of the visions as well as confronting the terrible price that they exacted.

Yet as I hope to have shown, there is no simple line to be drawn between metaphor and materiality, between the figuration of a thing and the thing itself. When missionaries see the hand of God in starving masses, and governors invoke divine Providence in promoting their own colonial designs, we see that metaphors and narrative norms have material effects. Jean and John Comaroff have identified as one of the misprisions of the colonial encounter the "misreading of mission metaphors" by Africans who "interpreted the admonitions and promises of the mission in highly literal, immediate terms."[94] But Europeans, too, misapprehended the cattle killing when they embraced the trope of reversal in order to project a linear progress narrative for which so little evidence of progress was to be found in nearly half a century of mission endeavor.

Notes

1. These figures come from the 1857 census of Commissioner John Maclean (J.C.B. Maclean, *A Compendium of Kafir Laws and Custom* [Grahamstown: J. Slater, 1906], 129), and from historian J. B. Peires's surmises about the tens of thousands who sought work in the colony surreptitiously, in addition to the twenty-nine thousand who formally entered the labor-channeling system set up as famine relief by Governor George Grey (*The Dead Will Arise: Nongqawuse and the Great Xhosa Cattle-Killing Movement of 1856–7* [Johannesburg: Ravan Press; Bloomington: Indiana University Press, 1989], 267). Peires claims that a total of 150,000 people were displaced by the cattle killing and the consequent attacks by the colony on the Xhosa

(*Dead*, 319–20). He estimates that 85% of Xhosa men complied with the order to kill cattle ("The Central Beliefs of the Xhosa Cattle-Killing," *Journal of African History* 28, no. 1 [1987]: 43).

2. Adam Ashforth, "The Xhosa Cattle Killing and the Politics of Memory," *Sociological Forum* 6, no. 3 (1991): 590.

3. Peires, *Dead*, 179.

4. "New people" is a term that pervades colonial sources in English and "does not correlate directly with any phrase in the surviving Xhosa-language texts" (Peires, "Central Beliefs," 53). Peires does find in the eyewitness account of William Wellington Gqoba words formed from -*tsha*, "new, young, healthy" (53); Bradford links "new people" to *Uhlanga*, which also denotes the cave from which the created world emerged as well as the creator god (Helen Bradford, "New Country, New Race, New Men: War, Gender, and Millenarianism in Xhosaland, 1855–57" [19th International Conference on Historical Sciences Session on Gender, Race, Xenophobia and Nationalism, Oslo, August 2000]). Jan Tzatzoe, the Christian chief of the amaTinde, wrote of "new people" (but also, idiosyncratically, of a returned Adam) in a report to British Kaffraria commissioner Maclean about the prophecies (Great Britain, Colonial Office, Cape of Good Hope, *Further Papers Relative to the State of the Kaffir Tribes*, Imperial Blue Book 2352 of 1857, Chief 1. Tzatzoe to Chief Commissioner, 15 October 1856, Annexure 11 in G. Grey to H. Labouchere, 25 March 1857).

5. See Jean and John Comaroff, *Of Revelation and Revolution: Christianity, Colonialism, and Consciousness in South Africa* (Chicago: University of Chicago Press, 1991), 75–78. For an additional account of how such projects were received by Africans, see Richard Elphick's "Africans and the Christian Campaign," in *The Frontier in History: North America and Southern Africa Compared*, ed. Howard Roberts Lamar and Leonard Monteath Thompson (New Haven: Yale University Press, 1981), 270–307. Elphick writes, "Missions also brought a new view of nature . . . and a new view of history (an 'open' one, in which God and man actively create a new world)" ("Africans," 305–6). Elphick maintains that the millennial aspects of the missionary message have been particularly appealing to many Africans, who "have come to see their personal and national travail as part of global historical patterns that will culminate in the establishment of a Kingdom of God on earth" ("Africans," 304).

6. R.H.W. Shepherd, *Lovedale, South Africa: The Story of a Century, 1841–1941* (Lovedale, C.P., South Africa: Lovedale Press, 1940), 67.

7. J. Maclean to W. Liddle, 4 August 1855, *Further Papers Relative to the State of the Kaffir Tribes*, Imperial Blue Book 2096 of 1856, p. 18.

8. When British settlers were slow to appear in what for decades had been either a war zone or a tense frontier, Grey would, in 1856, encourage the settlement of German mercenaries recruited for the Crimean War effort. A group of Germans arrived in the eastern Cape at the height of cattle-killing expectations in early 1857, and the magistrate John Gawler acknowledged the ironic connection between colonial schemes and Xhosa dreams: he brought Xhosa believers to the shore to watch "'*our* new people come out'" (Bradford, "New Country"; emphasis added).

9. Encl. in G. Grey to G. Grey, 17 March 1855, *Further Papers*, Imperial Blue Book 1969 of 1854–55, pp. 56, 58.

10. Nosipho Majeke, *The Role of the Missionaries in Conquest* (Alexandra Township, Johannesburg: Society of Young Africa, 1952), 69. The name Nosipho Majeke was revealed in the 1980s to be the pseudonym of Dora Taylor, a white amateur historian and member of the Non-European Unity Movement. See Bill Nasson, "The Unity Movement: Its Legacy in Historical Consciousness," *Radical History Review* 46/7 (1990): 189–211.

11. G. Grey to H. Labouchere, 6 March 1857, *Further Papers*, Imperial Blue Book 2352 of 1857–58, p. 67. I have chosen to retain the terminology and spellings used in quotations and to use currently accepted terminology and spelling in my own sentences: Kaf(f)ir/Xhosa; Nongqause/Nongqawuse; Chumie/Tyhume; Kreli/Sarhili; Umlakasa/Mhlakaza.

12. Speech before Parliament, 7 April 1857, *Further Papers*, Imperial Blue Book 2352 of 1857–58, p. 90.

13. G. Grey to H. Labouchere, 27 August 1856, ibid., p. 22.

14. Leon de Kock, *Civilising Barbarians: Missionary Narrative and African Textual Response in Nineteenth-Century South Africa* (Johannesburg: Witwatersrand University Press and Lovedale Press, 1996), 27.

15. David Chanaiwa, "African Humanism in Southern Africa: The Utopian, Traditionalist, and Colonialist Worlds of Mission-Educated Elites," in *Independence without Freedom: The Political Economy of Colonial Education in Southern Africa*, ed. Agrippa T. Mugomba and Mougo Nyaggah (Santa Barbara, CA: ABC-Clio, 1980), 34.

16. Janet Hodgson, *The God of the Xhosa: A Study of the Origins and Development of the Traditional Concepts of the Supreme Being* (Cape Town: Oxford University Press, 1982), 19; Bradford, "New Country."

17. Donovan Williams, *Umfundisi: A Biography of Tiyo Soga, 1829–1871* (Lovedale, South Africa: Lovedale Press, 1978), 4.

18. The London Missionary Society missionary F. G. Kayser was told by a Xhosa man in 1842, "'We have for a long time resisted the Word of God, but now [that you have dug a watercourse] we will come nearer to it and lead the water out lower down from you'" (Donovan Williams, *When Races Meet: The Life and Times of William Ritchie Thomson, Glasgow Society Missionary, Government Agent and Dutch Reformed Church Minister, 1794–1891* [Johannesburg: A.P.B. Publishers, 1967], 45). Noting that digging irrigation channels was among missionaries' first priorities, Donovan Williams asserts that the severe droughts to which Xhosaland was prone were a crucial factor in what success the missions had ("The Missionaries on the Eastern Frontier of the Cape Colony, 1799–1853" [PhD diss., University of the Witwatersrand, 1959], 65).

19. Shepherd, *Lovedale*, 62–63.

20. Ibid., 65. A suggestive typographical error in R. W. Shepherd's *Bantu Literature and Life* recasts Bennie's description of the Xhosa language as that which had "hitherto floated in the mind" (Lovedale, South Africa: Lovedale Press, 1955), 27.

21. Nongqawuse's prophecy drew on earlier nineteenth-century prophecies, the earliest of which was articulated in the 1810s by Nxele (or Makana), who had significant contact with European missionaries and subsequently articulated his own Christian-influenced but anti-European theology. Thixo, the Christian god, was actually the god of Europeans, according to Nxele; Mdalidephu was the god of black peoples. Nxele claimed to be a messianic son of the creator god Uhlanga as well as the brother of Christ, for whose murder Europeans were to be punished. Nxele's insistence

that his followers kill some of their cattle and give up witchcraft, in anticipation of the emergence of ancestors and cattle, was an early precursor of the events of the mid-1850s; Nxele was also a war doctor (*itola*) who claimed that he could make his followers bulletproof. There is no evidence that Nongqawuse herself had direct contact with missionaries. See Peires' s *Dead*, 134–38, for a discussion of the relationships between Xhosa prophecy and Christian theology.

22. William Beinart and Colin Bundy, "The Union, the Nation and the Talking Crow: The Ideology and Tactics of the Independent ICU in East London," in *Hidden Struggles in Rural South Africa: Politics and Popular Movements in the Transkei and Eastern Cape, 1890–1930*, ed. William Beinart and Colin Bundy (London: J. Currey; Berkeley: University of California Press, 1987), 294.

23. One of the major achievements of Jean Comaroff and John Comaroff's *Of Revelation and Revolution* is its articulation of the epistemological coherence of missionary endeavor among the southern Tswana: the economic, architectural, social, sexual, and sartorial changes urged by the missionaries are not merely trivial, mundane lifestyle choices but part of a broader understanding of Christian identity and society. This is not to say that these missionaries were not ethnocentric, but rather that they aimed beyond simply increasing the numbers of people who professed a belief in Jesus. We see a similar scope of ambition in the case of missions among the amaXhosa.

24. Williams, "Missionaries," 232; emphasis in the original.

25. J. A. Chalmers, *Tiyo Soga: A Page of South African Mission Work* (Edinburgh: A. Elliott, 1877), 5–6.

26. Clifton C. Crais, *White Supremacy and Black Resistance in Pre-industrial South Africa: The Making of the Colonial Order in the Eastern Cape, 1770–1865* (Cambridge: Cambridge University Press, 1992), 18–22.

27. John L. Comaroff and Jean Comaroff, "Goodly Beasts and Beastly Goods: Cattle in Tswana Economy and Society," *American Ethnologist* 17, no. 2 (1990): 210. William Kentridge's 2003 short film, *Tide Table*, suggests these contested regimes of value, juxtaposing images of cattle reduced to commodities and images of cattle elevated as indexes of a re-creative life cycle in the era of HIV/AIDS. In an excised passage in Chalmers's manuscript, Stretch cites noneconomic value forms of cattle (and Eurocentric disdain for Xhosa gender roles) as a reason for not granting Soga's request: "'If you had oxen you would not use them to cultivate your garden, your weak and poor women are the oxen you employ to provide grain for consumption. The oxen you would only race through the country for amusement & admiration & praise the one that ran in front.' Soga assented by a very significant laugh." Chalmers, "Tiyo Soga," Ms. PR3988.

28. Marx, *Capital*, 163.

29. Williams, "Missionaries," 228.

30. James Stewart, *Dawn in the Dark Continent, or Africa and Its Missions* (Edinburgh: Oliphant Anderson & Ferrier, 1903), 190.

31. De Kock, *Civilising*, 30, 33–34.

32. Chalmers, *Tiyo Soga*, 37.

33. "Kuba mhla kwafik' abefundisi / Babelek' iBhayibhile ngaphambili / Kanti baxway' imfakadolo ngasemva." Jeff Opland, "Imbongi Nezibongo: The Xhosa Tribal Poet and the Contemporary Poetic Tradition," *PMLA* 90, no. 2 (1975): 199.

34. Jeff Opland, *Xhosa Poets and Poetry* (Cape Town: David Philip Publishers, 1998), 322. Early European missionaries saw themselves as combating the settler conviction that "powder and ball" were the only means of civilizing the amaXhosa; by the time of the 1834–35 frontier war, disillusionment would lead the missionary John Ayliff to write, "They are now escaping the reward of their iniquity. . . . They have rejected the Gospel which was benevolently sent unto them . . . and now they have the sword." The Wesleyan Missionary Society deleted Ayliff's comment from its official correspondence (Williams, "Missionaries," 366, 173). Charles Henry Matshaya recalls an encounter with a British soldier who brandished his gun and said, "This is our book. Begone" (Charles Henry Matshaya and John Laing, "Charles Henry Matshaya: A Follower and Convert," in *Ntsikana: The Story of an African Convert*, ed. J. K. Bokwe [Lovedale: Lovedale Press, 1914], 34). Kenyan novelist and critic Ngugi wa Thiong'o has written that in the late-nineteenth-century scramble for Africa, "the night of the sword and the bullet was followed by the morning of the chalk and the blackboard" (*Decolonising the Mind: The Politics of Language in African Literature* [London: J. Currey; Portsmouth, NH: Heinemann, 1986], 9). Effectively reversing this trope, former freedom fighters in Umkhonto we Sizwe, the armed wing of the African National Congress that trained across South Africa's borders from the late 1970s, reminisce about revising old hymns for militant ends: "Changing a word here, changing a word there; put in an AK[47] there, take out a bible there" (*Amandla!: A Revolution in Four Part Harmony*, dir. Lee Hirsch, Lionsgate/Fox/Artisan Home Entertainment, 2002).

35. Chalmers, *Tiyo Soga*, 327.

36. Early missionaries to the Xhosa from 1818 to 1830, including Joseph Williams, John Brownlee, and William Ritchie Thomson, held the combined offices of missionary and government agent; their dual charge was the "'inculcation of civilisation'" and the "'transmission of information to the Colonial Government'" (Williams, *When Races Meet*, 4, 24).

37. Tiyo Soga, *The Journal and Selected Writings of the Reverend Tiyo Soga*, ed. Donovan Williams (Cape Town: Published for Rhodes University, Grahamstown, A. A. Balkema, 1983), 86–87.

38. W. J. Ong, *Orality and Literacy: The Technologizing of the Word* (London: Methuen, 1982), 15.

39. Ibid., 81.

40. See Bhekisizwe Peterson, *Monarchs, Missionaries and African Intellectuals: African Theatre and the Unmaking of Colonial Marginality* (Trenton: Africa World Press, 2000), 72.

41. Ong's broader arguments about a gulf between oral and literate cognition and culture have rightly been challenged, and, like Ong's critics, I see the technologies of literacy not as neutral or autonomous but as deployed, contested, and appropriated ideologically. For critiques of Ong and his place within literacy studies, see Ruth H. Finnegan, *Literacy and Orality: Studies in the Technology of Communication* (Oxford: Blackwell, 1988), and B. V. Street, *Cross-Cultural Approaches to Literacy* (Cambridge: Cambridge University Press, 1993).

42. Peires, *Dead*, 237; emphasis added, and brackets in the original.

43. Ong, *Orality*, 78–79.

44. In literary terms, the word "peripety" refers to a reversal in the plot; "peripeteia" is an important element of Aristotle's definition of tragedy, as I discuss below.

45. Chalmers, *Tiyo Soga*, 103; emphasis added. Peires surmises that Mhlakaza had literally been a Christian "gospel man" named Wilhelm Goliath, who was a servant of Nathaniel Merriman, archdeacon of Grahamstown, before he left disillusioned and became a diviner and spiritual healer in the Xhosa tradition (in colonial discourse, "witchdoctor"; in isiXhosa, *igqira*). Other historians are skeptical of Peires's reading of his evidence for the identification of Mhlakaza as Wilhelm Goliath.

46. Ibid., 129.

47. A similar dynamic appears in the official correspondence of Charles Brownlee, commissioner to the Ngqika Xhosa in British Kaffraria, who recounted for the chief Sandile and his councillors the Christian story of God's creation of the earth in six days and the eschatological promise of resurrection, judgment, and fiery destruction of the earth. Brownlee concluded, "But the time is not yet. Umhlakaza professes to have his revelations from God. God is a God of Truth, and what he has once revealed to man stands as unchangeable as himself. There will be no resurrection of men or beasts, as predicted by Umhlakaza, for his resurrection is opposed to the Word of God." Brownlee figures his own position at this crucial meeting, where he tried to dissuade Sandile from ordering his people to kill their cattle, as that of a prophet more reliable than Xhosa prophets like Mhlakaza or the earlier prophet Mlanjeni, who had called in 1850 for limited cattle killing, noncultivation, and cessation of witchcraft and had promised invulnerability in battle: "Did Umlanjeni perform an iota of what he had promised, and which of my words proved false?" C. Brownlee to J. Maclean, 5 August 1856, *Further Papers*, Imperial Blue Book 2202 of 1857, p. 53.

48. Hayden V. White, *The Content of the Form: Narrative Discourse and Historical Representation* (Baltimore: Johns Hopkins University Press, 1987), 2.

49. For a discussion of Theal's monumental status within South African historiography—problematic because of Theal's racial bias, his failure to cite sources, and his enormous influence on the writing of history textbooks—see Leonard Thompson, *The Political Mythology of Apartheid* (New Haven: Yale University Press, 1985).

50. George McCall Theal, *Compendium of the History and Geography of South Africa*, 3rd ed. (Lovedale, South Africa: Lovedale Press, 1877), 51.

51. Ibid., 49.

52. George McCall Theal, *History of South Africa* (Cape Town: C. Struik, 1964).

53. An exhaustive examination of the treatment of the cattle killing within Theal's entire body of work is beyond the scope of my argument. Theal uses the same account in *South Africa (The Union of South Africa, Rhodesia, and All Other Territories South of the Zambesi)* (London: Unwin, 1894). In *The Progress of South Africa in the Century*, part of a Nineteenth Century Series, the account is substantially condensed to three paragraphs (Edinburgh: Linscott, 1902).

54. Theal, *History*, 202. British Kaffraria chief commissioner John Maclean argued that aspects of the prophecy concerning anticipated atmospheric disturbances such as earthquakes and unnatural oceanic or celestial movements were "'remembrances of Scripture statements,'" implying that the prophecy was borrowed from the Bible (Peires, "Central Beliefs," 61).

55. Charles Pacalt Brownlee, *Reminiscences of Kafir Life and History and Other Papers*, ed. Christopher C. Saunders (Pietermaritzburg, South Africa: University of Natal Press, 1977), 143–44.

56. A version of Mrs. Brownlee's account also appears in Charles Brownlee's *Reminiscences of Kaffir Life and History* (Lovedale, 1896). Mrs. Brownlee was the former Frances Thomson, daughter of Rev. William Ritchie Thomson of the Glasgow Missionary Society's Tyhume mission station, which had been established by her father-in-law, John Brownlee of the London Missionary Society (Brownlee, *Reminiscences*, 439, 372).

57. W. C. Holden, *The Past and Future of the Kaffir Races* (Johannesburg: Struik, 1963), 289.

58. Holden's imputation of the prophecy as "jugglery" brings to mind Stephen Greenblatt's discussion of what he terms "Machiavellian anthropology," which posits "religion as a set of beliefs manipulated by the subtlety of priests to help instill obedience and respect for authority" (*Shakespearean Negotiations: The Circulation of Social Energy in Renaissance England* [Berkeley: University of California Press, 1988], 26). Greenblatt traces the containment of subversive notions of Christianity as a "confidence trick" used to exert European control over inhabitants of the New World; as will become clear in my discussion, Holden's reading of the Xhosa prophecy as evidence of the need for European intervention emerges from a similar ambivalence, yet Holden's text allows far less scope to the subversive thrust than the early modern texts that Greenblatt considers.

59. J. H. Soga, *The Ama-Xosa: Life and Customs* (Lovedale: Lovedale Press, 1932), 121.

60. Holden, *Past*, 294.

61. Chalmers, *Tiyo Soga*, 120.

62. Ibid.

63. Theal, *History*, 204.

64. Brownlee, *Reminiscences*, 148. A passage in the manuscript of Chalmers's biography (in which Mrs. Brownlee's account appears) contrasts the physical state of "weak emaciated objects" with their mental state, an "already overfed imagination" (J. A. Chalmers, *Tiyo Soga: A Page of South African Mission Work*, Ms. PR3988, Cory Library for Historical Research, Rhodes University, Grahamstown, South Africa, 157).

65. Fitzgerald Letterbook, Ts. PR3624, Cory Library for Historical Research, 31 August 1857.

66. Brownlee, *Reminiscences*, 144. In narrative theory, "prolepsis" refers to an anticipatory reference to an event that occurs later in the plot.

67. Ibid., 148.

68. The manuscript of Chalmers's biography contains the following disclosure from Frances Brownlee, struck through and excised from the published version: "I almost began to feel a little superstitious myself, left as I was day after day alone," since Charles Brownlee was away consulting with various chiefs (143). She describes his return from a meeting with Sandile in another excised passage: "I fancy I see them now as they appeared on the Sunday morning, returning from that melancholy conference, 'Napakadi' [Brownlee], his followers, dragged, dispirited, wet, weary, sorrowful, & sorry company they looked, as they passed the little church at Bethel, where I had gone, uneasy and anxious, one felt it was the only place where one could be at rest" (149).

69. Brownlee, *Reminiscences*, 148.

70. Holden, *Past*, 283.

71. Ibid., 292, 160, 295–96; emphasis in the original.

72. Ibid., 286.

73. Chalmers, *Tiyo Soga*, 103.

74. Brownlee, *Reminiscences*, 137; Chalmers, *Tiyo Soga*, 106.

75. Theal, *Compendium*, 53; James Laing, *Memorials of the Missionary Career of the Rev. James Laing, Missionary of the Free Church of Scotland in Kaffraria*, ed. C. W. Govan (Glasgow: David Bryce & Son, 1875), 182.

76. Brownlee, *Reminiscences*, 145.

77. The conviction about the chiefs' plot thesis coalesces rather suddenly in Grey's official correspondence during the week of 20 September 1856. Previously he or his informants indicated that the prospect of war is largely a rumor circulating among European settlers (see J. Maclean to G. Grey, 4 and 11 August 1856, *Further Papers*, Imperial Blue Book 2352 of 1857–58. Also compare G. Grey to H. Labouchere, 20 and 27 September 1856).

78. Brownlee to J. Maclean, 2 August 1856, *Further Papers*, Imperial Blue Book 2352 of 1857–58, p. 13.

79. See, for example, Bradford, "New Country"; Peires, *Dead*, 107; Timothy Stapleton, "'They No Longer Care for Their Chiefs': Another Look at the Xhosa Cattle-Killing of 1856–1857," *International Journal of African Historical Studies* 24, no. 2 (1991): 383–92, and "Reluctant Slaughter: Rethinking Maqoma's Role in the Xhosa Cattle-Killing (1853–1857)," *International Journal of African Historical Studies* 26, no. 2 (1993): 345–69; Jack Lewis, "Materialism and Idealism in the Historiography of the Xhosa Cattle-Killing Movement, 1856–7," *South African Historical Journal* 25 (1991): 244–68.

80. Theal, *Compendium*, 55. Similarly, the chiefs' plot thesis so dominates the otherwise remarkably sympathetic chapter on the cattle killing in William Rees and Lily Rees's hagiographic *Life and Times of Sir George Grey, K.C.B.* (London: Hutchinson, 1897) that the resurrected cattle are mentioned only as a kind of bonus prize for an anticipated military victory over the British, and the authors do not mention the resurrected ancestors at all: the amaXhosa were to go directly from noncultivation and slaughter to attack, with no magical copula.

81. Some of the Xhosa survivors were literally driven into the sea, loaded onto boats headed for prisons and schools in Cape Town; this fate was not insignificant, given the Xhosa taboos concerning the ocean.

82. Chalmers, *Tiyo Soga*, 129.

83. "After Ntsikana's story, the most fertile episode in 19th century history for telling the story of Christian emergence was the Cattle Killing" (David Attwell, *Rewriting Modernity: Studies in Black South African Literary History* [Scottsville, South Africa: University of KwaZulu-Natal Press, 2005], 64).

84. We see a similar economy of Xhosa hostility and European charity at work in a 31 August 1857 letter to Maclean by Dr. John FitzGerald, head of the King Williams Town Native Hospital: "I cannot speak too highly of the exertions made by the Ladies and Gentlemen of King William's Town to save human life in the present distressing state of destitution in which the Kaffirs are placed by their own reckless folly and perverse obstinacy!" (FitzGerald Letterbook, 94). It is difficult not to read symptomatically the missionary William C. Holden's assertion in this vein: "As, in days gone by, the English came nobly forward to save the starving population of the Emerald Isle, although the Irish had accused them of every foul deed; so also, the colonists put forth herculean efforts to keep alive these starving creatures, although their sires and friends had been engaged in desolating war, and might be so again" (Holden, *Past*, 294).

85. See, for example, the convoluted attributions of agency in the account of the cattle killing in Laing, *Memorials*:

> The country from which, by a mysterious providence, they had, through their own insane folly, been made the blind instruments of their own expulsion, is all but entirely deserted, the inhabitants having passed in swarms into the Colony, not, as repeatedly in bygone years to spread the horrors of barbarous warfare, but to cast themselves on the compassion of those who had so lately, apparently not without good reason, been anticipating a repetition of those dread, and really dreadful invasions, to which, in recent years, they had been too much accustomed. (189)

86. G. Grey to H. Labouchere, 27 March 1857, *Further Papers*, Imperial Blue Book 2352 of 1857–58, p. 85.

87. Maclean to Douglas, 6 August 1857, Fitzgerald Letterbook. In explaining why it was not operating in New Orleans after Hurricane Katrina in August 2005, the American Red Cross heeded similar logic from the Department of Homeland Security: "Our presence would keep people from evacuating and encourage others to come into the city." This while tens of thousands were kept from leaving the Superdome, the Convention Center, and the city itself—often at gunpoint (American Red Cross, "Disaster FAQs: Hurricane Katrina; Why Is the Red Cross Not in New Orleans?" (2005), available at http://chicago.indymedia.org/newswire/display/62547/index.php (accessed 29 December 2009).

88. I am thinking of the famous passage from Benjamin's "Theses on the Philosophy of History": "There is no document of civilization which is not at the same time a document of barbarism. And just as such a document is not free of barbarism, barbarism taints also the manner in which it was transmitted from one owner to another. A historical materialist therefore dissociates himself from it as far as possible. He regards it as his task to brush history against the grain" ("Theses on the Philosophy of History," in *Illuminations*, ed. Hannah Arendt, trans. Harry Zohn [New York: Schocken Books, 1969], 253–64, 256–67). In the South African context, Adam Ashforth identifies the perils in the intersection of academic historiography and the cattle killing, "the problem of writing a history of a process of colonial conquest in the terms and languages of the victors, which does not simply replicate in historiographical discourse the imperial encounter by translating the colonized people's experiences into the terms of dominant discourses" ("Xhosa Cattle Killing," 590).

89. Ranajit Guha identifies a similar dynamic in secondary histories of nineteenth-century peasant rebellions in India, in which the authors would both express sympathy for the peasants' suffering under native landlords, traders, and moneylenders and uphold the British Empire as the ultimate source of law, order, and benign "civilization" for the peasants ("The Prose of Counter-Insurgency," in *Selected Subaltern Studies*, ed. Ranajit Guha and Gayatri Chakravorty Spivak [New York: Oxford University Press, 1988], 345–88).

90. Theal, *Compendium*, 52.

91. White, *Content*, 24.

92. Frank Kermode, *The Sense of an Ending; Studies in the Theory of Fiction* (New York: Oxford University Press, 1967), 83.

93. Ibid., 18.

94. Comaroff and Comaroff, *Of Revelation and Revolution*, 236. Critic David Attwell wonders, however, whether colonized intellectuals "merely accepted the metaphorics of the civilizing mission, or whether they appropriated them to serve their own interests. In all probability, the answer cannot simply be either-or" (Attwell, *Rewriting*, 52–53).

3.

DIPESH CHAKRABARTY

Bourgeois Categories Made Global: The Utopian and Actual Lives of Historical Documents in India

JÜRGEN HABERMAS, in coining and exploring the expression "public sphere," wisely characterized it as a "category" of bourgeois society.[1] It was a "category" of thought, an ideational entity, not to be found anywhere on the ground in a full-fledged form, though it could be approximated by certain institutions. Not every modern nation in the history of the last two hundred and fifty or so years has felt obliged to mint replicas of the so-called European bourgeoisie, but none, one could argue, has been quite able to escape the ghosts of the categories and themes of public life forged in bourgeois Europe. The ghost of the "public sphere" haunts us all in many different forms. One such form, globally speaking, is the discipline of history. Born in nineteenth-century Europe as a knowledge form nestled in and nourished by the university—though, of course, with complex and entangled roots reaching back to distant and diverse pasts—the discipline of history had the utopian ideal of the public sphere written all over it. Take, for example, one of the most elementary rules of evidence in academic history writing: that the documents a historian uses as his or her sources must be verifiable. The rule derives from a fundamental principle of debate in the construction of modern "public life" (or, after Habermas, the public sphere): that such debates should be based on equal access to information. Equal access to information is what a modern archive represents to researchers in history. History writing is thus very much the act of the "public man" (I do not gloss "man" for obvious reasons). The discipline of history has the story and the *telos* of the public sphere built into it.

Equal access to historical information—a principle so important to the growth of the discipline of history as a public discourse—requires, as a condition of possibility, a process whereby documents held in private possession or available to a restricted group of people turn into public records. For this to happen, however, there has to be in place some abstracting mechanisms that actually abstract—that is, remove—documents from the particular relations within which they originate and circulate (family, bureaucracy, religious institutions, and so on). Both the state and the market have historically acted as such abstracting forces. The state, for instance, could pass legislation such as the Public

Records Acts and thus create official or public archives. But the market could also be such an abstracting force. Leopold von Ranke used to procure some of his key documents in the Venetian marketplace for ancient documents.[2] Without this developed trade in historical records, historians such as Ranke would not have been able to build their private research libraries. (For now, I will keep the accompanying development of the institution of the university to one side.)

Let us call these two processes of abstraction of documents—that of the state acting as a mechanism that abstracts documents from their points of origin and makes them into the signifiers of an abstract entity called "history," and that of the market performing this function of abstraction—by two different names (though, clearly, their connotations overlap): the processes, respectively, of reification and commodification of documents. The state reifies papers. It declares some papers to be of "permanent" value to the nation's history and hence to be preserved for posterity. It even designates a place for their preservation. As Derrida writes, "Archives is not a living memory. It's a location—that's why the political power of the *archons* is so essential to the definition of the archive. So that you need the exteriority of the place in order to get something archived."[3] One could say that in being a particular place removed from all the diverse places where archived papers actually originate, the archives embody the reified state of these documents. The market, on the other hand, makes ancient documents and books into commodities, available for purchase and sale. We may thus say that modern ideas about history and historical research impart "value" to old documents, and this "value" finds expression through two different logics, both of them, however, logics of abstraction. I have called them the reification (archives) and commodification (market) of documents.

Yet it is easy to see that these processes of abstraction represent not only the ideal of the public sphere but also some operation of power as well. For no society—my concrete examples come from colonial India—is premised on this principle of equal access to information. Information, that is knowledge, is always privileged in any society. It belongs and circulates in the numerous and particularistic networks of power, kinship, community, gendered spaces, aging structures, and so on.[4] If that is true, then the archives and the market, insofar as they appear to operate successfully, hide the conflict-ridden history of the public sphere in the same way as the dance of commodities in the marketplace—I am mixing the languages of Marx and Benjamin here—hides the inequalities that go into the production of commodities. The reification and commodification of documents, one can then argue, are never processes that come to a final conclusion. Even in the most effectively functioning archives or marketplaces one might have to have recourse to some relation outside the logic of bureaucracy or the marketplace to be able to access certain documents (friendship, family connections, and so on). In other words, the public sphere—a domain where one can discuss and debate matters of public interest on the basis of unfettered access to information—remains a utopia after all, but because it is a utopian ideal, it retains an ideological function as well. The process whereby we create "unfettered" access to historical information can also be seen as the prying open of information that was otherwise accessible only to a "privileged" community. This tension is central to the very idea of the public sphere: it can act both as a utopia of "bourgeois" equality and as an ideology of domination. It can be simultaneously democratic and undemocratic. The agents and advocates of the public sphere are often the bearers of this tension, for we never find a society where all its members, inspired by the social value we call history, volunteer to convert willingly all "private" documents into "public" records. Of course, the general social acceptance of a subject called history imparts value to old documents, and some democratic and historically minded citizens may indeed feel inspired to make "private" papers "public," but a complete correspondence between a particular individual and the figure of the citizen is exceedingly rare, if not altogether impossible. The rendering of private papers into public documents must remain, in the end, a political question.

The Indian Historical Records Commission

I illustrate this proposition by looking at a fragment of the history of history in colonial India in the twentieth century. At the center of my story is the Indian historian Sir Jadunath Sarkar, who lived between 1870 and 1958 and who may be regarded as one of the earliest proponents in the subcontinent of the Rankean ideals of "scientific" history. All his life he struggled, unsuccessfully, to create the conditions for historical research in India, conditions that included the question of unfettered access to historical records on the part of "qualified" researchers. Usually regarded as "the doyen of history" in India, he is also seen as someone superseded by later research. During most of his working life, his official duties had to do with teaching literature (and history in the last few years of his career) at undergraduate institutions such as Ripon College, Calcutta, Patna College in Bihar, and Ravenshaw College in Cuttack, Orissa. He retired in 1926 when he was appointed vice chancellor of the University of Calcutta for two years. Sarkar became a self-taught historian with a strong interest in the last phase of the history of the Mughal Empire. He wrote a five-volume history of the last great Mughal, Aurangzeb, published between 1912 and 1924. Between 1932 and 1950, he published four volumes titled *The Fall of the Mughal Empire*.[5] He wrote numerous other books and essays. For the purpose of this exposition, we come into his life around 1919, the year that saw the publication of his book on the seventeenth-century Maratha king Shivaji and when he was nominated to the Indian Historical Records Commission that the government set up that year. To put matters in historical context, one needs to remember that the University of Calcutta started the first department of modern history in 1919, and other Indian universities followed suit in the 1920s and '30s. Sarkar retired from employment in 1929—the year he was knighted—but remained an active researcher into the early 1950s.

The career of the discipline of history in colonial India is interesting because the discipline developed at a time when neither of the two processes mentioned earlier—the state reifying and the market commodifying historical records—was in operation. The colonial government preserved documents but was extremely reluctant to open them for public examination, even though writing history in a modern form became a popular activity among educated and nationalist Indians from the 1890s onwards.[6] A market for antique books in India also did not develop until some time after independence in 1947. In his autobiography, the historian Rameshchandra Majumdar (1888–1980), for instance, speaks of how, as a young researcher at the University of Calcutta in the late 1910s, he could sometimes bid successfully at British auctions on antique books only when the then vice chancellor of the university, Sir Ashutosh Mukherjee, waived all time-consuming rules and granted him immediate money and authority to do so. When Majumdar moved to the University of Dhaka in 1921, he found it impossible to acquire antique books from abroad, as that required obtaining clearance not only from the vice chancellor but also from the Finance Committee and the Executive Council of the university, leaving him no time in which to bid.[7]

Historians in colonial India also labored without the benefit of public archives. There is a long history in British India of the government's dragging its feet on the question of—as contemporary officials put it—"removing obstacles to historical research" in the country. Soon after they assumed the formal charge of India in 1858, the British formed a state that required a sense of historical documentation for its daily operation.[8] But the question of throwing open the records of the central and provincial governments in British India was not raised until 1914, when the Report of the Royal Commission on Public Records was published. The India Office now wanted the government of India to take responsibility for the use by researchers of their own records.[9] The response of the officials of the government of India to this issue leaves us in no doubt that, from the very beginning, the matter of opening up records to Indian researchers touched some raw political nerves of the colonial administration.

The correspondence that passed between the Marquess of Crewe, the secretary of state for India at the India Office, London, and the governor of Madras in 1913 clearly showed that insofar as the administration in India was concerned, the very idea of letting researchers into colonial record rooms had something unnerving about it. Crewe felt the need to reassure a nervous Madras government, who were "under a misapprehension" that India Office was proposing to "allow private persons unrestricted access to . . . unpublished [public] records." He enclosed with his letter a copy of rules "regarding applications to search the India Office records," showing that no one was allowed such unrestricted access even in London. Every request, he wrote, was "carefully considered"; the applicant was "required to state the object he has in view" and, if necessary, to "submit notes or extracts he may have made" and was not "allowed to make use of any to which objection is raised."[10]

However, Crewe wrote again the following year, in February 1914, to the governor-general of India, nudging him to open records to researchers by pointing out that the records in London were "largely duplicates of those in India" and that "it [was] obviously undesirable that there should be any difference . . . between the practice adopted by . . . [the India] Office and that obtaining in India [with regard to researchers in history]."[11] A. F. Scholfield, the officer in charge of Records in the Imperial Record Department in Calcutta, disagreed strongly and in terms that revealed the political fear that guided the government in India in these matters. In a note dated 28 April 1914 and addressed to his colleagues and superiors, Scholfield countered Crewe's letter by writing that "the argument from the Records in the India Office is specious. If the Records in London are the same as those in Calcutta, the 'public' is different." Elaborating, he added that there had never been "any wide-felt want, any loud or insistent demand for the throwing open of the Records." Indian scholars, in his opinion, had "no knowledge of what is evidence and how to use it." "There is in India," he wrote in words that must have guided him in 1919 when he was appointed, ex officio, the first secretary to the newly formed Indian Historical Records Commission, "no Aristocracy of erudition, no school of history; historical research, scientific use of evidence[, and] critical scholarship are rarely understood and seldom achieved."[12] He would rather prevent any "abuse of records" by (a) "admitting only persons who have given proof that they are serious researchers" and (b) "publishing press-lists and calendars of all of our Records, forestalling those who for whatever ends would distort or suppress evidence, by placing the whole in the hands of the public."[13]

An official letter dated 4 February 1915 addressed to Lord Crewe and signed by the governor-general and several provincial governors summed up the position of the government of India. There was no question of "placing the whole [archives] in the hands of the public," as historical research was "still in its infancy in India." In such a situation, the "encouragement and opportunities which the opening of records would afford to irresponsible writers . . . might be a source of inconvenience to the Government."[14] Clearly, a colonial government was not going to be favorably inclined to the idea of facilitating the emergence of a "public sphere," even in a domain that pertained to the past.

The government of India's hands were eventually forced, it seems, by the home government in England, which adopted some of the recommendations of the Royal Commission on the question of allowing private scholars access to government records in the interest of promoting historical research. In itself, this development is perhaps a testimony to the growing importance at this time, globally, of the idea of "historical research," arguably a German invention in the nineteenth century. Perhaps also at issue was another factor: the changing legal status of the records of the India Office in England. So long as the India Office was maintained "out of Indian revenue," there was some doubt as to "whether its records could be looked upon as coming within the scope of the [English] Public Records Acts." "But the same hesitation," noted an official, "no longer seems to exist in England[,] for the India Office records have lately come within the purview of the Royal Commission on Public Records in England." In theory, then, the Master of the Rolls in England could legally compel the India Office "to deposit its records down to the year 1837 in the Public Record Office."[15] This looming change in the legal situation must have also weighed on the minds of the otherwise conservative colonial administrators in India.

As a compromise, then, the government of India decided to constitute not anything resembling the English Public Record Office in India—a national archive, that is—but the Indian Historical Records Commission, which would consist of both government officials and four historians (for a term of three to five years) nominated to be "Ordinary Members" by the government of India. The argument received broad endorsement from the historian-cum-politician Ramsay Muir, whose opinions the government of India appears to have solicited in 1917. Muir agreed with others that the number of historical researchers in India did not justify the opening of records in the way they had been in England. But he emphasized the pedagogical role that the "permanent Historical Materials Commission" could play in the development of history as an academic subject in India. One of "the gravest defects of the Indian mind," wrote Muir, "is its lack of the historical sense. We will never remedy this by compelling Indian students to learn by heart any number of half-crown text books; we can only do it by introducing the method and spirit of historical enquiry and criticism, and that must be done, in the first instance, among the teachers." Muir underlined the importance of this point by enunciating a principle of what may be called an "imperial liberalism": "The remedying of this defect seems to me to be of primary importance, not merely from an intellectual but a political point of view; if educated India is to attain full political sanity, it must be by training in criticism and in the evaluation of evidence."[16] It was with such educational aims in mind that Professor Muir suggested that the proposed commission be headed by a "trained historian brought out from Europe," "a man stronger . . . on the historical than on the archival side."[17]

A gap remained between the principles of "imperial liberalism" that Ramsay Muir spelled out in his letter and the sentiments of the officials involved in running the commission, which was finally set up in 1919. The official resolution that led to the establishment of the Indian Historical Records Commission made "the training of Indian students . . . in methods of historical research and the selection of competent editors" the very last of the "duties" of the commission, the highest being that of advising the government "on the treatment of archives for the purposes of historical study," for example, "the cataloguing, calendaring and reprinting of documents" and "the extent and the manner in which documents should be open to inspection by the public."[18] The latter is what the government meant by the phrase "removal of obstacles to historical research."[19] It remained opposed for a long time to the idea of opening, wholesale, all governmental records to Indian researchers. It would rather have Jadunath Sarkar or other trusted historians produce selections of old documents. The Records Commission was to help make such selections.

Sarkar was one of the first Indian scholars to be nominated to the commission. In the 1920s and '30s (except for the years 1931 to 1936, when for financial reasons the commission was held in "suspended animation"), Sarkar remained the intellectual center of the commission and a vital force behind its activities and annual meetings.[20] For him, the Indian Historical Records Commission represented an opportunity; it provided a pedagogical and intellectual platform from which to propagate a particular vision of historical research and argue for the indispensability of public archives for the writing of history. (Like Ranke's, the history Sarkar wrote was mostly political.) Sarkar was acutely aware that the absence of proper archives hindered the progress of modern historiography in India. In a paper presented at the 1925 session of the commission, he focused on the question of archives as the condition of possibility for writing Mughal history. "The problem of Indian history in the Mughal period," he wrote, "is to find out the most original sources of information."[21] This Rankean enterprise, he explained, was constantly frustrated by the history of the very peculiar nature of the Mughal state. "In pre-British days," he wrote by way of explanation, "the records of every department of the Mughal Government or a feudatory state were usually kept in the house of the secretary of that department and not in any Government building or archives. . . . Administrative convenience dictated this practice, as, in the absence of a State archivist or general record-keeper, the secretary to a department was the only 'walking index' to the old records of that department." "The result of this old practice," concluded Sarkar, "was disastrous for history. . . . With the decay of the old families . . . much valuable material of first-rate importance has perished. Masses of old paper have rotted in their houses."[22]

Sarkar returned to this problem in a paper he presented at the twelfth meeting of the commission, held in Gwalior in December 1929. Speaking of "The House of Jaipur" and the records in their private holdings, he alluded directly to Ranke's experience. "In mediaeval conditions of society, State archives often did not exist, and even when they existed and have survived, they are usually surpassed in the extent and importance of their contents by private family records, as von Ranke pointed out long ago." Sarkar then quoted from

Ranke's famous introduction to "his monumental *History of the Popes*": "The freedom of access which I could have wished was by no means accorded to me. . . . A large part of the State-papers . . . constituted a part of the family endowments. Thus, to a certain extent the private collections of Rome may be regarded as the public ones." "Even a transcendent historical genius like Ranke," Sarkar went on to write, "failed to give fullness and finality to his *History of the Popes* because he could not open those closed treasuries of information."[23] What hope would Indian history have without a collective effort to imbibe the Rankean love of primary sources? Clearly this question engaged Sarkar's passion. As he said in the very first paper he presented to the commission: "I have come across very few historical letters in Persian for these three [second, third, and fourth] decades of Aurangzeb's reign. . . . The missing materials can be discovered only by the combined search of many men at many places."[24]

Sarkar thus was a man with a mission. As the chair of the meeting of the Records Commission in Patna in 1930, he emphasized that the commission needed to interest the research community and the general public in historical documents, for unless the papers in the possession of "historical families" and private persons were "made known and available to scholars, it would be as impossible to write a true and full history of India as it would be to write the history of England without using the papers in the possession of the Cecil and Walsingham, Buckingham and Grenville families." The idea, therefore, was to "interest the outer public" in the work of the commission and "to tempt private records out of their seclusion by . . . [having] a public session." To the public session was also added the attraction of an exhibition of historical artifacts and documents. As Sarkar put it in the same speech: "The exhibition has been our most helpful auxiliary for this purpose."[25]

Sarkar and Sardesai

In what follows, I read Sarkar as someone engaged in precisely the struggle to produce the preconditions that would enable the discipline of history to be a part of the "public sphere" in India. I thus read his frustrations for what they tell us about the nature of that struggle and about the visions, utopian or otherwise, that sustained him. Much of my information comes from the thirteen hundred original letters exchanged between Sarkar and his friend and collaborator, the Marathi historian G. S. Sardesai, which are now preserved at the National Library in Calcutta and span the years 1909 to 1956. Their friendship is a fascinating indicator of the new kinds of closeness that modern disciplines made possible between two scholars sharing the same intellectual passion. We do not know of any precolonial historians in India who were such close friends on the basis of a shared and complementary interest in "sources." Sardesai writes:

> Sometime in the year 1904 a letter in an unknown handwriting indicating vigour and precision with contents severely formal and businesslike, took me by surprise at Baroda. The name of the writer did not solve the mystery as I had not till then heard of him. . . . However, this letter came like a divine windfall . . . [he] required my help in supplementing with Marathi sources his vast source of Persian materials regarding . . . Aurangzib. And I myself in my scheme of the *Marathi Riyasat* was just then sorely feeling the need of utilizing Persian sources. . . . In short, this letter became the pledge of future co-operation between the Mughal and the Maratha.[26]

Friends for life, the two historians would travel together to different parts of India in search of sources relating to Maratha and Mughal history of the seventeenth and eighteenth centuries held by the descendants of older princely or administrative families of the region. Reading their letters, however, makes it manifestly clear that contrary to their own Rankean beliefs, Sarkar and Sardesai operated in a society where documents seldom had the character of "public" records. Kept by families in an often neglectful state, these documents were caught up in invisible but palpable webs of intrigue, rivalry, and regional or family pride and thus lay outside the control of the forces of the market or those of the colonial state.

The situation was complicated by the fact that the popularity of history as a subject newly imported from Europe and the dissemination of the Rankean idea, however badly assimilated, that "original" sources were of supreme value in the matter of narrating the past, had combined to create, by the beginning of the twentieth century, cadres of young scholars in different parts of the country who were already engaged in scouting the land in search of family papers. This was nowhere more so than in Maharashtra, where much of Sarkar's and Sardesai's research was located. These other scholars openly competed with Sarkar and his friend in searching for historical papers. Their competition reveals another process—distinct from the processes I named reification and commodification of documents in the opening section of this chapter—that one may liken to the process of fetishization. Instead of collecting documents to make them available to all researchers, the early hunters and collectors of historical papers in India often wanted to corner and hoard such documents for their exclusive use and restrict, at least for the time being, other scholars' access to them. It was as though the "originality" of these documents, instead of being valued for its usefulness in historical analysis, was in itself a value. The documents thus took on the aura of fetishes, and simply being in possession of them lent the owner of such documents some of the glory of the fetish!

It is striking, for instance, how often in the letters they wrote to each other Sarkar and Sardesai would emphasize the need for caution and secrecy to keep others off the scent of old documents. Their rivals, on the other hand, as the following letter shows, would go to great lengths to make access difficult for the duo. I quote a letter from Sarkar to Sardesai, dated 14 August 1931, which is typical of the letters of this genre:

> Please keep our tour programme next winter strictly secret, or better still, mislead the Poona rascals by carelessly saying that you would accompany me next December on a tour of Panipat, Delhi and Lahore—i.e. exactly the opposite direction. You talk too freely and too unsuspiciously, while you are surrounded by men who, when not rogues, are fools and proclaim your plans and words to the Poona circle the very next morning, either out of maliciousness or a simple desire to display their own knowledge of your se-crets. *Our Maval tour of 1930 was preceded by a hostile printed handbill signed by Potdar* and one of his tools, only because you had beaten the drum in advance in Poona. This time never mention Tanjore to anyone there, or if you have done so, say that I am unable to go and you have aban-doned the Tanjore project for a new programme of tour in North West India.[27]

The "Poona rascals" of Sarkar's description referred to the historians and collectors associated with the Bharat Itihas Samshodhak Mandal (Association of Researchers in Indian History), a voluntary organization for amateur re-search in history, established in Poona in 1910. The "Potdar" of the passage quoted was Datta Vaman Potdar, who by 1931 was the secretary of the Mandal. The founding scholars of the Mandal—Rajwade, Parasnis, Sane, and Khare—people Sarkar would write essays about in the 1920s, as most of them passed away in that decade—had been engaged in collecting historical documents from old Maratha families. A letter from Sardesai, dated 14 April 1927, sug-gests that the process had rather unsavory beginnings: "It is the extremely hos-tile attitude of these Poona people which has retarded the progress of history in the university and with Government. They are extremely jealous of other workers and would rather damage all other work in the hope of pushing on their own hobbies." He continued:

> Whatever the Poona apologists of Rajwade might say, the whole method of obtaining papers from private houses is nauseating. Of course, we must re-member that all sorts of contrivances have to be used in getting hold of pa-pers. There was a scramble between Parasnis, Bhave, Chandorkar, Rajwade, and Mawji[?] and Poona Mandal for a time. But recently the crase [sic] has subsided: people have now begun to understand the value of papers and are themselves coming out with them. But the methods about 10 years ago were altogether reproachable.[28]

The correspondence between Sardesai and Sarkar does not support the optimism Sardesai expressed in those last lines. There were occasions when Sarkar himself would accompany Sardesai on these document-hunting trips dressed as a dumb Maratha Brahman, since his spoken Marathi would have given him away. When Sarkar wrote to Sardesai on 10 August 1935, "When you next visit Poona . . . please quietly pick out all the letters of General Arthur Wellesley (Lord Wellington) . . . and send them to me," Sardesai made a note in the margin of the letter to remind himself to "keep this a secret from the A[lienation] O[ffice] [the records office] staff and all others."[29] In any case, the need for secrecy in looking for documents is repeated in several letters, covering a span of nearly twenty years. Of the two, Sarkar was the scholar more intent on discovering "original" documents, so it should not surprise us that notes for the need for caution and secrecy often came from him. Besides, it also shows that his commitment to the idea of public records or his search for documents was not uncontaminated by what I have called "the fetish of the original." Here are a few more examples:

> Sarkar to Sardesai, 21 August 1925: "From Gwalior I shall take you privately to Indore, where you must examine the vast State records in Modi in charge of Bhagwat, and also the Wagh Raje daftar. . . . Your presence at Indore can be kept secret, if you desire."[30]

> Sarkar to Sardesai, 1 November 1931: "Please see if you can join me in Bombay, but keep our dates and programme strictly secret from the Poona gang."[31]

> Sarkar to Sardesai, 18 December 1934: "It would be [a] matter of good policy to keep *strictly* silent there about the mournful fact that the Imperial Record Office, Calcutta, possesses ten times as much records about Maratha affairs after 1785 as the Residency Records of Poona, and that our volumes when issued will be found to be indebted to Calcutta *thrice* as much as to Poona; —and in the case of Mahadji, it is ten to one."[32]

> Sarkar to Sardesai, 22 October 1940: "Make your confidential arrangements beforehand for securing access to the records in Bangalore."[33]

The Parasnis Affair

Sarkar's struggle to access historical documents was not confined simply to the matter of rivalry with Poona historians. Quite a substantial amount of the correspondence between Sardesai and Sarkar related to what may be called the Parasnis affair. This again gives us some insights into the politics of the process whereby old papers could or could not be converted into public documents for use by researchers in history and the ideas that informed this process.

While working on the history of the eighteenth-century Maratha ruler Mah-
daji Sindhia (1764–94) of the Gwalior state, Sarkar and Sardesai discovered
that many of the relevant documents of the Sindhia family—still an important
political family in India—were in the custody of one of the Poona historians,
D. B. Parasnis, who was an inveterate collector of historical documents, which
he published in his journal *Itihas Sangraha* (History Collections).[34] He collected a vast amount of primary material from the Sindhia family and died in
1926 before he could publish it all. Some of these documents formed the collections of a private historical museum he had created, known as the Satara
Museum, after the town of Satara, where he lived.[35] Parasnis had been granted
a lifelong pension of two hundred rupees a month by the government of Bombay for this task. On his death, both the papers and the pension went to his son
Amritrao Parasnis, or A. D. Parasnis, who, as far as I can make out, was not a
scholar of history but simply held on to these papers without making them
available to other historians.

Sarkar and Sardesai tried for many years to gain access to these documents
and thought long and hard about how they might put pressure on the young
Parasnis and force him to release the documents for research. Interestingly,
many of their attempts turned around legal questions, such as what might
have been the nature of the contract between Parasnis and the Sindhias and
who might be the legal owners of these documents. In itself, this was a new
way of thinking about historical records. However, Sarkar and Sardesai failed
to resolve this question successfully, but their correspondence shows both the
utopian and the pragmatic role that the idea of the law and the public sphere
played in their arguments. The letters also suggest how they understood
the junior Parasnis's attachment to these documents.

For quite some time to come, Sarkar and Sardesai were convinced that it
was the prospect of making money that made Amritrao hold on to the Gwalior
documents. Sarkar writes in March 1931: "Is young Amrit Rao Parasnis trying
to play the game of getting more money out of the Gwalior Darbar as the price
of yielding these documents up? If so, he deserves no sympathy."[36] Sardesai
also was clear from the beginning that Parasnis was after money. He would
part with the documents only if he could make money out of this. In a letter
to Sarkar dated 20 January 1927, he wrote that the young Parasnis was prepared to sell the unsold but printed volumes of these documents that his father
had prepared: "He is in distressing circumstances and would like to secure as
much monetary return for these copies as he can." But Sardesai's letter also
raised another question, indispensable in discussions of the public life of historical documents; this was the question of the law, especially the law pertaining to the ownership of documents. Sardesai was not sure that legally Sarkar
and Sardesai could simply buy these papers: "We do not know what Parasnis's
arrangement with Gwalior was, i.e. whether he has received full payment

for all the 15 volumes that he had promised to print for them: and whether the 90 copies now found have been retained by him [were so retained] with the permission of Gwalior." Otherwise, "all the printed works and perhaps even the mss. papers, now in the Satara museum, will form property of Gwalior."[37]

There were two main prongs to Sarkar and Sardesai's strategy—as Sarkar phrased it in a letter of 1932, for "put[ting] the screw on young Parasnis."[38] One was to bring him under financial pressure by using their contacts in the government to threaten him with a cut in his pension. The other was to convince the government about its own, that is, the colonial state's, legitimate ownership of these papers, which once belonged to a ruling Maratha family. The second entailed the exposition of a certain kind of political theory on the part of Sarkar, but of that more later.

Parasnis, noted Sardesai in a letter dated 25 June 1932, owed the raja of Sangli "over a lac and a half [Rs. 150,000]." "The Raja is quite irritated with young Parasnis and yet he is too shy to take strong action. . . . Barve asks me to make a case against Parasnis. The originals of all papers printed or unprinted by Parasnis must form the property of the museum. . . . If on the day of the opening ceremony Parasnis had not brought all Daftars into the new building, and did not subsequently send them in, it was a fraud and the allowance the family gets can be made liable for it."[39] He later returned to his point about "a kind of fraud played by Parasnis upon Government. . . . We have to move more carefully and threaten him with a cut in his grant."[40] Sarkar concurred in his reply: "I entirely agree . . . that unless he is threatened by Government with a cut in his perpetual pension, he will not disgorge the illegally detained records. Furnish me with full details so that I may approach the Government on the subject. A personal visit from me to the Hon'ble Revenue Member would have been most effective, but it is impossible for me before December next."[41] Writing a few years later on the subject, he repeated, using a Bengali expression about "straightness" that saw "crookedness" as belonging to the ordinary order of things:

This young man can be made to walk straight only by being put in fear of starvation or when he has some additional favour to expect from Government,—and not by appeals to justice or the interests of history. . . . I strongly suspect that ADP, just before his father's death, removed (1) all the pictures, (2) all the Sanskrit illuminated (costly) mss., (3) all the Persian mss., and (4) the letters of Sir F. Currie, Ellenborough, & c.—which I had seen in DBP's house in 1916, as well as the Menavli daftar. . . . These are not in the museum.

I am convinced that valuable Sindhia papers remain unprinted and in ADP's possession . . . ADP is mainly trying to enhance his importance— and chance of making more money—by pretending he has several rumals [a piece of cloth used to put documents into a bundle] not covered by the material published in *Itihas Sangraha* [in Nagari] and the 5 Gwalior volumes.[42]

As it became clear, however, that "Gwalior Darbar has no legal claims to Parasnis's Modi daftar," Sarkar also considered the question of a money suit, though "one shadow," he said, "crosses my mind: will not a money suit be barred by time limitations in 1938?" It turned out that Parasnis Senior owed some money to the Gwalior family.

> All the letters written by [the late] D.B.P. to the late Maharaja deeply commit him, by stating his remuneration and printing costs per volume. . . . His receipts for Rs. 63,150 are there. These will be copied now and sent to V. S. Bakhle [a lawyer] confidentially for his opinion as to . . . whether the sum of Rs 48,150 not cleared by D.B.P. (whose 5 volumes of his own valuation discharge Rs 5 x 3000 = Rs 15,000 only) can be claimed from DBP's remaining assets, viz., his house Happy Vale and his pictures, and his heirs called upon to pay the amount or bring a lawsuit upon their heads. . . . Thereafter Bakhle will formally serve notice of demand on ADP. This, it is hoped, will bring that young man down on [his] knees. If he appeals for mercy to the Gwalior Darbar, Sir Manubhai has agreed to take all the unprinted Modi papers (Mahadji-Nana correspondence) from him and give him a formal quittance.[43]

When these methods failed to produce the desired results, Sarkar and Sardesai experienced much despair about these seemingly unrecoverable sources, which they considered indispensable for writing the eighteenth-century history of the Marathas.[44] They made one last desperate bid to move the colonial government by exhorting them to take action to recover the documents from the young Parasnis on the ground that these documents were of public life and hence belonged to the colonial sovereign power, the state that inherited the rulership of Maharashtra from the eighteenth-century Peshwas. On 27 November 1949 Sardesai reported that he had had a talk with a Mr. Lad, "who is the present legal Advisor to the Bombay Government," regarding "the question of recovering historical documents from Amrit Parasnis, "to which he [Parasnis] has no right." Lad proposed to issue a notice to Amritrao "recounting the fraudulent dealings and [threatening that] unless he would deliver all that he has wrongly withheld, the Bombay government would be compelled to suspend his allowances."[45] He urged Sarkar to draft such a note.

It says something about the commitment of these two men to the rendering of old papers into historical documents that Sarkar actually composed a note for possible use by the government. The note is remarkable for the political theory that informs it. It was also interesting that Sarkar was prepared to do the government's work for this cause. He drafted a quasi-legal letter, for he said in a short prefatory note to the draft: "It will have to be put in a lawyer-like form . . . remember that a Government Legal Adviser only makes himself ridiculous if he issues an ultimatum which he cannot substantiate in a law-court." Here is the letter that Sarkar drafted:

To A. D. Parasnis,
Happy Vale,
Satara.

In connection with the perpetual pension of Rs 2400 a year granted by the Government of Bombay to the late Rao B[ahadur] D. B. Parasnis's heirs, I have to draw your attention to the following points.

(1) Throughout his correspondence with the Government of Bombay, the late Rao B. had always given the assurance that all the historical records collected by him would be kept in one place and made available to scholars in an unbroken mass, and for ensuring this object he had solicited government aid. That aid was given conditionally upon this avowed object being fulfilled. . . .

That on the above clear understanding Government built the Satara His[torical] Museum, gave your father in his lifetime money aid to the extent of Rs 12,900, and finally sanctioned the perpetual pension to his heir.

(2) But after his death, you as the representative of his heirs, withheld from Government a large portion of historical records, without revealing the fact to Government. This was a direct contravention of the contract made by your father, and an act of fraudulent concealment and misappropriation against Government. The grant is therefore liable to cancellation on grounds of fraud.

(3) You should know that the historical records of a sovereign state belong to the state (and its successors) even though state papers many have been addressed to some minister of the state (like Nana Phadnis) and stored in his private house (which was the usual practice in pre-British days in India and also in medieval European countries). The Government's right to these national records cannot be barred by limitation or adverse possession in the hands of others. The Menavli Daftar and other state papers that you hold in your hands are the lawful property of the Bombay Government alone, and you cannot claim them to the property of Gwalior darbar or any other party. Your duty is through these to inspection and recovery by an accredited agent of the Government of Bombay, and you should take notice that by objecting to or delaying such an investigation you are committing a criminal offence.

For your information, I will tell you that Mr. Elphinstone, the first Governor, on taking possession of the Peshwa dominions, found many of the state records in the hands of the old hereditary officers of the Peshwa, and all these were removed by him to the control of the Government and housed in the Alienation Office. The records that then escaped and reached your father are equally government property.[46]

None of these ploys by Sarkar and Sardesai worked. It is possible that the colonial government, now facing the growing tempo of the nationalist movement and realizing that independence could not be very far off for India, did not want to stir up matters that concerned only Indians. The secretary of the General Department of the Government of Bombay informed Sir Jadunath on 30 November 1934 that "the Govt. have carefully examined the question of recovering from the de[s]cendants of late Rao Bahadur Parasnis the historical papers forming the bulk of the volumes composed by Rao Bahadur Parasnis for the Gwalior state. They have been advised that they have no legally valid claim to papers relating to the Scindia family referred to by you, as these were among documents housed in the Historical Museum, Satara, in respect of which argument was entered into with the heirs of the late Rao Bahadur Parasnis." Sarkar's proposal for intervention by the government was simply "not practicable."[47] The issue was dead by the early 1950s as far as either the provincial or the central government was concerned. In 1951 Sarkar reported to Sardesai that the Sindhia papers in possession of the central government were being removed to the newly set up National Archives of India: "No hope of [looking?] into the hands of Amrit D. Parasnis."[48] And in 1955 he reported again that the historian Dr. Saltore had written to him "some weeks ago that the Gwalior Government has entirely forgotten the case of the last Parasnis bundle." "No hope," he added, "of our doing anything."[49] He also realized, with much sadness, that he was never going to see anything like a Public Records Act in India.

Public and Private

Thus both in the practical and the "principled" ways in which Sarkar and Sardesai had imagined they would be able to wrest old historical papers out of the hands of the junior Parasnis—by getting the government to reduce his pension or by instituting a money suit—or in their political theory (that one sovereign power simply inherits the documents pertaining to public life created during a previous regime), they were proved wrong. Yet it is remarkable how central the utopian and bourgeois distinction of the private and the public was to their theoretical and practical thinking. "Parasnis will have to disgorge all he has gulped," wrote Sardesai in a letter to Sarkar in 1936. Notice the use of the word "public" in the text of this letter: "The main point is [that] . . . it was fraudulent on the part of Parasnis in keeping back these and several other original papers which have been printed by him in his magazines: - that all these should be available to *students of history* as the Parasnis family is granted Rs 200 in perpetuity out of *public* funds."[50] Or his optimism in November 1937 when he felt that an upcoming meeting between Sarkar and the commissioner of the Central Division of the Bombay Presidency could be "utilized for setting right the affairs of the Satara Museum." Sarkar could perhaps explain to the commissioner "how Parasnis defrauded Government and how the originals of the Sindia papers are still possessed by Parasnis." "I feel sure," he added, "they would threaten Parasnis with suspension of his allowance if he does not produce Sindia originals, as these are no more *private* property, having been *publicly* given out."[51] The political theory postulated in Sarkar's draft of the semi-legal letter I have reproduced above also turns on this distinction between private and public documents, public documents being seen in his letter as "national" as well: "You should know that the historical records of a sovereign state belong to the state (and its successors) even though state papers many have been addressed to some minister of the state (like Nana Phadnis) and stored in his *private* house. . . . The Government's right to these *national* records cannot be barred by limitation or adverse possession in the hands of others" (emphasis added).

What was remarkable about this application—by the most preeminent Indian historian of British India—of the private/public distinction to pre-British records pertaining to rule in eighteenth-century India was its anachronism. For it did some violence to the very understanding of Indian society through which Sarkar had initially posed the problem of historical sources. Recall Sarkar's own explanation of why it was difficult to find original, eyewitness accounts for the Mughal period: it stemmed from the fact that "in pre-British days . . . the records of every department of the Mughal Government or a feudatory state were usually kept in the house of the secretary of that department," for there were no home/office, and hence private/public, distinctions in that period. Surely, the point made by Sarkar and Sardesai that the documents found in the possession of old Maratha families were public documents needs to be squared with this observation. Sarkar and Sardesai's blindness to this problem points not only to the utopian nature of the "public" and "the archive" they worked with in thinking politically about historical documents but to their ideological nature as well. For them these bourgeois categories were not just visions of the future but also weapons to wield in the present.

There is, however, something to learn about these European categories from their failure. A successful functioning of archives and historical research as part of a public sphere entails the formation of a particular kind of state, a state that has managed to tame the past through the creation of archives, something that Achille Mbembe has called "chronophagy." This happens precisely through what I have previously called "reification." Archiving means, as Mbembe puts it, placing documents "under a seal of secrecy—for a period of time, which varies according to the nature of the documents and local legislation."[52] The documents thus become abstracted from their roles in the present—even if present and extant practices lead to their eventual physical decay and destruction—and they are not available for conversion into popular memory. Bourgeois categories of thought are perhaps about imagining politics that tame the past by "eating" memory. Politics in India in Sarkar's time and later—modern but not bourgeois, though laboring under the spectral presence of bourgeois Europe—was such that it ended up resisting the idea of the archive. How else would one think about all those amateur collectors (such as the Poona historians) who, out of their passions of the present, hunted, hoarded, and fought over old papers in ways that precisely prevented their transformation into historical documents? Admittedly, their hoarding practices and publications based on such practices created new publics that were modern but not bourgeois.[53] Sarkar and Sardesai, on the other hand, looked to the colonial government with pretensions to the ideals of an empire to perform the principled duties of a modern state in creating conditions in which the spirit of the bourgeois public sphere could animate research in history. This utopian vision was flawed—for Sarkar never understood the difference between a modern bourgeois state and a colonial-imperial government—but powerful for the influence it wielded in molding the career of history in colonial India.

Notes

I am grateful to the American Institute of Indian Studies for a grant that funded the research for this paper and to Arvind Elangovan for assistance with the research. Thanks are also due to my audience at Princeton University, where the first version of this paper was presented, and to Gautam Bhadra, Prachi Deshpande, Anthony Low, Rochona Majumdar, and Thomas Metcalf for helpful discussions.

1. Jürgen Habermas, *The Structural Transformation of the Public Sphere: An Inquiry into a Category of Bourgeois Society*, trans. Thomas Burger with assistance from Frederick Lawrence (Cambridge, MA: MIT Press, 1989).

2. Ugo Tucci, "Ranke and the Venetian Document Market," in *Leopold von Ranke and the Shaping of the Historical Discipline*, ed. Georg G. Iggers and James M. Powell (Syracuse, NY: Syracuse University Press, 1990), 99–108.

3. Jacques Derrida, "Archive Fever in South Africa," in *Refiguring the Archive*, ed. Carolyn Hamilton et al. (Dordrecht: Kluwer Academic Publishers, 2002), 42.

4. In this and the preceding paragraph, I draw on some thoughts I have lived with for a long time. See my "Trafficking in Theory and History: *Subaltern Studies*," in *Beyond the Disciplines: The New Humanities*, ed. K. K. Ruthven (Canberra: Australian Academy of the Humanities, 1992), 106.

5. H. R. Gupta, ed., *Life and Letters of Sir Jadunath Sarkar* (Hoshiarpur: Punjab University, 1957), 108–9; Anil Chandra Banerjee, *Jadunath Sarkar* (Delhi: Sahitya

Akademi, 1989), 6–7; Moni Bagchi, *Acharya Jadunath: Jibon o shadhona* (Calcutta: Jijnasha, 1975), 47–49.

6. See my "Public Life of History: An Argument Out of India," *Public Culture* 20, no. 1 (Winter 2008): 143–68.

7. Rameshchandra Majumdar, *Jiboner smritideep* [The Memory Lamp of Life] (Calcutta: General Printers, 1978), 28–29.

8. *Indian Historical Records Commission* [hereafter *IHRC*] *Retrospect* (Delhi: Government of India, 1951), 1.

9. Ibid., 2.

10. National Archives of India, Delhi (hereafter NAI), Imperial Record Department (hereafter IRD), April 1914, Proceeding (hereafter Prog.) No. 53, India Office to His Excellency the Right Honourable the Governor General of India in Council, 5 December 1913, Fort St. George, Madras.

11. Ibid., India Office to His Excellency the Right Honourable the Governor General of India in Council, 27 February 1914.

12. Ibid., note by A. F. Scholfield dated 28 April 1914. Alwyn Faber Scholfield succeeded Edward Denison Ross (later director, School of Oriental and African Studies, University of London) to the position of the officer in charge of Records of the Imperial Record Department in 1914 and retired soon after the first session of the Indian Historical Records Commission (1919), having been its first ex officio secretary. See *IHRC Retrospect*, 48–52.

13. Ibid.

14. Ibid., June 1915, Prog. No. 94, and IRD, April 1918, Prog. No 47, appendix.

15. NAI, IRD, April 1920, Prog. No. 41, K.W., R. H. Blaker's note on "questions of making the official records in India more accessible to students of history and the public," 27 November 1919.

16. NAI, IRD, December 1917, Prog. No. 18 and K.W. Demi-official letter, Professor Ramsay Muir to Sir Edward D. Maclagan, Secretary, Education Department, Government of India, 7 December 1917.

17. Ibid.

18. Government of India, Department of Education, Resolution No. 77 (General), 21 March 1919, reproduced as Appendix A in *Indian Historical Records Commission, Proceedings of the Meetings*, vol. 1, first held in Simla, June 1919 (Calcutta: Superintendent of Government Printing, 1920).

19. *A Hand-Book to the Records of the Government of India in the Imperial Record Department, 1748 to 1859* (Calcutta: Government of India, Central Publication Branch, 1925). Foreword by A.F.M. Abdul Latif.

20. The expression "suspended animation" was Sarkar's. He used it in welcoming delegates to the 1937 meeting of the commission: "Today, the . . . Commission meets again after seven years of suspended animation due to the financial difficulties of the Government." *IHRC Proceedings of Meetings*, vol. 14, *Fourteenth Meeting Held at Lahore, December 1937* (Delhi: Manager of Publications, GOI, 1938), 7. See also the discussion in NAI, IRD, January 1937, Prog. No. 18, note by "S.D.U" dated 10 September 1936: "The meetings of the . . . Commission were held in abeyance in 1931 as a measure of retrenchment. It has not yet been possible to revive them though the question is raised by the K[eeper of] R[ecords] from year to year. Last year efforts were

made for their revival but they proved unsuccessful. The question will be taken up again shortly in connection with the budget estimates for 1937–38."

21. Jadunath Sarkar, "Historical Records Relating to Northern India, 1700–1817," in *IHRC Proceedings*, vol. 7, *Seventh Meeting Held at Poona, January 1925* (Calcutta: Government of India, Central Publishing Branch, 1925), 28.

22. Ibid., 30–31. Throughout his life, Sarkar would return to this point. He repeated it in his foreword to *Selections from the Peshwa Daftar* (Bombay: Superintendent, Government Printing and Stationery, 1933), 2–3. He later remarked of Sardesai's exploratory research in Hyderabad in the late 1930s that it had

> only proved what I had believed, namely, that the Nizam's archives do not contain any state papers of the pre-Panipat period because all the despatches received and copies of despatches sent out were kept in the houses of the secretaries concerned—exactly like the Peshwa's statepapers during Nana Fadnis's regime finding their refuge at Manawali, and not in the Peshwa Daftar at Poona. These Moghlai officers lived in Aurangabad and their houses are now in ruins. So farewell to one of your dreams.

Sarkar to Sardesai, 18 March 1937, Letter no. 454, Darjiling, in Jadunath Sarkar Papers (hereafter JSP), National Library (hereafter NL), Calcutta.

23. Jadunath Sarkar, "The House of Jaipur," in *IHRC Proceedings*, vol. 12, *Gwalior, December 1929*, 18.

24. Sarkar, "The Missing Link in the History of Mughal India from 1658 to 1761," in *IHRC Proceedings* 2:7, 8.

25. See speech by Jadunath Sarkar in *IHRC Proceedings*, vol. 12, *Thirteenth Meeting Held at Patna, December 1930* (Calcutta: Government of India, Central Publication Branch, 1932), 7.

26. G. S. Sardesai, "Jadunath Sarkar as I Know Him," in *Sir Jadunath Sarkar Commemoration Volume*, vol. 1, ed. H. R. Gupta (Hoshiarpur: Department of History, Punjab University, 1957), 18.

27. Sarkar to Sardesai, No. 168, 14 August 1931, Darjiling, JSP, NL; emphasis in the original.

28. Sardesai to Sarkar, No. 64, 14 April 1927, Girgaum, Bombay, JSP, NL.

29. Sarkar to Sardesai, No. 364, 10 August 1935, Darjiling, JSP, NL.

30. Moradpur, P.O., JSP, NL.

31. No. 172, Darjiling, JSP, NL.

32. No. 328, Calcutta, JSP, NL; emphasis in the original.

33. No. 648, Calcutta, JSP, NL.

34. NAI, IRD, March 1920, Prog. No. 44, shows the Bombay government financing in part the publication of Parasnis's *Itihasa Sangraha*, which did not have a wide readership.

35. See Sarkar's question: "Will the Satara museum ever be open to the public?" in Sarkar to Sardesai, No. 67, 18 April 1927, Darjiling, JSP, NL.

36. Sarkar to Sardesai, No. 150, 1 March 1931, Calcutta, JSP, NL.

37. No. 58, Girgaum, Bombay, JSP, NL.

38. Sarkar to Sardesai, No. 197, 11 March 1932, Calcutta, JSP, NL.

39. Sardesai to Sarkar, No. 215, Alienation Office, Poona, JSP, NL.

40. Sardesai to Sarkar, No. 218, 16 July 1932, Kamshet, JSP, NL.

41. Sarkar to Sardesai, No. 221, 22 July 1932, Darjiling, JSP, NL.

42. Sarkar to Sardesai, No. 342, 8 April 1935, Darjiling, JSP, NL.

43. Sarkar to Sardesai, No. 496, 26 December 1937, c/o Rai Bahadur Bhaduri, Morar, Gwalior, labeled "Confidential," JSP, NL.

44. Sarkar to Sardesai, No. 792, 4 March 1944, Calcutta, JSP, NL.

45. No. 1022, Kamshet, JSP, NL.

46. Sarkar to Parasnis, No. 1023, 4 December 1949, Calcutta, JSP, NL.

47. Secretary to Jadunath Sarkar, Miscellaneous File, General Department, Govt of Bombay, Bombay Castle. This was a reply to Sarkar's letter to the Hon'ble Minister of Education, 10 November 1934, JSP, NL.

48. No. 1084, 6 October 1951, Calcutta, JSP, NL.

49. Sarkar to Sardesai, No. 1188, 8 September 1955, Calcutta, JSP, NL.

50. No. 396, 21 February 1936, Chhindvada, Central Provinces, JSP, NL; emphasis added.

51. Sardesai to Sarkar, No. 491, 19 November 1937, Kamshet, JSP, NL; emphasis added.

52. Achille Mbembe, "The Power of the Archive and Its Limits," in *Reconfiguring the Archive*, ed. Hamilton et al. (Dordrecht: Kluwer Academic Publishers, 2002), 20.

53. See Prachi Deshpande, *Creative Pasts: Historical Memory and Identity in Western India* (New York: Columbia University Press, 2007).

4.

Luise White

The Utopia of Working Phones: Rhodesian Independence and the Place of Race in Decolonization

When Rhodesia's white minority unilaterally declared itself independent from Britain in 1965, it denied that its independence was racist in any way. Among its many claims was the statement that it was forced to take its own independence because of the racism of decolonization—the idea, dear to Britain and African nationalists alike, that independence for African territories had to be based on universal suffrage, which would mean majority rule, which would be racist, as only one race would govern. Rhodesians insisted that their independence was based not on race but on the need to maintain "standards," to stand up for "civilization," and to struggle against the Communist menace. Such broad ideals made Rhodesians' notions about their own statehood some-what vague, but the claims Rhodesia made for itself and its independence implied comparisons. Rhodesia insisted it was far better than the African states that Europe had summarily abandoned to independence and to the one-man, one-vote system, and a lot better than the Britain that had done the abandoning, but that was the limit of its vision. Rhodesians called their illegal independence the rebellion, a deliberate act of defiance against decolonization and membership in the world community of nations, including former African colonies, which were now declared equal. This seems to have made many people around the world think Rhodesia was a last stand of empire. It was, but as a racialized and simplified idea of what the British Empire—or indeed any empire—had been. But the longer Rhodesia survived, the more it came to represent another sort of meaning to another sort of white men around the globe: Rhodesia was the place where white people dared to stand up for themselves, where they did what needed to be done. In these representations, Rhodesia became a state in which race trumped all else, especially any notion of nation.

Within Rhodesia, the mechanics of declaring itself independent, combined with a heady dose of the most regressive kind of nineteenth-century liberalism, seemed to coalesce into an ideal of progress, of efficiency, and of modern conveniences that could be maintained only through the hard work of quali-fied men and women. That these men and women were white was the coincidence of history that made Rhodesia what it was. Outside Rhodesia, however, the independent state was considered a white supremacist's dream, a country that had taken its own independence rather than let white people live under black rule. Even as Rhodesia edged toward majority rule in the late 1970s, the racialized imaginary submerged the more mundane one, and Rhodesia became, to its supporters and to itself, a racial utopia, a locus of ideas about white rule that had no history, no specificity, and no real loyalty to place. In this chapter I argue that Rhodesia's racial utopia was relative: Rhodesia was the most responsible government in Africa. This meant it had the best hospitals, telephone service, and road repair crews on the continent, but that was because the government maintained standards. What made such a government utopian was that responsible people refused to give up the phones and hospitals to black rule. The white minority's claims to rule by the rights conferred by history were gradually undone, in part, by international claims of racialized rights and protections.

In what has become a seepage between popular and academic histories, Rhodesia has been seen not as utopian in any way but as a racist anomaly, the last stand of white folk against the end of empire, an eager imitation of South Africa's apartheid.[1] Certainly white-ruled Rhodesia was racist—and there is no need for another essay proving it—but it was also a functioning and fractious state, often at odds with the army defending it, and the product of specific ideas about politics and the cultural norms that should support political life. The problem in this chapter, and indeed of a significant part of the history of decolonization, is how to interrogate a state when the state is represented in the vocabulary of race. Rhodesia's racism came to define the state, and as I argue here, it came to obscure it as well.

Race and Decolonization

In 1923 Southern Rhodesia, a chartered colony of Cecil Rhodes's British South Africa Company, was granted the status of "responsible government" by Great Britain. This meant that Rhodesia had a British governor and that its parliament could enact any legislation so long as the Crown approved of it. Rhodesia had its own army and civil service, but it did not have control over its international relations. In 1953 it became part of the Central African Federation. This was a final compromise on ideas about territorial unification that had been floated by white politicians and white trade unionists for years, a federation of copper-rich Northern Rhodesia, Southern Rhodesia, and the labor reserve of Nyasaland. The federation was also the last gasp of an imperial imaginary, a unit based on a set of ideas called multiracialism that were in direct opposition to majority rule; these ideas were in large part about how to manage African advancement while preserving white privilege. Opposition to the federation, mainly by African nationalist groups and quite a few Southern Rhodesian politicians, weakened it from the start.[2] By 1960—the year Harold Macmillan warned settlers in Africa with his "winds of change" speech—a royal commission recommended that the federation be dissolved, and that Northern Rhodesia and Nyasaland be given independence as separate states. For Rhodesia—the name was changed when Northern Rhodesia became Zambia—this precipitated a crisis. Many thought they could go on as before, but that was impossible in Africa in the 1960s. From 1960 to 1965 there were frosty negotiations with Britain over the future status of Rhodesia. In the midst of these, in 1962, a new political party, the Rhodesian Front (RF), proclaiming the segregationist sentiments that had long characterized Rhodesia's opposition parties, was elected and began to carefully plan for independence. Its first leader, Winston Field, was ousted because he did not pursue independence aggressively enough; Ian Smith replaced him. The RF was well funded; although it began as a coalition between large landowners and defectors from older political parties, it grew in popularity the longer it remained in power.[3]

Rhodesia's Unilateral Declaration of Independence in November 1965 quickly became an acronym (UDI) that referred both to the status and the period of Rhodesian statehood, which lasted, with one revision, for fourteen years. At first, Rhodesia was not wholly sure what to make of its own independence. The bloodless revolution seemed to have left its perpetrators "glum," wrote one journalist; another noted that no one spoke of the promise of independence but of the "chaos" of majority rule from which Rhodesia was saved by UDI.[4] After the first legal challenges to UDI—especially the African detainees' lawsuits of 1966—the RF was relieved to be called the de facto government.[5] Also in 1966 Rhodesia became the first modern pariah state; no other country recognized it, and mandatory, worldwide sanctions were imposed on it years before even limited sanctions were imposed on South Africa. All of this seems to have given Rhodesia the equivalent status of a state. Sanctions lasted longer, and took a greater toll, than anyone had anticipated, although almost everyone traded with Rhodesia, albeit illegally. In spite of sanctions, in spite of a war fought against two African guerrilla armies that drained the country's resources from 1977 to 1979, in spite of a dramatic political shift toward majority rule—calculated, wrongly, to get sanctions lifted—and in spite of a new name, Zimbabwe-Rhodesia (locally known as Rhobabwe), Rhodesia managed to survive, with economy and army intact, for fourteen years. The story of how Rhodesia survived has generated an enormous literature about how various Western nations secretly approved of minority rule and about who traded with it and who refused to invade it.[6] The main questions of this essay are somewhat different: how did the Rhodesian Front, and its supporters, understand their independence, and what did the racializing of the Rhodesian state, both in Africa and in the wider world, do to their ideas?

There are two broad and linked answers to what Rhodesians, both in and out of the RF, thought they were doing, one concerning the form of the state and the other the form of racial domination. The idea of Rhodesia in the mid-1960s was conceived as a rightful state, one legitimated by its history, its wealth, and the quality of its governance. Many imagined it to be a worthy successor to empire. Several politicians, even those opposed to UDI, repeated the story of the Conservative Commonwealth Secretary Duncan Sandys, explaining to a small group of federal politicians in 1962 that Britain had lost the will to rule. An otherwise moderate Rhodesian parliamentarian blurted out, "But *we* haven't."[7] Opponents and proponents of UDI insisted that Britain secretly wanted Rhodesia to take its own independence, as Britain could not give it to them. Indeed, Rhodesians assumed that if they were to become independent, their state would occupy a weighty geopolitical place in the cold war world. "History," Ian Smith told the nation, "has cast us in a heroic role." The RF took it for granted that Rhodesia would be recognized by South Africa and Portugal out of sheer self-interest and by France, which would want to upset Britain and provide a precedent for an independent Quebec. International recognition was the way that new states acquired legal and equivalent status with each other, however new and non-European they were. Had Rhodesia been widely recognized as a state, it would have recuperated the legitimacy it had lost with UDI.[8] Everyone in the RF leader-ship knew of the intensive lobbying that had tried to make Britain recognize the breakaway state of Katanga in 1960 and 1961; they assumed, not without reason, that the Rhodesia lobby would do the same for an independent Rhodesia.[9]

The very example of Katanga begs the question of race. Katanga was ruled by Africans; the secessionist state did not succeed as an independent state because no other country (not even Belgium, whose interests it served) recognized it and because it violated the integrity of colonial borders.[10] No one questioned the right of the government in Katanga to rule the territory so long as the territory did not declare its independence from the Congo. The question of Rhodesia's independence was not about territory but about population: how could a white minority declare independence so that it could claim to legally rule a country with an African majority? Caroline Elkins has argued that after 1945, white settlers in Africa dug in against the colonial retreat and claimed a popular sovereignty for themselves alone.[11] This does not fully apply to Rhodesia, where white settlers had controlled the state for more than forty years and where the notions of sovereignty, popular or not, were specific. One race should be allowed to rule another, but that right was based on history, not innate qualities. Almost all Rhodesian political parties had constructed arguments that minority rule was legitimate, if not legal, because of how well its rulers had ruled for forty years. The wickedness of decolonization created what Ian Smith, announcing UDI to the nation, called the "absurd situation" in which "people such as ourselves, who have ruled ourselves with an impressive record for over 40 years, are denied what is freely granted to other countries," some of which had not ruled themselves for more than a year. Rhodesians required "the separate and equal status to which they were entitled."[12]

These separate but equal entitlements were racial; they were to be protected by independence. Among the racialized rights was that of not having to call white people white—they were civilized, they maintained standards, they governed responsibly, but they did not rule by race or skin color alone. It was the British who wanted rule by one race: majority rule. Many of the men who demanded Rhodesian independence had been MPs of the governing party of the Central African Federation; they were well aware of some of the tendencies in that party to redefine what being white, or black, meant. In 1961, for example, the Southern Rhodesia organizing secretary for the United Federal Party (UFP) hoped to do away with the term "Federation." He asked the party rank and file to recommend a better name. He himself liked "Rhonasia. . . . Friends, let us love 'Rhonasia.' Let us build it into a glorious country. Let us be big enough to forget this silly bickering about race."[13] Indeed, Rhodesia's policies never had a straightforward notion of white supremacy or, as I will show, whiteness. Many in the RF had never lost their fear of non-British immigrants, and others had never recovered from the eager inclusion of Africaners—and speeches in Afrikaans—in federal electoral politics.[14] This was more than a matter of language and culture; South Africa represented the racial practices from which Rhodesians desperately tried to distance themselves.[15] Rhodesians liked to think of themselves as Africans, with tenuous ties to settler colonies or the UK. Ian Smith, born in Rhodesia in 1919 and a former UFP chief whip, loved to say, "I am an African just as much as any black man is." Indeed, in October 1965 he was unmoved when Harold Wilson suggested that UDI might endanger whites elsewhere in Africa.[16] A month later, the RF frantically invoked white Rhodesians' ties to Britain—the oft-quoted phrase that Britons were their "kith and kin" was first used in the declaration of independence—to claim a special relationship so that Rhodesia would not be penalized for taking its own independence.

How much kinship to Britain—and British subjects everywhere—was required to make Rhodesia a settler society or a settler state, where white men clung to the distant land they tamed by animating their metropolitan ties?[17] Settler society is one of those tropes that insist race be placed before history in understanding colonial formations; it is not an inaccurate turn of phrase, but it does nothing to explain how racial privilege was legislated and instantiated in these societies, and how those laws and their vitality changed over time. It flattens the historical specificity I foreground in this chapter, one example of which was the way members of the RF evaluated the attitudes of civil servants and soldiers and purged those who might oppose UDI. The RF had already gotten rid of a prime minister who was reluctant to demand independence; it was not about to tolerate opponents who were high-ranking civil servants: loyalty to fellow white men, who shared histories and schools and regiments, was secondary to assessing their loyalty to a specific political goal. RF cabinet ministers boasted that they made sure the army was loyal; they "got rid of" the commander of the army and the permanent secretary in the Ministry of Defense, both of whom resigned. It took twenty months of such research and pressure before UDI was declared, but the time spent was well worth the effort. "It would have been the simplest matter in the world for the Army to have stepped in and had a coup . . . we had to find out exactly whether the army was with us and whether in fact the civil service was with us," although, of course, "there were odd ones who weren't." The odd ones who were not behind the RF were barely tolerated; some left the country as soon as they could afford to, and others called it the worst years of their lives.[18] Another example of the historical specificity of Rhodesian independence was that the date of UDI was postponed in order to preserve "the shape of the state that had been under federation." When it became clear that Britain would not approve an extension of the preventive detention law—which allowed Rhodesia to keep one thousand African politicians in detention—the RF cabinet waited until the British governor, amid unremarkable township violence, declared a state of emergency. A week later UDI was declared.[19]

The Utopia of Working Phones

The tried and true vocabularies of conquest and settler power were frequently deployed in the first days of UDI. Rhodesia was compared to Sparta and Lepanto, which fought off the "hordes from the east"; RF party hacks claimed Rhodesia was like Britain at the height of empire, or like Britain in the 1940s, or like Rhodesia in the 1920s and '30s. Sometimes they insisted that if Winston Churchill were alive, he would immediately immigrate to Rhodesia because only there could he find all the admirable qualities he had once loved in Britain.[20] Not everyone—and maybe no one—believed the hyperboles. These stock phrases and comparisons had limited resonance because UDI was, more than anything else, a product of its time. The RF itself had been constructed in the space between the ever-embarrassing segregationist Dominion Party and some of the multiracial, Rhonasian excesses of the territorial branches of the UFP party. But as a party in power, the RF's only real ideology was to oppose decolonization, to decry the horrors of one man, one vote, and to call cynical the transfer of power to an unqualified electorate by a weakened Britain (or France or Belgium), throwing up its imperial hands and leaving Africans to their own devices. Rhodesia's legitimacy seemed based on the examples of Rwanda, Zanzibar, and above all the "ghastly chaos" in the Congo two weeks after independence, which calcified Rhodesian ideas about decolonization. After 1965, there were coups in Ghana, Mali, and Togo and pogroms in Nigeria, which added, albeit retroactively, to the justifications for UDI.[21]

Rhodesians feared majority rule, of course, but bundled into Rhodesians' use of the term were coups, ethnic violence, and Africans on the rampage.[22]

If majority rule meant chaos—"the word that dominates political discussion among white Rhodesians"—UDI meant much, much more than the opposite. It meant efficiency, standards, technology, and working telephones. Calvin Trillin, visiting Rhodesia in 1966, was told over and over again that telephones in neighboring Zambia were so bad Rhodesian businessmen preferred to drive hundreds of miles to the Copperbelt rather than wait for a connection. Trillin became the first of many visitors to disparage what Rhodesians bragged about. There was something constricting, he wrote, about a country "where the national aspiration can be stated in terms of preserving an efficient telephone system."[23] Ten years later, David Caute, reporting on Rhodesia for the *New Statesman*, interviewed a company director. He had the usual praise for Rhodesian standards of sanitation, hygiene, "and medicine second to none in Africa" and "telephones that work."[24] But a reliable phone service and all that was necessary to maintain it underscored the rights by which Rhodesia justified its independence. Natural rights could not make the telephones work or the hospitals function. Rhodesia was legitimated because it could uphold what Zambia, two years after independence, could not sustain.

How did working telephones become a way to talk about civilization and the advantages of minority rule? By no means was there a straight line between the self-reliance of white settlers and their pride in a really reliable phone service; once again, the belief in working phones, like the belief in UDI, was a product of postwar politics and postwar white populations. The idea of Rhodesian independence had been around since the early 1930s,[25] but the idea of Rhodesia taking its own independence, of unilaterally withdrawing from the British Empire, was a product of postwar ideas and postwar populations. The conventional demographic history is one of population growth. There were the pioneers and pre-1920 settlers, a group of great mythology and even greater gravitas: they were known to work hard, often alongside Africans, and dwell in modest circumstances while building agricultural fortunes.[26] There were 82,000 whites in Rhodesia in 1945. After World War II, and after the early boom of the federation, the white population of Rhodesia all but trebled between 1946 and 1965, when it peaked at 228,000. The postwar immigrants told striking stories. A valley in the eastern highlands that was uninhabited in 1947 had a dozen white farms three years later. The white population of Salisbury, the capital, quadrupled between 1946 and 1961. Immigrants came from England and South Africa—although many of those immigrants were British born—and internees and refugees from Poland, Greece, Italy, and Germany stayed after the war. Rhodesia's postwar immigrants were categorized by country of origin whether or not they spoke English; their attitudes were studied and quantified.[27] The new immigrants, however, were thrilled to be of a wave; they boasted that Salisbury was now the most cosmopolitan, polyglot city in Africa and that they were making their mark on the country.[28] But the anecdotes, the numbers, and the studies are misleading. Rhodesia's steady population growth was marked by a large number of whites leaving every year. Between 1955 and 1960, for example, more than half as many whites left Rhodesia as immigrated; in 1961–65, years of great uncertainty, eight thousand whites immigrated, but almost thirteen thousand left. These proportions were nearly reversed between 1966 and 1972, years in which Rhodesia thrived. Not until 1976 did more whites emigrate than immigrate. Some of this movement was part of an older pattern of skilled white workers' migrations around the mining industries of Central and Southern Africa, and some of it was a disengagement from the Rhodesian project, but the comings and goings of the "good time Charlies" meant that the white population was far more fluid, and possibly smaller, than anyone admitted.[29]

What does this do to the idea of whiteness, which historians of the United States have shown to be critical to understanding how race and racism operate? Labor historians in particular have argued that whiteness was constructed in opposition to an imaginary of blackness—servile, foreign, erotic—even as whiteness had no fixed constituency. Throughout the nineteenth century certain white European immigrant groups, such as Italians and Hungarians, came to be called white only after a long and contentious process.[30] Rhodesia's immigration figures throw such a notion of whiteness into question. If most of the new immigrants circulated between the United Kingdom, South Africa, Rhodesia, and possibly Mozambique, how well could the mechanics of exclusion and subsequent inclusion operate? If whiteness was not a core identity, how did its proponents deploy the category? Rhodesians—at least long-term residents—seemed to make race a matter of history and culture. As late as 1973, Ian Smith asked that the Ministry of Internal Affairs (formerly Native Affairs) form a committee that could declare people white; there was already a committee to classify Africans and Coloureds. Smith was concerned about the case of two children who could not be admitted to the government school reserved for whites in a provincial town. Their grandfather had married a "creole" woman, but their mother was married to a white man and was accepted as white in the European community of Fort Victoria. Surely there should be some committee that could declare people white, as similar problems could be found throughout the country.[31]

If race could be decided by committee, what did whiteness mean in Rhodesia? Warwick Anderson's work on Australia may provide the greatest insight. Anderson has argued that for Australia, "white" was an imprecise term, at once too simple and too ambiguous. For Australian doctors and researchers, using the term "white" was not so much about fixing membership in a community as the entry point into the debates of the day.[32] In Rhodesia, especially after 1960, these debates were not about the vulnerability of white bodies in the colonies but about the white polities therein. The term "white" was not so simplistic as it was vulgar; it was much better to say "responsible" or "civilized." The bureaucratic power to declare someone white—as in children with a "creole" grandmother—was the discursive ability to mark white Rhodesians in place; it was a way to animate heritage and history. For Rhodesians, arguing about who was white and what someone had to do to become fully white was too close to some of the evolutionary models behind decolonization. Declaring Rhodesian children white was one thing; deciding what to do about Portuguese immigrants (11% of new arrivals in 1970) and their relations with Coloured and African prostitutes was another. The problem was that these men, the cabinet was told, had come from colonies with policies of assimilation, which "contradicted the Rhodesian way of life."[33]

The timing of Rhodesia's rebellion meant that the country had to put up with Portuguese immigrants from Mozambique and Angola. The politics of the rebellion, however, meant that even those Rhodesians most enamored with the idea of white settlers had no force of empire to support their claims. Within a few years of UDI, their claims to the right to rule were translated into a very broad notion of what might constitute white or Western supremacy. Some of the wealthy men and retired officers who immigrated to Rhodesia after 1945 produced most—but not all—of the grandiose descriptions of Rhodesian independence. One boasted that the RF had stopped "'the black flood' at the Zambezi." Another wrote that Rhodesia alone was turning back "the Eastern tide," as had been done before only at Thermopylae and Lepanto.[34]

The black floods and the eastern tides and the working telephones meant that Rhodesian political thought remained a hodgepodge, easily parodied.[35] Well into the 1980s, UDI was described as a struggle against Britain, not against anything Africans might do. "The people were fed up with being pushed around by Britain," said an RF MP; "we felt like we were giving perfidious Albion a kick in the teeth," said a farmer.[36] Many RF politicians, including Smith, had started their careers as federalists. They had the language of partnership and multiracialism down pat: they spoke of gradualism, of African advancement; they spoke with authority, if disingenuousness, about their knowledge of Africans, how happy Rhodesia's Africans were, and how much they appreciated a qualified franchise. The meaning of these words might have shifted, but they remained in place because so much of the RF's statecraft was about maintaining the status quo.[37] What was anti-African was packaged in the language of anticommunism. At the same time, the antifascist rhetoric of World War II was put to work: decolonization was nothing more than appeasement, which Rhodesians rejected. It was Britain's "socialist government" that was "hell-bent on appeasing the cult of Marxism-Leninism, at the expense of the old traditional values of the British Empire."[38]

Yet the inclusive nature of empires was at odds with the growing exclusions of independent Rhodesia. At the dissolution of the Central African Federation, it was fairly easy to establish citizenship in Southern Rhodesia: one could have been born there, lived there, or one's father could have done so. Federal citizens had the option of dual citizenship, which various committees encouraged them to have.[39] But demands for Rhodesian independence paralleled the breakup of the federation, and many in the RF believed there could be no such thing as dual loyalties, as one member of the government insisted: "You're either British—English, Scots or whatever you'd like to call it—or you're Rhodesian, one of the two."[40] In the first months of UDI, there was a strong, if not Spartan, sense of patriotism, a loyalty to place and to history and a resourceful enthusiasm for the task at hand. Civil servants were praised for staying at their posts in the face of vague threats from Britain; they were offered cash rewards if they could find ways of saving their departments money.[41] The Royal Air Force quietly allowed Rhodesian officers and airmen to resign and join the Rhodesian Air Force, which in turn allowed British subjects to do the same.[42] When Rhodesia became a republic in 1969, however, citizenship became a problem for a country at war. Until then, Rhodesia consisted of British subjects, South African citizens, and aliens; now it was a land of citizens and aliens, many of whom had British passports. If only Rhodesian citizens were called up, there would soon be a dire shortage of manpower; moreover, if only citizens were conscripted, it might make new arrivals loath to become citizens. After much debate, it was decided to conscript aliens as well as citizens. This was fairer, and it would not drive citizens out of the country. Besides, most of the treaties forbidding British subjects to serve in foreign armies were more than a hundred years old and were made with "banana republics of little concern to us."[43]

In this, as in much else, Rhodesia in the 1960s was keenly aware of where and when it was: UDI was the response to a specific understanding of time and place. UDI's rhetoric, Thermopylae and all, was about cold war politics and institutions.[44] "The forces of the East," wrote the last Rhodesian high commissioner to Britain, used communism "to exploit world organisations originally dedicated to the cause of peace." But those forces were now halted because Rhodesia "assumed the mantle of the champion of Western civilisation."[45] P. K. Van der Byl, the most flamboyant RF cabinet minister and one of the men most given to talk of Spartans, announced that Rhodesians were "a breed of men the like of which has not been seen for many a long age" but who could set an example that would "go some way towards redeeming the squalid and shameful times in which we live."[46] The shameful times were decolonial; the example set was to reject the worldwide trend of universal franchise and majority rule. Even the most intense claims of settler legitimacy slipped into attacks on the UN, the Commonwealth, and, of course, Communists. As Ian Smith ended his radio address announcing UDI to the nation, "The decision we have taken today is a refusal by Rhodesians to sell their birthright. And, even if we were to surrender, does anyone believe that Rhodesia would be the last target of the Communists in the Afro-Asian bloc?"[47]

UDI was more than a racist response to majority rule all over Africa; it was a hedge against the fact of international bodies, constituted in part by these new African states, which could constrain the practices of a racially consti- tuted state. Even those in the RF who believed they could let the issue of in- dependence slide, that Rhodesia could act as it had done before, were fearful of international and inter-African organizations. After the founding of the Or- ganization of African Unity (OAU) in 1963, party leaders thought there would be "too many difficulties." It would be best to make a "complete and utter break and take the consequences. Let us paddle our own canoe rather than there be an opportunity every now and then for some kind of special inquiry into what we were doing."[48] The goal of UDI, Rhodesian cabinet ministers told Conservative supporters, was to free Rhodesia "from the shackles of Brit- ain" and to be left alone "to deal with our own problems in our own way." As long as Rhodesia was tied to Britain, they said, it was fair game for "the Com- monwealth, the OAU, and the United Nations and every other ignorant busy- body meddling in our affairs and exciting our Africans to ever greater violence and bitterness."[49]

Rhodesia's rebellion was against not just Britain but also against all that decolonization had become a shorthand for: to be postcolonial, to become a nation-state in a world of formal horizontal relationships between states in which rights and relations were based on nature (as in human rights) rather than culture (as in civilization).[50] Rhodesia was to be the exception to the or- derly processes of decolonization and transnational realignments that insisted that all modular states could be equal—the very things that made the "shame- ful times" such a shame. The concept of one man, one vote, it turned out, was only one evil; worse was the equivalency between nations and the one-nation, one-vote phenomena of the UN. In 1964 Roy Welensky, prime minister of the moribund Central African Federation, wrote that he did not worry that the African and Arab nations in Africa could "subdue" South Africa or Southern Rhodesia. Instead he feared that "by the very make up of the United Nations," they might be able to intervene in the internal workings of either country.[51]

In this way, Rhodesia's right to exist, its legitimacy, came to have less and less to do with the specific history of the country or its population. Rhodesia's legitimacy was that it deliberately defied the processes of decolonization, that it scorned the orderly creation of new modular nations, and that it rejected the idea that these nations belonged in international forums that could police each other. These exceptions made the nation. They did not make the nation sovereign, as Carl Schmitt has been so easily paraphrased; instead the set of decisions that resulted in UDI created a space for a sovereign state, however unacknowledged and penalized it was. The decision to remove Rhodesia from what was, by 1965, the routinized process of decolonization also removed it from ideas about rights inherent in natural law. It gave the state powers that were greater than those of its laws.[52] These decisions encouraged claims to a

Rhodesian utopia, not because of the exceptions, but because they marked the specific ideas of racial domination and civilization that were at the core of Rhodesia's claims to sovereignty. These ideas were common to settler communities in colonial Africa, but for the most part they had died a natural death by the late1950s.[53]

Far more central to Rhodesia's exceptionalism was its struggle to become legitimate, to gain international recognition—in short, to be given the status of a modular nation that UDI had eschewed. Rhodesians constantly whined that Rhodesia was not thought to be a legitimate state in the world of nations— the very thing UDI was the exception to. There was a long litany of the injustices Rhodesia and Rhodesians suffered. Rhodesia was not allowed to compete in the 1968 Olympics.[54] Anyone who held a Rhodesian passport was banned from entering Britain and most UN-member countries, although that was subject to appeal and negotiation. Rhodesian residents with British passports had to wait in the Commonwealth line when returning to England.[55] Rhodesia had the good fortune to be cast out of the sterling zone well before the devaluation of 1967; the cabinet, however, worried less about the value of the currency than its new name. Many wanted something local, like the sable (for the antelope) or the Rhodes (for Cecil), but the Ministry of Finance refused; it was unlikely that such a unique currency would "enjoy a reputable position in the eyes of the world," so they settled on the dollar.[56] Even so called, Rhodesian currency could not be used outside the country without criminalizing the trade that brought it there, so Rhodesia tended to trade in Central African francs and keep accounts under false names in French banks.[57] There were constant complaints that Rhodesia was not accorded the same rights or respect that other nations, especially African nations, enjoyed. In 1973, for example, a Rhodesian resident (carrying a British passport) was wounded by Zambian soldiers for inadvertently crossing the border; one weekly newspaper asked its readers to "imagine what would have happened if the incident was perpetrated in reverse. . . . The world would have gone hoarse with shouting and the United Nations would have gone up in arms."[58]

What gave Rhodesia the abject legitimacy it did have was the combination of ideas about civilization, of standards, and of the practice of empire (when no one else was willing to do it). All this constituted Rhodesia's utopia: the right of racial domination had been asserted, without regard for time or place or law. This utopian legitimacy was fashioned in large part through all the talk about the wickedness of the UN and the OAU and later the World Council of Churches (which gave a small grant to one of the guerrilla armies). The Rhodesian state was defined and constituted by what it stood against, and how firmly it stood against it, all the things bundled into Rhodesia's courage to tell Britain and the world, "So far and no further!" Yet Rhodesia's legitimacy could not be expressed without referencing the horrors of decolonized Africa. As Smith wrote in his memoirs, "The most compelling argument for our taking of independence was the rest of Africa."[59] A chauvinistic immigrant compared the good health of political prisoners in Rhodesia with the appalling state of those in Kwame Nkrumah's Ghana.[60] And, of course, there were those telephones in Zambia.

Race and Place

A peculiar dialectic of Rhodesia began in the mid-1960s but was firmly in place by 1969: every other place in Africa (or the world) was so bad, and because Rhodesia was so much better, it had the right to exist as an independent state. Rhodesia's history was initially part of what made the country so much better, but the history was soon displaced by the vague utopia of independent Rhodesia. When white people, whatever their politics, immigrated to independent Rhodesia, their recollections followed a particular pattern: "I came from a bad place, now I am in good place." A man came from England in the mid-1960s and quickly saw how happy Rhodesians were. It was he who was weighed down from "the sorrow of editorials, the UNO, trade unions, pundits, culture and the rest." Taffy Bryce, a Rhodesian hit man, came to Rhodesia in 1970 from Zambia, where he was working in construction. One trip across the border for a weekend's drinking and he was hooked, determined to stay and fight for this oasis of peace and civilization in central Africa.[61] Denis Hills came to Rhodesia in 1975; he had been sentenced to death in Idi Amin's Uganda for an unpublished manuscript; freed by British intervention, a year later he was deported from Northern Nigeria on some pretext or other. He took up a teaching position in Rhodesia in 1975 and immediately felt safe among the Yorkshire accents, swimming pools, and superb gardens. Another man who arrived in Rhodesia in 1976 just wanted to be out of Britain: "Anything would be better than being ground to a powder under the crushing weight of income tax and creeping bureaucracy."[62]

Such narratives were at odds with the uneven patterns of population growth and decline, but the "good time Charlies" who came and went—and perhaps came again—were part of the myth of the Rhodesian way of life.[63] With UDI, Rhodesia became a place defined by what it was not, not by what it was. Rhodesia was not permissive and immoral like Britain, it was not violent like the United States, and it was not like South Africa in its racial laws. Visitors crowed that Rhodesia was a "valiant country riding out the storm of world hostility and not afraid to refuse plays like *Oh Calcutta*."[64] Such praise raised a larger question: if Rhodesia was not a place like any other—however wonderful or horrible that might be—what was it? Rhodesians loved to joke that they were a nation wandering in the wilderness in shorts, that when you landed at the airport the stewardess told you to set your watch back twenty years, but no one seemed to be able to get beyond the homilies of a brave nation going it alone, abandoned by a Britain it no longer recognized.[65] A 1977 survey of morale in the Rhodesian Army revealed that soldiers repeatedly complained that they knew what they were fighting against, but not what they were fighting for. The response by the army's psychological action team, which carried out the survey, was not reassuring. They suggested a small poster of the Moscow May Day parade, overprinted with "Not in Rhodesia," or stickers in the shape of Rhodesia with a hammer and a sickle in the corner overprinted with "Not on your Nellie."[66]

As the war progressed, and as Rhodesia became increasingly uncertain about how to identify itself, the country came to occupy an even more specific kind of political imaginary, one that had no other location in the world in the mid-1970s. Colonel Mike Hoare, who raised Moise Tshombe's mercenary force in Katanga, tried to convince the Rhodesian Army to let him form a French-speaking Rhodesian Foreign Legion, which would recruit only white anti-Communist youths in Europe. Portugal offered the services of 2,000 white Portuguese soldiers who had fought with UNITA in Angola; there were 100 more white Portuguese in South Africa, ready to fight for Rhodesia if Rhodesia could pay for their passage.[67] The exiled King Zog of Albania offered to send 500 men.[68] The number of foreign (and foreign-born) soldiers fighting for Rhodesia was watched intensely by the army and journalists,[69] as were the motivations that made these men come and fight in an African war.

Robin Moore, an American novelist and the amanuensis of the Green Berets, arrived in Rhodesia in the early 1970s and set himself up as the unofficial American ambassador. He founded an organization for U.S. soldiers who came to fight for Rhodesia: Crippled Eagles, so called because they were crippled by U.S. government harassment. The younger of these Americans, resting beside Moore's swimming pool in 1977, explained their disinterest in Rhodesia to the journalists Moore invited on Sundays. One told David Caute that he had answered an ad in *Soldier of Fortune* because after Vietnam and Angola, "we can't afford to lose any more countries." Another one cheerfully informed Christopher Hitchens that he did not care "about the rich white guys and their farms and their dough. But I'm fighting for them because they're white, and the white man is running out all over."[70] In a book published in 1977 specifically to inform the American public of the situation in Rhodesia—and the need to end the sanctions—Moore produced eight vignettes about individual Crippled Eagles. One man explained why he came to Rhodesia with a question about Angola, which seems to have had all the power for these young men that Sparta had for a generation of RF party hacks. "If we were willing to send men to Vietnam and ask them to fight communism, how can it be wrong to intervene in critical places like Angola?" Another came because of the United States: he said he was in Rhodesia because he was ashamed of "my own government" and "the way the United States is heading." And a third came out of loyalty to "other Anglo-Saxons . . . who were trying to fight for their own freedom and to determine their own destiny. I just couldn't stay in the United States any longer, on the other side of the world and not do anything about it."[71] Not everyone was recruited by Moore or magazines. One young American said he joined the Rhodesian Army in 1972 to protest the "revolutionary conspiracy of internationalists" who now controlled and weakened the United States.[72]

These immigrants and soldiers and the proposed Rhodesian Foreign Legion raise critical questions about the peculiar problem of Rhodesia: as the country's history and self-inflated nationhood became irrelevant to its supporters, only politics—and racialized and caricatured politics at that—mattered. And those politics were literally utopian: communism had to be stopped, men had to stand up against terrorism, and the Western world had to stand fast against the eastern hordes. Where this took place did not matter at all. These men were fighting a war in Africa, however, where the context for these terms was profoundly racialized; they were fighting against a black government. But race, as Benedict Anderson pointed out years ago, is decidedly unnational: each of the words used to disparage the guerrillas—*gooks, terrorists,* or *CTs*—"*erases nation-ness*" from the enemy, who becomes a racial or political embodiment.[73] Rhodesia suggests that the opposite is also true, that travel to the other side of the world to support Anglo-Saxons fighting for their freedom occurred without any loyalty to a nation, without any historical specificity or even a sense of place.

Young Rhodesian men were not much better. History, place, and patriotism ceased to matter as Rhodesia became a locus of poorly globalized ideas about white privilege. A young man in the all-white Rhodesian SAS (Special Air Services) complained to David Caute in 1978 that "we can't survive without outside help. It's about time Europeans looked after Europeans—it's the white man's getting a raw deal throughout the world."[74] As Zimbabwe-Rhodesia was proclaimed in 1979 and the war escalated, a young national serviceman wrote in his diary, "A lot of guys are ratty about serving a black government, but in the last resort they'll fight because they're told to. Personally, I'm fighting for a way of life; if the government starts wrecking those standards, I'll fight the government instead. Or go to Spain."[75] Eventually, Ian Smith, in his memoirs, could find nothing very specific about Rhodesia that led to Rhodesia's demise. Instead, he blamed South Africa for aggressively demanding a settlement in Rhodesia that could provide a moderate and pro–South African black government to help them, not Rhodesia, maintain minority rule. Noting that the presidents of Tanzania and Zambia did not tell African nationalist Rhodesians what to do, Smith offered this "object lesson for South Africa": "When the crunch comes the blacks will stand together, but with the white people dog starts eating dog."[76]

Conclusion

This chapter does not suggest that Rhodesia was not a racist state; instead, it argues that it is racism of a specific, if not utopian, sort, a racism in which anticommunism, efficiency, and working phones replaced history. The historic claims of settlers survived the instability of postwar white populations but not the postwar ideas about states in Africa or anywhere else. Rhodesia was such an egregious roadblock on the orderly path to decolonization and the nation-states so created, its meaning—first outside Rhodesia and later within the country—came to be solely about race, about the power and privileges that made for good roads and working phones. The much-heralded Rhodesian way of life was flattened into the idea that white men had to be protected from whatever hordes were at their gates; part of that flattening obliterated almost every claim Rhodesia made for its right to independence based on its specific history. Rhodesia might have been a certain kind of white man's utopia on a certain global stage, but at home, in barracks and cabinet rooms, the floundering state had so cloaked itself in racialized ideas and imaginaries that it obscured its own history.

Notes

1. Despite some superb studies of white politics in Rhodesia (see n. 3), there has been no real history of the Rhodesian state. Indeed, Rhodesia remains such an exception to the historical trends of the post-1945 era that most historical studies of it end in 1963 (the end of the Central African Federation) or in 1965, with the unilateral declaration of independence (UDI). There have been, however, some excellent studies of how the Rhodesian state acted upon Africans and how Africans resisted those actions; see Robin Palmer, *Land and Racial Domination in Rhodesia* (Berkeley: University of California Press, 1977); William A. Munro, *The Moral Economy of the State: Conservation, Community Development, and State Making in Zimbabwe* (Athens, OH: Ohio University Press, 1998); Jocelyn Alexander, JoAnn McGregor, and Terence Ranger, *Violence and Memory: One Hundred Years in the "Dark Forests" of Matabeleland* (Oxford: James Currey, 2000), chaps. 3–7.

2. Thirty percent of the white electorate in Southern Rhodesia voted against joining the federation, some because it weakened the country's political autonomy, and others because they feared whites would be "swamped by Africans." See George Rudland, Sinoia, 5 September 1972, National Archives of Zimbabwe (NAZ)/RU3; Robert Francis Halsted, Bulawayo, 19 March 1974, NAZ/HA10; Sir John Caldicott, Salisbury, 7 March 1976, NAZ/ORAL/CA5; Sir Athol Donald Evans, Salisbury, April and September 1979, NAZ/EV1; Noel Allison Hunt, London, November 1983, NAZ/ORAL/240. All intereviews were conducted in cities in Rhodesia or Zimbabwe, or in London.

3. This section is based on Martin Chanock's *Unconsummated Union: Britain, Rhodesia and South Africa, 1900–45* (Manchester: Manchester University Press, 1977);

Colin Leys, *European Politics in Southern Rhodesia* (Oxford: Clarendon Press, 1960);
Ian Phimister, *An Economic and Social History of Zimbabwe, 1890–1948: Capital
Accumulation and Class Struggle* (London: Longman Group, 1988); Bennie Goldin,
The Judge, the Prince, and the Usurper: From UDI to Zimbabwe (New York: Vantage
Press, 1990); *Southern Rhodesia: Documents Relating to the Negotiations between the
United Kingdom and Southern Rhodesian Governments, November 1963–November
1965,* Cmd. 2807 (London: HMSO, 1965); Larry W. Bowman, *Politics in Rhodesia:
White Power in an African State* (Cambridge, MA: Harvard University Press, 1973);
J.R.T. Wood, *So Far and No Further! Rhodesia's Bid for Independence during the Re-
treat from Empire, 1959–65* (Victoria, BC: Trafford Publishing, 2005).

4. Marion Kaplan, "Their Rhodesia," *Transition* 23 (1965): 32–44; Calvin Trillin,
"Letter from Salisbury," *New Yorker*, 12 November 1966, 134–93.

5. Goldin, *The Judge*, 62–68; Luise White, "What Does It Take to Be a State? Sovereignty and Sanctions in Rhodesia, 1965–1980," in *The State of Sovereignty: Territories, Laws, Populations*, ed. Douglas Howland and Luise White (Bloomington: Indiana
University Press, 2009), 148–68.

6. For example, International Defense and Aid Fund, *Rhodesia: Why Minority Rule
Survives* (London: International Defense and Aid, 1969); Anthony Lake, *The "Tar
Baby" Option: American Policy toward Southern Rhodesia* (New York: Columbia University Press, 1976); Martin Bailey, *Oilgate: The Sanctions Scandal* (London: Hodder
and Stoughton, 1979); Andrew DeRoche, *Black, White and Chrome: The United States
and Zimbabwe, 1953–1998* (Trenton, NJ: Red Sea Press, 2001); Gerald Horne, *From
the Barrel of a Gun: The United States and the War against Zimbabwe, 1965–1980*
(Chapel Hill: University of North Carolina Press, 2001).

7. Exchange between Duncan Sandys, Commonwealth secretary, and Julian Green-
field, quoted in *Welensky's 4000 Days: The Life and Death of the Federation of Rhodesia and Nyasaland*, by Sir Roy Welensky (London: Collins, 1964), 319; J. M. Green-
field, *Testimony of a Rhodesian Federal* (Bulawayo: Books of Rhodesia, 1978), 251.
According to Welensky, Lord Alport, British high commissioner to the federation, went
home and vomited, so sickened was he by this rejection of empire. Alport later wrote
that he got angry, not sick or mortified. Lord Alport, *The Sudden Assignment: Central
Africa, 1961–63* (London: Hodder and Stoughton, 1965), 168.

8. Ian Smith, *The Great Betrayal: The Memoirs of Ian Douglas Smith* (London:
Blake, 1997), 53–54, 106; Goldin, *The Judge*, 26–30; Wood, *So Far*, 156–58. On recog-
nition, see Antony Anghie, *Imperialism, Sovereignty, and the Making of International
Law* (Cambridge: Cambridge University Press, 2004), 75–77.

9. Smith, *Great Betrayal*, 53–54; Alport, *Sudden Assignment*, 208–9; Goldin, *The
Judge*, 19, 26–27; Philip Murphy, *Party Politics and Decolonization: The Conservative
Party and British Colonial Policy in Tropical Africa, 1951–1964* (Oxford: Clarendon
Press, 1995), 113–17.

10. Preserving the integrity of colonial borders was part of the canon on which the
Organization of African Unity was founded in 1963.

11. Caroline Elkins, "Race, Citizenship, and Governance: Settler Tyranny and the
End of Empire," in *Settler Colonialism in the Twentieth Century: Projects, Practices,
Legacies*, ed. Caroline Elkins and Susan Pedersen (New York: Routledge, 2005), 203–
22, esp. 206–7.

12. The text of the address is in Smith's *Great Betrayal*, 104–5.

13. Steve Kock, *Ukuru!* vol. 1, mimeograph, Salisbury, Rhodesia. Kock did not want anyone to recommend any "silly names like 'Zimbabwe'!" Sir Edgar Whitehead Papers, personal file, October 1960–September 1962, Rhodes House, Oxford RH Mss Afr s 1482/2.

14. Barry M. Schutz, "European Population Patterns, Cultural Persistence, and Political Change in Rhodesia," *Canadian Journal of African Studies* 7, no. 1 (1973): 21–23; George W. Rudland, Sinoia, 5 September 1972, NAZ/ORAL/RU3. The Rhodesian Army could barely control its contempt for the fifteen hundred South African police seconded to them between 1972 and 1974. Minutes, Commanders' Secretariat, Operations Coordinating Committee, 20 April, 20 July 1974, Rhodesian Army Association Archives (RAA)/2001/086/026(A)/157, British Empire and Commonwealth Museum, Bristol.

15. For years, white politicians had threatened the white electorate that unless they supported "reasonable change" and an increased African franchise, they would prove themselves "as people overseas imagine them—like the platteland voters in the Union." Hardwick Holderness, in *Lost Chance: Southern Rhodesia, 1945–58* (Harare: Zimbabwe Publishing House, 1985), 227, quoting a United Rhodesia Party pamphlet from 1958; David Caute, *Under the Skin: The Death of White Rhodesia* (Harmondsworth: Penguin, 1983), 88.

16. Record of a meeting held at 10 Downing Street, 8 October 1965, *Southern Rhodesia: Documents Relating to Negotiations*, 83.

17. Settler societies, and states, are by definition comparative categories that historians and social scientists have tended to see as a broad homogenous group, characterized by race and global ties of wealth, privilege, and tenacious access to state power. Louis Hartz, ed., *The Founding of New Societies* (New York: Harcourt, Brace, and World, 1964); D. K. Fieldhouse, *The Colonial Empires: A Comparative Survey from the Eighteenth Century* (New York: Weidenfeld and Nicholson, 1966); Paul Mosely, *The Settler Economies: Studies in the Economic Histories of Kenya and Southern Rhodesia, 1900–1963* (Cambridge: Cambridge University Press, 1980); Donald Denoon, *Settler Capitalism: The Dynamics of Dependent Development in the Southern Hemisphere* (Oxford: Oxford University Press, 1983); Dane Kennedy, *Islands of White: Settler Society and Culture in Kenya and Southern Rhodesia, 1900–1939* (Durham: Duke University Press, 1987); Stanley B. Greenberg, *Race and State in Capitalist Development: Comparative Perspectives* (New Haven: Yale University Press, 1980); Elkins and Pederson, eds., *Settler Colonialism*. Even when settlers are seen as beleaguered and misrepresented, they are a transnational category. See L. H. Gann and P. Duignan, *White Settlers in Tropical Africa* (Harmondsworth, 1962); Sarah Gertrude Millin, ed., *White Africans Are Also People* (*Cape Town: Howard Timmons, 1967*); and Keith Meadows, *Sometimes When It Rains: White Africans in Black Africa* (Bulawayo: Thorntree Press, 1998). Scholarship on Rhodesia and Zimbabwe has done much to show local patterns and practices among white settlers; see Phimister, *Economic and Social History*; Anthony Chennells, "Rhodesian Discourse, Rhodesian Novels, and the Zimbabwe Liberation War," in *Society in Zimbabwe's Liberation War*, ed. Ngwabi Bhebe and Terence Ranger, vol. 2. (Harare: University of Zimbabwe Press, 1995), 102–29, and David McDermott Hughes, "Whites and Water: How Euro-Africans Made Nature at Kariba Dam," *J. Southern African Studies* 32, no. 4 (2006): 823–38.

18. William Joseph John Cary, Gwelo, September 1971, February 1972, NAZ/ORAL/CA 4; Rupert Meredith Davies, Hampshire, 17 November 1983, NAZ/ORAL/

241; author's field notes, Harare, 13 July 2001. Such statements trouble the published claims of neutral obedience to the government; see, for example, the memoirs of Ken Flower, *Serving Secretly: Rhodesia's CIO Chief on Record* (Alberton, South Africa: Galago, 1987).

19. Clifford DuPont, Salisbury, June 1967 and January 1977, NAZ/ORAL/DU4.

20. Andrew Skeen, introduction to *Prelude to Independence* (Cape Town: Nationale Boekhandel, 1968); John Parker, *Rhodesia: Little White Island* (London: Pitman, 1972), 13; Kenneth Skelton, *Bishop in Smith's Rhodesia: Notes from a Turbulent Octave, 1962–1970* (Gweru: Mambo Press, 1983), 87; Caute, *Under the Skin*, 90; Denis Hills, *Rebel People* (London: G. Allen & Unwin, 1978), 87, 204–5. The liberal judge Robert Tredgold, for example, thought it inconceivable that Britain had lost all that made it great in less than a generation while "this little pool of white people in the heart of Africa have become the repository of those qualities; as if the small branch of a great tree can live on when the roots have been destroyed." Sir Robert Tredgold, *The Rhodesia that Was My Life* (London: George Allen & Unwin, 1968), 255. Rhodesian liberals liked to joke that there were not even enough white people to run Aberdeen, let alone a country. Author's field notes, Harare, 16 July 1995.

21. Desmond Lardner-Burke, *Rhodesia: The Story of a Crisis* (London: Oldbourne Books, 1966), 11–12; Michael Auret, quoted in Meadows's *Sometimes When It Rains*, 205; Welenksy, *4000 Days*, 206; Smith, *Great Betrayal*, 44, 108. For voting, see Epiphany Azinge, "The Right to Vote in Nigeria: A Critical Commentary on the Open Ballot System," *J. African Law* 38, no. 2 (1994): 173–75.

22. As Welensky wrote to the colonial secretary in 1960, "I am living next door to the Belgian Congo and the tragedy that occurred there. You just don't realise the effect on Rhodesians of having had some 10,000 to 13,000 refugees living in their homes and having to listen to the stories of rape, murder, and atrocities that took place." Welensky, *4000 Days*, 206.

23. Trillin, "Letter from Salisbury," 139, 162. For other authors who found Rhodesian life shallow, see Hills, *Rebel People*, 199; Frances Strauss, *My Rhodesia: A Personal Story of the Two* (New York: Gambit, 1969); George M. Daniels, ed., *Drums of War: The Continuing Crisis in Rhodesia* (New York: Third Press, 1974), 101–11.

24. Caute, *Under the Skin*, 27.

25. Several politicians thought that Southern Rhodesia's status would evolve into independence, but many more sought an amalgamation with Northern Rhodesia — in which copper would do for the region "what coal did in Britain and gold did in South Africa"—which would become a unified, independent state. Carl Hubert Fox, Salisbury, 7 November 1973, NAZ/ORAL/FO3; Sir George Rudland, NAZ/ORAL/RU3; Robert Francis Halsted, Bulawayo, March 1974, NAZ/ORAL/HA10; Sir Athol Donald Evans, Salisbury, April and September 1979, NAZ/ORAL/EV1; Sir John Caldicott, Salisbury, March 1976, NAZ/ORAL/CA5.

26. Lord Alport, *Sudden Assignment*, 120; N. H. Brettell, *Side-Gate and Stile: An Essay in Autobiography* (Bulawayo: Books of Zimbabwe, 1981), 68; W. E. Arnold, *The Goldbergs of Leigh Ranch* (Bulawayo: Books of Zimbabwe, 1980), 43, 52.

27. One study carefully measured the degree to which new immigrants disapproved of social contact between Europeans and Africans and concluded that after five years immigrants were as "conservative" as men and women who had lived in the country for more than thirty years. Charles Frantz and Cyril A. Rogers, "Length of Residence and

Race Attitudes in Southern Rhodesia," *Race* 3 (1962): 46–54. See also J. M. McEwan, "The European Population of Southern Rhodesia," *Civilisations* 13, no. 4 (1963): 429–41; Schutz, "European Population Patterns," 3–25; A. S. Mlambo, *White Immigration into Rhodesia: From Occupation to Federation* (Harare: University of Zimbabwe Press, 2002), 52–67.

28. Hills, *Rebel People*, 87; Parker, *Little White Island*, 10–11, 69–71.

29. Josiah Brownell, "The Hole in Rhodesia's Bucket: White Emigration and the End of Settler Rule," *J. Southern African Studies* 34, no. 3 (2008): 591–610.

30. David Roediger, *The Wages of Whiteness: The Making of the American Working Class* (London: Verso, 1990), and Noel Ignatiev, *How the Irish Became White* (New York: Routledge, 1996); John Hartigan, "Establishing the Fact of Whiteness," *American Anthropologist* 99, no. 3 (1997): 495–505; Peter Kolchin, "Whiteness Studies: The New History of Race in America," *J. American History* 89, no. 1 (2002): 154–73.

31. Cabinet Minutes, 26 June 1973; Cory Library (CL), Rhodes University, Grahamstown, South Africa, CL/Box 26.

32. Warwick Anderson, *The Cultivation of Whiteness: Science, Health and Racial Destiny in Australia* (Melbourne: Melbourne University Press, 2002).

33. Miscegenation, Prostitution, and Allied Problems, Cabinet Minutes, 24 August 1971, CL/Box 24.

34. Clifford DuPont, Salisbury, six sessions between June 1976 and January 1977, NAZ/ORAL/DU4; Skeen, introduction to *Prelude to Independence*.

35. An anonymously written play, *A Guide to the Thought of Ian Douglas Smith*, attributed to David Astor of the *Observer*, was the best-seller of 1971; two thousand copies had been printed in England, and an unknown number mimeographed and circulated in Rhodesia. Most of the dialogue was taken from parliamentary debates. Judith Todd, *The Right to Say No* (London: Sidgwick and Jackson, 1972), 17–18; Judith Todd, Bulawayo, 7 March 1988, NAZ/ORAL/Unprocessed.

36. Lancelot Bales Smith, Banket, 22 November 1985, NAZ/ORAL/250; Thomas Albert Holloway, Harare, 24 October 1986, NAZ/ORAL/235.

37. Richard Hodder-Williams, "White Attitudes and the Unilateral Declaration of Independence: A Case Study," *J. of Commonwealth and Comparative Politics* 8 (1970): 241–65; Munro, *Moral Economy*, 149–54.

38. Smith, *Great Betrayal*, 101, 106.

39. Dissolution of the Federation, Committee A, 53rd report, 29 October 1963, Cabinet Memoranda, 1963, CL/Box 17.

40. Brig. Andrew Dunlop, Salisbury, 24 February and 13 April 1972, NAZ/ORAL/DU2.

41. Loyalty to Rhodesian Government, November 1965–January 1966, NAZ/S3279/11/211; "Dollars and Sense," mimeograph, December 1965, NAZ/S3279/11/209.

42. Beryl Salt, *A Pride of Eagles: The Definitive History of the Rhodesian Air Force, 1920–1980* (Johannesburg: Covos-Day, 1980), 397–98; author's field notes, Bristol, 18 July 2003.

43. J. H. Howman, Minister of Defence, Military Service: Rhodesian Citizens and Aliens, 11 June 1970, Cabinet Memoranda, 1970, CL/Box 24.

44. Dean Acheson, Rhodesia's most articulate supporter in the United States, had made extensive references to the independence of the thirteen colonies, and Rhodesians hoped this would lead to increased support from the United States, or at least

some of its further-right elements. Rhodesian Information Office, *Dean Acheson on the Rhodesian Question* (Washington, DC, n.d.); Lake, *"Tar Baby" Option*, 112–16; Douglas Brinkley, *Dean Acheson: The Cold War Years, 1953–71* (New Haven: Yale University Press, 1992), 303–5, 315–28. Another sporadic fantasy was that Cubans would fight in Mozambique, and the United States would immediately begin to support Rhodesia; see Hills, *Rebel People*, 81.

45. Skeen, introduction to *Prelude to Independence*.

46. Quoted in Paul A. Moorcraft's *A Short Thousand Years: The End of Rhodesia's Rebellion* (Salisbury: Galaxie, 1980), 3, and Hills, *Rebel People*, 204–5.

47. Smith, *Great Betrayal*, 106.

48. Goldin, *The Judge*, 19–22, 26–30; Smith, *Great Betrayal*, 52–60; Sir John Caldicott, Salisbury, 7 March 1976, NAZ/ORAL/CA5; William Joseph John Cary, Gwelo, September 1971 and February 1972, NAZ/ORAL/CA4. After the "happy occasion" of a dinner party in England in late 1964, attended by both Labour and Conservative MPs, Smith concluded that "had it not been for the OAU, the UN and such there would have been no difficulty in striking an agreement, even with the Labour Party." Smith, *Great Betrayal*, 76.

49. Miles Hudson, *Triumph or Tragedy? Rhodesia to Zimbabwe* (London: Hamish Hamilton, 1981), 47–48. Nevertheless, RF tried to avoid any appearance of "pure racialism," or racialism at the national level, and left segregation to local councils; within a decade, an RF MP admitted that this led to "bonkers stuff." Lancelot Bales Smith, NAZ/ORAL/250; see also Lardner-Burke, *Story of a Crisis*, 19–20, 28.

50. I take this point and much of my thinking here from John D. Kelly and Martha Kaplan's *Represented Communities: Fiji and World Decolonization* (Chicago: University of Chicago Press, 2001).

51. Roy Welensky, "The United Nations and Colonialism in Africa," *Annals of the American Academy of Political and Social Science* 354 (1964): 145–52. South Africa, which had been a much more active member of the UN than it ever had been of the Commonwealth—it had, for example, sent troops to Korea—did not share this view in the early 1960s. Neta C. Crawford, "Trump Card or Theater? An Introduction to Two Sanctions Debates," in *How Sanctions Work: Lessons from South Africa*, ed. Neta C. Crawford and Audie Klotz (New York: Palgrave Macmillan, 1999), 2–24.

52. Carl Schmitt, *Political Theology: Four Chapters on the Concept of Sovereignty*, trans. George Schwab (Chicago: University of Chicago Press, 1985), 5–12. Schmitt is important here, not only because of how he theorized states' breaking their own laws, but because many in the RF and many of their supporters in Britain knew their way around Schmitt's thought.

53. The place where UDI had the greatest traction was Northern Ireland, perhaps the only other place left where anyone imagined that the men who had come to civilize and colonize it should be protected from the people they dominated because they upheld traditions and went on about standards. For years, politicians in Central Africa and the United Kingdom had joked that Northern Ireland was like Rhodesia, but in 1966 the Northern Irish premier felt compelled to announce in a television broadcast that Rhodesia, "in defying Britain from thousands of miles away, at least had an air force and an army of its own." Donal Lowry, "Ulster Resistance and Loyalist Rebellion in the Empire," in *"An Irish Empire"? Aspects of Ireland and the British Empire*, ed. Keith Jeffrey (Manchester: Manchester University Press, 1996), 191–215.

54. John Cheffers, A *Wilderness of Spite, or Rhodesia Denied* (New York: Vantage Press, 1972).

55. Arthur R. Lewis, *Too Bright the Vision? African Adventures of a Rhodesian Rebel* (London: Covenant Books, 1992), 246; Caute, *Under the Skin*, 113–14, 155; Harvey Ward, London, 4 July 1984, NAZ/ORAL/246. Residents forcibly sent back to England were thought to be worst of all. A soon-to-be-deported clergyman was denounced in a speech in Parliament as living in "wonderland": he refused to call the government or its courts legal. Rhodesians might have expected this "from ignorant and unsympathetic people in the early days of our independence," but not now, in 1971. Guy and Molly Clutton-Brock, *Cold Comfort Confronted* (London: Mowbrays, 1972), 162–63.

56. Decimal Currency: Unit of Currency, Cabinet Memorandum, 6 July 1966; Cabinet minutes, Decimal Currency, 26 July 1966, CL, Box 20. Rhodesia introduced the Rhodesian dollar in 1967; it was locally designed and printed with a watermark of Cecil Rhodes. Replacing the old sterling notes, specially printed for Rhodesia but in GBP, had proved difficult. German authorities seized a series of ten-shilling notes in 1966 as counterfeit; weeks later German courts ruled that being a country need not have international recognition to print specie. See Goldin, *The Judge*, 135–37.

57. For trade in CFA, see Derek Arthur Collings van der Syde, Harare, 27 November 1987, NAZ/ORAL/267; White, "Sovereignty and Sanctions," 160.

58. *The Citizen*, Salisbury, 30 November 1973, 2.

59. Smith, *Great Betrayal*, 107–8.

60. James Barlow, *Goodbye, England* (London: Hamish Hamilton, 1969), 94.

61. Ibid., 136; Peter Stiff, *See You in November* (Alberton, South Africa: Galago, 1985), 88–90.

62. Hills, *Rebel People*, 1–66; Dick Pitman, *You Must Be New Around Here* (Bulawayo: Books of Rhodesia, 1979), 1.

63. Brownell, "Rhodesia's Bucket," 600. There was a firm belief in official circles that Rhodesians who left the country would return, and some did. See, for example, Lauren St. John, *Rainbow's End: A Memoir of Childhood, War and an African Farm* (London: Scribner, 2007), 1–16.

64. Ruth Lady Crauford, *Six Letters from Rhodesia*, pamphlet (Berkhamsted, Herts., 1970), Sterling Memorial Library, Yale University, Africa 605/42/731. The liberal judge Tredgold wrote that the only play London Rhodesians should import was *Stop the World—I Want to Get Off.* Tredgold, *Rhodesia*, 224.

65. Moorcraft, *Short Thousand Years*, 3; Peter Godwin, *Mukiwa: A White Boy in Africa* (London: Macmillan, 1996), 400–401.

66. Survey of morale in the Rhodesian Army, Appendix A-3, 16 May 1977, RAA/2001/086/342/237.

67. Commander's Secretariat, Operations Coordinating Committee (OCC), 12 March and 25 March 1976, RAA/2001/086/241/159; Joint Planning Staff, Ministry of Defence, Salisbury, 12 April 1976, RAA/2001/086/277/122. The Rhodesian Army fretted over being accused of hiring mercenaries, although many groups insisted they did just that. It is not altogether clear that Rhodesia could afford mercenaries, if the amounts the CIA offered in Angola in the mid-1970s are anything to go by; see Odd Arne Westad, *The Global Cold War: Third World Interventions and the Making of Our Times* (Cambridge: Cambridge University Press, 2005), 222–28.

68. The king hoped that these men would be trained as an expeditionary force to eventually invade Albania. Minutes, Operations Coordinating Committee, 16 September 1977, RAA/2001/086/223/248.

69. As with mercenaries, everyone involved had a reason to distort the actual numbers, so that estimates, which range from 500 to 1,500, are all anecdotal. See Luise White, "Civic Virtue, National Service, and the Family: The State and Conscription in Rhodesia," *International Journal of African Historical Studies* 37, no. 1 (2004): 103–21.

70. Caute, *Under the Skin*, 138. See also the interview with David Crowley, Marine, Vietnam Center, Texas Tech University, Lubbock, Texas; Crowley claimed that many Americans were attracted by the romance of the Rhodesian Army: they had a cavalry.

71. Robin Moore, *Rhodesia* (New York: Condor, 1977), 201, 208, 217, 232.

72. John Alan Coey, *A Martyr Speaks: Journal of the Late John Alan Coey* (n.p.: CPA Book Publishers, 1994), 9.

73. Benedict Anderson, *Imagined Communities: Reflections on the Origin and Spread of Nationalism* (London: Verso, 1983), 135; italics in the original. CT stands for "communist terrorist," a term selected by Rhodesian Army psychologists when they learned that their first-choice term, "barbarian terrorist," could refer only to nonnationals. Army HQ, Salisbury, Change in Terminology, 7 May 1967, RAA 2001/086/131.

74. Caute, *Under the Skin*, 288–89. The youth insisted that the reason there were no Africans in the SAS (unlike other Rhodesian counterinsurgency units) was that there was no point at which you could not be weeded out of the SAS, and "Blacks would take umbrage." Chris Cocks, an infantryman turned novelist, gave another reason: "There were no black soldiers in the Long Range Desert Group, the forerunner of the SAS, during World War II. There had been no black soldiers in Malaya, so for what sane reason would anyone think it necessary to have black troops in an African SAS?" Chris Cocks, *Survival Course* (Weltrevreden Park, South Africa: Covos-Day, 1999), 104.

75. Dan Wylie, *Dead Leaves: Two Years in the Rhodesian Army* (Pietermaritzburg, South Africa: University of Natal Press, 2002), 39.

76. Smith, *Great Betrayal*, 182.

5.

Timothy Mitchell

Hydrocarbon Utopia

FOSSIL FUELS HAVE PLAYED an ambiguous role in our utopian imagination. In the twentieth century they helped to form the most prosperous, healthy, and democratic communities in human history.[1] They enabled these communities to live according to the utopian principle that the growth of wealth and well-being could continue without any foreseeable limit. Yet hydrocarbon energy also now appears as a curse. Oil is said to be a cause of violence and war. Societies that possess it in abundance appear more liable to suffer from a special degree of tyranny.

What is the relationship between petroleum and political freedom? In the wake of the U.S. invasion of Iraq in 2003, one aspect of this relationship was widely discussed. A distinctive feature of the Middle East, many said, is the region's lack of democracy. In several of the scholarly accounts, this lack had something to do with oil. Countries that depend upon petroleum resources for a large part of their earnings from exports tend to be less democratic.[2] However, most of those who write about the question of the "rentier state" or the "oil curse," as the problem is known, have little to say about the nature of oil and how it is produced, distributed, and used.[3] They merely discuss the oil rents, the income that accrues after petroleum is converted to government revenue. So the reasons proposed for the antidemocratic properties of oil— that it gives government the resources to relieve social pressures, buy political support, and repress dissent—have little to do with the ways in which oil is extracted, processed, shipped, and consumed, the forms of agency and control these processes involve, or the powers of oil as a concentrated source of energy.

The tendency to ignore the properties of oil reflects an underlying conception of democracy. This is the conception shared by the American democracy expert who addressed a local council in southern Iraq. "Welcome to your new democracy," he said. "I have met you before. I have met you in Cambodia. I have met you in Russia. I have met you in Nigeria." At that point, we are told, two members of the council walked out.[4] This conception of democracy sees it as fundamentally the same everywhere, defined by universal principles that are to be reproduced in every successful instance of democratization, as though democracy occurs only as a carbon copy of itself. If it fails, as it seems to in oil states, the reason must be that some universal element is missing or malfunctioning.

By failing to follow the oil, accounts of the oil curse diagnose it as a malady located within only one set of nodes of the networks through which oil flows and is converted into energy, profits, and political power: in the decision-making organs of individual producer states. Its etiology involves isolating the symptoms found in producer states that are not found in nonoil states. But what if democracies are not carbon copies but carbon based? Are they tied in specific ways to the history of carbon fuels? Can we follow the carbon, the oil, so as to connect the problem afflicting oil-producing states to other limits of a carbon democracy?

The leading industrialized countries are also oil states. Without the energy they derive from oil, their current forms of political and economic life would not exist. Their citizens have developed ways of eating, traveling, housing themselves, and consuming other goods and services that require very large amounts of energy from oil and other fossil fuels. These ways of life are unsustainable, and they now face the twin crises that will end them: although calculating reserves of fossil fuels is a political process involving rival calculative techniques, there is substantial evidence that those reserves are running out;[5] and in the process of using them up, we have taken carbon that was previously stored underground and placed it in the atmosphere, where it is causing increases in global temperatures that may lead to catastrophic climate change.[6] A larger limit that oil represents for democracy is that the political machinery that emerged to govern the age of fossil fuels may be incapable of addressing the events that will end it.

To follow the carbon does not mean replacing the idealist schemes of the democracy experts with a materialist account, or tracing political outcomes back to the forms of energy that determine them—as though the powers of carbon were transmitted unchanged from the oil well or coal face to the hands of those who control the state. The carbon itself must be transformed, beginning with the work done by those who bring it out of the ground. The transformations involve establishing connections and building alliances that do not respect any divide between material and ideal, economic and political, natural and social, human and nonhuman, or violence and representation. The connections make it possible to translate one form of power into another. Understanding the relations between fossil fuels and democracy requires tracing how these connections are built, the vulnerabilities and opportunities they create, and the narrow points of passage where control is particularly effective.[7] Political possibilities were opened up or narrowed down by different ways of organizing the flow and concentration of energy, and these possibilities were enhanced or limited by arrangements of people, finance, expertise, and violence that were assembled in relationship to the distribution and control of energy.

Buried Sunshine

Like mass democracy, fossil fuels are a relatively recent phenomenon. The histories of the two kinds of forces have been connected, in several ways. This chapter traces four sets of connections, the first two concerned with coal and the rise of mass politics in the late-nineteenth and early-twentieth centuries, the second two with oil and organizing limits to democratic politics in the mid-twentieth century.

The first connection is that fossil fuel allowed the reorganization of energy systems that made possible, in conjunction with other changes, the novel forms of collective life out of which late-nineteenth-century mass politics developed.

Until two hundred years ago, the energy needed to sustain human existence came almost entirely from renewable sources, which obtain their force from the sun. Solar energy was converted into grain and other crops to provide fuel for humans, into grasslands to raise animals for labor and further human fuel, into woodlands to provide firewood, and into wind- and waterpower to drive transportation and machinery.[8]

For most of the world, the capture of solar radiation in replenishable forms continued to be the main source of energy until perhaps the mid-twentieth century.[9] From around 1800, however, these renewable sources were steadily replaced with highly concentrated stores of buried solar energy, the deposits of carbon laid down 150 to 350 million years ago, when the decay of peat-bog forests and of marine organisms in particular oxygen-deficient environments converted biomass into the relatively rare but extraordinarily potent deposits of coal and oil.[10]

The earth's stock of this "capital bequeathed to mankind by other living beings," as Sartre once described it,[11] will have been exhausted in a remarkably short period—most of it in the one hundred years between 1950 and 2050.[12] To give an idea of the concentration of energy we will be depleting, compared with the plant-based and other forms of captured solar energy that preceded the hydrocarbon age, here is an apt metric: a single liter of gasoline used today needed about twenty-five metric tons of ancient marine life as precursor material, and organic matter the equivalent of the earth's entire production of plant and animal life for four hundred years was required to produce the fossil fuels we burn in a single year.[13]

Compared with these concentrated hydrocarbon stores, solar radiation is a weak form of energy. However, it is very widely distributed. Historically, its use encouraged relatively dispersed forms of human settlement—along rivers, close to pastureland, and within reach of large reserves of land set aside as woods to provide fuel. The switch to coal over the last two centuries enabled the concentration of populations in cities, in part because it freed urban populations from the need for adjacent pastures and woods. In Great Britain, substitution of wood by coal created a quantity of energy that would have required forests many times the size of existing wooded areas if energy had still depended on solar radiation. By the 1820s, coal "freed," as it were, an area of land equivalent to the total surface area of the country. By the 1840s, coal was providing energy that in timber would have required forests covering twice the country's area, double that amount by the 1860s, and double again by the 1890s.[14] Thanks to coal, Great Britain, the United States, Germany, and other coal-producing regions could be catapulted into a new "energetic metabolism," based on cities and large-scale manufacturing.[15]

We associate industrialization with the growth of cities, but it was equally an agrarian phenomenon. It required access to extensive new crop-producing territories, both to provide the increased food supplies on which the growth of cities and manufacturing depended and to produce the raw materials for industry, especially cotton. By freeing land previously reserved as woodland for the supply of fuel, fossil energy contributed to this agrarian transformation. As Pomeranz argues, the switch to coal in northwest Europe interacted with another land-releasing factor: the acquisition of colonial territories, which could be converted into plantations for the production of additional food and of cotton and other industrial crops.[16] Europe now controlled surplus land that could be used to produce agricultural goods in quantities that, together with novel ways of governing labor—slavery, sharecropping, and debt bondage— allowed the development of coal-based mass production, centered in cities.

This points to the first set of connections between fossil fuels and democracy. Limited forms of representative government had developed in parts of Europe and its settler colonies in the eighteenth and nineteenth centuries. From the 1870s on, however, the emergence of mass political movements and organized political parties shaped the period that Hobsbawm calls both "the age of democratization" and "the age of empire."[17] The mobilization of new political forces depended upon the concentration of population in cities and in manufacturing, made possible in part by the control of colonized territories and enslaved or coerced labor forces, but equally associated with the forms of mass collective life made possible by organizing the flow of unprecedented concentrations of nonrenewable stores of carbon.

Controlling Carbon Channels

Fossil fuels are connected with the mass democracy of the late-nineteenth and early-twentieth centuries in a second way. Large stores of high-quality coal were discovered and developed in relatively few sites—central and northern England, South Wales, the Ruhr Valley, Upper Silesia, Appalachia, and the Powder River Basin of Montana and Wyoming.[18] Most of the world's industrial regions grew above or adjacent to supplies of coal.[19] However, coal was so concentrated in carbon content that it became cost-effective to transport energy overland or on waterways across greater distances than timber or other renewable fuel supplies. In Britain the first canal acts were passed to dig canals for the movement of coal.[20] The development of steam transport, whose original function was to serve coal mining and which in turn was fueled by coal, facilitated this movement. Large urban and industrial populations could now accumulate at sites that were no longer adjacent to sources of energy. By the end of the nineteenth century, industrialized regions had built networks that moved concentrated carbon stores from the underground coal face to the surface, to railways, to ports, to cities, and to sites of manufacturing and electrical-power generation.

Great quantities of energy now flowed along very narrow channels. Large numbers of workers had to be concentrated at the main junctions of these channels. Their position and concentration gave them, at certain moments, a new kind of political power. The power derived not just from the organizations they formed, the ideas they began to share, or the political alliances they built, but also from the extraordinary concentrations of carbon energy whose flow they could now slow, disrupt, or cut off.

Coal miners played a leading role in contesting labor regimes and the powers of employers in the labor activism and political mobilization of the 1880s and onward. Between 1881 and 1905, coal miners in the United States went on strike at a rate of about three times the average for workers in all major industries and at double the rate of the next-highest industry, tobacco manufacturing. Coal-mining strikes also lasted much longer than strikes in other industries.[21] The same pattern existed in Europe.[22] Bruce Podobnik has documented the wave of industrial action that swept across the world's coal-mining regions in the later nineteenth century and early-twentieth century, and again after World War I.[23]

The militancy of the miners can be attributed in part to the fact that moving carbon stores from the coal seam to the surface created unusually autonomous places and methods of work. The old argument that mining communities enjoyed a special isolation compared with other industrial workers, making their militancy "a kind of colonial revolt against far-removed authority," misrepresents this autonomy.[24] More recent accounts stress the diversity of mining communities and the complexity of their political engagements with other groups, with mine owners, and with state authorities.[25] As Goodrich had argued in 1925, "the miner's freedom" was a product not of the geographic isolation of coal-mining regions from political authority but of "the very geography of the working places inside a mine."[26] In the traditional room-and-pillar method of mining, a pair of miners worked a section of the coal seam, leaving pillars or walls of coal in place between their own chamber and adjacent chambers to support the roof. They usually made their own decisions about where to cut and how much rock to leave in place to prevent cave-ins. Before the widespread mechanization of mining, "the miner's freedom from supervision [was] at the opposite extreme from the carefully ordered and regimented work of the modern machine-feeder."[27]

The militancy that formed in these workplaces was typically an effort to defend this autonomy against the threats of mechanization, or against the pressure to accept more dangerous work practices, longer working hours, or lower rates of pay. Strikes were effective not because of mining's colonial isolation but, on the contrary, because of the flows of carbon that connected chambers beneath the ground to every factory, office, home, or means of transportation that depended on steam or electric power.

Large coal strikes could trigger wider mobilizations, as with the violent strike that followed the 1906 Courrières colliery disaster in northern France, which helped provoke a general strike that paralyzed Paris.[28] The most common pattern, however, was for strikes to spread through the interconnected industries of coal mining, railways, dockworkers, and shipping.[29] During World War I, U.S. and British coalfields and railroads were placed under the direction of government administrators, and coal and rail workers were in some cases exempt from conscription and integrated into the war effort. The number of strikes was reduced, but the critical role of these energy networks became more visible.[30] After the war, from the West Virginia coal strikes of 1919 to the British General Strike of 1926, a "triple alliance" developed between mine workers, dockers, and railway men, who had the power to shut down energy nodes. The dispersed energy systems of solar radiation had never allowed groups of workers this kind of power.

The strikes were not always successful, but the new vulnerability the owners of mines, railways, and docks experienced, together with those of the steel mills and other large manufacturing enterprises dependent on coal, had its effects. One can note, for example, the role of a figure such as MacKenzie King, the Canadian political economist and politician hired by the Rockefellers to help them through the political crisis that followed the massacre of striking coal miners at Ludlow in 1914, who went on to become an architect of the Canadian welfare state.[31] The difficult fight against the resources of a labor movement that, for a few decades, could threaten a country's carbonenergy networks helped impel them to accept the forms of welfare democracy and universal suffrage that would weaken working-class mobilization.

From Coal to Oil

After World War II, the coal miners of Europe again appeared as the core of a militant threat to corporatist democratic politics. As U.S. planners worked to engineer the postwar political order in Europe, they came up with a new mechanism to defeat the coal miners: to convert Europe's energy system from one based on coal to one based predominantly on oil. Western Europe had no oil fields, so the additional oil would come from the Middle East. Scarce supplies of steel and construction equipment were shipped from the United States to the Persian Gulf to build a pipeline from eastern Saudi Arabia to the Mediterranean and to enable a rapid increase in oil supplies to Europe. The diversion of steel and of Marshall Plan funds for this purpose was justified in part by the need to undermine the political power of Europe's coal miners.[32]

Like coal, oil gave workers new kinds of power. Decisive industrial action was organized at Baku in 1905 in the Russian-controlled Caucasus, in the Maracaibo strikes of 1922 and 1936 in Venezuela, in the 1937 Mexican oil strike, and in the 1945–46 strike in Iran. These conflicts were a training ground for later confrontations. Joseph Stalin, a young labor activist in Baku, later said that the advanced organizing skills of the Azeri oil workers and the intensity of their conflict with the oil industrialists gave him an experience that qualified him as "a journeyman for the revolution."[33]

However, the material qualities and physical locations of oil made things different from coal. Since oil comes to the surface driven by underground pressure, either from the water trapped beneath it or the gas above it, it required a smaller workforce than coal in relation to the quantity of energy it produced. Workers remained on the surface, under continuous supervision and surveillance. Since the carbon occurs in liquid form, pumping stations and pipelines could replace railways as a means of transporting energy from the site of production to the places where it was used or shipped abroad. Pipelines were vulnerable, as we will see, but not as easy to incapacitate through strike actions as were the railways that carried coal.[34] Diesel oil and petrol are also lighter than coal and vaporize more easily, and their combustion leaves little residue compared with the burning of coal. For these reasons, as Lewis Mumford noted in 1934, "they could be stowed away easily, in odds and ends of space where coal could not be placed or reached: being fed by gravity or pressure the engine had no need for a stoker. The effect of introducing liquid fuel and of mechanical stokers for coal, in electric steam plants, and on steamships, was to emancipate a race of galley slaves, the stokers."[35]

The relative lightness and fluidity of oil made it feasible to ship it in large quantities across oceans. Historically, very little coal crossed oceans.[36] In 1912 Britain exported one-third of its coal and was responsible for two-thirds of the world's seaborne exported coal. But almost 90% of its exports went to the adjacent regions of Europe and the Mediterranean.[37] Over the course of the twentieth century, the proportion of coal exported internationally stabilized at about 15%. By contrast, from the 1920s onward, about 60 to 80% of oil was exported.[38] So much oil was moved across oceans that by 1970, 60% of all seaborne cargo consisted of oil.[39]

Moving oil by sea eliminated the labor of coal heavers and stokers, and thus the power of organized workers to withdraw their labor from a critical point in the energy system. Transoceanic shipping operated beyond the territorial spaces governed by the labor regulations and democratic rights won in the era of widespread coal and railway strikes. In fact, shipping companies could escape the regulation of labor laws altogether (as well as the payment of taxes) by resorting to international registry, or so-called flags of convenience, thus removing whatever limited powers of labor organizing might have been left.

Unlike railways, ocean shipping was not constrained by the need to run on a network of purpose-built tracks of a certain capacity, layout, and gauge. Oil tankers frequently left port without knowing their final destination. They would steam to a waypoint, and then receive a destination determined by the level of demand in different regions. This flexibility carried risks (in March 1967 it was one of the causes of the world's first giant oil spill, the Torrey Canyon disaster, which helped trigger the emergence of the environmental movement, a later threat to the carbon fuel industry), but it further weakened the powers of local forces that tried to control sites of energy production.[40] If a labor strike, for example, or the nationalization of an industry affected one production site, oil tankers could be quickly rerouted to supply oil from alternative sites. In other words, whereas the movement of coal tended to follow dendritic networks, with branches at each end but a single main channel, creating potential choke points at several junctures, oil flowed along networks that often had the properties of a grid, like an electrical grid, where there is more than one possible path and the flow of energy can switch to avoid blockages or overcome breakdowns.

These changes in the way forms of fossil energy were extracted, transported, and used made energy networks less vulnerable to the political claims of those whose labor kept them running. At the same time, the fluidity and flexibility of oil presented new problems for those who owned or managed the production sites and distribution networks. It was no longer sufficient to control production and distribution in one particular region. Since oil could move easily from one region to another, petroleum companies were always vulnerable to the arrival of cheaper oil from elsewhere. This vulnerability, seldom recognized in accounts of the oil industry, set further limits to the democratizing potential of petroleum.

Market competition destroyed profits and ruined companies and had, if possible, to be prevented. Thanks to the difficulty of transporting coal across oceans, coal producers faced competition only within their own region. They prevented it either by forming cartels, as in Germany and the United States, or by creating new organizations to regulate production, such as the postwar European Coal and Steel Community. In Britain producers were ruined by competition and taken over by the state. Oil companies faced similar threats, but on a transoceanic scale. The two world wars helped restrict the supply and movement of oil, but between the wars a new set of devices was needed to limit the production and distribution of energy. The devices that were developed included government quotas and price controls in the United States, consortium agreements to restrict the development of new oil discoveries in the Middle East, and cartel arrangements to govern the worldwide distribution and marketing of oil. These techniques and controls shaped the development of the transnational oil corporation, which emerged as a long-distance machinery for maintaining limits to the supply of oil.[41] One could think of this development as the formation of what Barry calls a "technical zone," a set of coordinated but widely dispersed regulations, calculative arrangements, infrastructures, and technical procedures that render certain objects or flows governable.[42]

After World War II, new devices were added to this machinery for the production of scarcity. There were two important techniques for transforming postwar carbon energy abundance into a system of limited supplies. The first was the new apparatus of peacetime "national security."[43] The Second World War had given U.S. oil companies the opportunity to reduce or shut down most of their production in the Middle East. In 1943, when Ibn Saud demanded funds to compensate for the loss of oil revenues, the oil companies persuaded Washington to extend Lend-Lease loans to the Saudi monarch. These payments for *not* producing oil were presented as a necessity for America's national security. They marked the start of a long relationship in which Saudi collaboration in restricting the flow of oil was organized as though it were a system for "protecting" the oil against others.

The second method of preventing energy abundance involved the rapid construction of lifestyles in the United States organized around extraordinary levels of energy consumption. In January 1948 James Forrestal, recently appointed as the country's first secretary of defense under the new National Security Act, discussed with Brewster Jennings, president of Socony-Vacuum (later renamed Mobil Oil), how, "unless we had access to Middle East oil, American motorcar companies would have to design a four-cylinder motorcar sometime within the next five years."[44] In the following years the U.S. car companies helped out by replacing standard six-cylinder engines with the new V8s as the dream of every middle-class family. While Forrestal spoke, the Morris Motor Company in Britain prepared to challenge the successful four-cylinder Volkswagen Beetle with the four-cylinder Morris Minor; Citroën did the same with the two-cylinder 2CV, and the German engine maker BMW with its first postwar passenger car, the one-cylinder Isetta 250. The European vehicles outsold and outlasted the badly engineered American cars. But the makers of the latter helped engineer something larger. They manufactured the utopia of a carbon-heavy middle-class American lifestyle, in which any concern about the cost of energy and its future availability dissolved away. Combined with new political arrangements in the Middle East, this utopian form of life helped the oil companies keep oil scarce enough to allow their profits to thrive.

If the ability of organized workers to disrupt the networks and nodal points of a coal-based energy system shaped the kinds of mass politics that emerged, or threatened to emerge, in the first half of the twentieth century, this postwar reorganization of fossil fuel networks altered the energetics of democracy.

Oil and Democracy

The points of vulnerability, where movements could organize and apply pressure, now included a series of oil wells, pipelines, refineries, railways, docks, and shipping lanes across the Middle East. The details of some of these struggles are worth recalling.

In Iraq, which Britain had reoccupied in 1941, less then a decade after granting the country nominal independence, postwar protests culminated in the popular uprising and student and worker strikes of 1948. The Communist Party of Iraq, one of the best-organized political movements in the region, demanded "the evacuation of foreign troops, the unshackling of democratic freedoms, . . . [and] the provision of decent bread to the people."[45] Hanna Batatu notes that the party had "concentrated the weight of its force in the colossal enterprises that were . . . most vital to the country," the railways, the port of Basra, and the oil fields. This focus on the most vulnerable points in the technical structures of a petroleum-based system of production "constituted the key to its basic strategy."[46]

In the railways, the party organized most of its resources at "the most fundamental point in the entire system, the railway workshops at Schalchiyyah," where the main stores and all repair and maintenance work were concentrated. "Stoppage of activity in this place for ten to fifteen days would have brought the movement of trains in the whole of Iraq to a complete standstill."[47] In the British-controlled oil fields, the party focused its activities at an even more vital site, "the point of bifurcation of the Kirkūk-Haifa and the Kirkūk-Tripoli pipelines, the K3 pumping station near Ḥadīthah."[48] A strike by oil workers in June 1946 demanding the right to a union, sickness and disability insurance, and a pension was crushed by force, with ten workers killed and twenty-seven injured.[49] During the 1948 uprising, however, the oil workers succeeded in shutting down K3. Since the pumping station supplied the gasoline for other pumping stations, the union posted guards to ensure that not "even a pint of gasoline" got out. The stoppage lasted two weeks, until the company surrounded the site with machine guns and armored cars and cut off supplies of food. Unable to risk an armed confrontation, the strikers decided to march on Baghdad, more than 150 miles away. After three days of marching, with increasing support along the way, they "entered Fallujah and fell into a police trap."[50] The oil workers were sent back to K3, and the strike leaders to prison.

The other end of the Kirkūk-Haifa pipeline, in Palestine, provided another site of struggle. In the 1936–39 Arab revolt, the most sustained anticolonial uprising against the British in the Middle East, a major target of the insurgency was the recently completed pipeline from Iraq. Initial efforts to weaken the British in August 1936 by organizing a strike at the oil refinery at Haifa, and at the port, the railway, and the Public Works department, were defeated when the British brought in Royal Navy engineers to run the trains and Jewish workers to run the port and the refinery.[51] The pipeline was more vulnerable. Palestinian forces destroyed it for the first time near Irbid on 15 July 1936. They later blew it up several times near the villages of Kaukab al-Hawa, Mahane Yisrael, and Iksal, between 'Afula and Beisān, and at Tel 'Adas, al-Bira, 'Ard al-Marj, Tamra, Kafr Misr, Jisr al-Majami', Jinjar, Beisan, and Indur.[52] Unable to protect the pipeline, the British created a force of armed Jewish settlers to assist with its defense, along with the protection of the Haifa-Lydda railway.[53] This British-officered force became the nucleus of the Zionist army that seized control of Palestine in 1948.

The construction of a pipeline to carry oil from the Saudi fields to the Mediterranean produced another set of political calculations and opportunities. The Trans-Arabian Pipeline Company, a joint venture by Exxon, Chevron, Texaco, and Mobil, originally planned to terminate the pipeline near the British refinery at Haifa.[54] In 1946 it altered the route to avoid Palestine and terminate instead on the Lebanese coast near Sidon, passing through southern Syria. The reason given was the uncertain political future of Palestine, but this uncertainty may have included more than just the threat of Zionism. The British refinery, located at the terminus of the existing pipeline from Iraq, was a site of the 1936 strike already mentioned, an earlier strike in February 1935, and a thirteen-day strike for better wages in March 1947.[55] In the summer of 1947, Samuel Mikunis, secretary of the Communist Party of Palestine, testifying in Jerusalem before the UN Special Committee on Palestine, raised a series of objections to the local political powers that the oil companies exercised:

> The oil refinery at Haifa (The Consolidated Refineries Limited) is a foreign concern exempted from all payment of customs duties. Monopoly concessions have been granted to the Iraq Petroleum Company and to the Trans-Arabian Oil Company. These concessions include the right—free of royalties, taxes, import duties or other payments, charges or compensations—to lay pipelines through any part of the country, to expropriate land, to seize any wood, stone, water and other local materials required, to import cheap labour regardless of existing immigration laws, to pass freely the border of Palestine, to build and use their own harbours, railroads, aerodromes and wireless stations, to exact port taxes for harbouring and loading, and to keep their own police force. The population of Palestine does not derive even cheaper oil and petrol from these concessions, granted by the Government without any consultation of the people.[56]

Rerouting the pipeline through Syria provided a way to avoid this kind of political contestation. When the Syrian parliament refused to ratify the terms of the agreement with the pipeline company, arguing for improved transit fees and a less one-sided U.S. position on Palestine, the oil companies had the CIA organize a coup to put a more accommodating colonel in power. The new military government suspended parliament and the constitution and completed the pipeline agreement.[57] It was in events such as these that the postwar relationship between oil and democracy was engineered.

In Lebanon, the United States pressured the government to sign a bilateral investment treaty that would exempt the oil companies from local labor law.[58] Labor protests beginning in the winter of 1943–44 that demanded union rights and improved pay and conditions had led to the passage of a labor code in 1946.[59] Kamal Junblat, the minister of national economy, represented a reformist faction that opposed generous concessions to foreign multinationals and favored the development of domestic manufacturing industry. His deputy warned that an earlier pipeline and refinery, the Kirkuk-Tripoli line, which was the other branch from the K3 pumping station in Iraq, had provided little employment or local development. "Two million tons of oil flow every year through Tripoli, but what does the huge installation represent in the economy of the town? Few perhaps know that a single cotton spinning and weaving plant in Tripoli itself employs four times as much labour as the whole Iraq Petroleum terminal and refinery together."[60] In the final negotiations over the pipeline concession, the Americans secured Junblat's removal from office.[61] When the pipeline began operations, the U.S. company used temporary employees and other measures to prevent the unionization of the workforce.[62]

In the case of Saudi Arabia, Vitalis has brought to light the extensive efforts of Aramco, the American-owned company with exclusive rights to the country's oil, to suppress labor organizing and political action.[63] The company imported the system of racially segregated workforces and worker housing, which were familiar features of oil and other extractive enterprises in the United States. In the mid-1940s a labor movement began to emerge among the oil workers, demanding better treatment and an end to racial discrimination in living conditions. A ten-day strike in 1953 led to a promise of reforms and the imposition of martial law in the oil fields. When the promises were not kept, a wave of protests, stoppages, and boycotts followed, culminating in a general strike in July 1956. The workers' demands included the introduction of a political constitution, the right to form labor unions, political parties, and national organizations, an end to Aramco's interference in the country's affairs, the closure of the U.S. military base, and the release of imprisoned workers. Aramco's security department identified the leaders to the Saudi security forces, and the leadership was imprisoned or deported.

There were similar pressures in Iran. In 1945–46 struggles for better pay and working conditions in the oil industry led to a series of strikes, including a three-day general strike in the refinery at Abadan and across the oil fields. The government gave in to the demands but then attempted to crush the union.[64] In 1949–51 the union and its allies in the Tudeh Party (the Communist Party of Iran) reemerged. As in Mexico in 1937, a reformist government tried to defuse the oil workers' power by nationalizing the country's oil industry, albeit on terms more favorable to the foreign oil company than those demanded by the union and the Communist Party. There followed a violent confrontation between the Mossadegh government and the oil workers, whose leaders were arrested. But the international oil companies refused to accept the nationalization, and in 1953 another CIA-organized coup reestablished foreign control over the country's oil.[65]

In Iraq a similar pattern of events followed the overthrow of the British-backed regime in 1958. The new leader, Abd al-Karim Qasim, survived the initial CIA attempts to assassinate him, including the gift of a monogrammed handkerchief laced with poison. As an uneasy alliance with the oil workers and the Communist Party broke down, Qasim proceeded with plans to take back 99.5% of the concession area granted to the foreign-owned Iraq Petroleum Company, leaving them only the currently producing fields in the north. He was removed and assassinated in the CIA-supported coup of 1963.[66]

If the construction of new energy networks replacing coal with oil was the basis for building a particular form of postwar democracy in Europe, those networks had different political properties from the coal-centered energy arrangements they replaced. Although the oil fields, pumping stations, pipelines, and refineries of the Middle East became sites of intense political struggle, they did not offer those involved the same powers to paralyze energy systems and build a more democratic order.

The Currency of Oil

When the heads of the Trans-Arabian Pipeline Company were deciding the route for transporting oil from the Gulf to the Mediterranean, they briefly considered a southerly route terminating on the northern coast of the Sinai Peninsula in Egypt. But like Palestine, Egypt fell within the British sphere of influence. That raised a further problem besides the issue of the troubles in Palestine. Egypt was a member of the sterling area, the group of former British colonies that issued their own local currencies but held their hard-currency earnings in a central pool in London. In fact, Egypt and Iraq were the only non-Commonwealth members of this exchange mechanism.[67] The American company wanted to use the route of the pipeline to undermine the sterling area. A further advantage of running the pipeline through Syria and Lebanon was to assist with this financial engineering.

This points to a third set of linkages that were established between fossil fuels and the forms of mid-twentieth-century democracy: the mechanisms that tied democracy in the West, oil, and the U.S. dollar.

The collapse of democracy in Europe in the 1920s and 1930s, the rise of fascism, and the path toward world war were understood to have been caused by the collapse of the international financial system. In central and eastern

Europe, countries were forced to abandon the attempt to base the value of their currencies on reserves of gold, and one by one their domestic financial systems collapsed, middle classes were pauperized, and interwar democracy was destroyed. "The breakdown of the international gold standard," Karl Polanyi wrote in 1944, was "the mechanism which railroaded Europe to its doom."[68]

After World War II the global financial order was reconstructed—on the basis not of reserves of gold but flows of oil.[69] Gold would no longer work because the European allies had been forced to send all their gold bullion to America to pay for imports of coal, oil, and other wartime supplies. By the end of the war, the United States had accumulated 80% of the world's gold reserves. The Bretton Woods Agreements of 1944 fixed the value of the U.S. dollar, on the basis of this gold, at $35 an ounce. Every other country pegged the value of its currency to the dollar and thus indirectly to the American gold monopoly. In practice, however, what sustained the value of the dollar was its convertibility not to gold but to oil. In 1945 the United States produced two-thirds of the world's oil. As production in the Middle East was developed and the routes of pipelines plotted, most of this overseas oil was also under American control. The rest of the world had to buy it using dollars.

The place of oil in postwar politics escapes most standard accounts of the postwar financial system. Yet it was visible in the sequence of meetings that established the new arrangements. Between the Bretton Woods talks in July 1944, which established the postwar financial regime, and those at Dumbarton Oaks from August through October of the same year laying out the new international political order, a third meeting was held: representatives of Britain and the United States met in Washington, DC, in early August to draw up the postwar petroleum order.[70] The Anglo-American Petroleum Agreement established the International Petroleum Commission, which would allocate production quotas and manage prices, much as the International Monetary Fund, created at Bretton Woods, would allocate borrowing quotas and manage the value of currencies.[71] The Petroleum Agreement was a successor to the 1928 cartel arrangement between U.S. and British oil corporations, concerned largely with limiting the flow, managing the distribution, and dividing the profits from the new oil fields of the Middle East.

Domestic U.S. oil companies used their influence in the Senate to kill the Petroleum Agreement, preferring existing arrangements in which the Texas Railroad Commission and other local regulators set production quotas and prices to an international scheme. The following February, however, Roosevelt met with King Ibn Saud of Saudi Arabia to cement the arrangement that would replace the International Petroleum Commission for Middle Eastern oil, American corporate control of Arabian oil in exchange for Washington's help in suppressing labor militancy and other populist threats to the oligarchs Britain had helped bring to power. Subsequently, the Marshall Plan paid for

Europe to postpone plans to rebuild its battered coalfields and instead to purchase oil—supplied from the Middle East but paid for in U.S. dollars.

Britain's attempt to defend the pound sterling as a rival international currency was a battle fought over oil fields. Oil was so large a component of its international trade that a 1955 report on the treatment of oil in the country's trade accounts suggested: "The international ramifications of the oil industry (including its tanker operations) are so large and so complex as *almost to constitute oil a currency in itself.*"[72]

Europe and other regions had to accumulate dollars, hold them, and then return them to the United States in payment for oil. Inflation in the United States slowly eroded the value of the dollar, so that when these countries purchased U.S. oil, the dollars they used were worth less than their value when they acquired them. These seigniorage privileges enabled Washington to extract a tax from every other country in the world, keeping its economy prosperous and thus its democracy popular.

In the same way that the working of carbon-fuel networks helped engender certain concentrations of power and points of political vulnerability in the coal era, and were transformed with the postwar transition to oil into new sites of democratic contestation and vulnerability, postwar democracy in Europe was built on international financial exchanges organized upon the flow of oil. Postwar democracy in the West appeared to require a stable financial order, an order engineered with the help of oil wells, pipelines, tanker operations, and the increasingly difficult control of oil workers. The fact that flows of oil were the basis for intersecting networks of global energy supply and global currency movements helped introduce a disjuncture that would become increasingly apparent by the end of the 1960s, leading to the 1971–74 energy, dollar, and Middle East crises. Before considering those interlocking crises, let us explore one more dimension of carbon democracy, a dimension that helped define the hydrocarbon utopia and that would also be transformed in the 1971–74 crises: the mid-twentieth-century politics of "the economy."

The Carbon Economy

In a memorable passage in *The General Theory*, John Maynard Keynes explains his novel theory of the economy in terms of banknotes buried in disused coal mines. "If the Treasury were to fill old bottles with bank notes, bury them at suitable depths in disused coal mines which are then filled up to the surface with town rubbish, and leave it to private enterprise on well-tried principles of *laissez-faire* to dig the notes up again . . . there need be no more unemployment and, with the help of the repercussions, the real income of the community, and its capital wealth also, would probably become a great deal greater than it actually is."[73]

British coal production had passed its peak in the 1920s. By the time Keynes wrote *The General Theory*, coal mines were being exhausted at an unprecedented rate.[74] William Stanley Jevons, the author of an earlier revolution in British economic thinking, the marginalist theory of the 1870s, had published a book warning of the coming exhaustion of coal reserves.[75] Keynes was reading that book as he published *The General Theory* and gave a lecture on Jevons in 1936 to the Royal Statistical Society.[76] It is indicative of the transformation in economic thinking in which Keynes played a role that the exhaustion of coal reserves no longer appeared as a crisis. The management of coal reserves could now be replaced in the mind, and in the textbooks of economics, with reserves of banknotes. In the era that Keynes's thinking helped to shape, the supply of carbon energy was no longer a practical limit to economic possibility. What mattered was the proper circulation of banknotes.

A fourth set of connections between oil and mid-twentieth century democratic politics concerns the role of economic expertise and the economy. Like twentieth-century democracy, twentieth-century economic expertise developed in a specific relationship to the utopian possibilities of the hydrocarbon age.

The shaping of Western democratic politics from the 1930s onward was carried out in part through the application of new kinds of economic expertise: the development and deployment of Keynesian economic knowledge, its expansion into different areas of policy and debate, its increasingly technical nature, and the efforts to claim an increasing variety of topics as subject to determination not by democratic debate but by economic planning and expertise.

The Keynesian and New Deal elaboration of economic knowledge was a response to the threat of populist politics, especially in the wake of the 1929 financial crisis and the labor militancy that accompanied the crisis and re-emerged a decade later. It provided a method of setting limits to democratic practice and maintaining them.

The deployment of expertise requires, and encourages, the making of worlds that it can master. In this case, what had to be made was "the economy." This was an object that no economist or planner prior to the 1930s spoke of or knew to exist. Of course, the term "economy" existed prior to the 1930s, but it referred to a process, not a thing. It meant "government" or the proper management of people and resources, as in the phrase "political economy."[77] The economy became the central object of democratic politics in the West (paralleled by the emergence of "development" outside the West), an object whose management was the central task of government, and which required the deployment of specialist knowledge.

The peculiar nature of the project of the "national economy" deployed by Keynesian planners and colonial development officers and its relationship to forms of democracy can be seen by comparing it with a rival project, formulated at the same time and destined to overtake it: neoliberalism. Launched at a colloquium in Paris organized in August 1938 to discuss the work of Walter

Lippmann criticizing the New Deal (as a movement against this new object of planning, the economy, and against planning as a method of concentrating and deploying expert knowledge), neoliberalism proposed an alternative ordering of knowledge, expertise, and political technology that it named "the market."[78] This was not the market of David Ricardo or Jevons, but a term that began to take on new meanings in the hands of the nascent neoliberal movement. Drawing on Lippmann's warnings in *The Phantom Public* and *The Good Society* about the dangers of public opinion and the need to expand the areas of concern that are reserved to the decisions of experts, neoliberalism was launched by Friedrich von Hayek and his collaborators as an alternative project to defeat the threat of populist democracy.

The development of neoliberalism was delayed by the war and the programs of postwar reconstruction. Its political challenge to the Keynesian consensus got under way a decade later, with the founding of a think tank called the Institute of Economic Affairs in London in 1955. The launch was triggered by the first postwar crisis in the oil-currency system: Britain's attempt to preserve the sterling area as a mechanism of currency regulation, despite the loss of its control of the hub of that mechanism, the Anglo-Iranian Oil Company's fields in Iran. The desperate measures with which London tried to retain the pound's value despite the loss of the oil wells through which its value had been manufactured provided the point of vulnerability where the neoliberal movement first aimed its weapons.[79]

Larger connections can be drawn between the assembling of "the economy" and the transition from a coal-based energy system to a predominantly oil-based one. One could argue that the new era of abundant and low-cost energy supplies undergirds the new conception of the economy and perhaps describes postwar Keynesian economics as a form of "petroknowledge."

The economy is conceived in a particular way. It is not the total of the nation's wealth—which had proven impossible to calculate. (There seemed no way to avoid continually counting everything twice, for example when wholesale goods were resold as retail.) It is imagined and measured, rather simply, as the phenomenon of banknotes changing hands. Even if it is the same money, every time it changes hands it is measured as part of the economy. The economy is the sum total of those monetary transactions.

This reconceptualization defined the main feature of the new object and gave it an underlying utopianism: it could expand without getting physically bigger. Older ways of thinking about wealth were based upon physical processes that suggested limits to growth: the expansion of cities and factories, the colonial enlargement of territory, the accumulation of gold reserves, the growth of population and absorption of migrants, the exploitation of new mineral reserves, the increase in volumes of trade in commodities; all of these were spatial and material processes that had physical limits. By the 1930s, many of those limits seemed to be approaching: population growth in the

West was leveling off, the colonial expansion of the United States and of the European imperial powers had ended and was threatened with reversal, coal mines were being exhausted, and agriculture and industry faced gluts of over-production. The economy, however, measured by the new calculative device of national income accounting, had no obvious limit. National income, later renamed the gross national product, was a measure not of the accumulation of wealth but of the speed and frequency with which paper money changed hands. It could grow without any physical or territorial limits.

Oil contributed to the new conception of the economy as an object that could grow without limits in two ways. First, oil prices declined continuously. Adjusting for inflation, the price of a barrel of oil in 1970 was one-third of what it sold for in 1920.[80] So although increasing quantities of energy were con-sumed, the cost of energy did not appear to represent a limit to growth. Sec-ond, thanks to its relative abundance and the ease of shipping it across oceans, oil could be treated as inexhaustible. Its cost included no calculation for the exhaustion of reserves. The growth of the economy, measured in terms of GDP, had no need to account for the depletion of energy resources. The lead-ing contributions to the academic formulation of the economy—Keynes's *General Theory*, Hicks's *Value and Capital*, Samuelson's *Foundations*, and the Arrow-Debreu model—paid no attention to the depletion of energy. The eco-nomics of growth of the 1950s and 1960s could conceive of long-run growth as unrestrained by the availability of energy.[81] Moreover, the costs of air pollu-tion, environmental disaster, climate change, and the other negative conse-quences of using fossil fuels were not deducted from the measurement of GDP. Since the measurement of the economy made no distinction between beneficial and harmful costs, the increased expenditure required to deal with the damage caused by fossil fuels appeared as an addition rather than an im-pediment to growth.[82] In all these ways, the availability and supply of oil con-tributed to the shaping of the economy and its growth as the new and utopian object of mid-twentieth-century politics.

The oil wells and pipelines of the Middle East and the political arrange-ments that were built with them helped make possible the idea of the Keynes-ian economy and the forms of democracy in which it played a central part.

The 1967–74 Reorganization

With all this in mind, we can turn briefly to the 1967–74 dollar-oil crisis, a pivotal episode in the story of postwar carbon democracy.[83] The linked crises of the dollar and the nationalization of oil in the Middle East brought into play and reconfigured the intersecting elements of carbon democracy.

Again, by following the oil one can trace how relations between oil produc-tion, the gold standard, the circulation of dollars, and Keynesian economic expertise were all transformed in the crisis, along with the possibilities for democratic politics in the Middle East. Following the balance-of-payments crisis of the late 1950s, Washington had introduced oil-import quotas to protect the value of the dollar and later tried to support its pegged gold price by interventions in the London gold market. When this scheme collapsed in November 1968, the United States tried to transform Bretton Woods into a mechanism that allowed the gold peg to float. In an effort to lower domestic oil prices, Washington removed the controls on oil imports in 1970, but this caused more dollars to flow abroad. By the following year, the United States had used up most of its nongold reserves, and only 22% of its currency reserves were backed by gold. When European banks requested payment for their dollars in gold, the United States defaulted. Described as "the abandoning of the gold standard," it amounted to a declaration of bankruptcy by the U.S. government.[84]

These developments coincided with the emergence of a politics of "the limits to growth" as an alternative project to that of "the economy," in which the oil companies helped trigger the production of the environment as a rival object of politics. They did this in part inadvertently, by adopting ways of drilling and transporting oil that led to giant oil spills, around which environmentalists were able to organize. But they also helped produce the environment as a matter of political concern, by changing the way they calculated the world's reserves of oil.

In 1971 the oil companies abruptly abandoned their utopian calculations of oil as an almost limitless resource (calculations that had underpinned postwar theories of the economy as an object capable of limitless growth) and began to forecast the end of oil.[85] The recalculations were needed to deal with the threat posed by the new Ba'athist government of Iraq, which was developing the first major oil production in the region independent of any Western oil company. When the oil majors tried to punish Iraq by cutting their own production in the country, Baghdad responded by nationalizing their assets.[86] To dissuade other Gulf states from following Iraq's lead, the oil companies now sought to accommodate or even encourage their demand for an unprecedented increase in the price of oil, a goal already supported by agencies of the U.S. government.[87] A doubling or tripling of the price of oil would enable the major oil companies to survive the transition to a much lower percentage share of Middle Eastern oil revenue, and this would make it feasible to develop the less accessible, high-cost oil fields of the North Sea and northern Alaska. No model of the economy or its future growth could rationalize such an unprecedented transformation in costs of energy or flows of finance. But if the world was reconfigured as a system of finite resources that were rapidly running out, then entirely new calculations became possible.

The need to conserve environmental resources and protect them for the long term also helped with another calculation. For the oil companies, the large increase in oil prices carried a risk. It threatened to make affordable a rival source of energy, nuclear power. However, if the oil companies could force the producers of nuclear power to include in the price of the energy they sold a payment to cover its long-term environmental effects —the cost of decontaminating reactors when they went out of service and of storing spent fuel for millennia—it would remain more expensive than oil. To promote such calculations, the oil companies joined the effort to frame the environment as a new object of politics and to define and calculate it in particular ways. Like the economy, the environment was not simply an external-reality principle against which the oil industry had to contend. It was a set of forces and calculations that rival groups attempted to mobilize.

The role of oil companies in framing the politics of the environment suggests another dimension of the relationship between oil and democracy: compared with the production of coal, oil production has a different way of deploying and distributing expertise. Earlier, I suggested that the democratic militancy of coal miners could be traced in part to the autonomy that miners exercised at the coal face, especially prior to the large-scale mechanization of production. The autonomy of those who mined the ore placed a significant amount of expertise in their hands. Oil, in contrast, leaves its workers on the surface and distributes more of the expertise of production into the offices of managers and engineers.

This difference extends further. Once mined, coal is ready to use. It may require cleaning and sorting, but it needs no chemical transformation. Oil comes out of the ground in an unusable form, known as crude oil. The crude must be heated in a furnace, separated into its different hydrocarbons by fractional distillation, and further processed into usable and uniform products. Initially its main use was in the form of heavy oils (kerosene) for domestic lighting and lubrication. Gasoline and other lighter byproducts of the refining process were treated as waste. To increase their profit margin, oil companies developed large research and development divisions to find uses for these unused byproducts, distribution and marketing divisions to promote their use, and political and public relations departments to help build the kinds of societies that would demand them.[88]

Compared with coal companies, oil companies developed much larger and more extended networks for the production of expertise, which became increasingly involved in making of the wider world a place where its products could thrive. They also collaborated to deny expertise to others, including the coal industry. The 1928 oil cartel, as Gregory Nowell has shown, was actually a broader hydrocarbon cartel because it consisted of an agreement not just to restrict the production of oil, but to prevent the use of patents that would allow coal companies to move into the production of synthetic oils.[89] After the 1967–74 crisis and the rise of environmentalist challenges to carbon democracy, the oil companies are well equipped to meet the challenge.

Finally, drawing on the work of Nitzan and Bichler, one can note the emergence of a new partner in the oil-democracy relationship: the arms industry. The export of weapons by U.S. and other manufacturers, previously a relatively small trade financed mostly through U.S. overseas development aid, was transformed into a highly profitable commercial industry. The commercialization of weapons exports was made possible by establishing a series of linkages between the Western import of oil from the Middle East, the flow of dollars to the producer countries, the production of political vulnerabilities and military threats to the further flow of oil, and producer countries' use of petrodollars to purchase arms from the West as protection against those threats.[90] The 1967–74 crisis represented the work of connecting these elements. The flow of weapons and related opportunities in construction, consulting, military assistance, and banking now depended on new levels of militarism, and indeed on a U.S. policy of prolonging and exacerbating local conflicts in the Middle East and on an increasingly disjunctive relationship with the Salafist forms of Islam that had helped defend the mid-twentieth-century oil order against nationalist and popular pressures in the region. The tensions between militarism, Salafism, and armed conflict would render the prospects for a more democratic politics of oil production even weaker in the post-1974 period.[91]

Conclusion

This chapter has not attempted to draw up a general theory of democracy. General theories of democracy, of which there are many, have no place for oil, except as an exception. Rather, the goal has been to follow closely a particular set of connections that were engineered between carbon fuels and certain kinds of democratic and undemocratic politics, and the utopianism that this relationship required and enabled.

The forms of democracy that emerged in leading industrialized countries by the middle decades of the twentieth century were enabled and shaped by the extraordinary concentrations of energy obtained from the world's limited stores of hydrocarbons and the sociotechnical arrangements required for extracting and distributing that energy. When the production of energy shifted to oil from the Middle East, however, the transformation provided opportunities to weaken rather than extend, both in the West and the Middle East, the forms of carbon-based political mobilization on which the emergence of industrial democracy had depended. Exploring the properties of oil, the networks along which it flowed, and the connections established between flows of energy, finance, and other objects provides a way of understanding how the relations among these different elements and forces were constructed. The relations we have followed connected energy and politics, materials and ideas, humans and nonhumans, calculations and the objects of calculation, representations and forms of violence, and the present and the future.

Democratic politics developed, thanks to oil, with a peculiar orientation toward the future: the future was a limitless horizon of growth. This utopian horizon was not some natural reflection of a time of plenty. It was the result of a particular way of organizing expert knowledge and its objects, in terms of a novel world called "the economy." Innovations in methods of calculation, the use of money, the measurement of transactions, and the compiling of national statistics made it possible to image the central object of politics as an object that could expand without any form of ultimate material constraint. In the 1967–74 crisis, the relations among these disparate elements were all transformed. Those relations are being transformed again in the present.

In their book *Afflicted Powers*, Ian Boal and his colleagues have suggested that understanding the contemporary politics of oil involves the difficult task of bringing together the violence that has been repeatedly deployed to secure arrangements for the production of oil and the forms of spectacle and representation that seem somehow an equally effective aspect of the undemocratic politics of oil—not least the representation of the latest rounds of U.S. militarism as a project to bring democracy to the Middle East.[92]

We can better understand the relationship between spectacle and violence, and between other apparently disparate or discordant features of the politics of oil, by following oil closely, not because the material properties or strategic necessity of oil determines everything else (on the contrary, as I suggested, a lot of hard work went into producing America's "strategic dependence" on the control of Middle Eastern oil, starting with those V8 engines), but because in tracing the connections that were made between pipelines and pumping stations, refineries and shipping routes, road systems and automobile cultures, dollar flows and economic knowledge, weapons experts and militarism, one discovers how a peculiar set of relations was engineered among oil, violence, finance, expertise, and democracy.

These relations are quite different from those of the coal age. If the emergence of the mass politics of the early twentieth century, out of which certain sites and episodes of welfare democracy were achieved, should be understood in relation to coal, the limits of contemporary democratic politics can be traced in relation to oil. The possibility of more democratic futures, in turn, depends on the political tools with which we address the passing of the era of fossil fuel.

Notes

1. An earlier version of this chapter has been published in *Economy and Society* 38, no. 3 (2009): 399–432. I am grateful for the help received from Robert Vitalis, Munir Fakher Eldin, Katayoun Shafiee, Andrew Barry, three anonymous referees for *Econ-*

omy and Society, and seminar participants at Rutgers, Cornell, Princeton, Binghamton, NYU, SOAS, the University of Illinois at Urbana-Champaign, and the University of California, Berkeley, where parts of this work were presented.

2. Michael L. Ross, in "Does Oil Hinder Democracy?" *World Politics* 53 (April 2001): 325–61, demonstrates a negative correlation between oil exports as a percentage of GDP and degree of democracy, as estimated in the Polity data set compiled by Keith Jaggers and Ted Robert Gurr. (The data are derived from an evaluation of the institutional procedures by which the candidate for chief executive is selected, elected, and held accountable; Keith Jaggers and Ted Robert Gurr, "Tracking Democracy's Third Wave with the Polity III Data," *Journal of Peace Research* 32, no. 4 [1995]: 469–82. The narrowness of this conception of democracy, the unreliability of its measurement, and the assumption that diverse institutional arrangements can be compared and ranked as differing degrees of a universal principle of democracy are among the many problems presented by the data.) Ross is unable to establish reasons for the statistical relationship between oil exports and Polity data ranking.

3. The problem of the rentier state was first formulated in Hussein Mahdavy's "The Patterns and Problems of Economic Development in Rentier States: The Case of Iran," in *Studies in Economic History of the Middle East*, ed. A. Cook (London: Oxford University Press, 1970); subsequent contributions on the Middle East include Hazem Beblawi and Giacomo Luciani, eds., *The Rentier State* (New York: Croom Helm, 1987), Ghassan Salame, ed., *Democracy without Democrats: The Renewal of Politics in the Muslim World* (London: I. B. Tauris, 1994), and Isam al-Khafaji, *Tormented Births: Passages to Modernity in Europe and the Middle East* (London: I. B. Tauris, 2004), 309–25. For other regions, see Terry Lynn Karl, *The Paradox of Plenty: Oil Booms and Petro-States* (Berkeley: University of California Press, 1997); Douglas A. Yates, *The Rentier State in Africa: Oil Rent Dependency and Neocolonialism in the Republic of Gabon* (Trenton, NJ: Africa World Press, 1996); Leonard Wantchekon, "Why Do Resource Dependent Countries Have Authoritarian Governments?" *Journal of African Finance and Economic Development* 5, no. 2 (2002); Andrew Rosser, "Escaping the Resource Curse: The Case of Indonesia," *Journal of Contemporary Asia* 37, no. 1 (2007). Among economists, the problem of natural resources is posed in terms of obstacles to economic growth rather than democracy; Jeffrey D. Sachs and Andrew M. Warner, "Natural Resource Abundance and Economic Growth" (development discussion paper no. 517a, Harvard Institute for International Development, Cambridge, MA, 1995).

4. Rory Stewart, *Occupational Hazards: My Time Governing in Iraq* (London: Picador, 2006), 280.

5. M. King Hubbert, "Nuclear Energy and the Fossil Fuels" (Exploration and Production Research Division, Shell Development Co., Publication no. 95, June 1956); Kjell Aleklett and Colin J. Campbell, "The Peak and Decline of World Oil and Gas Production," *Minerals and Energy* 18, no. 1 (2003): 5–20; Kenneth S. Deffeyes, *Beyond Oil: The View from Hubbert's Peak* (New York: Farrar, Straus and Giroux, 2005); on the history of peak oil estimates, see Gary Bowden, "The Social Construction of Validity in Estimates of US Crude Oil Reserves," *Social Studies of Science* 15, no. 2 (1985): 207–40.

6. Intergovernmental Panel on Climate Change, "Climate Change 2007: Synthesis Report," available at http://www.ipcc.ch/publications_and_data/publications_ipcc_

fourth_assessment_report_synthesis_report.htm (accessed 3 January 2010). Research by James Hansen and his colleagues on paleoclimate data suggests that feedback loops in the melting of ice can cause a rapid acceleration in the loss of ice cover, forcing much more extreme climate change, with potentially cataclysmic consequences. These findings make even the dire warnings from the IPCC look absurdly optimistic. James Hansen et al., "Climate Change and Trace Gases," *Philosophical Transactions of the Royal Society* A 365 (2007): 1925–54.

7. On the sociology of translation and "obligatory passage points," see Michel Callon, "Some Elements of a Sociology of Translation: Domestication of the Scallops and the Fishermen of St Brieuc Bay," in *Power, Action and Belief: A New Sociology of Knowledge*, ed. John Law (London: Routledge & Kegan Paul, 1986), 196–233. See also Timothy Mitchell, *Rule of Experts* (Berkeley: University of California Press, 2002), chap. 1.

8. Rolf Peter Sieferle, *The Subterranean Forest: Energy Systems and the Industrial Revolution* (Cambridge: White Horse Press, 2001).

9. Bruce Podobnik, in *Global Energy Shifts: Fostering Sustainability in a Turbulent Age* (Philadelphia: Temple University Press, 2006), 5, calculates that coal replaced wood and other biomass materials as the main source of the world's commercial energy as early as the 1880s. But until well into the twentieth century, the bulk of this fossil energy was consumed by just a handful of countries.

10. The use of coal, and also peat, another fossil fuel, was already known in antiquity. But its use was generally restricted to the localities where it was found and to particular trades that required large quantities of process heat, such as limestone burning and metal smithing. Shortages of wood, especially in Britain, led to a gradual rise in the use of coal as a general substitute for wood from the sixteenth century on. Sieferle, *Subterranean Forest*, 78–89.

11. Jean-Paul Sartre, *Critique of Dialectical Reason*, vol. 1, *Theory of Practical Ensembles* (London: Verso, 1977), 154.

12. On the depletion of oil reserves, see Aleklett and Campbell, "Peak and Decline," and Kenneth S. Deffeyes, *Beyond Oil: The View from Hubbert's Peak*. Until recently, it was assumed that coal reserves would long outlast oil, with plentiful supplies for hundreds of years. Recent studies suggest that estimates of coal reserves are even less reliable than those for oil, that production in the United States, the country with the largest reserves, has already peaked and begun to decline, and that global production may peak as early as 2025. Werner Zittel and Jörg Schindler, "Coal: Resources and Future Production" (EWG Paper no. 1/01, 10 July 2007), available at http://www.energywatchgroup.org/Studien.24+M5d637b1e38d.0.html (accessed 3 January 2010). See also Iain Boal's warnings about the risks of Malthusianism in discussions of oil depletion, in Iain Boal and David Martinez's "Feast and Famine: A Conversation with Iain Boal on Scarcity and Catastrophe," 3 January 2006, available at http://www.beyondthecommons.com/boal.html (accessed 3 January 2010).

13. Jeffrey S. Dukes, "Burning Buried Sunshine: Human Consumption of Ancient Solar Energy," *Climatic Change* 61, nos. 1–2 (November 2003): 33–41 (figures from 1997); Helmut Haberl, "The Global Socioeconomic Energetic Metabolism as a Sustainability Problem," *Energy* 31, no. 1 (January 2006): 87–99.

14. Sieferle, *Subterranean Forest*; Kenneth Pomeranz, *The Great Divergence: China, Europe, and the Making of the Modern World Economy* (Princeton: Princeton University Press, 2000).

15. Haberl, "Energetic Metabolism." Sidney Pollard, in *Peaceful Conquest: The Industrialization of Europe, 1760–1970* (Oxford: Oxford University Press, 1981), documents the link between coal-producing regions (rather than states) and industrial development in Europe.

16. Pomeranz, *Great Divergence*.

17. Eric J. Hobsbawm, *Age of Empire, 1875–1914* (New York: Vintage, 1989), 88. As Hobsbawm points out, democratization came slowly. In most countries with systems of representative rule, property qualifications and registration procedures restricted the electorate to between 30 and 40% of adult males. Voting rights for the majority of men, and for women, were won only in the twentieth century. For the restrictions in the British case, see Neal Blewett, "The Franchise in the United Kingdom, 1885–1918," *Past and Present*, no. 32 (December 1965): 27–56.

18. Britain also developed coal resources in the colonies—Natal and the Transvaal, parts of Queensland and New South Wales, and West Bengal. Coal production was also developed in the Donets Basin in Russia and in China.

19. Daniel T. Rodgers, *Atlantic Crossings: Social Politics in a Progressive Age* (Cambridge, MA: Belknap Press, 1998), 45.

20. William Stanley Jevons, *The Coal Question: An Inquiry Concerning the Progress of the Nation and the Probable Exhaustion of Our Coal-Mines* (London: Macmillan, 1865), 87–88.

21. The strike rates per one thousand employees for coal mining and for all industries were, respectively, 134 and 72.0 (1881–86); 241 and 73.3 (1887–99); 215 and 66.4 (1894–1900); and 208 and 86.9 (1901–5). P. K. Edwards, *Strikes in the United States, 1881–1974* (New York: St. Martin's Press, 1981), 106.

22. Coal was also associated with labor militancy beyond the main centers of the industrialized world. Donald Quataert notes the repeated strikes among the workers of the Zonguldak coalfield on the Black Sea coast of Ottoman Anatolia (*Miners and the State in the Ottoman Empire: The Zonguldak Coalfield, 1822–1920* [New York: Berghahn Books, 2006]). In Egypt an April 1882 strike by the coal heavers at Port Said, the world's largest coaling station, is recorded as the first collective action by indigenous workers in the country (Joel Beinin and Zachary Lockman, *Workers on the Nile: Nationalism, Communism, Islam, and the Egyptian Working Class, 1882–1954* [Princeton: Princeton University Press, 1987], 23, 27–31). But without the linkages that connected coal to centers of industrial production within the country, these actions could not paralyze local energy systems and gain the political force of strikes in northern Europe and the United States.

23. Podobnik, *Global Energy Shifts*. On the central role of the Left in creating democracy in Europe, see Geoff Eley, *Forging Democracy: The History of the Left in Europe* (Oxford: Oxford University Press, 2002).

24. Clark Kerr and Abraham Siegel, "The Interindustry Propensity to Strike: An International Comparison," in *Industrial Conflict*, ed. Arthur Kornhauser, Robert Dubin, and Arthur M. Ross (New York: McGraw-Hill, 1954), 192.

25. Royden Harrison, ed., *Independent Collier: The Coal Miner as Archetypal Proletarian Reconsidered* (Hassocks, Sussex: Harvester Press, 1978); Roger Fagge, *Power, Culture, and Conflict in the Coalfields: West Virginia and South Wales, 1900–1922* (Manchester: Manchester University Press, 1996); John H. M. Laslett, *Colliers across the Sea: A Comparative Study of Class Formation in Scotland and the American Midwest, 1830–1924* (Champaign: University of Illinois Press, 2000); Roy A. Church,

Quentin Outram, and David N. Smith, "The Militancy of British Miners, 1893–1986: Interdisciplinary Problems and Perspectives," *Journal of Interdisciplinary History* 22, no. 1 (Summer 1991): 49–66.

26. Carter Goodrich, *The Miner's Freedom: A Study of the Working Life in a Changing Industry* (Boston: Marshall Jones, 1925), 19.

27. Ibid., 14; Podobnik, *Global Energy Shifts*, 82–85. Other discussions of the relative autonomy of coal miners and its loss under mechanization include K. Dix's *What's a Coal Miner to Do? The Mechanization of Coal Mining* (Pittsburgh: University of Pittsburgh Press, 1988); see also Chris Tilly and Charles Tilly, *Work under Capitalism* (Boulder, CO: Westview Press, 1998), 43–51.

28. In one of the world's worst pit disasters, on 10 March 1906 a gas explosion destroyed the Courrières mine, leaving eleven hundred dead. Robert G. Neville, "The Courrières Colliery Disaster, 1906," *Journal of Contemporary History* 13, no. 1 (January 1978): 33–52.

29. Beverly J. Silver, *Forces of Labor: Workers' Movements and Globalization since 1870* (Cambridge: Cambridge University Press, 2003); fig. 3.3, p. 98, shows that strikes were concentrated in these industries rather than in manufacturing.

30. David Corbin, *Life, Work, and Rebellion in the Coal Fields: The Southern West Virginia Miners, 1880–1922* (Champaign: University of Illinois Press, 1981). Thomas Reifer, "Labor, Race and Empire: Transport Workers and Transnational Empires of Trade, Production, and Finance," in *Labor versus Empire: Race, Gender, and Migration*, ed. Gilbert G. Gonzalez et al. (London: Routledge, 2004), 17–36.

31. Detailed in Ron Chernow's *Titan: The Life of John D. Rockefeller, Sr.* (New York: Random House, 1998).

32. David Painter, "Oil and the Marshall Plan," *Business History Review* 58, no. 3 (1984): 361; James Forrestal, Diaries, vols. 9–10, November 1947–April 1948, 6 January 1948, James V. Forrestal Papers, 1941–1949, Public Policy Papers, Seeley G. Mudd Manuscript Library, Princeton, p. 2005. See also James Forrestal, *The Forrestal Diaries*, ed. W. Millis and E. S. Duffield (New York: Viking, 1951), vols. 7–8, April 1947–October 1947, 2 May 1947. See also Nathan Citino, "The Rise of Consumer Society: Postwar American US Oil Policies and the Modernization of the Middle East" (paper presented at the 14th International Economic History Congress, Helsinki, 2006), http://www.helsinki.fi/iehc2006/papers3/Citino.pdf (accessed 12 December 2008), and Fred Block, *The Origins of International Economic Disorder: A Study of United States International Monetary Policy from World War II to the Present* (Berkeley: University of California Press, 1977).

33. Stalin's words, from a 1926 speech to railway workers, are cited in Ronald Grigor Suny's "A Journeyman for the Revolution: Stalin and the Labour Movement in Baku, June 1907–May 1908," *Soviet Studies* 23, no. 3 (January 1972): 373.

34. On some of the more recent politics of pipelines, see Andrew Barry, "Technological Zones," *European Journal of Social Theory* 9, no. 2 (2006): 239–53, and Michael Watts, "Resource Curse? Governmentality, Oil and Power in the Niger Delta, Nigeria," *Geopolitics* 9, no. 1 (2004): 50–80.

35. Lewis Mumford, *Technics and Civilization* (New York: Harcourt Brace, 1934), 235.

36. The main exception was high-quality steam coal from South Wales, essential for the navy and fast liners; it was shipped to British coaling stations around the world.

H. Stanley Jevons, *The British Coal Trade* (London: E. P. Dutton, 1915), 684. Historically, long-distance coal shipments from Britain could be used as ballast or makeweight and benefited from low rates for back carriage. Jevons, *The Coal Question*, 227.

37. Jevons, *British Coal Trade*, 676–84. Charles P. Kindleberger, an economist with the Office of Strategic Services in 1942–44, recalled that at the outbreak of World War II,

> coal was regarded as something that didn't move across big bodies of water. It was shipped to British coaling stations but you wouldn't expect international transoceanic trade as a regular thing. And yet when the war came along, and we needed to get coal to Europe we started to move coal out. . . . They were loading it in clam shell buckets on to barges in Puget Sound to go to Europe, a landing in Texas, Portland, Maine, everywhere. Coal was being loaded all over this United States to be shipped all over the area. It was a fantastic operation, expensive as hell; boy it was expensive, you know. It was just awful the price they paid for it, but price was no object in these matters, you see. This used up the available monetary resources very rapidly.

Richard D. McKinzie, Oral History Interview with Charles P. Kindleberger, Economist with the Office of Strategic Services, 1942–44, '45; chief, Division of German and Austrian Economic Affairs, Department of State, Washington, DC, 1945–48; and Intelligence Officer, Twelfth U.S. Army Group, 1944–45, 16 July 1973, Harry S. Truman Library, Independence, MO, pp. 108–9, http://www.trumanlibrary.org/oralhist/kindbrgr .htm (accessed 3 January 2010). After World War II, Japan built a steel industry based on coal and ore shipped from Australia. Today, however, 80% of coal is consumed within the country of production (see Zittel and Schindler, "Coal: Resources and Future Production," 6).

38. Podobnik, *Global Energy Shifts*, 79.

39. UNCTAD, "Review of Maritime Transport" (since 1968). More than half of the freight carried by rail consisted of coal (see www.unctad.org [accessed 3 January 2010] for figures since the 1960s).

40. The *Torrey Canyon*, an oil tanker owned by a Bermuda-based subsidiary of the Union Oil Company of California, registered in Liberia, chartered to BP, built in 1959, and rebuilt in 1966 in a Japanese shipyard to increase her size from 66,000 to 119,000 deadweight tons, ran aground off the coast of Cornwall, England, in March 1967. The tanker had set sail without knowing its final destination and lacked detailed navigation charts for the coast of South West England. The environmental disaster was exacerbated by the lack of methods that could handle large oil spills. The British government tried to set fire to the oil by having air defense forces bomb it with napalm, creating further damage and inadvertently revealing its possession of the controversial weapon and the inaccuracy of the bombers (more than a quarter of the bombs missed their target). John Sheail, "Torrey Canyon: The Political Dimension," *Journal of Contemporary History* 42, no. 3 (2007): 485–504; H.M.S.O., *The Torrey Canyon*, Cabinet Office Publication, 1967.

41. Timothy Mitchell, "McJihad: Islam in the U.S. Global Order," *Social Text*, no. 73 (Winter 2003): 1–18.

42. Andrew Barry, "Technological Zones," *European Journal of Social Theory* 9, no. 2 (2006): 239–53.

43. On the ability of the U.S. oil majors to frame their program in terms of "national security" and the reproduction of this perspective in scholarship, see Robert Vitalis's

America's Kingdom: Mythmaking on the Saudi Oil Frontier (Palo Alto: Stanford University Press, 2006).

44. Forrestal, *Diaries*, p. 2005. He made the same argument at a Cabinet meeting on 16 January 1948 (p. 2026).

45. Prison letter from Comrade Fahd, early February 1948, cited in Hanna Batatu's *The Old Social Classes and the Revolutionary Movements of Iraq: A Study of Iraq's Old Landed and Commercial Classes and of Its Communists, Ba'thists, and Free Officers* (London: Saqi Books, 2004), 564.

46. Batatu, *Old Social Classes*, 616.

47. Ibid., 617.

48. Ibid., 622.

49. Ibid., 624.

50. Ibid., 625.

51. Zachary Lockman, *Comrades and Enemies: Arab and Jewish Workers in Palestine, 1906–1948* (Berkeley: University of California Press, 1996), 243.

52. Ghassan Kanafani, "The 1936–39 Revolt in Palestine" (New York: Committee for a Democratic Palestine, 1972), 109, http://www.newjerseysolidarity.org/resources/kanafani/kanafani4.html (accessed 3 January 2010). Kanafani twice mentions the place-name Bashan, which is not shown on any historical maps. I assume this is a translator's error and have corrected it to Beisan; I have also corrected Ain Dur to Indur. 'Ard al-Marj is probably Marj ibn Amir, known in English as the Plain of Esdralon or the Jizreel Valley.

53. Ibid. On the British-Zionist collaboration in defending the pipeline, see David Ben-Gurion, "Our Friend: What Wingate Did for Us," *Jewish Observer and Middle East Review*, 27 September 1963, 15–16, reprinted in *From Haven to Conquest: Readings in Zionism and the Palestine Problem until 1948*, ed. Walid Khalidi (Washington, DC: Institute for Palestine Studies, 1971), 382–87, and Leonard Mosely, *Gideon Goes to War* (London: Arthur Barker, 1955), chap. 4, excerpted as "Orde Wingate and Moshe Dayan," in *From Haven to Conquest*, ed. Khalidi, 375–82.

54. The four corporations, then known as Standard Oil of New Jersey (Exxon), Standard Oil of California (Chevron), the Texas Company (Texaco), and Socony-Vacuum (Mobil), were, from 1947, the joint owners of Aramco, the company with exclusive rights to Saudi oil.

55. Lockman, *Comrades and Enemies*, 327, 331.

56. Testimony of Samuel Mikunis (secretary of the Communist Party of Palestine), to UN Special Committee on Palestine, public hearing, held at the Y.M.C.A. Building, Jerusalem, Palestine, 13 July 1947, UN General Assembly, A/364/Add.2 PV, http://unispal.un.org/unispal.nsf/0/77d468d8893712ce85256e83005fbc53?OpenDocument (accessed 3 January 2010).

57. Douglas Little, "Cold War and Covert Action: The United States and Syria, 1945–1958," *Middle East Journal* 44, no. 1 (Winter 1990): 55–56; Irene Gendzier, *Notes from the Minefield: United States Intervention in Lebanon, 1945–1958*, 2nd ed. (New York: Columbia University Press, 2006), 97–98.

58. Gendzier, *Notes from the Minefield*, 111–14, 131–32.

59. Irene C. Soltau, "Social Responsibility in the Lebanon," *International Affairs* 25, no. 3 (July 1949): 307–17; Elizabeth Thompson, *Colonial Citizens: Republican Rights, Paternal Privilege, and Gender in French Syria and Lebanon* (New York: Co-

lumbia University Press, 2000), 277–81; Malek Abisaab, "'Unruly' Factory Women in Lebanon: Contesting French Colonialism and the National State, 1940–1946," *Journal of Women's History* 16, no. 3 (2004): 55–82.

60. Na'im Amiouni [Amyuni], "A Short History of Our Pre-war and Post-war Economic Problems," 3 July 1946, cited in Gendzier's *Notes from the Minefield*, 48.

61. Gendzier, *Notes from the Minefield*, 47–48, 145.

62. Ibid., 112, 117.

63. Vitalis, *America's Kingdom*. See also Alexei Vassiliev, *The History of Saudi Arabia* (New York: New York University Press, 2000).

64. Ervand Abrahamian, *Iran between Two Revolutions* (Princeton: Princeton University Press, 1982); Fred Halliday, "Trade Unions and the Working Class Opposition," *MERIP Reports*, no. 71 (October 1978): 7–13.

65. Ervand Abrahamian, "The 1953 Coup in Iran," *Science and Society* 65, no. 2 (Summer 2001): 185–215.

66. Douglas Little, "Mission Impossible: The CIA and the Cult of Covert Action in the Middle East," *Diplomatic History* 28, no. 5 (2004): 663–701.

67. For an explanation of the currency mechanism, see Elliot Zupnick, "The Sterling Area's Central Pooling System Re-examined," *Quarterly Journal of Economics* 69, no. 1 (February 1955): 71–84. Egypt formally left the sterling area in 1947, hoping to convert its sterling balances, accumulated in London during the Second World War, into dollars. Britain responded by imposing restrictions on the convertibility of sterling. Raymond F. Mikesell, "Sterling Area Currencies of the Middle East," *Middle East Journal* 2, no. 2 (April 1948): 160–74.

68. Karl Polanyi, *The Great Transformation* (New York: Farrar & Rinehart, 1944), 20.

69. Standard economic histories typically ignore the question of oil. For example, Barry Eichengreen, in "The British Economy Between the Wars," in *The Cambridge Economic History of Modern Britain*, vol. 2, *Economic Maturity, 1860–1939*, ed. Rodrick Floud and Paul Johnson (Cambridge: Cambridge University Press, 2004), l. 2, makes no mention of oil.

70. Harry Dexter White, the chief architect of the two Bretton Woods institutions, the IMF and the World Bank, had argued for a third institution, an "international essential raw material development corporation" whose function would be "increasing the world supply of essential raw materials and assuring member countries of an adequate supply at reasonable prices." Harry Dexter White, "United Nations Stabilization Fund and a Bank for Reconstruction and Development of the United and Associated Nations," preliminary draft, March 1942, chap. 3, p. 30, Harry Dexter White Papers, 1920–55, Box 6, Folder 6, Public Policy Papers, Seeley G. Mudd Manuscript Library, Princeton.

71. Herbert Feis, "The Anglo-American Oil Agreement," *Yale Law Journal* 55, no. 5 (August 1946): 1174–90. Michael B. Stoff, "The Anglo-American Oil Agreement and the Wartime Search for Foreign Oil Policy," *Business History Review* 55, no. 1 (Spring 1981): 59–74.

72. Steven Gary Galpern, in "Britain, Middle East Oil, and the Struggle to Save Sterling, 1944–1971" (PhD diss., University of Texas, 2002), writes:

> In 1955, a paper prepared for the Working Party on the Treatment of Oil in the Balance of Payments, the Treasury and the Ministry of Fuel and Power wrote: "The international ramifications of the oil industry (including its tanker operations) are so large and so

complex as almost to constitute oil a currency in itself. Its size and complexity, and the fact that the fullest statistics are those relating to currency movements, and that any other basis of treatment would mean very substantial corrections in a Balance of Payments account, are, in our view, sufficient reasons for treating oil differently from other trade." (Pp. xix–xx, citing "Paper for the Working Party on the Treatment of Oil in the Balance of Payments," Note by the Treasury and Ministry of Fuel and Power, T.O.[55]2, 28 January 1955, T 277/506)

73. John Maynard Keynes, *The General Theory of Employment, Interest and Money* (London: Macmillan, 1936), 129.

74. On the peak of British coal production in the 1920s, see Ugo Bardi, "Peak Oil's Ancestor: The Peak of British Coal Production in the 1920s," *Newsletter of the Association for the Study of Peak Oil and Gas* 73 (January 2007): 5–7; M. Kirby, *The British Coalmining Industry, 1870–1946: A Political and Economic History* (Hamden, CT: Archon Books, 1977); Andrew Martin Neuman, *The Economic Organization of the British Coal Industry* (London: Routledge, 1934).

75. Jevons, *The Coal Question*. Jevons's son, H. Stanley Jevons, returned to the question of the exhaustion of coal reserves in *British Coal Trade*. He revised his father's estimate of the date of the possible exhaustion of British coal mines from one hundred years to "less then two hundred years" (756–57).

76. J. M. Keynes, "William Stanley Jevons, 1835–1882: A Centenary Allocation on His Life and Work as Economist and Statistician," *Journal of the Royal Statistical Society* 99, no. 3 (1936): 516–55; lecture delivered on 21 April 1936. Keynes mentions *The Coal Question* on p. 517.

77. Timothy Mitchell, "Fixing the Economy," *Cultural Studies* 12, no. 1 (1998): 82–101; idem, *Rule of Experts*; idem, "Economists and the Economy in the Twentieth Century," in *The Politics of Method in the Human Sciences: Positivism and Its Epistemological Others*, ed. George Steinmetz (Durham: Duke University Press, 2005), 126–41; and idem, "Culture and Economy," in *Handbook of Cultural Studies*, ed. Tony Bennett and John Frow (London: Sage Publications, 2008), 447–66.

78. François Denord, "Aux origines du néo-libéralisme en France: Louis Rougier et le Colloque Walter Lippmann de 1938," *Le mouvement social*, no. 195 (2001): 9–34.

79. As John Blundell noted:

Fifty years ago this summer [in 1955] a little book was published in London. It was entitled The Free Convertibility of Sterling and was authored by an experienced financial journalist George Winder. In the front, Antony Fisher wrote as director of the Institute of Economic Affairs, 'It [the book] is of vital concern to all those who are interested in their own freedom and the freedom of their country.' Henry Hazlitt gave the book a brilliant review in Newsweek on July 25th 1955 and all 2,000 sold out. One can make a very good case for saying this was the start of the free market public policy institute movement that today encircles the world. That little book did so well that Fisher was emboldened to approach a young economist named Ralph Harris. Harris in turn saw a chance to do good by challenging the post–World War II Keynesian consensus." (John Blundell, "IEA Turns 50: Celebrating Fisher Meeting Hayek," *Atlas Investor Report* [Spring 2005]: 6, http://www .atlasusa.org/V2/files/pdfs/2005_Spring_IR.pdf [accessed 3 January 2009])

80. The price of oil fell from $31 a barrel in 1920 to $9 in 1970 (in 2006 prices). The average price per decade also declined, from $18 per barrel in the 1920s to $15 in the 1930s and 1940s, $14 in the 1950s, and $12 in the 1960s. "BP Statistical Review of World Energy 2009," available at http://www.bp.com/IntermediateSearchAction.

do?url=http%3A%2F%2Fwww.bp.com%2Fliveassets%2Fbp_internet%2Fglobalbp%2
Fglobalbp_uk_english%2Freports_and_publications%2Fstatistical_energy_review_
2008%2FSTAGING%2Flocal_assets%2Fdownloads%2Fpdf%2Foil_table_proved_
oil_reserves_2008.pdf&kw=%E2%80%9CBP+Statistical+Review+of+World+Energy
+2007%2C%E2%80%9D&currentPage=1&scope=Site&resultNumber=1&type=sea
rch&Host=http://www.bp.com&homeId=1 (accessed 3 January 2010).

81. Geoffrey M. Heal and Partha S. Dasgupta, *Economic Theory and Exhaustible Resources* (Cambridge: Cambridge University Press, 1979), p. 1.

82. Herman Daly, *Steady-State Economics* (Washington, DC: Island Press, 1991), chap. 5.

83. This section summarizes a longer discussion in Timothy Mitchell's "The Resources of Economics: Making the 1973 Oil Crisis," *Journal of Cultural Economy* (in press).

84. Fred Block, *The Origins of International Economic Disorder: A Study of United States International Monetary Policy from World War II to the Present* (Berkeley: University of California Press, 1977), 164–202. Block makes no mention of the oil dimension of the crisis.

85. Bowden, "Social Construction of Validity."

86. In 1961 Iraq had reduced the concession area of the foreign-owned Iraq Petroleum Company (IPC) to the fields currently in production, in the Kirkuk region in the north. In 1969 Iraq signed an agreement with the Soviet Union to help develop oil production in the south and to build a pipeline to a new refinery on the Persian Gulf. When production from the new field began in April 1972, IPC cut its production at Kirkuk by 50%. The government nationalized IPC in June. Charles Tripp, *A History of Iraq*, 3rd ed. (Cambridge: Cambridge University Press, 2007), 200. James Bamberg, *British Petroleum and Global Oil, 1950–1975: The Challenge of Nationalism*, History of British Petroleum series, vol. 3 (Cambridge: Cambridge University Press, 2000), 163–71. Algeria had taken 51% control of its French-owned oil industry in February 1971, and Libya began to nationalize foreign-owned oil production in December 1971. Syria had nationalized its small oil industry in 1964.

87. V. H. Oppenheim, "Why Oil Prices Go Up (1): The Past; We Pushed Them," *Foreign Policy*, no. 25 (Winter 1976–77): 24–57. John M. Blair, *The Control of Oil* (New York: Pantheon Books, 1976); Simon Bromley, *American Hegemony and World Oil: The Industry, the State System and the World Economy* (University Park: Pennsylvania State University Press, 1991).

88. In *Global Energy Shifts*, Podobnik discusses the question of the differing types of expertise relating to coal and oil.

89. Gregory P. Nowell, *Mercantile States and the World Oil Cartel, 1900–1930* (Ithaca, NY: Cornell University Press, 1994).

90. Jonathan Nitzan and Shimshon Bichler, "The Weapondollar-Petrodollar Coalition," in *The Global Political Economy of Israel* (London: Pluto Press, 2002), 198–273.

91. Subsequent developments are discussed in Mitchell's "McJihad."

92. Retort [Iain Boal, T. J. Clark, Joseph Matthews, and Michael Watts], *Afflicted Powers: Capital and Spectacle in a New Age of War* (New York: Verso, 2005).

PART TWO

ARTIFICE

6.

John Krige

Techno-Utopian Dreams, Techno-Political Realities: The Education of Desire for the Peaceful Atom

> In order to obtain the full benefit of Western tech-
> nology through its cultural diffusion, Africans and
> Asians had first to free themselves from colonial rule
> and then—a more arduous task—learn to under-
> stand, and not just desire, the alien machinery.
> —Daniel Headrick, *The Tentacles of Progress*

On August 8, 1955, almost ten years to the day after the first atomic bombs had been dropped on Hiroshima and Nagasaki, an international conference on the peaceful uses of atomic energy got under way at the United Nations Building in Geneva, Switzerland.[1] It lasted until August 20 and was attended by about 1,400 delegates and the same number of observers from 73 countries, as well as some 900 journalists.[2] A large amount of recently declassified material on nuclear science and technology was made available for the first time by the major nuclear powers. More than 500 papers were presented by the U.S. delegation alone. They described the results of research in fields as diverse as reactor physics and engineering, nuclear chemistry, the biological effects of radiation, and the use of radioisotopes in medicine, agriculture, and industry.[3] In the words of one hardened British scientific observer, the conference in Geneva, "which started out as if it was going to be a dull and almost formal affair, was suddenly brought to life after about three days by the discovery that it was becoming the most momentous scientific occasion the post war world had ever seen."[4]

The excitement in Geneva was fueled by the freewheeling exchanges that marked a thaw in relationships between the United States and the Soviet Union ("It was not an unusual sight to see small groups having spirited conversations as they walked along the Rhone River at dusk").[5] But it was also born of the utopian conviction that a new age was dawning. In his presidential address that opened the conference, Homi J. Bhabha, Secretary to the Indian Department of Atomic Energy, emphasized the revolutionary potential of the power of the atom, its potential not simply to destroy but to improve the lives of millions. "The acquisition by man of the knowledge of how to release and use atomic energy must be recognized as the third great epoch in human history," said Bhabha. First there was muscle power, then chemical and mechanical work during the Industrial Revolution, and now the atom. "For the full industrialization of the under-developed areas, for the continuation of our civilization and its further development, atomic energy is not merely an aid; it is an absolute necessity," Bhabha enthused.[6] Here was a technological fix to the "lag" that was the curse of colonialism, the "quantum jump" that would propel the power-starved areas of the world to modernity.[7] Improvements in agriculture, industry, and medicine, but above all the production of cheap and abundant energy, would transform the surface of the globe. Everyone, even in a country as vast as India, would eventually be able *to reach a standard of living equivalent to the present US level*," as Bhabha put it.[8] A magnificent future for India lay dormant in the atom. Once unlocked, it would impose its telos and propel the country along the path of inevitable progress toward a utopian world of plenty. Science, and nuclear science in particular, was going "to authorize an enormous leap into modernity, and anchor the entire edifice of modern culture, identity, politics and the economy."[9]

Atoms for Peace had been formally launched by President Eisenhower in December 1953.[10] No single narrative can capture its many dimensions; nor is it easy to unravel the tangled skein of interconnected meanings that it had both in the United States and in the multitude of countries that used it as an opportunity to enter the nuclear age under the watchful eye of Washington and the International Atomic Energy Agency (IAEA), the most enduring institutional fruit of the initiative. That initiative has been characterized variously as a copybook example of cold war propaganda,[11] as a Marshall Plan for atomic energy,[12] as an instrument of informal intelligence gathering,[13] as an imperialist strategy to create export markets for American utility companies in the postcolonial world,[14] as a major contribution to the controlled spread of nuclear science and technology,[15] as a naive and misguided attempt to demilitarize a dual-use technology, and as a major factor in the proliferation of nuclear weapons.[16] In this chapter I parse it in a somewhat different register and think about Atoms for Peace in the mid-1950s as an exercise in the "education of desire."

To think about Atoms for Peace as the education of desire (at least for the non-nuclear states) is to put the body at the center of the analysis, that body that so preoccupied Bhabha.[17] That body had no time for anything but survival in an impoverished and power-starved region of the globe. The collective body was the object of Bhabha's modernist utopian project, a project that would unlock a "mass of desires whose realization [was] not beyond the capacity of man's present means of action on the material world, but only beyond the capacity of the old social organization."[18] For Bhabha, the atom would not only be a new source of energy for India. It would also be the bearer of a universal-izing ideology that would transcend social divisions and schisms, liberate bodily desires and pleasures, reshape the "needs" of his people in line with those liv-ing in the rich, industrialized West, free them from the shackles of poverty, and allow them to participate in the society of mass consumption.[19]

The joyful expression of creativity that is implicit in the celebration of de-sire is incompatible with the constraints imposed by the already-frozen con-tours of the imagined futures that characterize the modernizing project. De-sire needed to be educated if the utopian journey was to be within the realm of the possible. As Daniel Headrick reminds us, in an age of high technology, the atom could be exploited independently only by those who had the requi-site scientific, engineering, and industrial capacity. There is an asymmetry embedded in the transformative urge that drives modernization forward, an asymmetry that maps knowledge/power onto stratified structures of inclusion/exclusion, both locally and globally. The education of desire for the peaceful atom was not achieved by "diffusion," as Headrick would have it. It was pur-sued by deliberate policies of the hegemonic authority, the United States in this case, working along with fragments of local elites who shared its aims and helped implement its policies. Those policies subverted the openness of the utopian project and restricted the agency of those who were embarking along it. While promising to supply "energy too cheap to meter"—the words are those of Atomic Energy Commissioner Lewis Strauss in 1954[20]—the United States diverted resources and ambitions down paths that cohered with its for-eign policy agenda. The collective body that desired to reap the fruits of the peaceful atom was subjected to the same contradictory logic that infused the politics of sexual desire in the colonial project. It was lured by "the promise of new possibilities for desiring male subjects and objects for them." It was con-strained by "policies that simultaneously closed those possibilities down."[21] In fusing desire for the nuclear with education on how to exploit it, the United States held out the promise of a new world to come. But it also combined its technological leadership with economic incentives to channel the allure of the nuclear and to direct it down specific paths, paths that shrank the imag-ined future to a point that was aligned with Washington's policy objectives. The new possibilities and objects that were embraced by non-nuclear states through the education of desire emerged in a knowledge/power nexus that was inspired by the technological hubris and self-serving propaganda of the early proponents of nuclear energy and implemented through the foreign policy agendas of the superpowers.

As Gabrielle Hecht has pointed out, the dominant narrative surrounding Eisenhower's 1953 speech and the establishment of the IAEA in 1957 is one that privileges cold war politics. It fails to recognize that the techno-political regime that was put in place was also a product of decolonization politics.[22]

"We are engaged in a life and death struggle against the communist movement in which our principal hope lies in the earliest exploitation of [peacetime] nuclear power," wrote the assistant secretary of defense to Lewis Strauss.[23] The board responsible for psychological warfare in the Eisenhower administration saw nuclear power as the leaven that would quickly bring those "cultural, economic and social improvements" that were needed to propel the newly independent states of the "third world" away from the Soviet model of development.[24] This chapter deals with this neglected dimension of Atoms for Peace by focusing on those countries in which the United States, in competition with other nuclear powers, hoped to embed its nuclear technology. It first focuses on the international conference in Geneva in 1955, for it was here that Washington put on display a working reactor that was identical to the type that it hoped to implant abroad. This meeting had an enormous impact on national elites, both as a showcase for American technology and as a stimulus to its export policy. Indeed, in the words of one official historian of the Atomic Energy Commission (AEC), "if anything it [and its successor in 1958] did too good a job of encouraging small and developing nations to invest scarce resources in the nuclear power option."[25] What he neglects to say, as the second part of this chapter explains, is that that "option" locked clients into relationships of dependency on American technology and American industry. Atoms for Peace aimed to export an advanced technology to many countries that were "not yet ready to exploit its full potential as a means of getting both a technological and economic foothold" for U.S. industry.[26] This then is a case study of a hegemonic practice that at once stimulates desire and restricts the possibilities for its fulfillment, that educates desire as to the "appropriate" forms of its expression not in the realm of personal liberation and social revolution that inspired Guy Debord, nor in that of biopolitics that interests Ann Laura Stoler, but in the techno-political realm of the nuclear.

Promise and Promotion

On 8 December 1953, U.S. president Dwight D. Eisenhower rose to his feet before the General Assembly of the United Nations.[27] In the light of what seemed to be a new willingness by the Soviet Union to work toward mutual disarmament, the president suggested that the time had come for the major world powers to dedicate some of their strength "to serve the needs rather than the fears of mankind." He proposed that the United States and the USSR take steps to "make joint contributions from their stockpile of normal uranium and fissionable materials" to an international atomic energy agency. This agency would devise methods whereby this nuclear "bank" could be used to serve socially useful purposes, especially in agriculture and medicine. Above all, the fissile material would be used "to provide abundant electrical energy in the power-starved areas of the world." This was Atoms for Peace, and the assembled delegates greeted it with rapturous applause.

The AEC was a civilian agency whose prime responsibility was designing and producing nuclear weapons. In an age of nuclear fear it was also concerned to construct a public image that highlighted the peaceful atom and its social benefits. At first this was achieved by making reactor-produced radio-isotopes available for research in industry, agriculture, biology, and medicine.[28] The program was initially restricted to American soil. With some exceptions (for example, tritium), it was soon internationalized in response to pressure from scientists abroad and in the United States, even though the possible dangers to national security always bothered Commissioner Lewis Strauss, who at times stopped the distribution of isotopes to some foreign laboratories.[29] Eisenhower's initiative in Geneva in 1953 was a major advance on this practice in that it lifted restrictions on the international circulation of knowledge and technology related to the production of nuclear power.

The timing was not coincidental, and the administration's motivations were multiple.[30] The scheme was intended to divert attention away from the continued expansion of a lethal nuclear arsenal, as required by Eisenhower's New Look military doctrine. It was a weapon of "psychological warfare," an attempt to counter Soviet propaganda that claimed the United States was a fundamentally bellicose power bent on world domination. It did duty as an attempt to counter the negative fallout from the Castle series of hydrogen-bomb tests that began in March 1954 and that caused unexpected damage in the Marshall Islands and to the United States' image abroad: the world, worried Eisenhower, thinks that "we're skunks, saber-rattlers and warmongers." It was an attempt to divert raw materials away from Moscow's military program and to restrict nuclear "have-nots" to civilian atomic programs under international control. It was also intended to provoke an otherwise reluctant U.S. private industry into developing commercially viable atomic energy; to facilitate this, a less restrictive Atomic Energy Act was signed into law in August 1954. In sum, by "promoting wider nuclear cooperation under international verification of peaceful uses, Atoms for Peace marked the end of the postwar nuclear policy of secrecy and denial enshrined in the U.S. Atomic Energy Act of 1946 and provided the framework for future U.S. peaceful nuclear trade, cooperation and non-proliferation policies."[31] It shifted the balance in American nuclear policy since the war, which had been marked by a tussle between restrictive nationalism and revelatory internationalism, firmly in favor of the latter.[32]

The 1955 Geneva conference was planned to provide scientific legitimacy to the Atoms for Peace program, as a forum to put nuclear technology on display, and as a focal point for the circulation of nonsensitive information on civilian nuclear reactors and their socially useful applications, from power production to neutron therapy. A technology fair in downtown Geneva complemented the scientific meeting and the exhibitions located at the United Nations head-quarters on the shores of the lake.[33]

The centerpiece of the American exhibit at the meeting was a working swimming pool–type research reactor. The reactor was designed, built, and tested at the Oak Ridge National Laboratory, which was operated at the time for the AEC by the Union Carbide and Carbon Corporation. It was flown to Geneva from Knoxville, Tennessee, in two military air-transport service planes, where it arrived on 2 July 1955. Within a little over two weeks, it had been installed in its new temporary home. It went critical for the first time on July 18. As it happened, there was a major four-power conference in Geneva at the time. President Eisenhower took the opportunity to operate the reactor in the presence of about 150 news representatives and photographers. The press could actually see the control rods being moved to manage the chain reaction under the demineralized water that served as coolant, moderator, and radia-tion shield. Eisenhower told them that the United States had already signed twenty-four bilateral agreements with foreign governments, enabling them to acquire reactor technology. Two hundred kilograms of 20% enriched uranium (enough for a couple of dozen research reactors, and double the amount gen-erally spoken of a few months earlier) had been made available to enable other countries to enter the nuclear age. The president concluded his press statement by encouraging governments, industry, and "professional men" the world over to find new ways in which atomic science could be used "for the benefit of mankind and not destruction."[34]

About sixty-three thousand people visited the reactor during the sixteen days it was open for viewing. Visitors approached the display via a ramp lined with exhibits explaining the multiple uses of a research reactor, paused to peer into the depths of the reactor core, and exited through a corridor lined with a further set of instructional panels. A variety of devices were deliberately de-ployed to replace fear with awe, ignorance with information, danger with do-mesticity, the bellicose with the benign.

The first notable feature of the display is the site itself: the reactor was in-stalled in the grounds of the United Nations Building, less than a mile from the downtown area. Here it nestled not in a concrete bunker but in a low structure measuring fifty by eighty feet, covered with stained redwood and a shed roof. The Atoms for Peace emblem adorned its facade.[35] Occupying a building that suggested a homely Swiss chalet rather than a secured bunker, the reactor was domesticated and semantically reinterpreted as a nonhazard-ous research tool.

The familiarity of the everyday was mingled with visual representations of the mysterious powers locked in the nucleus. Underwater lights illuminated the pool when the reactor was not operating. Every fifteen minutes during tours, they were turned off, and the reactor was slowly brought to criticality. As the control rods were removed further and its power climbed to one hundred kilowatts, the entire pool was bathed in an eerie bluish green glow (the so-called Cerenkov radiation).[36] Capitalizing fully on the beauty, a color photograph of the reactor core "when the Cerenkov effect was at its height" adorned the cover of the forty-five thousand brochures describing the reactor that were distributed to visitors in the four official languages of the conference.[37]

The hazards of radiation were managed by persuading the anxious that "respect, not fear, was the key to working safely with radiation."[38] The active core of the reactor was 16.5 feet below the surface of the pool—enough "shielding" (it was claimed) to reduce the radiation at floor level to a quarter of the intensity of that given off by a radium-dial wristwatch. A panel in the exhibit stressed that "radiation could be detected through the use of proper instruments, and that personnel could be protected through proper precaution." It included pictures of "standard items of laboratory wear, such as coveralls, shoe covers, gas masks, cotton and rubber gloves," along with a selection of radiation-detection instruments including Geiger and scintillation counters, pocket dosimeters, and film badges.

The homely, benign atom was not simply a symbol of scientific and technological progress; it was also a source of social good. One panel described some of the possibilities, from education in reactor design and nuclear research to biomedical applications, including the use of tracers to identify the location of tumors.[39] Another stressed the importance of radioisotopes for use in agriculture, medicine, and industry and gave a brief technical account of how to use a reactor for this purpose. Many of these themes were elaborated on in detail in additional panels.

In many respects the American display at Geneva was typical of any world's fair that staged science and technology: it was intended to reinforce "social and political trends, creating empathy for order and progress, industrial society and modernity."[40] Before the Second World War, popularizing efforts such as those in Chicago in 1933–34 ("Science discovers, industry applies, man conforms") and in Paris in 1937 (Le Palais de la Découverte) consciously embodied the interests of the scientific community and sought to justify the social value of disinterested research (and its entitlement to funding). After Hiroshima and Nagasaki, there was a deliberate effort to detach the atom from the horrors of war and to confirm it and science in general as forces for progress and social benefit. Oak Ridge, which had played a key role in producing raw material for the bomb dropped on Hiroshima, opened the American Museum of Atomic Energy in 1949. The museum's mission was "to serve as an exhibition and education center for advocating the peaceful uses of atomic energy."[41] Similarly, the Festival of Britain, which opened in May 1951, emphasized the positive, peaceful uses of the atom and simply ignored the military dimension.[42] As the cold war got into stride, this systematic bias in the representation of the nuclear was amplified by being situated at the core of superpower rivalry: world fairs became the battleground for displays of superior scientific and technological prowess between the Soviet Union and the United States.

The American exhibit in Geneva in 1955 shared several features of this genre. It was intended to persuade the public to dissociate the atom from the bomb and to see the tamed nucleus as a benign tool that was both an essential source of energy and a flexible research instrument of immense social benefit. It certainly upstaged the Soviets. They were actually ahead of the United States in developing an electricity-generating nuclear power station, but they sent only a model of their reactor to Geneva. Piqued, they hastily organized an international atomic energy conference of their own in Moscow the month before the Geneva meeting.[43] Those who came—and one Indian visitor noted that "countries receiving the Marshall aid were conspicuous by their absence"—were taken on a guided tour of the Soviet facility.[44] But the American display had another crucial function: it was an instrument for the education of desire, a tool intended to urge enthusiastic visitors from states that did not already have a nuclear program to embark on one with American help.

Access to the reactor was restricted. For seven hours a day, six days a week, only official conference delegates were allowed to enter the chalet. A couple of days before the meeting started, Lewis Strauss sent a letter to the heads of the seventy-three national delegations represented at the conference and of the eight specialized agencies. They were asked to name those in their entourage who wished to have an individual showing of the exhibit. These delegates were also invited "to operate the reactor. For many delegates," the official U.S. report of the meeting stated, "it was the first time they had ever seen a reactor," let alone brought one up to power.[45] By targeting members of the delegations specifically chosen for a private viewing, Strauss ensured that the United States had a list of key contact points in foreign countries that could be exploited when the conference was over.

Visual display and hands-on operation were supplemented by thousands of pages of scientific and technical information.[46] The United States provided all delegations with a handsome boxed eight-volume set of reference material.[47] Four volumes dealt with the physics, engineering, and materials of reactors for power generation and for research. One contained an eight-year summary of isotope work. Volume 8, *Information Sources*, listed hundreds of scientific titles describing "the vital foundation upon which present power-reactor development in the United States is proceeding"; it was a comprehensive guide to all relevant declassified material.[48] This volume also included a list of the more than 6,500 technical reports and over 50,000 abstracts that dealt with nuclear science and technology that the AEC was putting together in a standard depository library. One such library had been installed in the UN Building for the use of conference delegates. Eisenhower wrote a dedication for the introductory volume ("The atom cannot be limited by national boundaries"); Strauss wrote a preface ("It is our sincere hope that this material will be of practical value to the men and women of science and engineering in whom the great power of the atom is becoming a benign force for world peace"). Not to be outdone, the Soviet Union placed two bound sets of the proceedings of their July 1955 conference in the library, along with several technical books in Russian.[49] A few years earlier, Homi Bhabha had written to his homologue in the United States offering to barter Indian thorium and uranium for "all declassified information on reactor theory, design and technology," and on how to operate a reactor; he was rebuffed by the AEC.[50] Now he, and anyone who sought it, had unrestricted access to a copious amount of scientific and technical literature that had been put in the public domain by the American authorities.

The other great need of those who wanted to enter the nuclear field—trained personnel who could gradually assume responsibility for a local, "independent" program—was also catered for. Many American universities (Columbia, MIT, Michigan, Tennessee) had programs in nuclear science and engineering. The AEC complemented these with its own educational program. Beginning in 1950, Oak Ridge established a school of reactor technology that offered a one-year course to students who had at least a bachelor's degree and showed outstanding academic potential.[51] Oak Ridge, along with the Brookhaven National Laboratory and other centers, also trained health physicists who were "responsible for radiation control and monitoring beyond the routine stage" and "for radiation protection in the university, hospital, small industrial plant or laboratory." Finally, Oak Ridge also took responsibility for the intensive training of scientists in how to handle radioactive isotopes, finding that the traditional university courses on offer were "not rapid enough to introduce these tools into the many areas in which they could be applied."

Before 1955, foreign students were seldom, if ever, admitted to these various courses; over a period of six years, only one hundred out of almost two thousand received training in handling radioisotopes, for example, even though the United States had long since put in place an important international distribution network.[52] Atoms for Peace changed all that. In May 1955 Oak Ridge held a special course on radioisotope techniques for non-U.S. students and hoped to repeat the exercise later that year to meet demand. The International School of Nuclear Science and Engineering was established at Argonne National Laboratory in 1955 "primarily to help carry out the intent of the President's Atoms-for-Peace Program." Within a couple of years it had graduated a hundred students, sixty-nine of them from twenty-eight foreign countries.[53] Eisenhower placed much store by these training programs that were so crucial to disseminating nuclear science. At the press conference at the site in Geneva two weeks before the conference, he made a point of telling the assembled gathering that students from many countries were being trained in the United States in reactor science and in how to handle radioisotopes.[54] To consolidate the point, the last panel at the exhibit, the goal on which all converged as it were, "summarized the uses of a pool-type reactor, and featured a montage of photographs taken at the Oak Ridge School of Reactor Technology, the Argonne National Laboratory, and elsewhere. Included were a series of typical graphs obtained by students during the course of instruction."[55] Between 1955 and 1974—the year of its first nuclear weapons test—India sent more than eleven hundred scientists and engineers to be trained at Argonne and other U.S. facilities.[56]

Atoms for Peace was calculated to enable every developing country to enter the nuclear age, to embark on the sure path to modernization. The immense attention paid in Geneva to education through visual representation, hands-on experience, and published technical literature was not directed primarily at the existing nuclear powers, of course; it was largely produced by the United States (along with Britain and France) for those who aspired to a civilian nuclear capability.[57] It is reminiscent of the exhibitions put on for peasants by the British in colonial India, where water lifts, irrigation pumps, and modern dairy machinery represented in one movement the superiority of rational, Western culture and the importance of science and technology as instruments of improvement.[58] The target audience in Geneva was not the peasant or even the "educated layman." It was competent scientists, budding engineers, and ambitious technocrats. Indeed, according to Gerald Tape, the deputy director of Brookhaven National Laboratory for eleven years and a member of the AEC from 1963 to 1969, Atoms for Peace attracted some of the best scientists and engineers from both the developed and the developing nations. Countries that had previously shown little interest in science and technology responded to the utopian promise of the peaceful atom. It not only helped educate people in the science and technology but also taught them about "organization, training, infrastructure, working together, and other useful aspects of major undertakings. High government officials in science, education and foreign service often got their start through the Atoms for Peace program in their own country," says Tape. This helped them to "break away from conventional paths" and to inject "new insights" into their national administrations.[59] In short, the "civilizing mission" was never far below the surface of the conference in Geneva, where the United States made a major effort to educate an elite and to co-opt them as local nodes for the proliferation of American nuclear technology in their own "power-starved" regions of the globe.

The scientific meeting in 1955 was just one element of what Kenneth Osgood has called a "carefully orchestrated psychological warfare campaign [that] was, in every sense of the word, massive in scope." Indeed, "Atoms for Peace was quite possibly the largest single propaganda campaign ever conducted by the American government," and it involved virtually every arm of the administration.[60] Eisenhower's speech to the United Nations in 1953 was broadcast live in more than thirty languages on Voice of America, and films of the event were dispatched to thirty-five countries. The United States Information Agency

(USIA) published pamphlets on the speech in seventeen languages and distributed more than sixteen million posters and booklets drawing attention to it.[61] The theme of the peaceful uses of atomic energy became a top priority for the agency in every country of the world, where it was disseminated through a series of twenty-six television films and dozens of documentary-style short films with titles such as *The Atom and Agriculture*.[62] The USIA also organized traveling Atoms for Peace exhibits intended to "bring the idea of peaceful atomic energy for the first time to the immediate consciousness of the lay viewer." Working models, colorful displays, short films, and lectures were intended to give visitors the impression that "the future of atomic energy rested with the United States," and thousands came: 188,000 in Frankfurt, about 196,000 in Buenos Aires, almost 136,000 in Ghana, and 155,000 in Kyoto.[63]

Atoms for Peace has been associated with the trope of American imperialism, just as the Green Revolution that followed it a decade later has been described as engaging "a new type of imperialism" based on "specialized knowledge generously given to backward peoples."[64] This language must be used with care, even if, or precisely because, it is currently fashionable and often serves as little more than a metaphor for American pretensions to global supremacy.[65] Analytically, it obscures the multiple strategies, including education, training, and propaganda, that the United States used to co-opt, rather than to coerce, national elites into sharing its nuclear priorities in the 1950s. It also fails to recognize that some countries, notably India, were determined to maintain an independent nuclear program and successfully resisted American approaches until the mid-1960s. Indeed, the imbalance in scientific and technological power between the United States and many of its clients for nuclear knowledge and equipment in this period is best compared to that between America and Western Europe in the late 1940s. Put differently, it is more instructive to think of Atoms for Peace as a Marshall Plan than as an imperialist adventure. The American promotion of the peaceful atom was not imposed; nor was it maintained by force. It was implemented through a regime that was built and sustained with the collaboration of local elites who desired the nuclear and who circulated between their home countries and the United States. Members of those elites were targeted at Geneva in 1955. Hundreds of them drew inspiration and information from the declassified material that the United States put in the public domain and the training schemes that it, and other nuclear powers, put in place. The social capital acquired along with their knowledge was reinforced by the conviction that science and technology were crucial tools for transforming their "backward" economies. Their domestic authority and political power were legitimated by the massive and immensely popular propaganda campaign launched by the USIA, the Voice of America, and other arms of the Eisenhower administration in their countries. For those who could take advantage of it, Atoms for Peace was not an imperial project; it was an exercise in "consensual hegemony."[66] For those whose utopian "expectations of modernity" foundered for lack of domestic political, financial, or technical support, Atoms for Peace served as a cruel reminder of the agendas that underpinned Western concepts and strategies of "development," and it forced them to redefine their horizons of possibility in line with local histories and contingencies.[67]

Distribution and Control

The education of desire was not designed simply to inform and inspire; it was also intended to orient its targets in line with American business and foreign policy interests in the region and to lock them into those relationships. Medhurst reminds us that "if U.S. industry could be the first to establish a nuclear presence in the various countries, those countries would almost inevitably be dependent upon the U.S. for design, construction, initial operation, educational materials and every other aspect of the infant industry." More to the point, once established, "the U.S. technology would be difficult, if not, impossible, to supplant."[68] The promotion of the peaceful atom in Geneva was, from this point of view, part of a deliberate policy both to stimulate techno-utopian dreams and to confine the techno-political possibilities through which they could be realized.

A brief technical detour is required if we are to grasp how the program served to channel aspirations and scarce resources down paths that cohered with American interests.[69] First, some basics. Naturally occurring uranium contains two major isotopes. Uranium-238, the most abundant (99.29%), is not fissionable (that is, it cannot disintegrate to release the power locked in its nucleus).[70] The other naturally occurring isotope of uranium, U-235 (abundance 0.71%), is, however, fissionable. Although U-238 cannot be a source of energy, it can be transformed into plutonium-239, which is also fissionable. The bomb dropped on Hiroshima used highly enriched uranium as a fuel (that is, uranium in which the weight fraction of U-235 had been increased, using complex technological processes on an industrial scale, to about 90%); that which devastated Nagasaki used plutonium.

After the war, several major industrial nations immediately embarked on nuclear programs. Britain, Canada, and France chose to use natural uranium for their reactors, relying on the fission of the small amount of U-235 and of the Pu-239 that was produced in the reactor for energy production. This relatively inefficient path was followed because of their wish to situate themselves rapidly at the forefront of the nuclear powers without making the huge financial and industrial investments required to enrich uranium or to produce plutonium (though the British did bring a weapons-dedicated plutonium production facility online in 1954). The United States, by contrast, already had the production plants for enriched uranium and plutonium available thanks to the wartime Manhattan Project, which produced the bombs dropped on Japan. Once the immediate postwar policy debates over the future shape and mission of the AEC had been settled, these facilities were recommissioned.

At first it was widely believed that to fuel these programs it was imperative to control the worldwide deposits of uranium and thorium.[71] It was assumed that these raw materials were scarce and that access to them had to be restricted to retain an American, or at least Western, monopoly over the exploitation of the atom. A landmark agreement between the governments of Britain, Canada, and the United States in November 1945 (the Groves-Anderson memorandum) committed the three nations to "secure control and possession, by purchase or otherwise, of all deposits" of the two materials on the territories or possessions of the three countries, and also to use "every endeavor" to acquire all available supplies from the members of the British Commonwealth and other countries.[72] The inauguration of a French nuclear program—its first small nuclear pile went critical in December 1948—and the explosion of the Soviet atomic bomb in August 1949, followed by the British bomb in 1952, demonstrated conclusively that the American nuclear monopoly was irreversibly over.

With its monopoly broken, Washington's aim now was to maintain leadership and domination by containing both vertical proliferation (that is, expanding nuclear arsenals within the weapons states, notably the Soviet Union) and horizontal proliferation (that is, the spread of nuclear weapons to countries that did not already have them, notably in the developing world).[73] To contain vertical proliferation, Eisenhower, in his speech of December 1953, proposed that both superpowers donate "x" kilograms of fissionable material from their stockpiles to the United Nations, to be used for peaceful purposes. The figure x was deliberately calculated to seriously retard the Soviet nuclear program while having a negligible impact on the buildup of Washington's nuclear arsenal. If Moscow refused to collaborate, the Soviets would look like warmongers; if the Kremlin accepted, the Soviets would be forced to slow down their nuclear buildup.[74] To contain horizontal proliferation, the United States signed bilateral agreements with countries that had nuclear ambitions, especially those with access to important uranium and thorium deposits. They offered uranium enriched to 20% in the U-235 isotope, and the associated nuclear reactor technology, in return for control over access to the deposits. The aim was to deprive rival powers of the basic raw materials, to secure a market niche that America's competitors could not match with their natural uranium devices, and to curb nuclear proliferation by offering a degree of enriched fuel that was just below the useful threshold for producing a weapon, along with a system of inspections and safeguards to ensure that it was not abused.[75]

The reactor installed in Geneva has to be situated in this technical, commercial, and strategic context. Union Carbide and Carbon developed the swimming pool–type reactor for the exhibit specifically "to demonstrate a type of research reactor which nations could expect to build under Bilateral Agreements of Cooperation with the United States, using uranium enriched to 20% in the fissionable 235 isotope—the type of fuel the United States had pledged to contribute to an international pool."[76] It also went out of its way in the exhibit to "show that an efficient working reactor can be designed, constructed, and operated in complete safety without elaborate preparations or complicated facilities."[77] The aim, of course, was dissemination. Its "ease of operation, low cost and inherently safe characteristics" had ensured its popularity in the United States, wrote Union Carbide. Pennsylvania State College, the University of Michigan, the Batelle Memorial Institute, and Vanderbilt University were all clients.[78] Now the next step was being taken. "Operation of this reactor in Switzerland should encourage other nations to engage in the peaceful development of atomic energy," the company suggested.

These words had weight for those who attended the conference. The mobility of the technology was proven by the ease and speed with which it had been brought from Tennessee, installed and rendered operational in Geneva within a fortnight. Its safety was confirmed by its proximity to the city. Its peaceful intent was symbolized by locating it in the grounds of the United Nations Building and reinforced by its installation in neutral Switzerland. What is more, on the last day of the conference, August 20, the reactor was formally transferred to the Swiss authorities, who paid $180,000 for it, "a greatly reduced price" for "the first nuclear reactor ever sold by one nation to another."[79] The Swiss would dismantle it and reinstall it just outside Zurich. The performance suggested that *anyone* could set up and operate the swimming pool–type reactor that had been put on show in Geneva, and it hinted at financial assistance for those who bought the American product.

In the two months leading up to the Geneva conferences, the AEC formalized more than a dozen bilateral agreements, beginning with Turkey (10 June 1955) and ending with Pakistan (11 August 1955). Partners included technologically backward NATO members (Greece and Turkey), Middle Eastern neighbors (Israel and Lebanon), and four countries in Latin America (Argentina, Brazil, Chile, and Venezuela). Some were overt political statements: China/Taiwan was one recipient. Mainland China was not, of course.

In the standard form of this agreement, the United States' partner was committed to pursuing a "research and development program looking toward the realization of the peaceful and humanitarian uses of atomic energy."[80] Washington would provide uranium enriched up to a maximum of 20% in U-235 for research reactors. No more than six kilograms of such material would be provided for the initial operation and replacement. Reactors would be refurbished at the discretion of the AEC "to permit the efficient and continuous operation of the reactor or reactors while replaced fuel elements [were] radioactively cooling" in the recipient country, "or while fuel elements [were] in transit" back to the United States, who had the facilities to reprocess them.

The hope was that the research reactor would be just the first phase of a fully fledged nuclear power program, and that "this initial Agreement of Cooperation [would] lead to consideration of further cooperation extending to the design, construction and operation of power producing reactors." In short, the partner was both dependent on the United States for enriched fuel and encouraged to see a research reactor as the first step toward the acquisition of a nuclear energy program built with American help and by American companies. The AEC maintained control over the fuel cycle to ensure that no material was diverted to a weapons program, or third party.

The choice of partners was shaped by a combination of foreign policy and geopolitical considerations, along with the determination to leave an American footprint on nations that had supplies of raw material. Take the case of Spain. This agreement was a response to the Franco regime's interest in developing a nuclear program. It was symptomatic of an improvement in the relations between Washington and Madrid that began with the entry of the country into the UN in 1950 and the signing of an important agreement for mutual military assistance in 1953.[81] Spain had valuable uranium deposits and established its own Nuclear Energy Board (Junta de Energiá Nuclear [JEN]) in October 1951. In 1954 it took concrete steps to produce uranium bars on a semi-industrial scale from deposits in the Sierra Morena while building its own zero-power reactor using Spanish natural uranium as fuel. In July 1955 Spain and the United States signed the standard bilateral agreement regarding the civil uses of atomic energy. JEN's first 3MW swimming pool–type reactor came into operation in October 1958. It was fueled with American enriched uranium, not Spanish natural uranium. It was constructed with American technological assistance and American economic aid (basic parts worth half of the $350,000 bill for the total cost of the reactor were provided free). In the words of its chroniclers, "During JEN's first two decades, at least, there is no doubt that this . . . agency which controlled the entire Spanish nuclear development program . . . was completely dependent on the supplies, materials and know-how of the United States."[82]

Key provisions in the standard agreement were waived for historical allies. Belgium, for example, was a major supplier of uranium to the United States from its mines in Katanga. It continued to be a "vitally important" supplier to Britain and the United States after the war. In recognition of this, the bilateral agreement signed with Brussels allowed for U.S. assistance to move beyond research reactors and to proceed immediately with the construction of power reactors in Belgium and its colonies (the Belgian Congo and Ruanda-Urundi). Belgian scientists and engineers were permitted, after security clearances, to participate in the construction and operation of the first American civilian power reactor at Shippingport, Pennsylvania. In fact, by 1958 the Belgians were in a position to build an 11,500-kilowatt power reactor, in collaboration with the United States, for the world's fair to be held in Brussels that year.[83] In return for this accelerated entry into the atomic age, the Belgian government agreed "not to transfer to any country other than the United States or the United Kingdom any special nuclear materials produced in Belgium, the Belgian Congo or Ruanda-Urundi unless the Government of Belgium is given assurance that the material will not be used for military purposes."[84]

Like Belgium, the United Kingdom and Canada also maintained a fair degree of independence in their bilateral agreements with the United States. So too did Euratom, formally established by the Treaties of Rome in 1957. Eisenhower was particularly invested in this agreement. He saw Euratom as promoting European integration along with bodies such as NATO and the Common Market and dreamed of an eventual United States of Europe. American industry was also engaged, in the belief that the high costs of electricity in Europe provided an economic window of opportunity for nuclear power plants abroad. For their part, the Europeans were willing to give firm guarantees that fissionable material and nuclear technology imported from the United States would be used only for peaceful purposes. They refused to allow either the United States or the IAEA to have direct safeguards inspections over their installations, however.[85]

It would be wrong to see the United States as dominating the nuclear power market outside the Soviet bloc. True, until the first half of the 1970s, American suppliers had more than 90% of the reactor export market and 100% of the enrichment market.[86] India, however, was one of the countries that managed to build its nuclear capacity without being locked into one major supplier.[87] This was partly because of Homi Bhabha's determination to strike the best deal he could, both technically and economically, with those who wooed him. India had important deposits of uranium and thorium, which he could use both as a bargaining chip in his dealings with Western powers and as the raw material for an indigenous reactor program. However, Bhabha knew that it would take a decade or two to build up a national scientific and engineering capability. Concessions to full autonomy had to be made. In September 1954 he thus jumped at the offer from Sir John Cockroft, the head of Britain's Atomic Energy Research Establishment, to provide India with a small 1MW research reactor using slightly enriched fuel, something that could be "set up in a very short time," as Bhabha told Cockroft, "so we have something to work with while our other plans mature."[88] Then at the meeting in Geneva in August 1955, he accepted the Canadian offer of a 40MW version of Canada's NRX reactor, which had been developed at Chalk River, Ontario, and formed the basis of the successful CANDU series of reactors. In 1960 India called for tenders for a power reactor system, and both Canada and, for the first time, the United States were awarded contracts.

India's decision to choose an American system that used 20% enriched uranium—which only Washington could supply, and which was subject to inspection—not only subverted a major policy enounced by Bhabha in 1958, which stated that India's nuclear future would be based on natural uranium. It was also orthogonal to India's spirited insistence in negotiations in the IAEA that the safeguards being called for by the Americans were an unacceptable violation of national sovereignty.[89] Further, it was a "turnkey" project, which restricted the transfer of knowledge and technology from the United States to India. Technological and economic arguments, along with an improved climate in U.S.-Indian relationships were central to the deal.[90] The AEC, along with representatives of General Electric and Westinghouse, persuaded the Indian authorities that reactors using enriched fuel were cheaper to build and operate. India was also given an $80 million loan from the Export-Import Bank (for ten years longer than the duration of the contract), at an interest rate of 0.75%.[91] When Bertrand Goldschmidt asked Bhabha why India had chosen an American reactor rather than a French one using unenriched fuel, Bhabha reputedly told him that the best reactor was "the one that one did not have to pay for."[92]

A footnote. In 1974 India conducted its first atomic weapons test using plutonium, some of which had been produced in the 40MW research reactor provided by Canada. The blueprints for the plant built to separate out the plutonium were provided by an American firm. For many observers the Indian test was conclusive proof of the incoherence of a policy that drove an imaginary wedge between atoms for peace and atoms for war and that hoped to contain horizontal weapons proliferation by sharing nuclear technology for putatively civilian purposes only.[93]

Concluding Remarks

Technology . . . is a type of rhetoric, an argument in the form of an object. . . . The political effects of a technology derive not primarily from the motivations behind its inception, but from the way the artifact is used to reveal and circumscribe the universe of priorities and possibilities.

The United States' insatiable appetite for nuclear material, and its determination to do all that it could to control the sources from which it came, were simply a reflection of the massive expansion of its nuclear stockpile that went along with, and was shielded from view by, the promotion of the peaceful atom.[94] During Eisenhower's presidency, the United States' nuclear stockpile increased from 1,436 nuclear warheads in 1953 to 24,173 warheads in 1961.[95] Indeed, in Martin Medhurst's view, Eisenhower's willingness to increase the amount of enriched uranium made available to the international pool for civilian purposes—from 100 kilograms to 200 kilograms in 1955, to 40,000 kilograms by 1956—simply indicated the "superabundance of materials already in the weapons stockpile."[96] As Spencer Weart has pointed out, the USAEC spent less than 10% of its budget on civilian uses in the mid-1950s. The much-vaunted use of radioisotopes, presented as one of the key social advantages of having a small research reactor, "relied upon a stock of isotopes that could have been stored in a closet," whereas the nuclear industry was dealing with uranium-235 and plutonium "by the ton."[97] Countries that desired the peaceful atom in return for supplying raw materials to the United States both legitimated the nonmilitary rhetoric that saturated the program and fueled that asymmetry in power—economic, political, and military—that placed them in a situation of semipermanent dependence on Washington. Indeed, for almost two decades the United States dominated the development and commercialization of nuclear technology through the supply of research reactors and power reactors, training in nuclear science and engineering, and the provision of enrichment and reprocessing facilities.

The swimming pool–type reactor in the U.S. exhibit in Geneva was an essential component of a strategy intended to educate the desire of elites determined to modernize their nations and persuaded that the path to development was paved with nuclear power. Together with formal training sessions, bilateral agreements, and economic incentives, it helped to fill out their imagined futures. At the same time, by locking them into an enriched uranium fuel cycle, it "circumscribed their universe of possibilities and priorities" and guided their aspirations and their limited resources down a particular nuclear path. That path cohered with the interests of U.S. foreign policy, ensured Washington access to nuclear raw materials, and ultimately benefited American business. By the early 1950s Washington realized that not only its allies Britain, France, and Canada but the Soviet Union too were ahead in the development of civilian nuclear power. The security restrictions surrounding the development of a reactor for a nuclear submarine, and the reluctance of corporations such as General Electric and Westinghouse to invest in a technology that was difficult and dangerous, and whose economic success was anything but assured, was leaving the field open to America's political and commercial rivals. The demand bubbling up from fractions of national elites who identified the nuclear with national independence and national prestige, with "progress" and "modernization," had to be met. Drastic action was needed, and drastic action was taken—in the form of the Atoms for Peace program. It replaced refusal and denial with cooperation and sharing. But it also channeled resources and dictated technological choices. Gerald Tape has pointed out that one of the three main objectives of Atoms for Peace was to limit horizontal proliferation through cooperation with, and international control of, civil nuclear programs. These would divert resources away from autonomous national programs that could easily harbor military ambitions.[98] What he did not say was that this deliberate attempt to restrict the scope of national nuclear programs to an agenda decided in advance by the major nuclear powers, and to demand of them a transparency and legibility that were not reciprocal, would inevitably be seen by some states as a violation of their national sovereignty and as a new form of imperialism to be resisted.

In a farewell statement at Princeton University in November 2006, the outgoing UN secretary-general Kofi Annan chose as his main theme "the danger of nuclear weapons, and the urgent need to confront that danger by preventing proliferation and promoting disarmament, both at once."[99] Atoms for Peace was intended to achieve those objectives, but with a systematic bias toward the United States and its Western European allies. Fifty years later that asymmetry is no longer tenable, and if it is not reversed, there is the gravest danger that the now-faded utopian dreams of the peaceful atom will be obliterated by the now-menacing dystopic nightmare of a nuclear conflagration.

Notes

1. I thank Angela Creager, Alex Glaser, Gabrielle Hecht, Zia Mann, and Tim Stoneman for helpful comments on an earlier draft of this chapter. The epigraph is by Daniel R. Headrick, *The Tentacles of Progress: Technology Transfer in the Age of Imperialism, 1850–1940* (New York: Oxford University, 1988), 16.

2. Laura Fermi, *Atoms for the World: United States Participation in the Conference on the Peaceful Uses of Atomic Energy* (Chicago: University of Chicago Press, 1957), 2. Fermi, the widow of Enrico Fermi, was enrolled to write the official history of the meeting on behalf of the U.S. delegation.

3. In all, there were sixteen volumes of conference proceedings. The names of the participants and the main topics covered are in *Proceedings of the International Conference on the Peaceful Uses of Atomic Energy, Held in Geneva, 8 August–20 August 1955,* vol. 16, *Record of the Conference* (New York: United Nations, 1956).

4. Geminus [pseud.], "It Seems to Me," *New Scientist,* September 4, 1955, 742.

5. "Background of the Geneva Conference," undated and unsigned report, pp. 6–7, Folder 7, Box 55, Rabi Papers, Library of Congress, Washington, DC. The Rhone is the river that flows out of Lake Geneva.

6. *Record of the Conference,* 31, 33. For an analysis of Bhabha's opening speech, see Itty Abraham, *The Making of the Indian Atomic Bomb* (London: Zed Press, 1998), 98–102.

The utopian potential of the atom was stressed from the moment the atomic bomb flattened two Japanese cities, and it was part of the rhetoric justifying its use; thus Bhabha echoes Truman's message to Congress in October 1945. The energy in the atom, said the president, heralded "a new era in the history of civilization" that "may some day prove more revolutionary in the development of human society than the invention of the wheel, the use of metals, or the steam or internal combustion engines." Message to Congress, 3 October 1945, in *Memoirs by Harry S. Truman,* vol. 1, *Year of Decisions* (Garden City, NY: Doubleday, 1955), 530.

7. For the idea that this was a quantum jump, see Marcelo Alonso, "The Impact in Latin America," in *Atoms for Peace: An Analysis after Thirty Years,* ed. Joseph F. Pilat, Robert E. Pendley, and Charles K. Ebinger (Boulder: Westview Press, 1985), 85. This

rhetoric was also used during the Green Revolution. Robert F. Chandler, director of the International Rice Research Institute in the Philippines in the 1960s, was not interested in making incremental improvements to existing strains of rice; he went for the "big jump." See Nick Cullather, "Miracles of Modernization: The Green Revolution and the Apotheosis of Technology," *Diplomatic History* 28, no. 2 (April 2004): 239.

8. Homi J. Bhabha, "The Role of Atomic Power in India and Its Immediate Possibilities," in *Proceedings, Geneva 1955*, vol. 1, *The World's Requirements for Energy: The Role of Nuclear Energy* (New York: United Nations, 1956), 106; emphasis in the original.

9. Gyan Prakash, *Another Reason: Science and the Imagination of Modern India* (Oxford: Oxford University Press, 1999), 12.

10. For a more comprehensive account, including references, see John Krige, "Atoms for Peace, Scientific Internationalism and Scientific Intelligence," in *Osiris*, ed. John Krige and Kai-Henrik Barth, vol. 21, *Global Power Knowledge: Science and Technology in International Affairs* (Chicago: University of Chicago Press, 2006), 161–81.

11. Kenneth Osgood, *Total Cold War: Eisenhower's Secret Propaganda Battle at Home and Abroad* (Lawrence: University Press of Kansas, 2006), chap. 5.

12. James R. Schlesinger, "Atoms for Peace Revisited," in *Atoms for Peace*, ed. Pilat, Pendley, and Ebinger, 5.

13. John Krige, "Atoms for Peace, Scientific Internationalism and Scientific Intelligence," in *Global Power Knowledge*, ed. Krige and Barth.

14. Martin J. Medhurst, "Atoms or Peace and Nuclear Hegemony: The Rhetorical Structure of a Cold War Campaign," *Armed Forces and Society* 23, no. 4 (Summer 1997): 571–93.

15. Gerald F. Tape, "The Fabric of Cooperation," in *Atoms for Peace*, ed. Pilat, Pendley, and Ebinger, 59–66.

16. Leonard Weiss, "Atoms for Peace and Nuclear Proliferation," ibid., 131–41.

17. I thank Shiv Vishnanathan for his helpful discussions on this point.

18. The quote is freely borrowed from the French situationist Guy Debord as discussed by David Pinder, "The Breath of the Possible: Utopianism and the Street in Modernist Urbanism" (paper presented in the weekly Davis seminar, 30 November 2006). French situationists writing in the 1960s were, of course, critics of the conspicuous consumption typical of a bourgeois "society of the spectacle"; Bhabha is not. I thank David Pinder for his insights.

19. Abraham, in *Making of the Indian Atomic Bomb*, 98–106, stresses this aspect of Bhabha's intervention.

20. "It is not too much to expect that our children will enjoy in their homes electrical energy too cheap to meter, will know of great periodic regional famines in the world only as matters of history, will travel effortlessly over the seas and under them and through the air with a minimum of danger and at great speeds, and will experience a lifespan far longer than ours as disease yields and man comes to understand what causes him to age." Lewis L. Strauss, "Too Cheap to Meter: It's Now True" (speech to the National Association of Science Writers, New York City, 16 September 1954), www.atomicinsights.com/AI_03–09–05.html (accessed 3 December 2006). Walter Marshall made the same claims in Britain: "Nuclear Doubts Gnaw Deeper," 15 June 2000, http://news.bbc.co.uk/1/hi/world/europe/792209.stm (accessed 3 December 2006).

21. Ann Stoler, *Race and the Education of Desire: Foucault's History of Sexuality and the Colonial Order of Things* (Durham: Duke University Press, 1995), 178–79.

22. Gabrielle Hecht, "Negotiating Global Nuclearities: Apartheid, Decolonization, and the Cold War in the Making of the IAEA," in *Global Power Knowledge*, ed. Krige and Barth, 26. See also Gabrielle Hecht, "Nuclear Ontologies," *Constellations* 13, no. 3 (2006): 320–31.

23. Quoted by Abraham, in *Making of the Indian Nuclear Bomb*, 86.

24. Osgood, *Total Cold War*, 169.

25. Richard G. Hewlett, "From Proposal to Program," in *Atoms for Peace*, ed. Pilat, Pendley, and Ebinger, 31.

26. Medhurst, "Atoms or Peace," 587–88.

27. This paragraph and the next are based on Krige's chapter "Atoms for Peace," in *Global Power Knowledge*, ed. Krige and Barth, where detailed references may be found.

28. Angela Creager is doing pioneering work in this area, most recently in "Nuclear Energy in the Service of Biomedicine: The U.S. Atomic Energy Commission's Radio-isotope Program, 1946–1950," *Journal of the History of Biology* 39 (2006): 649–84. See also Angela N. H. Creager, "Tracing the Politics of Changing Postwar Research Practices: The Export of 'American' Radioisotopes to European Biologists," *Studies in History and Philosophy of Biology and Biomedical Science* 33C (2002): 367–88; also "The Industrialization of Radioisotopes by the U.S. Atomic Energy Commission," in *The Science-Industry Nexus: History, Policy, Implications*, ed. Karl Grandin, Nina Wormbs, and Sven Widmalm (Sagamore Beach, MA: Science History Publications, 2004), 141–67.

29. French researchers were particularly badly hit, especially after their own small pile went critical in December 1948 and as the cold war warmed up; see Jean Paul Gaudillière, "Normal Pathways: Controlling Isotopes and Building Biomedical Research in Postwar France," *Journal of the History of Biology* 39 (2006): 737–64. For a "successful" export and its foreign policy implications, see John Krige, "The Politics of Phosphorus-32: A Cold War Fable Based on Fact," *Hist. Stud. in Phys. Biol. Sci.* 36 (2005): 71–91.

30. I have discussed this at greater length in Krige's chapter "Atoms for Peace," in *Global Power Knowledge*, ed. Krige and Barth.

31. Introduction to *Atoms for Peace*, ed. Pilat, Pendley, and Ebinger, 16.

32. Ian Smart, "A Defective Dream," ibid., 73–82, at 76. This point has also been made by Mallard, who speaks of "the oscillation between two radically opposed positions, that which advocated secrecy and national nuclear policy dominated by military concerns, and that which called for the transparency that goes along with the formation of a supranational nuclear community dedicated to peaceful uses"; Grégoire Mallard, "Quand l'expertise se heurte au pouvoir souverein: La nation américaine face à la prolifération nucléaire, 1945–1953," *Sociologie du Travail* 48 (2006): 368 (my translation).

33. For the fair, see Michael L. Hoffman, "Britain Exploits Atomic Market, Takes a Big Lead over U.S. in Display of Commercial Equipment in Geneva," *New York Times*, 8 August 1955.

34. United States Delegation to the International Conference on the Peaceful Uses of Atomic Energy, "Appendix V: Research Reactor Exhibit at Geneva," in "Technical Exhibition of the United States of America," vol. 2, 314–15, Special Collections Division, Georgetown University Library, Washington, DC.

35. See the photograph in Fermi, *Atoms for the World*, between pp. 52 and 53.

36. Cerenkov radiation is electromagnetic radiation emitted when a charged particle passes through an insulator at a speed greater than the speed of light in that medium. The speed of light in water is 0.75c.

37. United States Delegation to the International Conference on the Peaceful Uses of Atomic Energy, "Technical Exhibition," 317.

38. Ibid., 322.

39. Union Carbide and Carbon Corporation, Memo, "Background Data: The United States Exhibit Reactor," undated, but about July 1955, Regenstein Library, University of Chicago, Chicago, IACF Papers, Box 259, Series 2, Folder 4.

40. Brigitte Schroeder-Gudehus and David Coulter, "Popularizing Science and Technology during the Cold War: Brussels 1958," in *Fair Representations: World's Fairs and the Modern World*, ed. Robert W. Rydell and Nancy E. Gwinn (Amsterdam: Vu University Press, 1994), 157–80.

41. Arthur Molella, "Exhibiting Atomic Culture: The View from Oak Ridge," *History and Technology* 19, no. 3 (2003): 211–26.

42. Sophie Forgan, "Atoms in Wonderland," *History and Technology* 19, no. 3 (2003): 177–96.

43. *Conference of the Academy of Sciences of the USSR on the Peaceful Uses of Atomic Energy, July 1–5, 1955*, English translation, Report AEC-TR-2435 (Washington, DC: United States Atomic Energy Commission, 1956). On the Soviet program, see Sonja D. Schmid, "Celebrating Tomorrow Today: The Peaceful Atom on Display in the Soviet Union," *Social Stud. of Science* 36, no. 3 (2006): 331–65. See also Paul R. Josephson, "Atomic Powered Communism: Nuclear Culture in the Postwar USSR," *Slavic Review* 55 (1996): 297–305; Paul Josephson, *Red Atom: Russia's Nuclear Power Program from Stalin to Today* (New York: W. H. Freeman, 2000).

44. *Science and Culture* 21, no. 22 (August 1955): 76.

45. United States Delegation to the International Conference on the Peaceful Uses of Atomic Energy, "Technical Exhibition," 315.

46. The revised Atomic Energy Act, passed in 1954, led to the declassification of material to enable American industry to benefit from government research previously done under wraps. Twenty-five thousand technical reports were declassified in about eighteen months. About one-third were unrestricted. About a quarter were classified "L" (limited clearance) and made available to engineers from U.S. industry: Richard G. Hewlett and Jack M. Holl, *Atoms for Peace and War, 1953–1961: Eisenhower and the Atomic Energy Commission* (Berkeley: University of California Press, 1989), 252.

47. USAEC, *Atoms for Peace. United States of America. Geneva 1955*.

48. Ibid., 37-A.

49. Fermi, *Atoms for the World*, 148–52.

50. Abraham, *Making of the Indian Atomic Bomb*, 80. Other organs in the U.S. administration were in favor of dealing with India.

51. For what follows, see E. E. Anderson, F. C. VonderLage, and R. T. Overman, "Education and Training in Nuclear Science and Engineering in the United States," in *Proceedings of the International Conference on the Peaceful Uses of Atomic Energy, Held in Geneva, 8 August–20 August 1955*, vol. 16, *Record of the Conference* (New York: United Nations, 1956), 1:463–70.

52. Creager, "Export of 'American' Radioisotopes" and "Industrialization of Radioisotopes."

53. AEC, "Reactor Development and Biology and Medicine: Domestic Educational and Training Programs," undated, but probably spring 1957, National Archives and Records Administration, College Park, MD, Record Group 59, Special Assistant to the Secretary for Energy and Outer Space, Atomic Energy Matters, 1944–63, Box 364, Folder 19.8, "Regional Programs. Euratom. General. March–April 1957," pt. 2 of 2.

54. United States Delegation to the International Conference on the Peaceful Uses of Atomic Energy, "Technical Exhibition," 314.

55. Union Carbide and Carbon Corporation, "Background Data."

56. George Perkovich, *India's Nuclear Bomb: The Impact on Global Proliferation* (Berkeley: University of California Press, 1999), 30.

57. For the British efforts to woo other countries to embrace the nuclear, including through educational programs, see Néstor Herran, "Spreading Nucleonics: The Isotope School at the Atomic Energy Research Establishment, 1951–67," *British J. for the History of Science* 39, no. 4 (2006): 569–86.

58. Prakash, *Another Reason*, chap. 2.

59. Tape, "Fabric of Cooperation,"63. For the Western seduction of national elites in third world countries, see also Arturo Escobar, *Encountering Development: The Making and Unmaking of the Third World* (Princeton: Princeton University Press, 1995).

60. Osgood, *Total Cold War*, 155, 156, 161. For a study of the role of the Voice of America in "psychological warfare" in the Truman administration, see Timothy Stoneman, "A Bold New Vision: Cold War Broadcasting and the VOA Radio Ring Plan, 1950–53," *Technology and Culture* 50, no. 2 (2009): 316–44.

61. Osgood, *Total Cold War*, 162–63.

62. Ibid., 170.

63. Ibid., 174–76. In his commentary on a previous version of this paper presented in the Davis seminar, Zia Mann remarked on the huge popular enthusiasm for these traveling exhibits in Pakistan in the 1950s.

64. The words are by Ralph T. Walker, the modernist architect of the luxurious and locally incongruous International Rice Research Institute building in the Philippines who described the experimental station in these terms; see Cullather, *Miracles of Modernization*, 234. Walker is famous for his designs of American military bases, suburban research campuses (Bell Labs, General Electric), and industrial pavilions at the 1939 World's Fair.

65. This lesson has been brought home in *Lessons of Empire: Imperial Histories and American Power*, ed. Craig Calhoun, Frederick Cooper, and Kevin W. Moore (New York: New Press, 2006). See also Charles S. Maier, *Among Empires: American Ascendancy and Its Predecessors* (Cambridge, MA: Harvard University Press, 2006). Against this prudence, especially when technology is factored in, see Michael Adas, *Dominance by Design: Technological Imperatives and America's Civilizing Mission* (Cambridge, MA: Belknap Press of Harvard University Press, 2006).

66. This is the thesis I defend in *American Hegemony and the Postwar Reconstruction of Science in Europe* (Cambridge, MA: MIT Press, 2006).

67. James Ferguson, *Expectations of Modernity: Myths and Meanings of Urban Life on the Zambian Copperbelt* (Berkeley: University of California Press, 1999). This situation occurred in many Latin American countries, where in the 1980s many reactors were still "underutilized and, in some instances, . . . shut down most of the time.

Moreover, many scientists who were trained in different fields of nuclear energy were not able to find jobs when they returned to their countries and either emigrated or worked on something different"; Alonso, "Impact in Latin America," 88.

68. Medhurst, "Atoms or Peace," 588.

69. I have stressed this general point elsewhere as regards an understanding of the politics of dual-use technologies: John Krige, "Technology, Foreign Policy, and International Cooperation in Space," in *Critical Issues in the History of Space Flight*, ed. Steven J. Dick and Roger D. Launius, NASA SP-2006–4702 (Washington, DC: NASA, 2006), 239–60.

70. The number following the symbol for the element is the sum of the protons and neutrons in the nucleus of the atom.

71. Thorium can also be used as a nuclear fuel by converting thorium-232 into uranium-233, which is fissile.

72. Margaret Gowing, *Independence and Deterrence: Britain and Atomic Energy, 1945–1952*, vol. 1, *Policy Making* (London: Macmillan, 1974), 85.

73. Today the term is broader and includes nonstate actors, notably terrorists.

74. Henry Sokolski, "The Arms Control Connection," in *Atoms for Peace*, ed. Pilat, Pendley, and Ebinger, 41, gives the primary source references. The Soviets pointed out, rightly, that this was meaningless from the point of view of arms control. Since plutonium was produced by natural uranium, any reactor was a potential source of weapons-grade material. What is more, as soon as uranium was defined as a strategic material, new deposits were immediately discovered; there seemed to be no limit to the amount available. The United States increased its contribution of fissile material for civil nuclear programs as the decade wore on, but for technical and political reasons, the IAEA never served the role of an atomic bank that Eisenhower foresaw for it in 1953.

75. Weapons designers estimate that the critical mass of a weapon built with uranium enriched to 20% or less is far too great for any practical weapon. It weighs approximately 375 kilograms at 20% and climbs to infinity as the degree of enrichment decreases: *Global Fissile Material Support 2006: First Report of the International Panel on Fissile Materials* (Program on Science and Global Security, Princeton University, 2006). See also Alex Glaser, "On the Proliferation Potential of Uranium Fuels for Research Reactors at Various Enrichment Levels," *Science and Global Security* 14 (2006): 1–24.

76. United States Delegation to the International Conference on the Peaceful Uses of Atomic Energy, "Technical Exhibition," 313.

77. Union Carbide and Carbon Corporation, "Background Data."

78. Ibid.

79. Ibid.; United States Delegation to the International Conference on the Peaceful Uses of Atomic Energy, "Technical Exhibition," 313.

80. Javier Ordoñez and José M. Sánchez Ron, "Nuclear Energy in Spain: From Hiroshima to the Sixties," in *National Military Establishments and the Advancement of Science and Technology: Studies in 20th Century History*, ed. Paul Forman and José M. Sánchez Ron (Dordrecht: Kluwer Academic Publishers, 1996), 196–97. This paragraph, and the material on Spain and Belgium, draws extensively from this chapter (185–213).

81. In the immediate postwar years, the regime had been publicly shunned by the State Department for its sympathies with the Axis powers. Franco's virulent anticommunism and the strategic location of Spain in Europe (Spain was soon dotted with U.S. Air Force bases) were assets the United States sought to exploit as the cold war got into its stride.

82. Ordoñez and Sánchez Ron, "Nuclear Energy in Spain," 200.

83. Schroeder-Gudehus and Cloutier, "Popularizing Science and Technology," 177.

84. For this information on Belgium, see Ordoñez and Sanchez Ron, "Nuclear Energy in Spain," 197–98.

85. John Krige, "The Peaceful Atom as Political Weapon: Euratom and American Foreign Policy in the Late 1950s," *Historical Studies in the Natural Sciences* 38, no. 1 (2008): 5–44.

86. William Walker and Måns Lönroth, "Arms Control or Anarchy?" in *Atoms for Peace*, ed. Pilat, Pendley, and Ebinger, 171.

87. Itty Abraham, "Excavating the Margins: Rare Earths and Travancore in the Annals of the Cold War, 1945–47" (unpublished MS, 2006).

88. As Itty Abraham has emphasized, the Indian atomic energy program was impregnated with a sense of urgency from its inception, this being an essential parameter of "postcolonial modernity"; *Making of the Indian Atomic Bomb*, 70–72.

89. On these negotiations, see, for example, Hecht, "Negotiating Global Nuclearities," and the references therein.

90. On the foreign policy context, see George Perkovich, *India's Nuclear Bomb: The Impact on Global Proliferation* (Berkeley: University of California Press, 1999), 40–59.

91. Ibid., 56.

92. Bertrand Goldschmidt, "From Nuclear Middle Ages to Nuclear Renaissance," in *Atoms for Peace*, ed. Pilat, Pendley, and Ebinger, 120.

93. But see also Itty Abraham, "The Ambivalence of Nuclear Histories," in *Global Power Knowledge*, ed. Krige and Barth, 49–65.

94. The epigraph is by Cullather, *Miracles of Modernization*, 229.

95. Jeremi Suri, *Power and Protest: Global Revolution and the Rise of Détente* (Cambridge, MA: Harvard University Press, 2005), 14.

96. Medhurst, "Atoms or Peace," 587.

97. Spencer Weart, *Nuclear Fear: A History of Images* (Cambridge, MA: Harvard University Press, 1988), 172.

98. Tape, "Fabric of Cooperation," 60.

99. "Secretary-General's Lecture at Princeton University," 28 November 2006, available at http://www.un.org/apps/sg/sgstats.asp?nid=2330 (accessed 11 December 2006).

7.

MARCI SHORE

On Cosmopolitanism, the Avant-Garde, and a Lost Innocence of Central Europe

MARX AND ENGELS GREETED the Springtime of Nations with a call for the workers of the world to unite. Thus in central Europe liberalism's nearly triumphal moment was also the beginning of its end. Liberalism placed its faith in reason, science, and progress; it insisted on individual rights and a social contract. Its teleology was optimistic, yet rational and measured. Hence its vulnerability; it proved emotionally unfulfilling.[1] Against this gradualist ethos and patience with human imperfection, liberalism's offspring rebelled; both nationalism and communism were utopian variations on liberalism. What made them utopian was not only a more fervent optimism but also an aspiration toward totality. In the postliberal world, the stakes were high. Nationalism and communism were thinking big, envisioning social engineering on a grand scale. National self-realization stood for personal self-realization, the free expression of a precious soul, and nationalism suggested that all of modernity's existential ailments—alienation, anomie, and the death of God—would find resolution in the nation-state. In part communism was born as a response to nationalism, and Marxism, in its turn, purported to explain everything. Once inside Marxist logic, there was no way out. Georg Lukács was one among many wonderful minds drawn to this Marxist notion of "the all-pervasive supremacy of the whole over the parts."[2] Then came Lenin, whose second fateful modification of Marxism (after the vanguard who could rush history) was a conciliatory approach to nationalist impulses. Henceforth the tension between national patriotism and Communist internationalism would haunt the Soviet project. Yet true believers knew this was all very temporary: one day soon the proletariat would rise up in a worldwide revolution; in time state borders would wither away. Internationalism was the way of the future.

The avant-garde felt similarly about internationalism. The critical issue was time, not place; generational identity, not ethnic or national identity. All sources of parochialism were to be relegated to history's dustbin, and Romantic poets "thrown off the steamboat of modernity."[3] The avant-garde shared with Lenin a certain audacity: national thinking was for the less ambitious. It was confining. It was also passé, and among the avant-garde's slogans was the battle against *passéisme*. The avant-garde disowned the past; come what may, it belonged to the future.

Yet in some sense the internationalist ideology of both the avant-gardists and the Communists was an appropriation of an older *Mitteleuropean* motif—an appropriation thinly veiling a rupture—for there was a cosmopolitanism that preceded Marxism and that was somewhat distinct from the internationalism of both the avant-garde and the Communists, both of which implicitly acknowledged the existence of the boundaries they strove to transgress. A genealogy of the avant-garde's internationalism would reveal that there was a time, not so long before, when those boundaries were still blurry. Stefan Zweig wrote of his youth in fin-de-siècle Vienna, "It was sweet to live here, in this atmosphere of spiritual conciliation, and subconsciously every citizen became supernational, cosmopolitan, a citizen of the world."[4] Zweig's world was that of a specific milieu; nonetheless it was the case that even as national paradigms came to be very much à la mode, a nontrivial part of the intelligentsia continued to share the aristocracy's traditional conviction that the world as a whole—or at the very least, Europe as a whole—belonged to them. Even as patriotic linguists were reviving forgotten grammars and Romantic poets were exalting the uniqueness of the national soul, a parallel intellectual elite continued to search for universal answers. Like its postliberal contemporaries and successors, cosmopolitanism practiced a willful denial of constraints. Yet there were important differences: if cosmopolitanism, too, harbored protoutopian impulses, its utopianism was a quieter one and its elitism less abashed. Its aspiration toward universality was not necessarily an aspiration toward totality. Polyglotism was its implicit ideology and its explicit practice.

The Cosmopolitanism of Central Europe

"We want to go back to the things themselves," Edmund Husserl wrote at the turn of the nineteenth to the twentieth century.[5] These things themselves (*die Sachen selbst*) were transcendent of any nation; they referred to our experience, to the act of thinking. Husserl was deeply concerned with the relationship between the self and the world. His slogan expressed an almost cheery optimism: the world *was* knowable.

If for Sigmund Freud everything of importance occurred in the unconscious, for Husserl everything of importance happened in human consciousness. Objects comprising the world were "transcendent" in the sense that they did not *constitute* but rather were *constituted* by, the subject's intentional consciousness. Human consciousness—a generic, purified human consciousness—was the starting point. Only consciousness was immanent, and phenomenology was consciousness reflecting upon itself. In turn, the world—the conviction of the existence of a world independent of our selves—needed to be not negated but rather only "bracketed," so as to be more clearly examined. For Husserl and his circle, the difference between the "natural attitude" and the "phenomenological attitude" was largely one of self-consciousness. The human subject was the source of all meaning. Yet unlike the Freudian subject, the Husserlian subject remained heir to a positivist legacy: phenomenology was modernist subjectivity meeting nineteenth-century science. Husserl's "I" was at once radically subjective and peculiarly impersonal.[6]

Like his contemporary Freud, Husserl was a Moravian Jew who studied in Vienna.[7] He studied in Leipzig as well, together with the young philosopher Tomáš Masaryk. In 1877 Masaryk left Leipzig for Vienna; the following year Husserl went on to Berlin. Peripateticism notwithstanding, they remained friends. Throughout his life Masaryk was on the move: between America and Europe, in France, England, Germany, and Russia. He married the American Charlotte Garrigue and in 1902 wrote to Husserl of his four children: one was studying history in Berlin, another was studying art in Antwerp, and the younger two were attending school in Prague.[8] When Czechoslovakia came into being, Masaryk envisioned his new state as one that would be *Mitteleuropa* in the very loftiest sense, a country that would embody "the synthesis of the European spirit."[9]

The circle of phenomenologists gathered around Masaryk's Moravian classmate, first in Göttingen, then in Freiburg, represented one of the last dazzling cosmopolitan moments in Central Europe's history. Among Husserl's friends from his student days was Kazimierz Twardowski; in the 1870s both had studied in Vienna with the philosopher of psychology Franz Brentano. Twardowski went on to become a professor in Austrian Lemberg, after World War I Polish Lwów; there he taught the talented Polish student Roman Ingarden, before sending Ingarden to Göttingen to write his doctorate with Husserl.[10] Among Husserl's other talented students were the Germans Hans Lipps and Martin Heidegger; the German Jews who embraced Christianity Max Scheler, Adolf Reinach, and Hedwig Conrad-Martius; the Russian Gustav Shpet; the Silesian from an Orthodox Jewish family Edith Stein; and (later) the Czech Jan Patočka and the Lithuanian Jew who had come to Göttingen from Kaunas via Kharkiv and Strasbourg, Emmanuel Levinas.[11] They came to Germany from Lwów, Vienna, Moscow, Breslau, Kraków, Strasbourg, and Prague.

Phenomenology reached Russia even before it did Germany's more immediate neighbors. Husserl's "Die Philosophie als strenge Wissenschaft" (Philosophy as Rigorous Science) appeared in Russia in 1911, the same year as in Germany. During the first year of World War I, a Moscow University philosophy seminar already included two of Husserl's main works.[12] Most significantly, phenomenology reached Russia in the person of Gustav Shpet, who returned from Göttingen in 1914. In turn it was through Shpet and the Kievan-turned-Muscovite philosopher-psychologist Georgii Ivanovich Chelpanov that the young linguist Roman Jakobson encountered Husserl's thought.[13] In the years following the First World War, Jakobson would bring Husserl's ideas to Prague, and thus did German phenomenology reach the Czech lands via Russia.[14]

Jakobson represented in his person the intersection of phenomenology and structuralism—among the great universalist strivings of the early-twentieth century. The precocious Muscovite, together with his friend Viktor Shklovsky, was among the young Russian intellectuals influenced by Jan Ignacy Niecisław Baudouin de Courtenay, a Warsaw-born scholar of French aristocratic ancestry who had lived in Austria and Latvia, considered himself a Pole, and by the 1910s was Russia's most influential linguist. De Courtenay had studied comparative Indo-European, Sanskrit, and Slavic philology in Prague, Berlin, Jena, Leipzig, and Petersburg; he had done fieldwork in Slovenia, attended lectures in Milan, and taught in Kazan, Dorpat, Kraków, Warsaw, and Petersburg. He spoke and wrote Polish, Russian, Slovenian, Czech, German, French, Italian, Lithuanian, and Yiddish; he was a specialist in Sanskrit, Latin, Slavic, Baltic, Turkic, Finno-Ugric, Ido, and Esperanto.[15] His contemporary the linguist Antoine Meillet said of de Courtenay that he "a eu le malheur de n'appartenir tout à fait à aucun pays" (had the misfortune of not fully belonging to any country).[16] Perhaps this was a misfortune, perhaps not. In any case, de Courtenay was not inclined to reify borders. A Slavicist, he rejected the idea that Slavic languages formed a closed linguistic group; he insisted on the need to study them in relation to other languages.[17] Any language, he believed, might in the right circumstances become a lingua franca: "'Every tongue shall glorify the Lord,' wrote the Apostle Paul. . . . And if every tongue is eligible for communication between man and God, then it is so much the more eligible for communication among people."[18]

In the first decade of the twentieth century, de Courtenay taught in Petersburg, where he was in dialogue with the like-minded Geneva-based linguist Ferdinand de Saussure. A Russian student named Sergei Karcevskii contemplated translating Saussure's posthumously published lectures, Cours de linguistique générale, into Russian.[19] This project never materialized, but when in 1917 Karcevskii returned to Russia from Geneva, he did bring with him some ideas Saussure held: language, considered unto and for itself, was the only true object of linguistic study. Language was a form, not a substance. The linguistic sign was arbitrary, defined only by contrast. All meaning was relational and existed only within a given system. Any given linguistic state possessed a "fortuitous character," and an absolute distinction had to be made between diachrony (evolution) and synchrony (simultaneity).[20]

Like phenomenology's return "to the things themselves," structuralist linguistics' return to the words themselves also involved a kind of bracketing—in this case of the referent (signified), which possessed no organic relationship to the sign (signifier).[21] In 1915 Roman Jakobson, together with a small group of

Moscow students including Petr Bogatyrev, founded the Moscow Linguistic Circle. The following year Viktor Shklovsky and Osip Brik were instrumental in forming the Moscow Linguistic Circle's Petersburg counterpart, the Society for the Study of Poetic Language. From these circles came Russian formalism, committed to "literature as such"—that is, to the autonomous nature of poetic language. Russian formalism was the study of aesthetic devices, considered unto and for themselves. "Art was always free of life," Shklovsky declared, "and its color never reflected the color of the flag which waved over the fortress of the city."[22]

Linguistic structuralism shared with phenomenology a search for universal principles. It shared much more than that, however. Among Russian formalism's most important contributions was Shklovsky's idea of *ostranenie* ("enstrangement"—that is, "making strange," or "defamiliarization"). In his 1917 essay, "Art as Device," Shklovsky proclaimed the purpose of art: to break the spell of automatization, the automatization that "eats away at things, at clothes, at furniture, at our wives, and at our fear of war."[23] Ostranenie shocks us out of our habitual state; it "returns sensation to our limbs."[24] In essence the aim of Shklovsky's ostranenie was that of Husserl's "bracketing": to make us self-conscious about what we were seeing, about how objects appeared to us. "Practical language" was to "poetic language" what the "natural attitude" was to the "phenomenological attitude."

The Twilight of the Age of Innocence

Of the last years of the Hapsburg Empire, Stefan Zweig wrote, "Nowhere was it easier to be a European."[25] He added, "[We] who once knew a world of individual freedom, know and can give testimony that Europe once, without a care, enjoyed its kaleidoscopic play of color."[26] Zweig wrote with a heavy nostalgia; in his great mourning for the Vienna of his youth, he necessarily idealized her. Yet, for a certain privileged milieu, that kaleidoscopic world had indeed existed. Even far from the imperial capital of Vienna, the cultural exchange that had long shaped central Europe's intellectual life survived for quite some time, and among intellectuals many resisted being defined by nation building. Among these was the Czech artist Bohumil Kubišta, who wrote in 1911, "In our time manifestations of national character have been elevated to the foremost criterion by which a work of art is assessed. . . . I personally doubt that this path could lead anywhere at all."[27]

Even provincial Kraków was a kaleidoscopic artistic center in the late imperial years.[28] The Polish writer Tadeusz Boy-Żeleński remembered his youth there: "Such an abundance of talent! It made the Kraków of that time the most extraordinary city that perhaps has ever existed; an intellectual capital of a great country grafted onto a city that, in other regards, was far from being a capital; a city relatively small, whose material means bore no proportion to the role she played."[29] The young writers who gathered in that intellectual capital were Poles and cosmopolitans, immersed in literature written in languages other than their own: "The devotion was then to the Scandinavians, to the Russian writers, to Ibsen, to Strindberg, to Dostoevsky, to Nietzsche, to Oscar Wilde, etc. We others, Poles, we have a great and beautiful literature of our own, but in the epoch of my youth we consumed enormous amounts of foreign literature."[30] Boy-Żeleński, having studied medicine and having become a doctor, began a cabaret. He wrote poetry and translated French literature. "I assure you," he later told a Parisian audience, "he who has not translated Rabelais does not know the pleasure of being alive."[31]

Life was not a pleasure for long, however. In 1908 came the crisis in Bosnia; six years later came the assassination of Archduke Franz Ferdinand, Vienna's ultimatum to Belgrade, and the First World War. Suddenly, Zweig writes, "society ladies swore . . . that never again would they speak a single word of French. Shakespeare was banned from the German stage, Mozart and Wagner from the French and English concerts, German professors declared that Dante had been Germanic, the French that Beethoven had been a Belgian, intellectual culture was requisitioned without scruple from the enemy countries like grain and ore."[32] Zweig and Romain Rolland were among those who stood in protest. The *Berliner Tageblatt* published Zweig's open letter: "I announced to all friends in foreign countries that, although relations were now impossible, I would remain loyal to them so that, at the very first opportunity, we might again collaborate in the reconstruction of European culture."[33] In response, Rolland sent a personal letter: "Non, je ne quitterai jamais mes amis" (No, I will never abandon my friends).[34]

Zweig, Jakobson, Shklovsky, and Boy-Żeleński all wrote of the Great War. And all wrote of their absorption in intellectual work; often they described those years as if the war happened only in the background, whereas literature happened in the foreground. In Jakobson's memoirs of his early "futurist years" in Russia, conspicuously missing amid Osip Brik's endless cigarettes, Vladimir Mayakovsky's stentorian voice, and Velimir Khlebnikov's exhilarating poetry was the First World War—and the Bolshevik Revolution. Shklovsky's jarringly graphic *Sentimental Journey* is in fact a story of the transcendent value of art in the midst of horror. When in Russia the First World War bled into the Bolshevik Revolution and civil war, Shklovsky was not only an observer but also a participant—yet in chronicling ghastly brutality he not infrequently paused to discuss literary theory.[35] Boy-Żeleński was possessed by a similar-seeming perversion. "As the Germans battled the Russians at the very walls of Kraków," he recalled, "I immersed myself with delight in the translation of Montaigne's 'Essays.' I translated Descartes in my little servant's quarters to the sounds of the farewell march played for the regiments departing for the Italian front, and I must say that the allegro rhythm was well suited to the triumphal thought of Descartes."[36]

After the war Zweig changed countries as often as he could, embarking on a personal campaign to restore cosmopolitanism. "In this spirit," he wrote, "I lectured in Switzerland and in Holland, I spoke in French in the Palais des Arts at Brussels, in Italian in Florence in the historic Sala dei Duecenti where once Michelangelo and Leonardo had sat, in English in America on a lecture tour from the Atlantic to the Pacific."[37] The age of innocence, though, had passed; one could no longer travel without a passport. Zweig was not the only one to learn quickly that the borders of the new nation-states were much less porous than those of the empires had been.

In the meantime, in the newly born Czechoslovakia, literary critic František Xaver Šalda tried to persuade other Czech intellectuals that nationalism was retrograde — and hardly innocuous:

> In spite of the fact that Mr. Dyk is attempting to convince myself and others of the legitimacy of the nationalism of himself and his comrades in arms by means commensurate to his ideal — that is, by means overblown and shoddy, by insults and detractions, I still continue to consider his nationalism as not only a pitiable antique, but also something *harmful to the nation*, something that is capable of thrusting us decades backwards and holding back the healthy discharge of energy, which by the logic of things is progressing in all of Europe. . . . Nationalism is something that lived to its end with Austria.[38]

The Persistence of Things

Even the great rupture of World War I was only the beginning of the end. For quite some time a cosmopolitan milieu persisted, with Roman Jakobson among its most compelling spokespersons. In 1920, in the midst of the Russian civil war, he arrived in Prague with an official mission of the Soviet Red Cross. At the end of that summer he wrote to Elsa Triolet, sister of the famous Lilia Brik, whose ménage à trois (in both the literal and conventional senses of the phrase) with her husband, Osip Brik, and the futurist poet Vladimir Mayakovsky stood at the center of the Russian formalist and avant-garde circles. By 1920 Lilia's sister Elsa had married the French officer Andrei Triolet and was living in Paris; both Jakobson and Shklovsky were very much in love with her. Jakobson wrote to Triolet:

> Really, each of us has lived through not one but ten lives in the last two years. In the last few years I, for example, was a counterrevolutionary, a scholar (and not the worst), the scholarly secretary of Brik, the head of

the Division of Arts, a deserter, a gambler, an irreplaceable specialist in the heating establishment, a writer, a humorist, a reporter, a diplomat, in every sort of romantic *emploi*, and so on and so forth. I assure you I was indeed a *roman d'aventures* and nothing else. And so it was with practically each of us.[39]

Once settled in Prague, Jakobson tried to persuade Shklovsky to join him.[40] Shklovsky preferred Berlin. "To live in Prague and believe that you're living in Europe is foolish," he told Jakobson. He added, "Do you wear round glasses? All the Jews are wearing them, don't be an assimilator."[41] About Prague, Jakobson thought otherwise and tried to persuade their breathtakingly handsome friend Mayakovsky to come as well. In February 1921 he wrote to Mayakovsky, telling him that although the right-wing newspapers were calling him a son of a bitch, in left-wing circles his popularity was only increasing, and that the best left-wing Czech poet, Stanislav K. Neumann, had translated his "150 Million." "Come, my dear," Jakobson wrote, urging Mayakovsky not to neglect Prague on his travels west.[42] Mayakovsky came to Prague only in 1927. The Moscow linguist Petr Bogatyrev accepted Jakobson's invitation much sooner. "When Roman left for Prague," Shklovsky wrote in Berlin in 1922, "he wrote for Bogatyrev to come. Bogatyrev went, with his pants short, his shoes unlaced and his suitcase filled with manuscripts and torn papers."[43]

In Prague Jakobson became the leading force behind the creation of the Prague Linguistic Circle.[44] From its outset the circle had an aura of fearlessness about it; its members rejected the distinction between art and scholarship. In 1929, at the International Congress of Slavists in Prague, the circle announced a set of "Theses." Poetic language was not identical to communicative language, but rather—following Russian formalism—was "directed at expression itself." "Questions of poetic language," the theses stated, "have for the most part played a subordinate role in literary historical studies. Yet *the organizing feature of art by which it differs from other semiotic structures is an orientation toward the sign rather than toward what is signified.*" Furthermore—and more generally—"from the functional standpoint *the independent existence of the word is completely evident.*" Moreover, the linguist was bound to "avoid egocentrism"—that is, to avoid "the analysis and evaluation of poetic facts of other periods or nations from the perspective of his own poetic habits and the artistic norms stressed in his education."[45]

Jakobson's milieu was devoted to thinking broadly—if possible, universally. N. S. Trubetzkoy, the Vienna-based Russian linguist who was his most important interlocutor during these years, wrote to Jakobson in 1928, "Among other things, I undertook a project that greatly interests me: I drew up the phonological vowel systems of the languages I remember by heart (thirty-four) and tried to compare them. Here, in Vienna, I continued this work, and now I have forty-six. I will go on until I get a hundred."[46] Likewise, the Prague

Linguistic Circle was radically cosmopolitan. One member recalled their meetings: "Seldom was Czech without an accent heard. Even those who hardly knew how to speak any other language but their native Czech acquired a queer pronunciation after some time. The guests from abroad added to this linguistic confusion. There would be, for example, a guest speaker from Denmark. He had to speak in French or German, or in a Slavic language, and this he did with an accent, of course."[47]

The Internationalism of the Avant-Garde

In Moscow and Petersburg the Russian formalists had been very close to the Russian futurist poets—especially to Mayakovsky and Khlebnikov. Formalist literary theory had very much been born of an "intoxication with verses."[48] Moreover, the formalists shared with both the avant-garde writers and the phenomenologists an inclination toward the "laying bare" (*obnazhenie*) of the device.[49] The Russian futurists Aleksei Kruchënykh and Velimir Khlebnikov's announcement that the future belonged to *slovo kak takovoe*, "the word as such," echoed linguistic structuralism's declaration of the arbitrariness of the connection between the signifier and signified. "The word as such" bore, too, an analogy to Husserl's call to return to "the things themselves": the essential was accessible.[50] Phenomenology, like structuralism, was an attempt to get at what was universally real. "Baring" very much appealed to the avant-garde, and nakedness became an avant-garde motif.[51]

Jakobson, one of those "intoxicated with verses," himself possessed an ability to intoxicate. People were drawn to him, things happened around him. Soon upon his arrival in Prague, at a reception organized by the Soviet mission, he met the Czech poet Jaroslav Seifert. "Within a few days," Seifert related, "he was sitting with us at the café, as if he had been coming there for years." Seifert noted as well that Jakobson learned Czech quickly: it took him all of three weeks.[52] Just months after arriving in Prague, he published a Czech translation of a fragment of one of Khlebnikov's poems.[53]

Jakobson stood at the intersection not only of phenomenology and structuralism, but also of the old cosmopolitanism of the east-central European intelligentsia and the new internationalism of the European avant-garde. He was a scholar who dabbled in poetry, a linguist who was also a futurist. This "bipolarity" was, for Seifert, "an inseparable component of the magic of his personality."[54] During his first winter in Czechoslovakia, Jakobson published an essay about Dada, the latest avant-garde movement that strove toward a "reification of contingency," an attempt to reify the aesthetic, in-itselfness. It was the device laid bare.[55]

Dada's creator, the Romanian Jewish Swiss Tristan Tzara, was a national nihilist par excellence who embraced disunity: "People are different. Diversity creates interest for life. There is no common basis in human minds. . . . It is often said to us that we are ununified, but it's difficult for me to grasp the offense contained in that word. Everything is ununified."[56] Of Tzara and the Dadaists, Jakobson wrote,

> They do not object to the war ("still today for war" [*heute noch für den Krieg*]), yet they are the first to proclaim the cause of erasing the boundaries between yesterday's warring powers ("me, I'm of many nationalities" [*Je suis, moi, de plusieurs nationalités*]). When it comes right down to it, they are satisfied and therefore prefer bars ("he holds war and peace in his toga, but decides in favor of a cherry brandy flip"). Here amid the "cosmopolitan mix of god and the bordello," in Tzara's testimonial, Dada is born.[57]

Soon Jakobson joined Devětsil, a group of Czech avant-garde artists founded in December 1920 whose members included Seifert, Karel Teige, and Vítěslav Nezval. For the Czech avant-gardists who were just a bit younger than Jakobson, cosmopolitanism was not so much a state of existence to be taken for granted as an ideology to be declared. The cover of a Czech avant-garde journal read "Disk, Internationální Revue/Le Disque, Revue Internationale, Der Diskus, Internat. Zeitschrift, The Disc, International Review, Il Disco, Riviste Internazionale." Its first issue of 1923 included an advertisement for Karel Teige's *Alexandr Archipenko*, the "monograph of a modern Ukrainian sculptor"; Philippe Soupault's poem "Le pirate" in French; Nezval's poem "Abeceda" in Czech with a French epigraph; Seifert's Czech poem "Marseilles"; Ivan Goll's column "Radio from Paris"; and V. Vančura's article "Der Amazonenstrom," translated from the original Czech into German.

In his 1927 "The Word, the Word, the Word," Devětsil's ideologue Karel Teige called for a turn away from "provincial and regional national horizons and nationality."[58] Into this internationalist *Weltanschauung* of the avant-garde, Jakobson fitted well. He was a mediator not only between Moscow and Prague, but also between Prague and Berlin, in the early 1920s a displaced center of Russian intellectual life, where constructivism was in vogue.[59] In Berlin the Russian graphic artist El Lissitzky and the novelist Ilya Ehrenburg were publishing the journal *Veshch'/Gegenstand/Object*; Shklovsky was there often, as were Elsa Triolet and the Hungarian avant-garde artist László Moholy-Nagy. The Polish poet Tadeusz Peiper wrote for a Polish avant-garde journal an account of his trip to Germany to visit Moholy-Nagy and his fellow Bauhaus artists: the German Walter Gropius, the Russian Wassily Kandinsky, and the Pole Kazimir Malewicz, who was a long-time resident of Russia.[60] The Polish Jewish graphic artist Henryk Berlewi spent the years 1921 to 1923 in Berlin, in the company of Moholy-Nagy, Lissitzky, and other artists from *Der Sturm* and the *Novembergruppe*. There in constructivist Berlin, Berlewi invented the theory of Mechano-Faktur and exhibited the first Mechano-Faktur picture at the 1922 Grosse Berliner Kunstaustellung.[61]

In 1923 Berlewi returned to Warsaw and, together with Aleksander Wat and another Polish futurist friend, founded a graphic design advertising agency. Among Reklama Mechano's projects was a brochure for the Warsaw chocolate manufacturer Plutos, with typography by Berlewi and text by Wat.[62] Like Berlewi and his constructivist friends in Berlin, the young polyglot futurist Wat had explicitly internationalist aspirations. In July 1921 he and two friends, "in the name of the Polish futurists"—that is, themselves—sent a letter to Vladimir Mayakovsky: "Polish futurists, establishing contact with futurists from all countries, send the Russian futurists fraternal greetings. Beginning in September of the present year we will publish in Warsaw the first large international journal-newspaper devoted to universal futurist poetry in all languages. In addition to Polish futurists, taking part are Italian, French, German and Spanish futurists. Now in turn we approach the Russian futurists with a request to participate in our international journal."[63] In the post–World War I years, internationalism had to be deliberately forged, and these invitations from East and Central European avant-gardists to their counterparts abroad represented their own internationalist literary genre. Henri Barbusse, "fellow traveler" and editor of the French *Monde*, wrote to M. Denissovskii asking for work by Soviet artists.[64] The editors of the French collection *L'art international d'aujourdhui* and the international PEN Congress in Vienna wrote to Mayakovsky.[65] The editors of the Czech avant-garde journal *Pásmo* wrote to Mayakovsky and Lissitzky.[66] The German-based Hungarian Moholy-Nagy, organizer of a new Bücher-Serie, wrote to Lissitzky.[67] In March 1924, following his return from Berlin, Berlewi wrote to Lissitzky as well. Another new journal was in the making, to be edited by Berlewi and the "famous Polish poet, the former pioneer of Dadaism in Poland, Aleksander Wat." The pair was inviting all similarly minded colleagues abroad to collaborate. "I hope," Berlewi wrote to Lissitzky, "that you will take an interest in this journal, the only one of its kind in Poland, and that you will send us interesting material (articles, reproductions) as soon as possible."[68]

Berlewi's working languages included Polish, Russian, German, French, and Yiddish. In 1925 he designed a Mechano-Faktur cover for a book by the Hebrew-language poet Gabriel Talfir, published in Warsaw. In 1928 he moved to Paris.[69] This was all quite in keeping with the inclinations of his Polish milieu: Polish avant-gardists considered themselves part of a Pan-European movement, and the section of their journal *Blok* devoted to an overview of modernist publications listed more than forty titles in French, English, German, Spanish, Dutch, Czech, Hungarian, and other languages: *Der Sturm, La revue européenne, L'esprit nouveau, Ma, Volné Směry, The Architectural Record, Zwrotnica, La pluma revista literaria, Futurist Aristocracy, La revue universelle, Der Querschnitt, Veraikon, Stavba, La revue de l'époque, The Broom, Egyseg, De Stijl, Mekano, F 24 Alamanch*, and others. A single issue of the Polish journal *Formiści* (The Formists) included an article on contemporary German poetry and drama and examples of French avant-garde poetry (Apollinaire); Russian futurist poetry (Mayakovsky and Khlebnikov); German Dada poetry (by an anonymous author); French Dada poetry (Georges Ribemont-Dessaignes); Italian "neofuturist poetry" (Aldo Palazzeschi); "the latest German poetry" (Ivan Goll); and "the latest Spanish poetry" (Humerto Rivas).[70] In the same issue an article on "new artistic paths" described the latest aesthetic innovations in Paris; the many exhibits of German and Russian expressionism; the newest Russian art that was causing a sensation in Germany ("Was it a transfusion of young Russian culture into the veins of the outmoded cultures of the West?"); and "the complete victory of futurism in Italy."[71]

Futurism disdained the past. Beyond, though, the common assertions of the freedom of words and an absolute chasm between the past and the future, Italian futurism in both aesthetics and philosophy was distinctly different from Russian futurism, and Marinetti's 1914 visit to Russia was not an unqualified success.[72] Nonetheless, the gesture of the visit was an important one. His eventual engagement with fascism aside, Marinetti played not a minor role in cultivating the internationalist ethos of the avant-garde. He corresponded with Karel Teige in Prague and with Mayakovsky in Moscow, to whom he wrote in 1925: "Notre ami futuriste italienne *ne s'arrêtera pas!*" (Our Italian futurist friend will not stop).[73] In 1923 he sent a letter to the editors of the Polish avant-garde journal *Zwrotnica* (The Switch), which they published in the original French: "I am a friar of the new religion of speed. I feel that *Zwrotnica* is a place inhabited by the Divine! . . . Today it is done: the past trembles. And this is the great joy of all the locomotives of Spirit. . . . To see you, my dear friends from *Zwrotnica*! When? Soon! Soon! Militarized revolution of my heart which rejoices at the idea of soon seeing the great strong intelligent Poland bolt forth!"[74]

Marinetti was a force, but he wrote in French for his Slavic interlocutors, and they all knew that Paris was special. Polish avant-garde journals (*Blok, Zwrotnica, Formiści*) published much contemporary French poetry, sometimes in the original, sometimes in Polish translation. *Zwrotnica* regularly published "letters from Paris," sometimes two or three in a single issue. In early 1920 *Formiści* published a letter from a Polish collaborator in Paris, who wrote about avant-garde happenings there; the participation of Tristan Tzara, the Russian Rochem Grey, and the Spaniard Huidobro; and the deep sense of absence that had followed Apollinaire's death in 1918.[75] In November 1922 *Zwrotnica* published a letter by the Polish futurist Tytus Czyżewski, who had returned to the French capital after some ten years. Having come from Poland, he wrote, he felt like one arriving in the muggy city "*de la campagne.*"[76] In the columns he sent back to Poland, he wrote of cubist painting, of Italian theater troupes, of Stanislavskii's Russian company performing in the theater on the Champs-Elysées, of the music of one of Stravinsky's students, of Picasso and Severini, of the cubist poet Jean Cocteau.[77] And if Paris was special, Apollinaire was even more so. For both the Polish and the Czech avant-gardes, Apollinaire, too, served as a model of the cosmopolitan-internationalist who "visited many countries and made the acquaintance of many languages" and who "could relate considerably more about the habits, customs, and tales of various lands than the Eternally Wandering Jew."[78]

In the 1920s, more than one avant-gardist in east and central Europe was confident in the coming of "Paneuropa."[79] The Ukrainian futurists created Aspanfut, an association of "Panfuturists." They published their manifestos in French, English, and German and included discussions of avant-garde doings throughout the continent. They, too, published Tzara and the Dadaists; they, too, wrote of Marinetti. The second issue of Aspanfut's journal *Katafalk mystetstv* (Catafalk of Arts) appeared in December 1922 in a trilingual version: Russian, Ukrainian, and Yiddish.[80] In 1927 leading Ukrainian futurist Mykhail' Semenko insisted that "we must follow the road of universal creative objectives and not stew in our own juice. . . . We must rid ourselves of provincialism."[81] In 1927 he published the article "Reflections about Why Ukrainian Nationalism Is Bad for Ukrainian Culture, or Why Internationalism Is Good for It."[82] In Soviet Ukraine, the futurists' journal *Nova generatsiia* (New Generation) of the late 1920s integrated French, German, English, and Esperanto; their prestigious editorial board was pan-European.[83]

Endgame

In 1932 the German writer Lion Feuchtwanger published the essay "The Novel of Today Is International." He wrote:

> Ever since economic and linguistic boundaries ceased to coincide, ever since the individual came to regard the planet rather than any politically bounded country as his homeland, native literature in the form of exclusively national writing has faced a difficult situation. Compared to the great writings of our time it looks like a Biedermeier display case filled with peasant knick-knacks next to a highrise outfitted with the most modern technology. Once a vital necessity, it has become a curiosity best suited to museums.[84]

Feuchtwanger began his essay with the words "It is obvious that the contemporary novel is international." In fact, it was not obvious, and just for that reason it needed to be vehemently asserted. Like František Xaver Šalda, who believed that nationalism had lived to its end with the Austrian empire, Feuchtwanger was a bit too quick to declare his own age a postnationalist one. On the contrary; by the 1930s, European antinationalists seemed to be fewer and fewer. The avant-garde persevered in its internationalist ideology, yet with the rise of the radical Right came a new insecurity. Beneath the enormous warmth of Czech poet Vítěslav Nezval's 1930s correspondence with French surrealists André Breton and Paul Éluard lay an undercurrent of desperation. Nezval traveled west and east, to Paris and to Moscow; he devoted himself to translations of the French surrealists into Czech. Collaborative desires were mutual. The year after Hitler took power in Germany, Breton wrote to Nezval, "I am more than ever before willing to recognize that in the future the surrealist movement should be given an international platform. More than at other times it seems necessary to me that we act in full agreement and that you and your friends have the possibility to express yourselves in all of our publications."[85]

In the spring of 1935, after lengthy organizing efforts and many financial difficulties, Nezval succeeded in bringing Breton and Éluard to Prague. For Nezval, as for the French surrealists, the visit was moving, even ecstatic. And Nezval and his fellow avant-garde poets were not alone in embracing the visitors; the two French poets were also befriended by an outstanding Marxist literary critic and fellow traveler of surrealism. Záviš Kalandra's critical writings were expansive in scope; he wrote of Czech structuralism, German philosophy, Russian literature, and French poetry; of Shakespeare, Kant, Masaryk and Mayakovsky; of Goethe, Dostoevsky, and Breton.[86] Kalandra wrote, too, of the nineteenth-century poet Karel Hynek Mácha, whose lyrical poem "Máj" (May) was the most revered text of Czech Romanticism. Mácha, Kalandra insisted, had nothing in common with present-day Czech patriots. On the contrary; all of these patriots "must have been offended and disturbed by the *cosmopolitanism* resounding from 'Máj.' The whole vast earth, not only that between Šumava and the Tatras, the *whole* earth without borders is here proclaimed as a 'single homeland'!"[87] Kalandra impressed the French surrealists with his intellect—and his openness.

After returning home, Éluard wrote to Nezval of how Paris seemed cold and sad after his time in Prague.[88] Breton wrote to Nezval that he had taken from Prague the most beautiful memories of his life, and that Nezval should know that "you have acquired me completely, that for you I'm willing to do *everything*, that you are my best friend."[89] The sentiments were reciprocated. "No feeling," Nezval told Breton, "has seemed to me so valuable, so sublime as the thought that I can call you my adored friend."[90] To Éluard, Nezval wrote:

> Dear friend, divine Éluard. . . . Now, when there's sun in Prague and when this city is created to please poets, missing here is you, you whose name, as I've said, is the synonym of poetry. Again I repeat to myself all of your words, I hear your voice, I see you. . . . You do not know, dear friend, what you are to me. . . . Believe me that your poetry will be translated into Czech with love and that the moments I dedicate to it are the happiest moments of my life.

Today I am sending you several of my poems in literal translation. Dear friend, that these lines have been permitted to find themselves before your eyes has already justified my entire life. No longer is it necessary for small nations to shed tears when the marvelous Paul Éluard, by his own hand, is able to render an invisible language visible. Only now, dear friend, does it seem to me that I am beginning to live, that I am beginning to feel again. I love you. We all love you.[91]

The Tragedy of Central Europe

An exiled Russian told Stefan Zweig, "Formerly man had only a body and a soul. Now he needs a passport as well for without it he will not be treated like a human being."[92] The years following the First World War were the years of passports—and the years of a polarizing political-ideological spectrum. Among the points of natural convergence between the avant-garde and communism was internationalism; and in fact throughout the 1920s, "New Art" and communism flirted, seduced, and coupled.[93] In Slovakia it was the talented Vladimír Clementis who, raised in the provincial town of Tisovec, studied in Prague, Germany, and France, and while at home founded the most important avant-garde journal in Slovakia, *DAV*.[94] He was both an avant-garde writer and a radical leftist; in his youth he had been a member of the Free Collective of Student-Socialists from Slovakia—"from Slovakia, not Slovak," as one of Clementis's comrades explained, "because we felt ourselves to be internationalists."[95] When Ilya Ehrenburg visited Slovakia, it was Clementis who hosted him. The two became friends, and Ehrenburg later wrote of Clementis: "He never turned his gaze for a moment from Moscow—for the DAVists each member of LEF possessed greater authority than all of the surrealists of the world."[96] Among young avant-garde writers, Clementis was far from alone in deciding that yes, Paris was special, but Moscow was still more so.

Clementis traveled to Soviet Kharkiv for the 1930 International Congress of Revolutionary Literature, as did the French surrealist poet Louis Aragon.[97] He and his Russian muse Elsa Triolet, together with Ehrenburg, Mayakovsky, and Henri Barbusse, were among the preeminent European emissaries of Communist internationalism.[98] In the case of Triolet and Aragon, she brought him closer to Russia, and he brought her closer to France. In the days of constructivism, Triolet had gone to Berlin; in later years both she and Aragon grew close to Czech writers in Prague; they organized French translations of Ukrainian literature.[99] "I loved foreigners—already when I was a small child," Aragon once said.[100]

Vladimir Mayakovsky was not present at the Kharkiv congress. Lilia and Osip Brik had been abroad in Berlin that spring of 1930 when at 6:47 on the evening of 14 April, the telegram arrived from Moscow: "This morning Volodia took his own life."[101] They hurried back to Russia. Two weeks later Triolet wrote to her sister, "I dream of him every single night. It's very difficult. A letter full of despair arrived from Roma [Jakobson]. The Ehrenburgs are going about in a fever. . . . [Aragon] has cried his eyes out over Volodia."[102] Mayakovsky's death was their dystopian moment, the symbolic failure of the new world. In Prague Jakobson composed a eulogy to his friend, whose unceasing theme had been "weariness with fixed and narrow confines, the urge to transcend static boundaries."[103] "It is our generation," Jakobson wrote, "that has suffered the loss."[104]

The Russian Revolution had mobilized the alluring poet as its European ambassador. Mayakovsky's role was important to the Bolsheviks, as was more generally Communist internationalism. Contained within this was perhaps both a deliberate attempt to forge a Communist unity and an adoption of a certain central European tradition. The internationalism of both the avant-garde and the Communists was ideologized and totalized; it was not the same as the largely unarticulated cosmopolitanism of nineteenth-century central Europe.[105] Yet nor was it unrelated. The avant-garde inherited from the cosmopolitan intellectuals, among other things, an assumption of multilingualism and an imagination that encompassed, but rarely transcended, the boundaries of Europe. For Stefan Zweig, it was the Great War and the subsequent introduction of passports that brought to European intellectuals a tragic loss of innocence.

While the moment of rupture was not quite so distinct, Zweig's intuition of a loss of innocence was apt: in its call for internationalism, the avant-garde implicitly—and despite itself—accepted the primacy of the nation- and state-building paradigm. Of folk traditions it is said that once the folklore collectors arrive, it is already too late: their very presence suggests that the thing they want to capture is disappearing. So it was with the internationalism of the avant-garde. By the time the futurists and surrealists arrived on the scene, internationalism had lost its unselfconsciousness. The change was perhaps more radical than it might appear. The very demand for the crossing of barriers suggested an acknowledgment that those barriers existed and had their own meaning. As it were, the avant-garde declared nationalism passé at the very moment when nationalism was taking on a radicalized form. It was a willful failure of discernment. The structuralists gathered around Roman Jakobson in Prague and the phenomenologists gathered around Edmund Husserl first in Göttingen, then in Freiburg represented, perhaps, the last great moments of cosmopolitanism à la *Mitteleuropa*. They very much still existed as the new avant-garde was arriving on the scene, and thus for a time, as if outside of the struggle between nationalism and internationalism, there lingered a cosmopolitan parallel polis—largely unarticulated as such and dedicated to discerning universal principles. In this sense, among so many others, the decades before the

Second World War were very much years of incongruent coexistence, of the *Ungleichzeitigkeit des Gleichzeitigen.*[106]

———

When in the midst of the First World War Husserl moved from Göttingen to Freiburg, his young assistant Edith Stein followed. There in Freiburg in 1916 Stein submitted her doctorate, "On the Problem of Empathy." Soon after, Husserl told her that she could only accept a man as her husband if this man were also to become Husserl's assistant. "Highly unpropitious!" she wrote of this condition to her friend Roman Ingarden.[107] Ingarden, the Polish patriot who loved Rainer Maria Rilke and hoped to write his habilitation thesis in Paris, had also followed Husserl from Göttingen to Freiburg.[108] It was he who in 1915 brought Husserl's ideas into Polish with a review of *Logische Untersuchungen* (Logical Investigations) in a Polish philosophical journal.[109] He did not marry Husserl's young assistant. Instead, Ingarden married a Pole from the eastern borderlands who had finished gymnasium in imperial Russian Kharkov and medical studies in Kiev and who spoke French and German as well as Polish and Russian. Soon after, in 1922, Edith Stein converted to Catholicism; she left Husserl to teach at a Dominican girls' school in the Rhineland. After Hitler came to power, she entered a Carmelite monastery in Cologne.

The last of Husserl's dazzling students was a young Czech philosopher, Jan Patočka, who had come to Freiburg in the early 1930s via Prague and Paris to study with the aging philosopher and his prodigy, Martin Heidegger. Patočka helped to found the Cercle philosophique de Prague, which in 1935, together with the Prague Linguistic Circle, invited Husserl to give a lecture.[110] By this time Husserl was no longer well. Upon his retirement in 1928, he had succeeded in having Heidegger appointed to his chair at the University of Freiburg. Five years later Heidegger joined the Nazi Party and became the university's rector. Very soon after, he sent a letter to all professors deemed Jewish by Nazi racial laws, forbidding them to enter the university premises. Husserl was among those who received the letter.[111] By this time Husserl's old friend, the former philosophy student who shared the elitism of central Europe's cosmopolitan intellectual milieu, was president of Czechoslovakia; Masaryk envisioned the country he would create as Zweig envisioned the Austria of his youth: multinational and humanist, located at the very center of Europe.[112] In January 1935 Husserl wrote to Masaryk of his decision to accept the invitation to Prague:

> Yes, I dare to take up our old, once natural conversation, and pass over the formidable distance in status which European history has created between us. Allow me to write to you today as if you were still a university lecturer in Vienna. How can I do this? This by way of explanation: A young Czech

philosopher, Dr. Jan Patočka, who won our favor two years ago, is spending the holidays with our family as a dear guest. . . . As I hear, there is a proposal in the newly formed Cercle philosophique of Prague to invite me for a guest lecture. Despite my age I would (provided I receive official permission) gladly come—for me there would also be the very welcome prospect of possibly seeing you. It is a pleasure in my old age that finally, and at the very end, a certain interest in my life's work has stirred in my homeland.

On Masaryk's own life's work Husserl added:

May your old ideal of a national ethical entity [*Dasein*] come true to the fullest, on this summit Providence has placed you and chosen you as guardian angel: a single *Staatsvolk*, bound through love for a common homeland and through the unity of the fatherland's history—a *Staatsvolk* not divided by the various languages, but rather mutually enriched and elevated by their participation in linguistically formed cultural achievements. You educated me to this ideal all those years ago in Leipzig! May the Republic through such political-ethical ennoblement become the foundation for the renewal of *European* culture, direly endangered by nationalist degeneracy.

"From the heart," Husserl signed the letter, "in unchanging reverence and friendship."[113]

Masaryk died in 1937, and Husserl the following year. In 1938 the novelist Karel Čapek said at a Prague PEN Club meeting of the Czechoslovakia created by Masaryk, "It is not so small a country—it is Europe in miniature, it is the continent's west and east brought together, so to speak, in a single hand."[114] Within months Czechoslovakia would be no more; when Roman Jakobson understood that the Germans would come to Prague, he headed for the train station. There, on the platform, he saw his old friend the Devětsil poet Jaroslav Seifert. "'I was glad to be in this country," he told Seifert in parting, "and I was happy here. And if it brings you any consolation, I can tell you that I feel myself to be Czech and I am sad."[115]

Epilogue: Terror

Jakobson escaped with his life. In this way, too, he was exceptional. For by then, fervent utopians had made much progress in their projects of social engineering on unprecedented scales: Europe was falling into totalitarian dystopia. Záviš Kalandra spent the long years of the Second World War in Nazi concentration camps. In 1941 Tadeusz Boy-Żeleński was shot to death by the Nazis in L'viv. In 1942 Edith Stein, the phenomenologist and Carmelite nun, was taken to Auschwitz and gassed as a Jew. That same year Stefan Zweig committed suicide in Brazil.

Then Stalin defeated Hitler, and Stalinism came to east-central Europe. Vladimír Clementis became minister of foreign affairs of the Communist Czechoslovak Republic. Soon, though, he and thirteen of his fellow Communists were arrested by their own comrades and tried as Trotskyites, Zionists, Titoists, bourgeois nationalists, traitors, spies, saboteurs, enemies of the Czechoslovak nation, and enemies of socialism. In prison their interrogators tortured them. The defendants all gave elaborate, self-flagellating confessions. Clementis was among the eleven who were hanged.

By this time Clementis had already been among the audience at similar shows. Two years earlier, he had watched his comrades sentence his fellow Marxist and avant-gardist Záviš Kalandra. After his sentencing, Kalandra asked that he be allowed to say good-bye to his wife and give her his manuscripts. Then he asked for cigarettes, soda water, and food.[116]

In Paris on 13 June 1950, André Breton wrote an open letter to his friend Paul Éluard, reminding him of the trip they had taken together to Prague some fifteen years earlier:

> In the slightly frantic bustle of those first few days, there is, if you recall, one man who comes by, who joins us as often as possible, who does his best to try and understand us, a man who is *open*. . . . I think you remember the name of that man: he is—or was—Záviš Kalandra. I dare not decide which tense to use since the papers have just announced that he was sentenced to death last Thursday by a Prague tribunal—after the usual "confession" in due form, naturally. . . . How can you tolerate, deep down, such degradation to be inflicted on a man who was a friend to you?[117]

Fourteen days later, at 4:36 a.m., Záviš Kalandra was taken to his hangman. He had no last words.[118] Paul Éluard, the utopian, did not intervene on his friend's behalf, for the joyous new world had arrived, and Éluard was too busy dancing.[119]

Notes

1. I am grateful to Amelia Glaser, Michael Gordin, Timothy Snyder, and the anonymous reviewer for comments on an earlier draft of this essay. For a Freudian reading of the failure of liberalism, see Carl Schorske, *Fin-de-siècle Vienna: Politics and Culture* (New York: Vintage Books, 1981).

2. Georg Lukács, *History and Class Consciousness*, trans. Rodney Livingstone (Cambridge, MA: MIT Press, 2002), 27. Slavoj Žižek similarly understands the Marxist revolution as "a situation of metaphorical condensation in which it finally becomes clear to the everyday consciousness that it is not possible to solve any particular question without solving them all." Slavoj Žižek, *The Sublime Object of Ideology* (London: Verso, 1989), 3.

3. See D. Burlyuk, A. Kruchenykh, V. Mayakovsky, and V. Khlebnikov, "A Slap in the Face of Public Taste," in *Russian Literature of the Twenties: An Anthology*, ed. Carl R. Proffer et al. (Ann Arbor: Ardis, 1987), 542.

4. Stefan Zweig, *The World of Yesterday*, trans. Harry Zohn (Lincoln: University of Nebraska Press, 1964), 13.

5. Edmund Husserl, *Logische Untersuchungen*, pt. 2 (Halle: Max Niemeyer, 1901), 7.

6. A clear exposition of Husserl's phenomenology can be found in Krzysztof Michalski's *Heidegger i filozofia współczesna* (Warsaw: Państwowy Instytut Wydawniczy, 1998).

7. Freud and psychoanalysis comprise a contemporaneous cosmopolitan milieu and are an interesting counterpoint to phenomenology.

8. Edmund Husserl, *Briefwechsel*, band 1, *Die Brentanoschule*, ed. Elisabeth Schumann and Karl Schumann (Dordrecht: Kluwer Academic Publishers, 1994), 106.

9. Quoted in Antoine Marès' "La Tchécoslovaquie entre l'est et l'ouest (1918–1938): Remarques introductives," *Prague entre l'est et l'ouest: L'émigration russe en Tchécoslovaquie, 1920–1938*, ed. Milan Burda (Paris: L'Harmattan, 2001), 15.

10. See the correspondence between Husserl and Twardowski in Husserl's *Briefwechsel*.

11. See Emmanuel Levinas, *Discovering Existence with Husserl*, trans. Richard A. Cohen and Michael B. Smith (Evanston: Northwestern University Press, 1998). See also Samuel Moyn, "Judaism against Paganism: Emmanuel Levinas's Response to Heidegger and Nazism in the 1930s," *History and Memory* 10, no. 1 (Spring 1998): 25–58.

12. Thomas Seifrid, *The Word Made Self: Russian Writings on Language, 1860–1930* (Ithaca, NY: Cornell University Press, 2005), 133.

13. Jindřich Toman, *The Magic of a Common Language: Jakobson, Mathesius, Trubetzkoy, and the Prague Linguistic Circle* (Cambridge, MA: MIT Press, 1995), 29–30.

14. See Maryse Dennes, "*L'École russe de phénoménologie* et son influence sur le *Cercle linguistique de Prague*: Gustav Špet et Roman Jakobson," in *Prague entre l'est et l'ouest*, ed. Burda, 32–63.

15. Edward Stankiewicz, "Baudouin de Courtenay: His Life and Work," in *A Baudouin de Courtenay Anthology: The Beginnings of Structural Linguistics*, by Jan Baudouin de Courtenay, trans. and ed. Edward Stankiewicz (Bloomington: Indiana University Press, 1972), 10–11. De Courtenay also protested tsarist political suppression of national minorities, and on one occasion he was imprisoned for several months as a result of his political brochure "The Territorial and National Mark in Autonomy," dedicated "to all patriots."

16. Quoted in Stankiewicz's "Baudouin de Courtenay," 8.

17. "A Survey of the Slavic Linguistic World with Relation to Other Indo-European Languages," in *A Baudouin de Courtenay Anthology*, trans. and ed. Stankiewicz, 308–18.

18. Ibid., 316.

19. See Sergei Kartsevskij to unknown, Geneva, 27 May 1916, in *Letters and Other Materials from the Moscow and Prague Linguistic Circles, 1912–1945*, ed. Jindřich Toman (Ann Arbor: Michigan Slavic Publications, 1994), 33–35.

20. Ferdinand de Saussure (1857–1913), *Course in General Linguistics*, trans. Roy Harris (Chicago: Open Court, 1996), 230. Also see Roman Jakobson, "Sergei Karcevskij: August 18, 1884–November 7, 1955," *Cahiers Ferdinand de Saussure* 14 (1956): 10.

21. "Jan Baudouin de Courtenay a poetyka formalistów," *Pamiętnik Literacki* 62, no. 1 (1971): 143–51.

22. Quoted in Victor Erlich's *Child of a Turbulent Century* (Evanston: Northwestern University Press, 2006), 129. On the Moscow Linguistic Circle (Moskovskii Lingvisticheskii Kruzhok) and the Society for the Study of Poetic Language (Obshchestvo izucheniia teorii poeticheskogo iazyka), see Victor Erlich, *Russian Formalism: History-Doctrine* (New Haven: Yale University Press, 1981).

23. Viktor Shklovsky, "Art as Device," in *Theory of Prose*, trans. Benjamin Sher (Normal, IL: Dalkey Archive Press, 1990), 5. Originally published as "Isskustvo kak priëm."

24. Shklovsky, "Art as Device," 6.

25. Zweig, *World of Yesterday*, 24.

26. Ibid., 127.

27. Bohumil Kubišta, "Josef Mánes Exhibition at the Topič Salon," in *Between Worlds: A Sourcebook of Central European Avant-Gardes, 1910–1930*, ed. Timothy O. Beson and Éva Forgács (Cambridge, MA: MIT Press, 2002), 57–58.

28. Stanisław Przybyszewski's Kraków-based fin-de-siècle journal *Życie* (Life), for example, was strikingly *à la page* with respect to politics and culture in Paris, Prague, and Berlin. On *Życie*, see Nathan Wood, "Becoming Metropolitan: Krakow Popular Press and the Representation of Modern Urban Life, 1900–1915" (PhD diss., Indiana University, 2004).

29. Tadeusz Boy-Żeleński, "Mes confessions" (Conférence donnée le 19 Février 1927, au Grand Amphithéâtre de la Sorbonne), published as a pamphlet, *Les amis de la Pologne* (1928), 16.

30. Ibid., 12.

31. Ibid., 18.

32. Zweig, *World of Yesterday*, 235.

33. Ibid., 238.

34. Ibid., 239.

35. Viktor Shklovskii, "Sentimental'noe puteshestvie: Vospominaniia, 1917–1922," in *"Eshche nichego ne konchilos'. . .",* ed. V. P. Kochetov (Moscow: Propaganda, 2002), 21–266. In English: Viktor Shklovsky, *A Sentimental Journey: Memoirs, 1917–1922*, trans. Richard Sheldon (Champaign, IL: Dalkey Archive Press, 2004).

36. Boy-Żeleński, "Mes confessions," 19–20.

37. Zweig, *World of Yesterday*, 326–27.

38. František Xaver Šalda, "Nacionalism a internacionalism," in *Soubor díla F. X. Šaldy: Kritické projevy-12, 1922–1924* (Prague: Československý spisovatel, 1959), 53–55.

39. Roman Jakobson to Elsa Triolet, Prague, 17 September [1920], in Roman Jakobson's *My Futurist Years*, ed. Beng Jangfeldt, trans. Stephen Rudy (New York: Marsilio Publishers, 1992), 112.

40. R. O. Iakobson to V. B. Shklovskii, 7 November 1922, in *Roman Jakobson: Texts, Documents, Studies* (Moscow: Rossiskii Gosudarstvennyi Gumanitarnyi Universitet, 1999), 111–13.

41. V. B. Shklovskii and G. O. Vinokur to R.O. Iakobson, 16 August 1924, ibid., 116–19.

42. Roman Jakobson to Vladimir Maiakovskii, Prague, 8 February 1921, fond 336, opis' 5, delo 119, Rossiiskii Gosudarstvennyi Arkhiv Literatury i Iskusstva, Moscow.

43. Viktor Shklovskii, *Zoo, or Letters Not about Love*, trans. and ed. Richard Sheldon (Ithaca, NY: Cornell University Press, 1971), 42.

44. On the origins of the Prague Linguistic Circle (Pražský linguistický kroužek), see Ladislav Matejka's preface to *Sound, Sign and Meaning: Quinquagenary of the Prague Linguistic Circle*, ed. Ladislav Matejka (Ann Arbor: University of Michigan, 1978), ix–xxxiv.

45. Prague Linguistic Circle, "Theses Presented to the First Congress of Slavic Philologists in Prague, 1929," in *The Prague School: Selected Writings, 1929–1946*, ed. Peter Steiner, trans. John Burbank et al. (Austin: University of Texas Press, 1982), 3–31. On the ways in which Czech structuralism developed in a different direction from that of Russian formalism, see Peter Steiner, "The Roots of Structuralist Esthetics," ibid., 174–219. On the seminal nature of Russian formalism and Czech structuralism, see Galin Tihanov, "Why Did Modern Literary Theory Originate in Central and Eastern Europe? (And Why Is It Now Dead?)," *Common Knowledge* 10, no. 1 (2004): 61–81.

46. N. S. Trubetzkoy to Roman Jakobson, 19 September 1928, in Trubetzkoy's *Studies in General Linguistics and Language Structure*, ed. Anatoly Liberman, trans. Marvin Taylor and Anatoly Liberman (Durham: Duke University Press, 2001), 187.

47. Milada Součková, "The Prague Linguistic Circle: A Collage," in *Sound, Sign and Meaning*, ed. Matejka, 2.

48. Erlich, *Child of a Turbulent Century*, 132.

49. See, for example, Roman Jakobson, "The Newest Russian Poetry: Velimir Xlebnikov [Excerpts]," in *My Futurist Years*, ed. Jangfeldt, trans. Rudy.

50. See Vladimir Markov, ed., *Manifesty i programmy russkikh futuristov* (Munich: Wilhelm Fink, 1967), 53–58.

51. See, for example, Anatol Stern, "Pierwszy grzech," in *Wiersze zebrane*, ed. Andrzej K. Waśkiewicz (Kraków: Wydawnictwo Literackie, 1986); Adam Ważyk, "Niedziela," in *Poezja polska okresu międzywojennego*, ed. Michał Głowiński, Janusz Sławiński, and Janusz Stradecki (Wrocław: Zakład Narodowy imienia Ossolińskich, 1987), 301–2; and Tadeusz Peiper, "Naga," in *Poezja polska*, 317.

52. Jaroslav Seifert, *Všecky krásy světa* (Prague: Československý spisovatel, 1993), 360.

53. Jindřich Toman, "A Marvelous Chemical Laboratory . . . and Its Deeper Meaning: Notes on Roman Jakobson and the Czech Avant-Garde between the Two Wars," in *Language, Poetry, Poetics, the Generation of the 1890s: Jakobson, Trubetzkoy, Majakovskij*, ed. Krystyna Pomorska et al. (Berlin: Mouton de Gruyter, 1987), 313–46, 314–15. The poem appeared in the 27 December 1920 issue of *Den* under the title "Sestry blýskavice."

54. Seifert, *Všecky krásy světa*, 364.

55. I owe the formulation "reification of contingency" to Katerina Clark, *Petersburg: Crucible of Revolution* (Cambridge, MA: Harvard University Press, 1995). On Dada and *obnazhenie*, see Stephen Rudy, introduction to Roman Jakobson's *My Futurist Years*, xxi–xxii.

56. Tristan Tzara, "Trzeci list z Paryża: DADA," *Zwrotnica* 3 (November 1922): 76–78.

57. Roman Jakobson, "Dada," in *Between Worlds*, ed. Beson and Forgács, 359–63.

58. "Nationality" here is "*státní příslušnosti*" and refers to *de jure* nationality in the sense of country of citizenship. Teige's "Slova, slova, slova," quoted in Jeanette Fabianová's "Ruku v ruce s básnictvím: Roman Jakobson a Umělecký svaz Devětsil," *Slovo*

a smysl/Word and Sense: A Journal of Interdisciplinary Theory and Criticism in Czech Studies, no. 4 (Summer 2006): 86.

59. Jindřich Toman makes this point in "Marvelous Chemical Laboratory," 321.

60. Tadeusz Peiper, "W Bauhausie," *Zwrotnica* 12 (June 1927): 255–56.

61. Henryk Berlewi, *Le graphisme fonctionnel polonais des années vingt/Funktionelle Grafik der zwanziger Jahre in Polen/Functional Design of the Twenties in Poland* (Paris: Separata aus 'Neue Grafik' no. 9/Spread of 'New Graphic Design' no. 9/Tirage à part de 'Graphisme actuel' no. 9). Also see Henryk Berlewi, "Mechano-Facture," in *Between Worlds*, ed. Beson and Forgács, 489–91.

62. Berlewi, *Graphisme fonctionnel*.

63. Bruno Iasenskii, Aleksander Vat, and Anatol' Stern to Vladimir Maiakovskii, Warsaw, 1 July 1921, fond 2852, opis' 1, delo 599, Rossiiskii Gosudarstvennyi Arkhiv Literatury i Iskusstva.

64. Henri Barbusse to M. Denissovsky, Aument par Senlin (Oise), 4 July 1929, fond 130, opis' 3, delo 54, Gosudarstvennyi Literaturnyi Muzei, Moscow.

65. A. M. Cassandre to V. Mayakovsky, Versailles, 11 December 1927, 7720, Arkhiv Maiakovskogo, Moscow; Felix Sallen to Vladimir Maiakovskii, Vienna, 22 May 1929, 7721, Arkhiv Maiakovskogo, Moscow.

66. Artuš Černik to Vladimir Maiakovskii, Prague, 25 April 1927, R-5532, Arkhiv Maiakovskogo.

67. L. Moholy-Nagy to El Lissitzky, 26 February 1924, 7 April 1924, and 17 April 1924, fond 2361, opis' 1, delo 47, Rossiiskii Gosudarstvennyi Arkhiv Literatury i Iskusstva.

68. Henryk Berlewi to El Lissitzky, Warsaw, 4 March 1924, fond 2361 (L. M. Lisitskii), opis' 1, delo 35, Rossiiskii Gosudarstvennyi Arkhiv Literatury i Iskusstva.

69. Berlewi, *Graphisme fonctionnel*.

70. See *Formiści* 6 (June 1921).

71. Konrad Winkler, "Na nowych drogach sztuki," *Formiści* 6 (June 1921): 2–3. Winkler was distinctly dissatisfied with Poland's comparative showing: "A u nas zacofanie, apatja, nuda i jakaś dziwna dusz i serc omdlałość" (And here in our country backwardness, apathy, boredom, and some kind of strange fatigue of the heart and soul).

72. The roles of technology and war, for instance, differed significantly between Italian and Russian futurism. On Marinetti's visit to Russia, see Jakobson, *My Futurist Years*; see also "Marinetti v Rossii," 1914, fond 177, delo 20, and "Marinetti," delo 159, Arkhiv i Otdel Rukopisei of the Gosudarstvennyi Russkii Muzei, Saint Petersburg.

73. F. T. Marinetti to Vladimir Maiakovskii, [1925], R-325, Arkhiv Maiakovskogo. Marinetti's letters to Teige can be found in fond Karel Teige, č. inv. 235–45, č. přír. 139/62, Literární archiv Památníku národního písemnictví, Prague.

74. F. T. Marinetti, "List," Milan, 1923, *Zwrotnica* 6 (October 1923): 161.

75. L. Markous, "Korespondencja z Paryza," *Formiści* 2 (April 1920): 12.

76. Tytus Czyżewski, "List z Paryża," *Zwrotnica* 3 (November 1922): 73–74.

77. See, for example, Tytus Czyżewski, "List z Paryża," *Zwrotnica* 4 (February 1923): 115–16.

78. Jean Bouchary, "Apollinaire," *Zwrotnica* 10 (September–October 1926): 234–35. See also Guillaume Apollinaire, *Guillaume Apollinaire*, trans. Milan Kundera et al. (Prague: Klub Přátel Poezji Československý, 1965), with an epigraph by Vítěslav

Nezval: "Veliký *Guillaume* bez kterého by nebylo poezie dvácatého století bez kterého by náš věk tápal a pabĕrkoval na klasicích parnasistech a symbolistech."

79. "Paneuropa," *Zwrotnica* 10 (September–October 1926): 236.

80. Oleh S. Ilnytzkyj, *Ukrainian Futurism, 1914–1930: A Historical and Critical Study* (Cambridge: Ukrainian Research Institute, 1997), 61. Oleh Ilnytzkyj, the author of a wonderfully thorough history of Ukrainian futurism, wants very much to make the Ukrainian futurists nationally conscious Ukrainians. And perhaps they were this, but what they wanted above all was to be internationalists. They wanted to speak to Europe. On a closely related subject: Kenneth Moss writes of the tension implicit in the endeavor of those Jewish intellectuals—Yiddishists and Hebraists alike—in the distintegrating Russian empire who wanted to produce "Jewish culture" (itself, Moss notes, a neologism), but at once wanted that authentically Jewish culture to be European, secular, and cosmopolitan. See Kenneth Moss, *Jewish Renaissance in the Russian Revolution* (Cambridge, MA: Harvard University Press, 2009).

81. Quoted in Ilnytzkyj's *Ukrainian Futurism*, 112.

82. Ibid., 113.

83. Ibid., 117.

84. Lion Feuchtwanger, "The Novel of Today Is International," *The Weimar Republic Sourcebook*, ed. Anton Kaes, Martin Jay, and Edward Dimendberg (Berkeley: University of California Press, 1994), 526. First published as "Der Roman von heute ist international," *Berliner Tageblatt*, 25 September 1932.

85. André Breton to Vítěslav Nezval, 26 June 1934, in *Korespondence Vítěslava Nezvala*, by Vítěslav Nezval et al. (Prague: Československý spisovatel, 1981), 63–64.

86. See Záviš Kalandra, *Intelektuál a Revoluce* (Prague: Edice Orientace, 1994).

87. Záviš Kalandra, "Mácha a Palacký," in *Ani labuť ani Lůna: Sborník k stému výročí K. H. Mácha*, ed. Vítěslav Nezval (Prague: Nová edice, 1936), 60. Copy of *Ani labuť ani Lůna* from Beinecke Rare Book and Manuscript Library, Yale University, New Haven, Connecticut.

88. Paul Éluard to Vítěslav Nezval, Paris, April 1935, in *Korespondence Vítěslava Nezvala*, by Nezval et al., 131.

89. André Breton to Vítěslav Nezval, Paris, 14 April 1935, ibid., 83; emphasis in the original.

90. Nezval to Breton, June 1936, ibid., 94.

91. Nezval to Éluard, 7 May 1935, ibid., 134.

92. Zweig, *World of Yesterday*, 409. The phrase in the subtitle is a reference to Milan Kundera's "The Tragedy of Central Europe," trans. Edmund White, *The New York Review of Books* 31, no. 7 (26 April 1984): 33–38.

93. I tell the story of the Polish avant-garde's encounter with Marxism in *Caviar and Ashes: A Warsaw Generation's Life and Death in Marxism, 1918–1968* (New Haven: Yale University Press, 2006). On the relationship between the avant-garde and Bolshevism, see also Clark, *Petersburg*, and Boris Groys, *The Total Art of Stalinism*, trans. Charles Rougle (Princeton: Princeton University Press, 1992).

94. Štefan Drug, *Vladimír Clementis: Kultúrny publicista* (Bratislava: Obzor, 1967). See also Il'ja Erenburg, "Vernosť srdcu a vernosť osodu," in *DAV: Spomienky a štúdie*, ed. Štefan Drug (Bratislava: Vydateľstvo Slovenskej akadémie vied, 1965), 475–81.

95. In the original: Voľne združenie studentov-socialistov zo Slovenska. Jan Poničan, "Svedectvo o Davistoch," in *DAV*, ed. Drug, 302–3.

96. Drug, *Vladimír Clementis*. See also Erenburg, "Vernosť srdcu a vernosť osodu," 476. The group Lef, or Left Front of the Arts, was formed in 1923 for the purpose of joining revolutionary politics and progressive art. The group included the literary figures Mayakovsky, Shklovsky, Nikolai Aseev, Osip Brik, and Sergei Treťiakov; the filmmakers Sergei Eisenstein and Dziga Vertov; and the theater director Vsevolod Meyerhold. Lef's theoretical mandate aimed toward an emphasis on and promotion of form as a vehicle of ideology. Lef existed between 1923 and 1925; subsequently Novyi Lef came into being in 1927 and lasted until 1928.

97. Vladimír Clementis, "Prejav na mezinárodnom kongrese revolučnej literatúry v Charkove 6.–15. Novembra 1930," in *Avantgarda známá a neznámá*, vol. 3 of *Generační diskuse 1929–1931*, ed. Štěpán Vlašín et al. (Prague: Svoboda, 1970), 337–39. On DAV and the Kharkov congress, see also "Otevřený dopis revolučním spisovatelům v Československu, II světova konference proletářské revoluční literatury v Charkově," *Tvorba* roč. 5 (1930): 794. Copy in fond Ladislav Novomeský, Literární archiv Památníku národního písemnictví, Prague.

98. On Ehrenburg's European sojourns and friendships in the 1920s, see Il'ia Erenburg, *Dai oglianut'sia: Pis'ma, 1908–1930*, ed. B. Ia. Frezinskim (Moscow: Agraf, 2004). On Mayakovsky's travels in Europe, see Vladimir Maiakovskii, "Ezdil ia tak," "Nemnogo o chekhe," "Cheshkii pioner," "Naruzhnost Varshavy," and "Poverkh Varshavy," in *Polnoe sobranie sochineniy*, vol. 2 (Kalingrad: FGUIPP Yantarny Skaz, 2002), 82–86, 86–87, 87–88, 88–89, 89–95, respectively. Mayakovsky was twice in Prague, the second and last time in 1928. On Mayakovsky in Prague, see Jiří Weil, "Vladimir Majakovskij a Praha," in fond Jiří Weil, Literární archiv Památníku národního písemnictví. See also Liubov' Feigel'man, *Maiakovskii v strankakh narodnoi demokratii: Chekhoslovakii, Bolgarii, Pol'she* (Moscow: Sovetskii Pisatel', 1952); L. F. Katsis, *Vladimir Maiakovskii: Poet v intellektual'nom kontekste epokhi* (Moscow: Rossiiskii Gosudarstevennyi Gumanitarnyi Universitet, 2004); S. E. Strikhneva, ed., "V tom, chto umiraiu, ne vinite nikogo"? . . . *Sledstvennoe delo V. V. Maiakovskogo: Dokumenty, vospominaniia sovremennikov* (Moscow: Ellis Lak 2000, 2005).

99. M. Bazhan, O. Korniejchuk, and Tychina to Elsa Triolet and Louis Aragon, Kiev, 15 June 1956, fond Elsa Triolet and Louis Aragon, file "Mikola Bazan," Bibilиothèque Nationale de France, Paris. Among the correspondence preserved in the fond Elsa Triolet and Louis Aragon at the Bibiliothèque Nationale de France in Paris is a remarkable series of letters by the Czech editor Antonín Liehm, mostly from the 1960s.

100. Quoted in Dominique Desanti's "Couple Royal, Couple Ambigu," *The Romantic Review* 92, nos. 1–2 (2001): 214.

101. "=segodnia utrom wolodia pokontschil soboi lewa fiania +." Plinkrugov [?] L. G. i F. to Lilia and Osip Brik, 14 April 1930, Moscow, fond 130, opis' 5, delo 27, Gosudarstvenyi Literaturnyi Muzei, Moscow.

102. Elsa Triolet to Lilia Brik, 28 April 1930, in Lilia Brik and Elsa Triolet's *Lilia Brik–El'za Triole: Neizdannaia perepiska (1921–1970)*, ed. Vasilii Katanian (Moscow: Ellis Lak, 2000), 38–39.

103. Roman Jakobson, "On a Generation That Squandered Its Poets," in *My Futurist Years* 214.

104. Ibid., 210.

105. After the Second World War, in 1948, Stalin initiated a campaign against "rootless cosmopolitans" (*bezrodnye kosmopolity*). The moment was one of irony: com-

munism had betrayed itself now not only implicitly, but also explicitly. The anticosmo-politan campaign was Soviet communism's rejection of its own founding ideology, an acknowledgment of the failure of utopia. The Soviet Union had been founded as an internationalist state; communism was never meant to have been "rooted' as such. "Rootless cosmopolitans," as Stalin conceived of them, were Jews, and the anticosmo-politan campaign was an anti-Semitic campaign by another name. Stalin, of course, was right about a certain Jewish predilection for cosmopolitanism. Jews *did* play a special role in central European cosmopolitanism—perhaps not by chance. Esperanto, the cosmopolitan tongue par excellence, was the invention of Ludwik Zamenhof, a Polish Jew from Białystok, and European Jews were among the most enthusiastic devo-tees of the new language. Freud, Husserl, Jakobson, Zweig, Tzara, Berlewi, Moholy-Nagy, Ehrenburg, Lissitzky, Wat, Stern, Stein, Levinas, Shklovsky, Elsa Triolet, and Lilia and Osip Brik were all Jews by birth, even if they declined to embrace a Jewish identity—as they most often did. This, however, is a somewhat separate subject.

106. I am grateful to Michael Wachtel for introducing me to this appealing formu-lation.

107. Edith Stein to Roman Ingarden, Freiburg, 28 January 1917. Edith Stein, *Self-Portrait in Letters, 1916–1942*, trans. Josephine Koeppel (Washington, DC: ICS Books, 1994).

108. See Edmund Husserl, *Briefe an Roman Ingarden* (The Hague: Martinus Nij-hoff, 1968). In 1922, while he was living in Toruń, Poland, and teaching at a secondary school there, Ingarden wrote to Twardowski, asking for his help in procuring a stipend to write his habilitation thesis in Paris. Twardowski responded that he was happy to accept him as his postdoctoral student, but that university politics made it impossi-ble for Twardowski to arrange a stipend for studying abroad the following year. Ingar-den subsequently completed his habilitation under Twardowski in Lwów and went to Paris only in 1927–28 on a fellowship from the Fundusz Kultury Narodowej. Roman Stanisław Ingarden, *Roman Witold Ingarden: Życie filozofa w okresie toruńskie (1921–1926)* (Toruń: Wydawnictwo Universytetu Mikołaja Kopernika, 2000).

109. Roman Ingarden, review of *Logische Untersuchungen*, by Edmund Husserl, *Przegląd Filozoficzny* 18, nos. 3–4 (1915): 305–11.

110. V. Mathesius to E. Husserl, Prague, 11 November 1935, PLK karton 2, Archiv Akademii Věd České Republiky, Prague.

111. On this episode, see Richard Wolin, ed., *The Heidegger Controversy: A Criti-cal Reader* (Cambridge, MA: MIT Press, 1992). See also Elżbieta Ettinger, *Hannah Arendt/Martin Heidegger* (New Haven: Yale University Press, 1995).

112. On Masaryk and the image he cultivated of Czechoslovakia, see Andrea Orzoff, *Battle for the Castle: The Myth of Czechoslovakia in Europe, 1914–1948* (New York: Oxford University Press, 2009).

113. Husserl to Masaryk, Freiburg, 3 January 1935, in Husserl's *Briefwechsel*, band 1, *Die Brentanoschule*, ed. Elisabeth Schumann and Karl Schumann (Dordrecht: Klu-wer Academic Publishers, 1994), 118–20.

114. Karel Čapek, "Au carrefour de l'Europe: Essais sur la Tchécoslovaquie place porte de l'esprit démocratique," PEN Club, Prague, 1938. Quoted in Antoine Marès' "La Tchécoslovaquie entre l'est et l'ouest (1918–1938): Remarques introductives," in *Prague entre l'est et l'ouest*, ed. Burda, 7.

115. Seifert, *Všecky krásy světa*, 365.

116. Karel Kaplan, *Největší politický proces: M. Horáková a spol.* (Brno: Edice Knihy Dokumenty, 1996), 163–64.

117. André Breton, "Open Letter to Paul Eluard," *Free Rein (La Clé des champs)*, trans. Michel Parmentier and Jacqueline d'Amboise (Lincoln: University of Nebraska Press, 1996), 230–31. Originally published as "Lettre ouverte à Paul Eluard," *Combat* (14 June 1950). See also Mark Polizzotti, *The Life of André Breton* (New York: Farrar, Straus and Giroux, 1995), 566–67.

118. Kaplan, *Největší politický proces*, 165.

119. The formulation of Éluard as dancing is from Milan Kundera, *The Book of Laughter and Forgetting*, trans. Michael Henry Heim (New York: Penguin, 1986), 66–67.

8.

DAVID PINDER

The Breath of the Possible:
Everyday Utopianism and the
Street in Modernist Urbanism

> Revolutionary urbanists will not limit their concern
> to the circulation of things, or to the circulation of
> human beings trapped in a world of things. They
> will try to break these topological chains, paving the
> way with their experiments for a human journey
> through authentic life.
> —Guy Debord, "Positions situationnistes sur la circulation"

Introduction

Streets have been prominent battlegrounds in modernist urbanism.[1] As "the terrain of social encounters and political protest, sites of domination and resistance, places of pleasure and anxiety,"[2] they have been continually fought over in architectural and planning discourses as well as through political negotiation, contestation, and struggle. "The very word *street* has a rough, dirty magic to it, summoning up the low, the common, the erotic, the dangerous, the revolutionary," notes Rebecca Solnit. For her the street means "life in the heady currents of the urban river in which everyone and everything can mingle," and she adds: "It is exactly this social mobility, this lack of compartments and distinctions, that gives the street its danger and its magic, the danger and magic of water in which everything runs together."[3] This mobility and mingling have also elicited contrary and often clashing reactions among many others, from delight and fascination to horror and repulsion. As a result, the very existence of the street has often been in question within modernist architectural and urban debate.

"The 'corridor street' must be destroyed!" famously declared Le Corbusier, scrawling these words at the head of an illustration for a lecture in Buenos Aires on 18 October 1929. A vociferous and influential critic, he depicted this space "plunged in eternal twilight" where the sky was "a remote hope far, far above it."[4] Not immune to the pleasures of urban strolling, he acknowledged elsewhere the dramatic spectacle of streets where "every aspect of human life pullulates throughout their length" and where amusement may be gained from watching "in this sea of lusts and faces." Yet the street was for him also an object of disgust, "a relic of the centuries, a dislocated organ that can no longer function," and something he wished was gone.[5] In presenting his utopian urban plans, Le Corbusier thus invited audiences and readers to imagine a contrasting scene in which they would walk free from jostling crowds and honking automobiles, in spacious parks between widely spaced crystal towers of offices. Promenading up gentle ramps, they would look down on "a tossing sea of verdure plumb beneath" while "gigantic and majestic prisms of purest transparency rear their heads one upon another in a dazzling spectacle of grandeur, serenity and gladness." Office workers would now enjoy light, fresh air, and absolute stillness. Meanwhile, the passage of cars along the highways would trace "luminous tracks that are like the tails of meteors flashing across the summer heavens." This, he insisted, had "nothing in common with those appalling nightmares, the down-town streets of New York"; nor was it a "Utopian flight of fancy."[6] Rather, it was based on what he claimed to be a rational, practical, and profitable solution to urban problems. Through a "water-tight formula,'" it separated and sorted the urban river and channeled its flows according to more efficient and less threatening arrangements so as to enhance speed and to avoid chaotic mingling.

Utopian projects to remake modern cities have long targeted streets. They have frequently imagined their reconstruction through spatial plans that project an ideal city or have sought to reshape or even abolish them through grand planning schemes. It was in this regard that Le Corbusier praised the earlier "titanic achievement" in his home city of Paris by Baron Haussmann, whose works during the Second Empire blasted boulevards through cramped working-class districts in an effort to open up the city to the circulation of people, traffic, air, and capital and to ensure the policing of its population. Along with many other planners and architects during the early twentieth century, Le Corbusier aimed to take such "surgery" much further by demolishing altogether the corridor street characterized by buildings on both sides and replacing it with a multileveled system of circulation whereby the street becomes "a traffic machine," "a sort of factory for producing speed."[7] Another admirer of Haussmann, Commissioner of Public Works Robert Moses, later confronted the "appalling nightmares" of downtown streets in New York City with urban clearances and the construction of highways through projects whose utopian dimension lay in their comprehensive effort to usher in what has been termed an "expressway world."[8] Meanwhile, the utopian dream of a city without streets was most fully realized in Brasília, whose design by Lúcio Costa and Oscar Niemeyer, influenced by Le Corbusier and the Congrès internationaux d'architecture moderne (CIAM), eliminated them completely in the belief that they were significant not only for harboring disease and clogging circulation but also for the ways in which they ordered forms of public and private urban life that the planners wished to overturn.[9]

But what of utopian perspectives that, in contrast, find inspiration in modern streets, that seek possibilities from within their "rough, dirty magic"? Such is the focus of this chapter, which addresses aspects of utopianism concerned with cities developed within twentieth-century European avant-gardes. My concern is not with grand planning projects but with recovering the significance of what might be termed an "everyday utopianism" that engaged critically with streets and urban life with a quite different intent. I will introduce that term shortly, but something of its tenor can be indicated through a contrasting depiction of Parisian streets from an inveterate urban walker writing at the same time that Le Corbusier was demanding their demolition. Far from recoiling from streets as spaces of disorder, disease, and threat, the surrealist André Breton emphasized their strong draw and the sense of possibility that could be found in them. "The street, which I imagined capable of communicating to my life its surprising detours, the street with its anxieties and its glances, was my true element," he wrote in his text Les pas perdus in 1924, the year the surrealist group formally emerged; "it was there I partook, as nowhere else, of the wind of possibility."[10]

In the streets one could become open to encounters and coincidences, so Breton and the surrealists believed, to the flow of events, signs, and messages that spoke of hidden desires and the potentiality of modern urban experience. There the hold of habit and routinized behaviors might be loosened, the boundaries between interior and exterior interrupted, and the breath of the possible sensed as one entered into charged relationships with other people, places, and objects and learned to perceive reality afresh. Breton shared the concern of many modernists, among them Le Corbusier, with how the powers of urban imagination had been constrained by old habits of thought and argued in the first Manifesto of Surrealism, also in 1924, that "imagination alone offers me some intimation of what can be."[11] Yet when he added that "imagination is perhaps on the verge of reasserting itself, of reclaiming its rights,"[12] and when he looked toward the prospects for revolutionary change and for the discovery of the marvelous within everyday spaces, he had in mind radically different values, desires, and geographies of Paris than those conjured in Le Corbusier's writings and utopian plans.

Positioning Breton against Le Corbusier in this way should not be taken as implying they were simply and diametrically opposed. Despite the polemics between them, their respective approaches to architecture and cities had points of interconnection and entanglement, as a number of critics have recently discussed.[13] The contrast nevertheless provides a way into considering a distinctive strand of utopianism, one that renounces an ordering perspective from on high and that is concerned explicitly with everyday life and space as well as with the potential for their radical transformation. It also underlines the importance of the street as a contested site in clashes between different utopian visions of urbanism and their demands for radical change, something that threads through the chapter. In the next section I discuss how drawing inspiration from streets has long been an important part of modernist and avant-garde urban culture, and I introduce distinctive aspects of an everyday utopianism concerned with their spaces. In the following sections I explore this theme by focusing primarily on its expression in ideas and practices that emerged in Paris several decades on from the activities of the early surrealist group based around Breton, and that were associated with the Letterist and Situationist Internationals of the 1950s and 1960s. My focus is on their uto-pian desire to transform everyday life and spaces based on the potentialities of the present, as first embodied in their explorations of Paris, and on contempo-raneous critiques of everyday urban life developed especially by the Marxist philosopher Henri Lefebvre. In their writings and activities, which were strongly influenced by surrealism even if they were in different ways critical of that group, streets and everyday life became key concerns for revolutionary politics. The situationists have been the subjects of an increasingly extensive literature since the early 1990s that has written them into histories of the twentieth-century avant-garde. At times this has been in conjunction with an important wider reconsideration of the histories and geographies of modernist urbanism in Europe and North America.[14] In addressing aspects of their utopianism, I seek to contribute to understandings of their spatial politics at a time when their political edge is often diluted.[15] I also want to argue more widely for the enduring value of forms of utopianism concerned with spatial and everyday practices against assumptions that they necessarily involve plans and blueprints for an ideal future, and against those who would only too read-ily dismiss them as such.

Shouts in the Street

There is a long history of modernist urban culture drawing inspiration from city streets and specifically from their activities, energy, clamor, and life. It finds expression in what Marshall Berman, borrowing from Stephen Dedalus in James Joyce's *Ulysses*, and writing about New York in the 1960s in his clas-sic study of experiences of modernity *All That Is Solid Melts into Air*, calls "a shout in the street."[16] Valuing the ordinariness of the street, the electrical charge of its crowds, the coming together of strangers within its spaces, the opportunities it provides for communication, embodied interaction, chance encounters, finding beauty where it is traditionally not supposed to be found, and the potential it embodies for claiming rights to an urban culture commit-ted to justice and freedom—these are the hallmarks of a progressive modern-ism as outlined by Berman. He traces this sensibility through a range of

modernist cultural forms and contexts from within Europe and North America, from Charles Baudelaire's prose poems about nineteenth-century Parisian
street life onward. In relation to New York City, he discusses how these creative and diverse "shouts in the street" confronted what he calls the "expressway world," which he represents in particular through the figure of Robert
Moses, who during the middle decades of the twentieth century sought to reconstruct the city. Moses oversaw vast building programs that led to the construction of new networks of parkways, bridges, and other structures in the city
and surrounding region, and later drove expressways through densely popu-
lated areas as he operated "with a meat ax."[17] Presenting the expressways as
symbols of modernity, he cast those who opposed them as being against progress and indeed against the modern spirit.

The expressway vision was thus marked by a deep antipathy toward urban
streets and their supposed disorderly life, according to Berman, a theme he
traces back to Le Corbusier's earlier demands for streets to be abolished and
replaced by machines for traffic, and to a wider discourse with modernist architecture and urban planning exemplified by the likes of Siegfried Giedion.
Writing in his canonical modernist text *Space, Time and Architecture* in 1938–
39, Giedion credited New York with the creation of the parkway and praised
the perspectives that it had forged. He claimed that the city and especially its
corridor streets were now out of scale with those parkways and bridges, however, and this necessitated changing the city. The current street system "cuts
off the organic development of the city like an iron ring around a tree," he
contended, with the result that the city becomes "deformed," and it "may even
be that the iron ring must burst or the tree die."[18] He looked forward to the
time when "the parkway will go through the city as it does today through the
landscape," that is unhindered, smoothly flowing, its meaning revealed by
driving that allowed the true experience of "the space-time feeling of our period." To enable this, surgery must be performed, and there must no longer be
any place for the city street, which he stressed "cannot possibly be permitted
to persist."[19] Given the importance Giedion attached to the parkway, his
space-time concept has been characterized in the U.S. context as a "Robert
Moses aesthetic";[20] and, indeed, his clinical talk of surgery was in turn soon
put into perspective by the massive scale of the building programs overseen
by Moses in New York City, especially by the brutal destruction of the center of the Bronx during the late 1950s and early 1960s to make way for the
Cross-Bronx Expressway. Berman notes that despite the large scale of these
works, they were only part of a more general new urban order centered on
automobiles in the United States during the postwar decades, an order that
"conceived of cities principally as obstructions to the flow of traffic, and as
junkyards of substandard housing and decaying neighbourhoods from which
Americans should be given every chance to escape."[21] In evoking shouts in the
street in this context, then, Berman refers to forms of opposition that especially

during the 1960s sought to show through alternative visions that other paths were possible, better directions could be charted. He suggests that the everyday life of the street provided a ground for many of these visions, becoming "a source of life and energy and affirmation that was just as modern as the expressway world, but radically opposed to the forms and motions of that world."[22]

A classic book Berman cited as having particular significance in this regard and subsequently shaping planning practices in New York City and far beyond is Jane Jacobs's *The Death and Life of Great American Cities*, from 1961. As is well known, Jacobs derided utopian planners for their supposed authoritarianism and prescriptive ideals. She targeted not only the grand public works promoted by Moses that were then threatening Manhattan but also visionaries such as Ebenezer Howard and Le Corbusier, claiming that the latters' concern with abstract principles about how cities *"ought* to work and what *ought* to be good for people and businesses within them" meant they were unable to appreciate the intricate reality of urban life and of streets, which they consequently depicted in terms of disorder and chaos.[23] She insisted that to comprehend the "real order" of the streets, a different perspective was needed. Starting from her own location of Hudson Street, in Greenwich Village, she eschewed urban utopias in which "the right to have plans of any significance belonged only to the planners in charge" and developed an account of urban vitality, diversity, and life that looked to serve rather than to replace what she saw as a potentially wondrous existing urban order: "a manifestation of the freedom of countless numbers of people to make and carry out countless plans."[24] Berman rightly notes a disturbing side to this vision, whose restrictive class and ethnic basis, and whose undertow of nostalgia for family and neighborhood, can make its appeals to "diversity" seem pastoral, and have made it susceptible to being taken up by those on the political Right to justify forms of exclusionary communitarianism. Yet he suggests that its radicalism stemmed from being locked in dialectical opposition to a modern movement that sought to destroy the street through "urban renewal."[25]

The rhetoric of Jacobs and many other critics of modernist planning visionaries was thus apparently antiutopian or postutopian, as was indeed much architecture and urbanism as it emerged under the sign of the postmodern during the 1970s.[26] Their criticisms are among the reasons why, at the level of urbanism as well as of a wider political debate, it is commonly held that the concept of utopia has waned.[27] A consideration of city streets and everyday urban life as a focus of utopian impulses, as in this chapter, must therefore be conducted against the grain of such perspectives. In particular it requires moving beyond common definitions of utopianism that bind it to the plan, model, or blueprint, which have been prominent in histories of utopian visions of cities, especially in late-nineteenth- and early-twentieth-century Europe, when many schemes were projected that had considerable influence on the discourses and practices of modernist planning and architecture.[28] Such utopias typically emphasize spatial form, with an ideal space being viewed as a key means of guiding urban (re)construction and of resolving social, political, and urban problems. For Le Corbusier and his colleagues within CIAM, for example, presenting a geometric, ordered, bounded, and planned space was a means to counter the consequences of the lack of proper urban planning, which, they contended, was "the cause of the anarchy that reigns in the organization of cities and the equipment of industry."[29] Also significant for many was an insistence on a tabula rasa, either through clearing the existing city or through turning to a fresh site; a break with the past and the announcement of a new beginning in time, enacted by the demolition of differences accumulated in space; and a perceptual shock or defamiliarization sought by imposing a new space on an old urban fabric. Protestations that plans were realistic and "no utopian flight of fancy" were another common move by those wanting to challenge existing norms and to ensure that their schemes were not too easily dismissed.

Referring to the emphasis on fixed spatial form in much utopian thought, David Harvey notes how an ordered space becomes a means of securing social process and history.[30] But while utopias are frequently portrayed in this vein as spaces that may be mapped out, complete with desired geographic configurations and in some cases proposed routes for their realization, the regulatory fixity of such conceptions has been widely challenged, including within the interdisciplinary realm of utopian studies. One common move has been to enlarge the utopian canon to include imaginations and projects that are more process-based and open-ended, involving a reaching toward what is not yet set (see also the introduction in this volume). The utopianism that I consider in what follows has this more open orientation, involving the desire and striving for radically better ways of living. The distinction is akin to that drawn by Fredric Jameson between the "utopian program," concerned with the realization of systemic demands for a new society, spatial totality, or city, and the "utopian impulse" that, following the lead of Ernst Bloch, may be discerned within a whole host of dreams, desires, and anticipations of the future as expressed in a myriad of ways in life and culture.[31] Yet, for the latter utopian impulse not to be free-floating and to move beyond wishful thinking to function critically in terms of willful action, it must engage not only with social processes but also with their spatialities. It must address both how space and time are currently produced and how they might be produced otherwise.[32]

A term I want to invoke here is "everyday utopianism," which might initially seem incongruous, given the ways in which, as Michael Gardiner comments, "utopia" and "everyday" are often understood. Yet, as Gardiner suggests, the term usefully indicates the shift alluded to above from the realm of plans and abstract models toward an understanding of utopianism as focused on "a series of forces, tendencies and possibilities that are immanent in the here and now, in the pragmatic activities of daily existence." It emphasizes the potentialities in the present situation rather than projecting them into another time or space, and it is concerned with "how the ordinary can become extraordinary not by eclipsing the everyday, or imagining we can leap beyond it arbitrarily to some 'higher' level of cognition, knowledge or action, but by fully appropriating and activating the possibilities that lie hidden, typically repressed, within it. Such an enriched experience can then be redirected back to daily life in order to transform it."[33] A core insight he traces through a range of Marxist thinkers is that "the everyday is permeated with political and ideological qualities, and constitutes the crucial terrain for both the exercise of domination and 'utopic' resistances to it."[34] In the hands of the situationists and Lefebvre, this utopian impulse had an explicitly spatial dimension; and in the remaining sections of this chapter, I explore their interest in engaging with and reclaiming streets as constituent elements of their effort to draw out the potential emancipatory qualities of the urban.

Cities on Foot

When Le Corbusier wanted to confront his readers with the horrors of Paris in 1925, to shock them into recognizing the mess around them and hence the need for his proposals for reconstruction, he reached for aerial photographs. Through these "denunciatory photographic documents," as he called them, he aimed to lift the viewer above the streets to demonstrate the terrible conditions in which ordinary people lived. He also hoped to pave the way for his solution, which would excise and replace vast tracts of the city center in the name of a glittering alternative: the Voisin Plan. He wrote: "Our city, which has crawled on the ground till now, suddenly rises to its feet in the most natural way, even for the moment going beyond the powers of our imaginations, which have been constrained by age-long habits of thought."[35] In the years that followed, the aerial view became central to his utopian urbanism as a means of setting cities at a distance and outlining how they should be remade through spatial plans. The airplane examines cities, he announced, it accuses them and indicts them. It was through the slow, calm, and unbroken gaze enabled by the airplane that the real face of the city could be revealed with all the accumulated horrors of its premachine age forms, and the urgency of a utopian plan could be most readily perceived.[36]

Three decades later aerial photographs of the same city were cut up and used to construct a map devoted to a quite different urban project. Four sections of the city appear to float in space. Black arrows link the areas or indicate movements into them, or curve off into the empty surrounds. The lower right corner features a color reproduction of Claude Lorrain's painting *Seaport: The Embarkation of St Ursula*, from 1641, suffused with golden sunlight. At the top a small photograph shows two men walking, their movement through the city suggested by an arrow toward one of the urban areas, with the figures accompanied by the words "La Contrescarpe notre promenade." This map was produced by Guy Debord and was entitled *Axe d'exploration et échec dans la recherche d'un Grand Passage situationniste*. It was among five "psychogeographical maps" by Debord that were advertised to be shown at the Taptoe Gallery in Brussels in February 1957, as part of the "first exhibition of psychogeography," organized by groups that would soon come together to found the Situationist International (SI). Other exhibits were promised from Asger Jorn, Yves Klein, Ralph Rumney, Michèle Bernstein, and Mohamed Dahou in addition to anonymous collective paintings and a drawing by a "mad psychogeographer." Debord's maps never reached the gallery, as he pulled out of the event at the final moment.[37] Instead, Debord appears to have given *Axe d'exploration* later that year to fellow situationist Piero Simondo around the time of the founding conference of the SI at Cosio d'Arroscia, in Italy, in July.[38]

In what ways can Debord's map be considered utopian? The map is both a trace of and a tribute to a walk through Paris that Debord conducted in 1953 with Ivan Chtcheglov, also known by his pseudonym, Gilles Ivain, shown in the photograph with Dahou to his right. The reference to Place Contrescarpe is to one of their favorite areas of Paris, a working-class district on the Left Bank that, following Chtcheglov's lead, they termed Contrescarpe Continent and commended for its "aptitude for play and forgetting."[39] Each section of the aerial photograph below shows what they called a "unity of ambience," through which they passed, initially in a southerly direction through the Contrescarpe Continent, and then seeking a passage to the southeast. The aerial photographs no longer act as "denunciatory documents" but are here cut and repositioned to adopt another perspective, that of the walker in the streets. Employing the technique that the letterists and situationists termed *détournement*, literally diverting or turning aside but also with the connotations of hijacking, Debord recontextualizes the photographs alongside the image of the figures walking and the arrows, and in the process he refunctions them so that they speak not of rising above the city and enabling its reordering, but rather of maneuvers and struggles to find a passage on the ground. The same technique was used in two other maps advertised to appear at the Taptoe Gallery that Debord published in 1957 and that have since been much more widely reproduced and discussed: *The Naked City* and *Discours sur les passions de l'amour* (also entitled *Guide psychogéographique de Paris*).[40] These fragmented and reworked standard cartographies of Paris show selected areas, or "unities of ambience," with red arrows between them suggesting connections, directions, movements, and collective currents.

The maps came out of experiences while Debord, Chtcheglov, Dahou, and Bernstein were members of the small Paris-based Letterist International (LI), established in 1952. They were not artists or writers as such but sought to use all means at their disposal to contest the values of dominant bourgeois society and to chart routes to its radical transformation. Acknowledging that new collective social structures could emerge only through the disappearance of the old, they pledged to contribute to the process by ruthless criticism, by contesting urban spaces, and by encouraging and fueling revolts. Appropriating from existing maps and aerial photographs to produce a "renovated cartography" became one such contestatory practice, a means of challenging dominant representations of urban space while using elements of them to register other desires, values, and ways of engaging with cities.[41] It was part of what Debord and the LI called psychogeography, a term they adopted before it was taken up as a central component of SI's early program and that involved the critical exploration of cities in terms of atmosphere, ambience, emotions, and desires. Primarily developed on foot through *dérives*, or urban drifts, in small groups of two or three people, this included attending to such "neglected" phenomena as the "sudden change of ambiance in a street within the space of a few meters; the evident division of a city into zones of distinct psychic atmospheres; the path of least resistance that is automatically followed in aimless strolls," and "the appealing or repelling character of certain places."[42] Understanding such issues required looking beyond the conditions of the physical environment to consider the social, cultural, and political constitution of spaces, and hence both the operation of powerful interests within cities and the possibilities that could be found and forged there.

Unlike Le Corbusier, who looked down on Paris to formulate a plan meant to make the city rise to its feet, Debord's psychogeographic engagement with the city was at street level and found sustenance and form in footsteps. One side of psychogeography apparent from his maps was its concern with consciously and critically studying spaces from the perspective of lived experience, with the aim of challenging dominant representations and practices and of considering how cities might be changed for the better. Subverting and refunctioning existing images were part of this process of contestation and struggle. But the maps also provide traces of ludic practices and experimental forms of playful behavior. Here the dérive's qualities as a passional journey came to a fore in which participants were meant to engage with the city's spaces through multiple senses, to feel those spaces come alive with an intensity that made every object, encounter, and event seem potentially loaded with significance, to find themselves in an adventurous game that embodied different values and desires. "Now the city would move like a map you were drawing," notes Greil Marcus. "Now you would begin to live your life like a book you were writing. Called forth by a street or a building, an ensemble of gestures might imply that a different street had to be found, that a building could be redesigned by the gestures performed within it, that new gestures had to be made, even that an unknown city had to be built or an old one over-thrown."[43]

Debord's street-level perspective brings to mind an apparently similar move to the streets made some years later by another French theorist, Michel de Certeau. In the first volume of *The Practice of Everyday Life*, originally published in France in 1980, Certeau famously referred critically to the godlike view from on high in which the city is immobilized before the eye and is rendered as a readable text, whether from an aerial perspective or a cartographic portrayal. Despite its importance for understandings of the city as a concept to be administered and ordered, the optical knowledge so produced was characterized as a fiction based on a voyeuristic and even deadening perspective that depends upon a distancing from everyday activities.[44] Relinquishing this view's supposed privileges, Certeau turned to ordinary practitioners of the city whose multiple interweaving practices and physical movements in the streets constitute an urban text that they do not themselves read or consciously write. Making an analogy with the speech act, he suggested that walkers "enunciate" spaces within the constructed order of the city. They do not simply follow ordained paths but drift over, play upon, rework, and overflow imposed terrains through ordinary practices and ways of operating. These ordinary practices became the primary focus of his attention as he invoked their "indeterminate trajectories" and "'traverses' that remain heterogeneous to the systems they infiltrate and in which they sketch out the guileful ruses of *different* interests and desires," and thus likened them to "the snowy waves of the sea slipping in among the rocks and defiles of an established order."[45]

Certeau's account of the spatializing actions of urban practitioners seems suggestive in relation to the trajectories enunciated through Debord's maps. Both refuse the distanced view from above in favor of the wandering, which operates within the realm of the everyday and depends upon a critical attitude to dominant ways of seeing. Both also cast such wandering in a deviant and transgressive light, as a means of resisting the "proper" uses of space. The connection between walking and the speech act that Certeau posited, specifically the procedures of synecdoche and asyndeton that he discusses as pedestrian figures, may further illuminate aspects of Debord's *The Naked City*. As Tom McDonough notes, through a synecdochic procedure the totality of the city map on which *The Naked City* is based—the *Guide taride de Paris* from 1951—is broken into fragments to indicate unities of atmosphere. Meanwhile, through a process of asyndeton, these are disconnected and gaps opened between them that take the form of white space. The result exposes the fabricated character of the original cartographic representation of Paris and, in the process, reveals the distinctions, conflicts, and contradictions that characterize capitalist abstract space but that are hidden in the map's utopian view from nowhere. Debord's map thus "brings these distinctions and differences into the open, the violence of its fragmentation suggesting the real violence involved in constructing [the original map's] homogeneity."[46]

Yet for all the suggestive connections between situationist and Certeauian perspectives on spatial practices, the politics as well as the context for their interventions are quite different. For Certeau the street appears as a relatively unproblematic and even aspatial zone, a site "of a kind of ludic avoidance of conformity and planification, a wily self-production of the self," to use the words of Kristin Ross.[47] Absent from Certeau's account of ordinary urban practices is an adequate sense of the historical geographies of the city through which they take place, and of what specifically they are supposed to "resist." This is despite the fact that, as Ross remarks, Paris had been profoundly transformed during the preceding years through an urban restructuring that produced new divided social geographies; the city had further been shaken by the revolutionary struggles of May 1968 that had contested the control and social ordering of its streets and spaces. In posing his celebratory account of ground-level everyday practices against a systemic power that is on high, Certeau effectively leaves unexamined the forces of political power and the prospects of more strategic forms of struggle. He provides a highly compelling and often poetic account of creative maneuvering, tactical incursions, ruses, ways of doing, and the like, but when it comes to the streets that are the medium for such activities, so Ross notes, confrontation or contradiction "has been ruled out in advance"; his ordinary walkers are presented in "a timeless vacuum, devoid of any contact with history, recent or otherwise."[48] His theory of the everyday more generally is detached from a totalizing critique of capitalism and leads instead, as John Roberts argues, toward a figure of the "creative consumer" and an account of resistance that has become familiar within Anglophone cultural studies, involving "the *recoding* and resymbolization of the signifying systems of bourgeois culture." Unattached from any counterhegemonic theory, this recoding "exists as a tactical insinuation of the voices and practices of the working class and marginalized into the spaces, traditions and forms of the dominating."[49] In contrast, the impacts of urban changes as well as the prospects for the revolutionary transformation of cities and everyday life were central concerns of letterist and situationist urban explorations, as I will discuss in the next section.

Street Oppositions

Letterist and situationist psychogeographies were developed in opposition to forces that were remaking urban spaces and streets in the postwar period. That context is vital for understanding a map such as *Axe d'exploration*, with its invocation of exploration and charting new paths. Initially emerging in Paris in the early 1950s, psychogeography became a means of confronting a city that was starting to change rapidly through a process of capitalist modernization that over the next twenty years involved the dramatic restructuring of its geographies. The scale of this transformation was comparable to that overseen by Haussmann the century before, as between the mid-1950s and the mid-1970s vast areas of the city were reconstructed and more than half a million residents were displaced, especially along class and ethnic lines. The center of the city became increasingly a space of privilege as rents soared and working-class districts were targeted for "renewal" and "cleaning up," with much of their population being dispersed to the new towns, or *grands ensembles*, on the periphery. Those living on the outskirts of Paris, in particular many immigrant workers from former colonies, were cast beyond the city. The city became increasingly oriented toward the requirements of the automobile, as planners and politicians sought to accommodate and embrace motorization as an aspect of modernization. It was a period in the city when streets, understood as a space of encounter and interaction, conducive to pedestrian movement, were reconstituted.[50]

Many letterists, in their early writings during the 1950s, were concerned with the role of architects and planners in such processes. Referring to how urban planning had "always found inspiration in police directives," they noted that "Haussmann only gave us these boulevards to make it easier to roll cannons through them." But they believed that housing was now increasingly based on the prison, and in this regard they saved their most vicious rhetoric for Le Corbusier—renamed Le Corbusier-Sing-Sing—who, they argued, is "trying to *do away with streets*." They added: "He even brags about it. His program? To divide life into closed, isolated units, into societies under perpetual surveillance," a project that would lead to "no more opportunities for uprisings or meaningful encounters; to enforced resignation."[51] Complaining about the "banalization" of streets, urban spaces, and homes in 1953, Chtcheglov also took a swipe at Le Corbusier's architectural style as being suitable for "factories and hospitals, and no doubt for prisons," but as "destroying the last remnants of joy."[52] Through their urban explorations, the letterists confronted more widely how political, economic, and cultural changes were being wrought through the production of new urban spaces, and their attention to commodification, control, and unfreedoms tempered the street romanticism that can be discerned in their accounts of urban wandering. Many letterist reports and maps focused on areas under threat and sought to document and defend them against the bulldozers. Examples included such favorite haunts as rue Sauvage in the thirteenth arrondissement, whose disappearance they deplored as the loss of "[o]ne of the most beautiful spontaneously psychogeographical places in Paris" whose status as a little-known street made it "more *alive* than the Champs Elysées for all its bright lights,"[53] and the central market area of Les Halles, with its mix of population and activities.[54] By 1967 Debord could write in *The Society of the Spectacle*: "The effort of all established

216

powers, since the experience of the French Revolution, to augment their means of keeping order in the street has eventually culminated in the suppression of the street itself."[55] He understood the attack on streets as part of an urbanist program that was intent on ensuring the fundamental isolation of people, as it functioned as "the technology of *separation itself.*"[56] As such, it was a key part of the society of the spectacle, a society marked by a new stage in the accumulation of capital and the mediation of social relationships by images as the commodity colonized ever more aspects of social life.

Among those sharing the situationists' critical concerns was Henri Lefebvre. His early writings on everyday life, developing out of his work on mystification and alienation during the 1930s that led to the first volume of his *Critique of Everyday Life* in 1947 and many subsequent studies, had been influential on the thinking of the younger Debord and situationists. Their interest in psychogeography and urbanism in turn influenced him through an intense, if later fractious, association at the end of the 1950s and beginning of the 1960s, a period when he increasingly turned to urban questions. In his writings on cities, Lefebvre similarly criticized Le Corbusier's approach, especially the emphasis on his urban plans on circulation. He reflected in a later interview that Le Corbusier was "a good architect but a catastrophic urbanist, who prevented us from thinking about the city as a place where different groups can meet, where they may be in conflict but also form alliances, and where they participate in a collective *oeuvre.*"[57]

For Lefebvre the street was threatened by the invasion of the automobile and the pressure of the automobile lobby, which had "turned the car into a key object, parking into an obsession, traffic into a priority, harmful to urban and social life."[58] More generally, he noted how the street may be emptied out, reduced to circulation and pure flow, and become a desert. The elimination of the street, he stated, something witnessed in many new towns where movements were channeled through commercialized and controlled walkways, leads to "the extinction of life, the reduction of the city to a dormitory, the aberrant functionalization of existence."[59] Like the letterists and situationists, he further noted how streets may be dominated by the commodity and the image. Streets may also be sites of repression, their speech and demonstrations silenced, or of harassment and persecution. Differential access to streets according to gender, ethnicity, and other axes of identity, as well as class, was important here, something to be remembered against overly celebratory discussions of the potential freedoms and adventures of their spaces.

At the same time, however, Lefebvre asserted that the street is more than a channel for circulation. It is, so he argued, a vital place for meetings, encounters, interactions, communication, and spontaneous theater. It is where the possibilities and choices characteristic of the city are offered. It changes and repeats itself continually, with varying rhythms. As such, the street embodies the everyday in condensed form, with more life than the places it links together.[60] Lefebvre thus pointed to functions of the street overlooked by Le Corbusier and by contemporary "technocrats" of space whose ideologies defined the city as a network of circulation and communication. These functions included "the informative function, the symbolic function, the ludic function." He added: "The street is a place to play and learn. The street is disorder. All the elements of urban life, which are fixed and redundant elsewhere, are free to fill the streets and through the streets flow to the centers, where they meet and interact, torn from their fixed abode. This disorder is alive. It informs. It surprises."[61] Lefebvre here cited the work of Jane Jacobs on the significance of a busy street in providing security against criminal violence and hence an order of its own. But he looked further toward radical sociospatial transformation in suggesting that through the appropriation of space, use and use value can gain prominence over exchange and exchange value. The street for him was important as a space for popular and rebellious energies to ferment. It could act as a place for different kinds of speech, communication, and writing, where speech can become wild and inscribe itself on walls. Lefebvre indeed looked to the street for stirrings of revolt, for gathering forces of opposition. It was where revolutionary events unfolded, something that he explored historically through his study of the Paris Commune of 1871, originally in dialogue with the situationists, and a process that he later commented on in relation to the uprisings of May 1968 when, so he wrote, it was "in the streets that spontaneity expressed itself—in an area of society not occupied by institutions."[62]

Significant to Lefebvre's critical position was the underlying thesis that there was "a *colonization* of the urban space, which takes place in the street through the image, through publicity, through the spectacle of objects—a 'system of objects' that has become symbol and spectacle."[63] This argument had roots in discussions with the situationists and especially Debord, who earlier had addressed what he called "the colonization of everyday life."[64] The phrase signaled what both Debord and Lefebvre understood as a move in the postwar years toward forms of interior colonization, in which new concentrations of capital, personnel, and administrative techniques turned toward urban space, consumption, leisure, domesticity, and ever more arenas of social life. The city and terrains of everyday life in this way became privileged sites of investment, exploitation, and "programming." This process of modernization was keenly felt in France, where it was bound up with decolonization, the reconfiguration of dominating and exploitative ties with colonial populations, and the embracing of American-style capitalism. As Kristin Ross has persuasively argued, this context was critical in the emergence of everyday life as a significant concept within French theory more generally in the postwar period, in the work of, among others, Barthes, Certeau, and Perec as well as Lefebvre and the situationists. She emphasizes that Lefebvre's analysis of the street and the city, by being situated in relation to such wider forces associated

with capitalist national and global networks, brings out the tensions and contradictions through which those spaces were constituted;[65] and in writing of
colonization in this manner, both Lefebvre and the situationists crucially focused attention on the prospects for resistance and for struggles for liberation.

Utopianism and Urban Desire

The initial forays in psychogeography by the letterists and situationists during
the 1950s played a significant role in developing their utopian spatial imagination. Forged within terrains not of their choosing, their psychogeographic
practices engaged with and contested dominant sociospatial relations. Representations, signs, and images were détourned for other ends, while mapping
was at times combined with direct interventions that included inscribing on
walls, reworking street signs, and experimenting with "architectural complexes" to alter spaces. A report on the Continent Contrescarpe in 1956, for
example, advocated the construction of several architectural complexes alongside the use of edifices to close streets and to alter behavior in the area.[66] A
strategic dimension, even a militaristic tone, was often apparent in such activities, for example when Debord referred to the potential of maps of
cities to reveal "their principal points of passage, their exits and defences."[67] At
the same time, however, psychogeography and the dérive were meant to embody values and desires radically at variance with those dominant within
capitalist bourgeois society and its space-time discipline. Through their rejection of work and commodified leisure as presently defined, the letterists saw
themselves as forming a provisional microsociety, as Debord advocated the
extension of the "will to playful creation'" characteristic of the dérive more
widely.[68]

Of particular significance were questions of desire and specifically of what
has been termed in utopian studies the education of desire. This was apparent
in the groups' mapping of geographies of attraction and repulsion, where they
investigated and speculated upon the interplay between desire and place with
the aim of constructing better places. But it was addressed directly by Debord
early on when he asserted that it was necessary to undermine "the passions,
compensations and habits" of the present exploitative society and "to define
new desires in relation to present possibilities."[69] He therefore called for the
promotion of "a mass of desires whose fulfilment is not beyond the capacity of
humanity's present means of action on the material world, but only beyond
the capacity of the old social organization."[70] By breaking topological chains,
the situationist city of desire promised to run with different currents. No longer dominated by channels of traffic and flows of capital, the "rough, dirty
magic" of the streets could move to alternative rhythms.

Psychogeography was in this way connected with other components of the situationists' early project, namely the "construction of situations" and "unitary urbanism." Not a doctrine or plan, the latter was presented by the SI as a critique of urbanism that looked toward the collective creation of the urban environment and the production of emancipatory spaces that would be dynamic, transcend current divisions and separations, and be lived by their creators. The fullest attempt to articulate and envision such an urbanism came with Constant's New Babylon, which he developed initially within, and later beyond, the SI into a remarkable utopian projection through a vast range of artworks and writings. Invoking what he insisted was an entirely realizable postrevolutionary urbanism constructed on play and free movement, this aimed to provoke and stimulate new ways of approaching urban space and culture.[71] If in later years Debord and fellow members of the SI moved away from such urban projects and explicitly distanced themselves from Constant's experiments that they professed to find technocratic, and if they increasingly devoted their energies to theoretical and political critique and questions of political organization whose significant contours stretch far beyond the confines of my particular focus here, their revolutionary perspectives still retained utopian dimensions in their efforts to realize what was hidden yet possible in modern life. They also still insisted that they must involve a *"critique of human geography."*[72]

For all the diversity and at times clashing currents within the SI, their utopian engagement with everyday life and its potential transformation, as Michael Gardiner suggests, allows them to be seen as part of a "subterranean" or "counter-tradition" of thinking about everyday life. Connecting them with Lefebvre as well as with the surrealists and Certeau, Gardiner proposes that they shared a wariness of what Bloch called abstract utopias and idealist projections of alternatives disconnected with the circumstances of the present, and addressed lived experience critically, based on a longing for a better way of living. In the process, they attended to "such phenomena as the body, sensuality, pleasure, play, fantasy and desire" and to "the role these might play in any truly emancipatory project."[73] Their utopianism did not entail a retreat into fantastical realms but remained "attuned to the dynamics of daily existence," as, in different ways, they aspired "to locate the utopian impulse and the pervasive desire for social transformation in the rhythms and textures of everyday life." In particular, they strove "to reconnect the aesthetic and the everyday realms and to introject the festival, the 'play impulse,' and the logic of the 'gift' into every area of personal and social experience." A distinctive aspect of their approach, Gardiner adds, was that in "searching for the signals and traces of a transfigured social existence in apparently 'trivial' acts of refusal, resistance and cultural appropriation," they argued that "a subversive imagination is not dead, that 'people' are capable of generating a utopian space that contests the functioning of an anonymous structure of technocratic power." At the same time they avoided claims to "finality or completeness" in the form of a fixed ideal and instead reached toward transformative possibilities and processes.[74]

Gardiner admits that to refer to a tradition in this context is contentious and that there were significant intellectual and political divergences between these individuals and groups. I go further in emphasizing certain differences, notably those between the utopian perspectives and trajectories of Lefebvre and the situationists on the one hand and the work of Certeau on the other. As already discussed, beyond recoding the possibilities of current conditions, the former were based on striving for fundamental social and spatial transformation that would revolutionize ways of living and would overturn the conditions and spaces through which those possibilities were defined. Their aim was to enter what Lefebvre termed a "possible-impossible" dialectic, based on the supposition that the full breath of the possible is most keenly felt when striving toward that currently deemed by dominant powers to be impossible and yet that is within reach.[75] Gardiner's assertion is nonetheless useful for drawing out distinctive elements of forms of critical utopianism that eschewed blueprints or vanguardist schemes for ideal futures and that were instead forged through critiques of everyday life. And what can be added to his discussion is the importance attached to the spatialities of everyday life, where a key site of political contestation became everyday urban spaces through which dominant social relations are reproduced, with the aim of intervening in those processes to produce new space-times appropriate to new ways of living.

Invitation to Voyage

The efforts outlined in this chapter to reclaim and remake streets as part of a wider revolutionary struggle have resonances with, and implications for, a range of other critical reactions to modernist urbanism and "shouts in the street" in Europe and North America during the 1950s and especially 1960s, including many whose influences are still strong today. The case of Jane Jacobs has already been mentioned, and she remains a highly prominent figure. This is not only through the efforts of supporters of "new urbanism" attempting to recapture aspects of traditional street life against the consequences of urban sprawl in the United States, but also as the counterpoint to recent attempts in New York City to rehabilitate Robert Moses and, with him, conceptions of modernist city building. Noting how views associated with Jacobs have typically been seen to prevail in determining planning priorities and procedures in recent decades, some critics have asserted that "the pendulum may have swung too far,"[76] and a number have sought to reappraise the role of her old archenemy, Moses, referring to him as, in the words of Hilary Ballon and

Kenneth T. Jackson—the curators of a major three-part exhibition on the subject in 2007—a "symbolic figure in discourse about the future of the city, its capacity to think and build big."[77] They have looked longingly and nostalgically at Moses's supposed ability to cut through bureaucracy, to tame opposition, and to get works built, claiming that his rising reputation in recent years has been "propelled by a fear that New York can no longer execute ambitious projects because of a multilayered process of citizen and governmental review."[78] This revisionism is far from politically innocent in an era of grand urban building projects and Bloomberg-sponsored initiatives that, for Jackson, "suggests a Moses era without Moses."[79] Not surprisingly, it has generated considerable public debate, with dividing lines often falling along a split between Moses as the master builder or "power broker" and Jacobs as defender of neighborhoods, streets, and local democratic engagement. As old adversaries, their positions still frame much of the debate about urban planning in New York and beyond, supposedly standing for opposed tendencies and approaches. Many critics line up accordingly, while some attempt to bridge the gulf between them by advocating the need to learn from both, arguing that the grand vision of Moses is required so long as it is tethered by the humane lessons that Jacobs taught.[80]

Returning to the utopian engagements with streets by the situationists and Lefebvre in the same period provides one means of disrupting this narrow framing of urban debate. It helps to open up senses of possibility by calling into question the bases of the visions associated with both Moses and Jacobs, and it invites the construction of alternatives. A primary concern for the situationists, as well as for Lefebvre, was reappropriating streets as part of a revolutionary struggle to transform everyday life and sociospatial relations. The targets of their critiques were the forces of capitalist development and state-led modernization that were then enabling the further colonization of space and social life by the commodity, and that were deepening forms of gentrification as well as control and surveillance in the streets. They demanded radically different urban worlds, but in so doing they did not pose as alternatives static spatial forms. Rather, theirs was a struggle for something not yet, a striving toward change beyond capitalist urbanization while of necessity not yet knowing the precise geographic and social form it would take.

Tensions involved in this utopianism are apparent in the construction of Debord's map discussed earlier in this chapter, *Axe d'exploration et échec dans la recherche d'un Grand Passage situationniste*. The map registers not only past journeys but also the effort to explore and to discover alternatives. It conveys a sense of seeking—and failing to find—passage through the streets. As with psychogeographic practices more generally, the emphasis was on the process of exploration and discovery rather than on plotting the precise coordinates of the desired destination. The arrows that connect the segments of aerial photographs thus evoke a quest through Paris undertaken in a spirit of adventure and uncertainty. Some of the protagonists are shown in the photograph at the top right, including Ivan Chtcheglov, whose presence is a tribute from Debord for his role in defining the early direction of the letterists.[81] The sense of exploration and adventure is also emphasized through the presence in the lower right-hand corner of the reproduction of Claude Lorrain's *Seaport*. This harbor scene shows Saint Ursula about to embark on a voyage, surrounded by her virgin entourage, as the bright sunlight is diffused through the atmosphere and plays on the water. Lorrain's paintings were strongly favored by Chtcheglov, who noted their "ambience of *perpetual* invitation to voyage" and "incitement to drifting." These are provoked by the "*unaccustomed architectural space*" that is produced through his depiction of palaces situated on the edge of the sea, he suggested, and by the proximity of the palace doors to the ships.[82] Debord, too, often wrote of the power and sense of expectation of Lorrain's harbor paintings in this regard and once referred to the beauty of two of his images of harbors at dusk at the Louvre, juxtaposing two highly different ambiences, as a matter of not "plastic beauty" but "simply the particularly moving presentation . . . of a *sum of possibilities*."[83]

Beyond tracing journeys through the city, Debord's map spoke of attempts to forge new paths, to find a "grand passage" toward new ways of living and new social spaces. Its utopian orientation, like that of situationist psychogeography more generally, was toward sensing and seizing possibilities found here and now in the city streets. It was some years before those same Parisian streets were literally seized in May 1968. As people took to the streets and barricades were thrown up, the city as a space of circulation was interrupted. Streets as conduits for flow, dominated by traffic and commerce, were reappropriated by those from whom they had been taken. They gave way to spaces and times of congregation, dialogue, encounter, and struggle and became arenas in which views were exchanged and horizontal connections were forged, in particular between workers and students, social categories typically kept apart, so bringing into question the specializations, assumptions of expertise, and spatial segregations associated with hierarchical categories. The significance of such spatial struggles was indicated in another situationist map of central Paris, reproduced in René Vienet's account of the uprisings of May 1968. This showed the location of barricades and the "defensive perimeter" of the fifth arrondissement on the night of clashes between demonstrators and the police on 10 May.[84] Beyond its immediate relevance to understandings of how forces were demarcated and deployed, it casts an interesting light on the prescient radicalism of the letterists' call, in their psychogeographic report on Contrescarpe Continent, twelve years earlier, to close streets in the same area and to produce architectural complexes to construct new situations.[85] It further provides a different perspective on Debord's maps with their own reference to exits, defenses, and the like, and with their arrows that in addition to indicating turns of direction taken by walkers in the streets, may connote strategic planning and insurgent action. At the founding conference of the SI in 1957, Debord insisted: "Something that changes our way of seeing the streets is more important than something that changes our ways of seeing paintings."[86] Maps such as *Axe d'exploration* and associated psychogeographic practices came out of this belief. But they were also underpinned by the statement with which he opened that report, and by his recognition of the importance of everyday life and social space to the endeavor so signaled: "First of all, we think the world must be changed."[87]

Notes

1. I would like to thank Gyan Prakash, Michael Gordin, Jennifer Houle, and participants in the Shelby Cullom Davis Center seminars in autumn 2006, especially John Krige, Anne-Maria Makhulu, Shira Robinson, and Mark Shiel, for providing a stimulating environment for research and debate. My thanks also go to Christine Boyer for her support and enthusiastic discussions about urban and utopian matters during my visit, and to Tom Levin, Greil Marcus, and Hal Foster for inspiring conversations. Thoughtful comments from Edward Eigen and other seminar participants when a version of this paper was delivered were appreciated, and I am grateful to the Arts and Humanities Research Council in the UK for its further support of this research. The epigraph is by Guy Debord, "Positions situationnistes sur la circulation," *Internationale situationniste (IS)* 3 (December 1959): 37, translated as "Situationist Theses on Traffic," in *Situationist International Anthology*, ed. Ken Knabb, rev. ed. (Berkeley: Bureau of Public Secrets, 2006), 69–70.

2. Nick Fyfe, "Introduction: Reading the Street," in *Images of the Street: Planning, Identity and Control in Public Space*, ed. Nick Fyfe (London: Routledge, 1998), 1.

3. Rebecca Solnit, *Wanderlust: A History of Walking* (London: Verso, 2001), 176.

4. From a lecture illustration reproduced in Le Corbusier's *Precisions on the Present State of Architecture and City Planning*, trans. Edith Schreiber Aujame (Cambridge, MA: MIT Press, 1991). The book was originally published as *Précisions sur un état présent de l'architecture et de l'urbanisme* (Paris: Crès et Cie, 1930).

5. Le Corbusier, "The Street," in *Oeuvre complète de 1910–1929*, by Le Corbusier and Pierre Jeanneret, ed. W. Boesiger and O. Stonorov, 5th ed. (Zurich: Éditions d'Architecture Erlenbach, 1948), 118. The essay was originally published in *L'intransigeant* in May 1929.

6. Ibid., 119.

7. Le Corbusier, *The City of Tomorrow and Its Planning*, trans. Frederick Etchells (London: Architectural Press, 1971), 131, 163. The book was originally published as *Urbanisme* (Paris: Éditions Crès, 1925).

8. Marshall Berman, *All That Is Solid Melts into Air: The Experience of Modernity* (London: Verso, 1983), pt. 5.

9. On "the death of the street" in Brasília, see James Holston, *The Modernist City: An Anthropological Critique of Brasília* (Chicago: University of Chicago Press, 1989), 101–44; and in relation to the ideas and practices of the "modern movement" more generally, see John R. Gold, "The Death of the Boulevard," in *Images of the Street*, by

Fyfe, 44–57. For the classic debates about street design and urban modernism in Vienna and Berlin, see David Frisby, "Streets, Imaginaries, and Modernity: Vienna Is Not Berlin," in *The Spaces of the Modern City: Imaginaries, Politics, and Everyday Life*, ed. Gyan Prakash and Kevin M. Kruse (Princeton: Princeton University Press, 2008), 21–57.

10. André Breton, *Les pas perdus* (Paris: Gallimard, 1924), in his *Oeuvres complètes* 1 (Paris: Gallimard, Pléiade, 1938), 196.

11. André Breton, "Manifesto of Surrealism" (1924), in his *Manifestoes of Surrealism*, trans. Richard Seaver and Helen R. Lane (Ann Arbor: University of Michigan Press, 1972), 4.

12. Ibid., p. 10.

13. See, for example, chapters by Alexander Gorlin, Nadir Lahiji, and David Pinder in *Surrealism and Architecture*, ed. Thomas Mical (London: Routledge, 2005); see also Anthony Vidler, "Fantasy, the Uncanny and Surrealist Theories of Architecture," *Papers of Surrealism* 1 (2003), available from http://www.surrealismcentre.ac.uk/papers ofsurrealism/journal1/index.htm (accessed 1 December 2007).

14. See David Pinder's *Visions of the City: Utopianism, Power and Politics in Twentieth-Century Urbanism* (Edinburgh: Edinburgh University Press, 2005), some of the arguments of which I seek to develop in this chapter. Among other texts that share my interest here in situationist critiques of urbanism are Libero Andreotti and Xavier Costa, eds., *Situacionistas: Arte, Política, Urbanismo / Situationists: Art, Politics, Urbanism* (Barcelona: Museu d'Art Contemporani/Actar, 1996); Simon Sadler, *The Situationist City* (Cambridge, MA: MIT Press, 1998); and Catherine de Zegher and Mark Wigley, eds., *The Activist Drawing: Retracing Situationist Architectures from Constant's New Babylon to Beyond* (New York: Drawing Center; Cambridge, MA: MIT Press, 2001). For original situationist writings in translation, see Libero Andreotti and Xavier Costa, eds., *Theory of the Dérive and Other Situationist Writings on the City* (Barcelona: Museu d'Art Contemporani/Actar, 1996).

15. See Erik Swyngedouw, "The Strange Respectability of the Situationist City in the Society of the Spectacle," *International Journal of Urban and Regional Research* 26, no. 1 (2002): 153–65.

16. Berman, *All That Is Solid Melts into Air*; see also the extension of this perspective in Peter Jukes, *A Shout in the Street: The Modern City* (London: Faber and Faber, 1990).

17. Moses's notorious maxim runs in full: "When you operate in an overbuilt metropolis, you have to hack your way with a meat ax"; in his *Public Works: A Dangerous Trade* (New York: McGraw-Hill, 1970), cited in Berman, *All That Is Solid Melts into Air*, 290.

18. Siegfried Giedion, *Space, Time and Architecture: The Growth of a New Tradition* (Cambridge, MA: Harvard University Press, 1941), 580.

19. Ibid., 559.

20. Fredric Jameson, "The Brick and the Balloon: Architecture, Idealism and Land Speculation," in *The Cultural Turn: Selected Writings on the Postmodern, 1983–1998* (London: Verso, 1998), 180.

21. Berman, *All That Is Solid*, 307.

22. Ibid., 314.

23. Jane Jacobs, *The Death and Life of Great American Cities* (Harmondsworth: Penguin, 1984), 18. This was originally published in 1961.

24. Ibid., 27, 405.

25. Berman, *All That Is Solid*, 314–18, 322–25. More recently Berman has noted: "Jacobs's vision seemed so direct and straightforward forty years ago. Today, we've got to wonder, is this pragmatism or pastoral? Is it direct experience of city life or a grid of prescribed happy meanings forcibly imposed on city life?"; in his "It Happens Every-day," in *The Pragmatist Imagination: Thinking about "Things in the Making,"* ed. Joan Ockman (New York: Princeton Architectural Press, 2000), 215. See also Herbert Gans, "Jane Jacobs: Toward an Understanding of *Death and Life of Great American Cities,*" *City and Community* 5, no. 3 (2006): 213–15.

26. When Paul Goldberger introduced "postmodern architecture" in the issue of *Architectural Design* that popularized the notion in 1977 under the editorship of Charles Jencks, for example, he argued that it had philosophical roots that emerged "from the modest, anti-utopian impulse, from a belief in incremental movement rather than cataclysmic change"; in his "Post-modernism: An Introduction," *Architectural Design* 47, no. 4 (1977): 257.

27. See also the comments on this in the introduction to this volume and in Chapter 1 by Fredric Jameson.

28. On the connections between utopianism and urbanism in twentieth-century western Europe, see my *Visions of the City*; Ruth Eaton, *Ideal Cities: Utopianism and the (Un)Built Environment* (London: Thames and Hudson, 2002); Robert Fishman, *Urban Utopias in the Twentieth Century: Ebenezer Howard, Frank Lloyd Wright, and Le Corbusier* (Cambridge, MA: MIT Press, 1982); and Peter Hall, *Cities of Tomorrow: An Intellectual History of Urban Planning and Design in the Twentieth Century,* 3rd ed. (Oxford: Blackwell, 2002).

29. Le Corbusier, ed., *The Athens Charter*, trans. Anthony Eardley (New York: Grossman Publishers, 1973). The charter was originally drawn up in 1933, and Le Corbusier's edited version was published in French in 1943.

30. David Harvey, *Spaces of Hope* (Edinburgh: Edinburgh University Press, 2000), 160.

31. Fredric Jameson, *Archaeologies of the Future: The Desire Called Utopia and Other Science Fictions* (London: Verso, 2005), 1–9; see also the elaboration in chapter 1 of this volume. For an important overview of different conceptualizations of utopia, see Ruth Levitas, *The Concept of Utopia* (Hemel Hempstead, Herts: Philip Allan, 1990).

32. Harvey deploys the term "dialectical" or "spatiotemporal utopianism," which he writes is "rooted in our present possibilities at the same time as it points towards different trajectories for human uneven geographical developments"; *Spaces of Hope*, 196.

33. Michael Gardiner, "Marxism and the Convergence of Utopia and the Every-day," *History of the Human Sciences* 19, no. 3 (2006): 2, 3. See also his "Utopia and Everyday Life in French Social Thought," *Utopian Studies* 6, no. 2 (1995): 90–123.

34. Gardiner, "Marxism," 27.

35. Le Corbusier, *City of Tomorrow*, 281.

36. On Le Corbusier's interest in the aerial view, see M. Christine Boyer, "Aviation and the Aerial View: Le Corbusier's Spatial Transformations in the 1930s and 1940s,"

Diacritics 33, nos. 3–4 (2003): 93–116. On aerial photography more specifically, see also Anthony Vidler, "Photourbanism: Planning the City from Above and Below," in *A Companion to the City*, ed. Gary Bridge and Sophie Watson (Oxford: Blackwell, 2000), 35–46.

37. Bernstein and Dahou's contributions also never appeared. Ralph Rumney provides firsthand recollections of his involvement with the exhibition and Debord's withdrawal in his *Le Consul* (Paris: Editions Allia, 1999), 47–54, translated by Malcolm Imrie as *The Consul* (San Francisco: City Lights, 2002), 40–46. He is unable to shed light on the offering by the "mad psychogeographer."

38. As recalled by Piero Simondo to curator Sandro Ricaldone, personal communication to author, 13 November 2004. The original measures 46 by 38 centimeters and on the back carries the title and the date 1953. Simondo suggests that Debord probably inscribed the title and date at the founding conference in 1957. The map was shown at an exhibition on Jorn in Italy curated by Ricaldone at Moncalieri, from March to April 1997. It is reproduced in *Una Mostra: Jorn in Italia gli anni del Bauhaus Immaginista, 1954–1957* (Moncalieri: Edizioni d'arte Fratelli Pozzo, 1997). It also appears in black and white in Guy Debord's *Oeuvres* (Paris: Quarto Gallimard, 2006), 282. I am grateful to Sandro Ricaldone for supplying information about this map.

39. Groupe de recherche psychogéographique de l'Internationale lettriste, "Position du Continent Contrescarpe," *Les lèvres nues* 9 (November 1956), reproduced in *Documents relatifs à la fondation de l'Internationale situationniste, 1948–1957*, ed. Gérard Berreby (Paris: Éditions Allia, 1985), 326.

40. Asger Jorn's International Movement for an Imaginist Bauhaus published both maps, and *The Naked City* also appeared in Jorn's book *Pour la forme* (Paris: Internationale situationniste, 1958). For discussions of their construction, see Tom McDonough, "Situationist Space," in *Guy Debord and the Situationist International: Texts and Documents*, ed. Tom McDonough (Cambridge, MA: MIT Press, 2002), 241–65; David Pinder, "Subverting Cartography: The Situationists and Maps of the City," *Environment and Planning A* 28 (1996): 405–27; and Sadler, *Situationist City*, 82–91.

41. Guy-Ernest Debord, "Introduction à une critique de la géographie urbaine," *Les lèvres nues* 6 (1955), reproduced in Berreby's *Documents*, 288–92; translated as "Introduction to a Critique of Urban Geography," in Knabb's *Anthology*, 8–12.

42. Ibid., 289; trans. 10. See also Guy Debord, "Théorie de la dérive," *IS* 2 (December 1958): 19–23, translated as "Theory of the Dérive," in Knabb's *Anthology*, 62–66. An earlier, slightly different version was first published in *Les lèvres nues* 9 (November 1956), reprinted in Berreby's *Documents*, 312–16.

43. Greil Marcus, *Lipstick Traces: A Secret History of the Twentieth Century* (London: Secker and Warburg, 1989), 166.

44. Michel de Certeau, *The Practice of Everyday Life*, trans. Steven Randall (Berkeley: University of California Press, 1984), 90–93.

45. Ibid., 34.

46. McDonough, "Situationist Space," 249. Referring to these operations, Certeau explains: "A space treated in this way and shaped by practices is transformed into enlarged singularities and separate islands. Through these swellings, shrinkings, and fragmentations, that is, through these rhetorical operations a spatial phrasing of an analogical (composed of juxtaposed citations) and elliptical (made of gaps, lapses and allusions) type is created"; in *Practice of Everyday Life*, by de Certeau, 101–2.

47. Kristin Ross, "Streetwise: The French Invention of Everyday Life," *Parallax* 2 (1996): 70.

48. Ibid., 70.

49. John Roberts, *Philosophizing the Everyday: Revolutionary Praxis and the Fate of Cultural Theory* (London: Pluto, 2006), 88.

50. Significant accounts include Louis Chevalier, *The Assassination of Paris*, trans. David Jordan (Chicago: University of Chicago Press, 1994), first published in French in 1977; Norma Evenson, *Paris: A Century of Change, 1878–1978* (New Haven: Yale University Press, 1979); and Kristin Ross, *Fast Cars, Clean Bodies: Decolonization and the Reordering of French Culture* (Cambridge, MA: MIT Press, 1995).

51. Internationale lettriste, "Les gratte-ciels par la racine," *Potlatch* 5 (20 July 1954), reprinted in *Potlatch (1954–1957)*, complete edition, introduced by Guy Debord (Paris: Gallimard, 1996), 38, translated by Gerardo Denís as "Skyscrapers by the Roots," in *Theory of the Dérive*, ed. Andreotti and Costa, 44–45.

52. Ivan Chtcheglov, "Formulaire pour un urbanisme nouveau," original 1953 version, reprinted in his *Écrits retrouvés*, ed. and intr. Jean-Marie Apostolidés and Boris Donné (Paris: Éditions Allia, 2006), 7; translated as "Formulary for a New Urbanism," in Knabb's *Anthology*, 2.

53. "On détruit la rue Sauvage," *Potlatch* 7 (3 August 1954), reprinted in *Potlatch (1954–1957)*, 54–55, translated by Gerardo Denís as "The Destruction of Rue Sauvage," in *Theory of the Dérive*, ed. Andreotti and Costa, 45. The letterists issued a further report on the process of the destruction of this street in *Potlatch* in January 1956.

54. See Abdelhafid Khatib, "Essai de description psychogéographique des Halles," *IS* 2 (December 1958): 13–18, translated by Paul Hammond as "Attempt at a Psychogeographical Description of Les Halles," in *Theory of the Dérive*, ed. Andreotti and Costa, 76.

55. Guy Debord, *La société du spectacle* (Paris: Buchet-Chastel, 1967), translated by Donald Nicholson-Smith as *The Society of the Spectacle* (New York: Zone Books, 1994), thesis 172.

56. Ibid., thesis 171.

57. Henri Lefebvre, "No Salvation Away from the Centre?" in his *Writings on Cities*, trans. and ed. Eleonore Kofman and Elizabeth Lebas (Oxford: Blackwell, 1996), 207. The interview was originally published in 1986.

58. Henri Lefebvre, *The Urban Revolution*, trans. Robert Bononno (Minneapolis: University of Minnesota Press, 2003), 18. The book was first published in French in 1970.

59. Ibid., 18.

60. Henri Lefebvre, *Critique of Everyday Life*, vol. 2, *Foundations for a Sociology of the Everyday*, trans. John Moore (London: Verso, 2002), 308–12. The book was first published in French in 1961.

61. Lefebvre, *Urban Revolution*, 18–19.

62. Henri Lefebvre, *The Explosion: Marxism and the French Revolution*, trans. Alfred Ehrenfeld (New York: Monthly Review Press, 1969), 71–72. This was originally published in French in 1968. See also Henri Lefebvre, *La proclamation de la commune* (Paris: Gallimard, 1965).

63. Lefebvre, *Urban Revolution*, 21.

64. Lefebvre, *Foundations for a Sociology*, 11. See especially Guy Debord, "Perspectives de modifications conscientes dans la vie quotidienne," *IS* 6 (August 1961):

20–27, translated as "Perspectives for Conscious Alterations in Everyday Life', in Knabb's *Anthology*, 68–75, where he references Lefebvre's idea of everyday life, understood through the lens of uneven development as a "lagging sector," and proposes that it should be termed "a colonized sector" (22, trans. 70). This text was originally presented as a talk at a conference of the Group for Research on Everyday Life organized by Lefebvre at the Centre National de la Recherche Scientifique (CNRS).

65. Ross, *Fast Cars* and "Streetwise." Lefebvre's account of the process of interior colonization is advanced especially in his *Everyday Life in the Modern World*, trans. Sacha Rabinovitch (New Brunswick, NJ: Transaction Publishers, 1984), first published in French in 1968. He returns to the theme in a self-critical spirit in *The Critique of Everyday Life*, vol. 3, *From Modernity to Modernism (Towards a Metaphilosophy of Daily Life)* (London: Verso, 2005), 26–28. The latter was first published in French in 1981.

66. Groupe de recherche psychogéographique de l'Internationale lettriste, "Position du Continent Contrescarpe," 326.

67. Debord, "Theory of the Dérive," 66.

68. Guy Debord, *Rapport sur la construction des situations et sur les conditions de l'organisation et de l'action de la tendance situationniste internationale* (Paris: n.p., 1957), reprinted in Berreby's *Documents*, 607–19; translated as "Report on the Construction of Situations and on the International Situationist Tendency's Conditions of Organization and Action," in Knabb's *Anthology*, 25–43.

69. Ibid., 36.

70. Debord, "Introduction to a Critique of Urban Geography," 10.

71. I discuss these themes in my *Visions of the City*, esp. 161–237. My concern with the utopianism and spatial politics of the work differs from Mark Wigley's influential writings on the subject, which resist its visionary components and situate it more in terms of postwar architecture culture; see especially his "The Hyper-architecture of Desire," in *Constant's New Babylon: The Hyper-architecture of Desire*, ed. Mark Wigley (Rotterdam: Witte de With Center for Contemporary Art/010 Publishers, 1998), 8–71.

72. Debord, *Society of the Spectacle*, thesis 178. Like many of the "utopian" theorists and activists addressed in this chapter, the situationists rejected the characterization of their positions as utopian, at least when that was understood to mean "unrealizable." They stated in 1964: "Reality is superseding utopia. There is no longer any point in projecting imaginary bridges between the wealth of present technological potentials and the poverty of their use by the rulers of every variety. . . . Everything we deal with is realizable, either immediately or in the short term, once our methods of research and activity begin to be put in practice"; in "Le questionnaire," *IS* 9 (August 1964): 25, translated as "Questionnaire" in Knabb's *Anthology*, 179–80.

73. Michael Gardiner, "Utopia and Everyday Life in French Social Thought," *Utopian Studies* 6, no. 2 (1995): 90–91.

74. Ibid., 116. For a careful exposition of the intellectual connections between Lefebvre and Certeau, as well as the connections between them and other critical writers on everyday life in France, especially as developed in the years from around 1960 to 1980, see Michael Sheringham, *Everyday Life: Theories and Practices from Surrealism to the Present* (Oxford: Oxford University Press, 2006).

75. This is not to mention, of course, significant differences between Lefebvre and the situationists that went well beyond the personal acrimony surrounding their break in the early 1960s.

76. Philip Lopate, "A Town Revived, a Villain Redeemed," *New York Times*, 11 February 2007, available from http://www.nytimes.com/2007/02/11/nyregion/thecity/ 11moses.html (accessed 1 January 2010). See also his "Rethinking Robert Moses: What if New York's Master Builder Wasn't Such a Bad Guy After All?" *Metropolis*, August/September 2002.

77. Hilary Ballon and Kenneth T. Jackson, introduction to *Robert Moses and the Modern City: The Transformation of New York*, ed. Hilary Ballon and Kenneth T. Jackson (New York: W.W. Norton, 2007), 66. The exhibitions held in early 2007 were Remaking the Metropolis, at the Museum of the City of New York; The Road to Recreation, at the Queens Museum of Art; and Slum Clearance and the Superblock Solution, at the Miriam and Ira D. Wallach Art Gallery at Columbia University. In calling for a fresh look at the achievements of Moses as a master builder, and in suggesting that he has been unfairly castigated for his authoritarian approach to urban renewal and slum clearance, these events sought to temper in particular the critical depiction of him made famous by Robert Caro's biography *The Power Broker: Robert Moses and the Fall of New York* (New York: Knopf, 1974).

78. Ibid., 65.

79. Kenneth T. Jackson, interview cited in Robert Pogrebin, "Rehabilitating Robert Moses," *New York Times*, 23 January 2007, available from http://www.nytimes. com/2007/01/23/arts/design/28pogr.html (accessed 1 January 2010).

80. "Jane Jacobs v. Robert Moses: How Stands the Debate Today?" was the title of a forum at the Gotham Center for New York City History, at the City University of New York, on 11 October 2006. See Amanda Burden, "Jane Jacobs, Robert Moses and City Planning Today," *Gotham Gazette*, 6 November 2006, available from http://www .gothamgazette.com/article/fea/20061106/202/2015 (accessed 1 January 2010); and the letters in response, published as "Robert Moses vs. Jane Jacobs," *New York Times*, 25 February 2007, available from http://query.nytimes.com/gst/fullpage.html?res=9C0 2E2DE113EF936A15751C0A9619C8B63 (accessed 1 January 2010).

Less often voiced is the important countervailing view that neither Moses nor Jacobs provides an adequate basis for building socially just and democratic forms of urbanism, as argued by Neil Smith and Scott Larson in "Beyond Moses and Jacobs," *Planetizen*, 13 August 2007, available from http://www.planetizen.com/node/26287 (accessed 1 January 2010). They assert: "Yet the standoff between Jacobs and Moses only ever sparred two separate wings of the middle class concerning how to build and rebuild the city for people of greater rather than lesser class privilege. . . . Where today's Moses revisionists and the Jacobs defenders meet, is in the politics of gentrification. They are for it, just by radically different means."

81. Debord later recalled: "But can I ever forget the one whom I see everywhere in the greatest moment of our adventures, he who in those uncertain days opened up a new path and forged ahead so rapidly, choosing those who would accompany him?" From his film *In girum imus nocte et consumimur igni* (1978), in his *Oeuvres cinématographiques complètes, 1952–1978* (Paris: Editions Champ Libre, 1978), 187– 278, translated under the same title in Guy Debord, *Complete Cinematic Works:*

Scripts, Stills, Documents, ed. and trans. Ken Knabb (Edinburgh: AK Press, 2003), 170–71. Despite Chtcheglov's exclusion from the LI in 1954, after which he was institutionalized in a psychiatric clinic, Debord often later paid tribute to his brief yet intense contribution, for example dedicating an edition of his *Mémoires* to him after they resumed correspondence during the 1960s and reminiscing in correspondence as the tenth anniversary of their early dérive approached.

82. Chtcheglov, "Formulary for a New Urbanism," 12, trans. 5. This passage was cut from the version of the essay published in *Internationale situationniste* in 1958.

83. Debord, "Introduction to a Critique of Urban Geography," 11. He further suggested that "Claude Lorrain is psychogeographical in the juxtaposition of a palace neighbourhood and the sea"; in his "Exercice de la psychogéographie," *Potlatch* 2 (29 June 1954), reprinted in *Potlatch (1954–1957)*, 20, translated by Gerardo Denís as "Exercise in Psychogeography," in *Theory of the Dérive*, ed. Andreotti and Costa, 42. Debord included two images of the harbor paintings in his film *La société du spectacle* (1973). There they were accompanied by the line "The point is to actually take part in the community of dialogue and the game with time that up until now have merely been *represented* by poetic and artistic works"; filmscript in his *Oeuvres cinématographiques completes*, translated as "The Society of the Spectacle," in Debord's *Complete Cinematic Works*, 52.

84. René Viénet, *Enragés et situationnistes dans le mouvement des occupations* (Paris: Gallimard, 1968).

85. Groupe de recherche psychogéographique, "Position du Continent Contrescarpe," 326. Tom Levin points out the prescience of the original report in his "Geopolitics of Hibernation: The Drift of Situationist Urbanism," in *Situacionistas*, ed. Andreotti and Costa, 136–37.

86. Debord, "Report on the Construction of Situations," 42.

87. Ibid., 25.

9.

IGAL HALFIN

Stalinist Confessions in an Age of Terror: Messianic Times at the Leningrad Communist Universities

ONE IS HARD-PRESSED to think of a set of events in the twentieth century that baffles us more than do Stalinist purges. The years 1934–38 witnessed the great Moscow show trials, as well as a large number of less prominent NKVD (People's Commissariat for Internal Affairs) investigations that ended with the execution or interior exile of countless Party members.[1] Historians find it difficult to explain the resolve of Stalin and his lieutenants to destroy the country's administrative and military elite, especially as war was looming on the horizon.[2] How could one come to terms with the mass psychosis the Great Purge generated, a flood of denunciations that turned Soviet society into a war of all against all?[3] No less astounding is the routine cooperation one finds between revolutionary veterans and their tormentors. Even as the firing squads lifted their rifles, they cried, "Long live Comrade Stalin!" Savagely beaten during his interrogations, Nikolai Chaplin, the former head of the Komsomol, kept repeating, "The Party, the Party the Party."[4] And the final words of the Siberian leader Robert Eikhe were "I will die believing in the rightness of the Party policy that guided my entire life."[5]

Defying every political and social logic, the party turned its violence against itself. "For twenty years the Bolsheviks lived without killing each other," the White general A. von Lampe observed in June 1937. "The next twenty years of their reign open with them doing just that. Internecine war is the normal outcome of every revolution."[6] If previous waves of arrests and executions that targeted Whites officers, kulaks, and priests, reprehensible as they may seem to us today, were at least understandable—the regime was attacking its real enemies—Stalin's onslaught on his own Party makes no sense.[7]

Indeed, no algorithm can tell us how the victims of the Great Purge were chosen. One can speak of probabilities: Mensheviks and Socialist Revolutionaries were seized, then former Trotskyists, then former Zinovievists. But the further we go, the less we understand. Communists with tainted biographies were arrested, but so were revolutionary heroes. Stalin's old foes died, but so did his friends. Many victims had impeccable records. In this modern-day witch hunt, anyone might prove to be a witch.[8]

Violence occurred routinely in the Communist polity: institutionalized violence, violence associated with the activity of the state, its courts, and its military. But the random violence of the wrecker and the saboteur could not be contained within the law. And by "law" I mean here not just the state's juridical framework, its legislation, and its courts, but also its legitimizing discourse—Marxism with its iron laws of historical development. Communists knew how to speak about the bourgeoisie and kulaks, how to analyze social forces. But when history was said to be consummated and the official language switched to abstract moral categories, objective indicators of identity turned out to be little more than indexes of subjective moral essence; they no longer predicted moral choice but registered it only after the fact. Once the party came to rely on tautologies to define the good and the bad, it short-circuited the Marxist argument, and all that remained of Soviet sociology was the empty shell of its scientific vocabulary.

The NKVD's pursuit of the inner enemy obsessively reenacted the boundary between the inside and the outside, the loyal comrade and the deserter. As if acknowledging the impossibility of the utopian messianic project of a radically egalitarian society, the Stalinist utopia structured itself around an incessant struggle against a deadly foe: the oppositionist interloper, the wrecker, and the spy; all were fetishistic embodiments of an immanent impossibility. Hardly the positive cause of social antagonism, "enemies of the people" (*vragi naroda*) embodied the obstacle that prevented the Communist brotherhood from its apotheosis as a closed, homogeneous totality. Under these conditions, the hunt for transgression had to be widespread and interminable.[9]

How can a nearly complete lack of resistance on the part of the high-ranking personnel be explained when party members knew they could face imminent death? Why, to the wonder of the whole world, did the majority of the accused prove willing to help in their own prosecution? It was as if, in the words of Bukharin, Communists put their heads into Stalin's mouth "knowing for sure that one day he will gobble us up."[10] The fact that the Communist revolutionary elite turned against itself with such single-mindedness of purpose, becoming an accomplice in its own destruction, remains a highly bewildering phenomenon defying simple explanation.

Stalinist eschatological diagnosis—paradoxical inasmuch as it interpreted the late 1930s both as a time of unrivaled purity in Soviet society and as the time of the last stand of the counterrevolution against Soviet society—explicated the Great Purge as something like the Communist apocalypse, a short reign of intraparty violence preceding the triumph of universal peace. What made the present so unique was that wicked deeds were carried out not by remnants of the old society but by Communists. "The source of Trotskyists' power, 'the wreckers of our times,'" Stalin stated, "is that they have a party card."[11]

The final showdown between the exploiters and the exploited, between the bourgeoisie and the proletariat, corresponded to the Judeo-Christian belief in a final battle between Christ and Antichrist in the concluding epoch of history. Stalin repeatedly declared that peaceful evolution was impossible because the opposition was intensifying with every step the Soviet Union took toward communism: "The further we move, the more successful we become, the more enraged the remains of the defeated exploiting classes will become. They will take the most extreme measures, harming the Soviet state and attempting the most desperate means, the last resort of the doomed."[12]

As things came to a head in 1936–37, the severity of the purges grew dramatically. The wheat now lay separated from the tare, and the time finally came to reveal the true nature of each and every individual. Party members were denied any additional time for refashioning their souls. No longer attributed to external circumstances, oppositionism came to be explained in terms of a fundamental quality of the soul. Soviet justice was now restructured along a binary principle. What in the 1920s had been an elaborate technique designed to establish one's distance from the light gave way to a much simpler procedure for separating "us" and "them."

When Nikolai Ezhov's secret police entered the picture, interrogations acquired a zealous, uncompromising form. Because the arrested were treated as calculating villains, there was no room for consideration or sympathy. The NKVD interrogation folders suggest that the confessions and conversions of the 1930s were devoid of the meaning we typically attribute to these terms. While the autobiographies of the 1920s did highlight sharp discontinuities in their authors' lives, a fundamental continuity of the narrating self was always presumed. But when the NKVD interrogator sat in front of him during the Great Purge, the accused was compelled to give up on his very self. He had to be broken, deprived, and made to profess, "Yes, I am a traitor, I am evil, I am irredeemable." Guilt was profound, unforgivable, and beyond appeal.

Within the messianic discourse that imbued the activity of the NKVD in the 1930s, it made no sense to distinguish truth and fiction. Once the revolutionary project was realized, the desired and the real became nearly indistinguishable, and the connection between the actual assumed the form of logical necessity—historical materialism took itself ad absurdum. The realm of possibility was wiped out; what happened had to happen, and what had to happen happened; one state of affairs turned into the necessary and sufficient cause of the other. There were no accidents or unpremeditated crimes in the universe of the security organs—all events were conditioned, and the chain of causality was unbreakable.

Because the enemy's course of action was predictable, acts of opposition, wrecking, and espionage could be foretold. So why should confessions not be prepared by the NKVD investigators themselves? After all, they knew what the enemy was supposed to be doing.[13] The prospective traitor became identical with the real traitor, and it was not that important whether he was caught before or after the act. What mattered more was that he fully externalized his potential and exposed the wicked creature he had always been. His counterrevolutionary

essence (*kontrrevoliutsionnaia sushchnost'*) had to be urgently drawn out so
that additional culprits could be disarmed. Individualized confession remained the medium of choice: whether actualized or not, destructive urges
remained a question of subjective attitude and could be captured only through
that medium alone. But now that the self reached the surface, compositional
work was easy.

If the interrogator was a soothsayer divining things, not to say an artist making things up, his creations must be examined in the light of the theory of
genre. The countless testimonies stored in the vaults of the archives of security
organs emerge as morbid works of art that should be read as one piece instead
of being sliced up into "wild fabrications," "unlikely insinuations," and "tidbits
of truth." A holistic approach that will examine the form of prisoners' confessions is in some ways more fruitful than exclusive preoccupation with their
contents. The plot was usually ghoulish but abstract—its images were magni-
fied but not developed. This was a piece of fictional criminological writing
placed upon a Stalinist slate. The wooden character of it all and the lack of
precise setting reflected the fact that much of the action took place in the
chamber of the investigator's mind. The situations created were not the ones
in which the accused actually had his escapades, but instead a world full of
sinister connections, ploys, and nightmarish images. The counterrevolutionary plot was taken out of the ordinary and catapulted into the air of a chilling,
if remarkably uninspired, spy novel where characters never develop and the
identity of the villain is known in advance.

Often the NKVD reinterpreted the actions of its prisoners rather than making them up—the tension between fact and narrative remained in interrogation transcripts even if the balance shifted toward fabrication dramatically.
Another important point is the question of agency: though it is obvious that
the investigator was in command, it was important for the investigators to retain a sense that a real person was sitting (or standing or lying) before them,
even if a totally wicked one. Unlike the Nazi industrial killing machine, the
NKVD interrogators treated individuals, not racial groups or collectivities—a
fact that is important to note if we are to unravel the discursive structure that
underlay the writing of confessions.

NKVD interrogations can be described as dialogues, provided we distinguish between the prisoner as the subject of dialogue and the prisoner as a
subject in dialogue. The former is a fictitious persona, a protagonist in a literary creation composed by the investigation team. The latter is a real individual, an author who participates in the composition of the protocol of his interrogation, an agent who introduces fissures into the flow of narrative.

Of course, more often than not, the NKVD fabricated the self of the accused, attributed to him wicked beliefs he had never entertained and treacher-
ous crimes he had not contemplated, let alone perpetrated. Unsubstantiated
confessions were designed to suit a threatening world in which conspiracies

ran rampant and conspirators looked like model citizens. But to the extent that the NKVD interrogation records were composed as confessions—subjective testimonies designed not only to establish a crime but also to pinpoint the moral outlook of the accused, his thoughts and motivations—they endowed the accused with a voice and in this sense forced him to become a subject of dialogue. In other, less frequent cases, the accused retained his ability to influence the course of the investigation, albeit in a very limited way. On occasion he would deny a charge, allege a lapse of memory, or even demand that a certain portion of the protocol be altered. When the accused was the coauthor of his interrogation protocol, he became a cause, an agent, and, as such, not just a subject of dialogue but a subject in dialogue as well.

The conflict in the self of the accused between the obligation to the party and the obligation to his conscience reached a climax with the Great Purge. During that period, Communist martyrology swelled to macabre proportions, as party leaders who had embraced oppositionism (for example, Kamenev and Zinoviev and later Bukharin) were commanded to renounce themselves. Most confessed to crimes they had not committed as a sort of parting gift to the party. Others, a small minority, clung to their personal truth and argued that they would rather die than betray their vision of history.

By interrogating the Communist notions of martyrdom, a different phenomenology of the Great Purge can be forged. The notion that only torture could have yielded the confessions Bolsheviks made to the most unlikely crimes suggests that the victims of terror were overwhelmed by what must have seemed to them a brute external force. Nonetheless, what follows will show that the victims shared much of the discourse of the perpetrators: for any Bolshevik, truth meant the truth of the proletariat as he conceived it, not his own personal truth as something standing outside history. As anyone could be mistaken regarding that truth, the anxiety surrounding that possibility tormented the victim from within.

———

The arrests of the mid-1930s rocked the Leningrad scholarly community. Students and teachers, described by the party's internal documents as shaken awake from a long slumber, saw for the first time that the headquarters of the Leningrad counterrevolution resided at one of the most prestigious academic systems in the country. Many were arrested, but this was less shocking than the stature of those revealed to be enemies. "Our seasoned instructors are imprisoned," students stated with clear amazement. And those instructors pleaded guilty to deliberately wrecking the teaching plan.

Let us consider a number of records that shed light on how the accused were broken and forced to sign confessions to heinous crimes they never perpetrated. The materials I draw on date from a period when the disfavor of a certain stratum of NKVD personnel loosed torrents of criticism: a number of letters of appeal that we shall examine were mailed in late 1936, when Ezhov was busy discrediting the henchmen of his predecessor as the lead of the NKVD, Genrikh Iagoda; others in 1939, when Lavrentii Beriia was doing the same to Ezhov and his cohort; the remaining petitions and recollections were composed following Khrushchev's thaw.

Only a handful of the many scholars arrested in the years 1933 to 1938 remained alive to tell their stories. Voitlovskaia, a young historian of the West and the wife of a convicted "Trotskyist," is one of those who survived; the details presented in her letter of appeal are priceless. In December 1955 Voitlovskaia petitioned the general prosecutor of the Soviet Union, requesting that she and her husband be exonerated of old, "trumped-up" charges. "When my husband, Karpov, was arrested in 1934 I was barely thirty," she stated in the preamble to her appeal. "Today I am fifty-two. During the intervening years the procuracy has not found the time to review the material and unmask the methods used by the NKVD in its investigations." Heartened by Khrushchev's excoriation of the lawlessness of Stalin's rule at the Twentieth Party Congress (1956), Voitlovskaia was eager to tell her story once again. "On April 1, 1936," she wrote, "I was arrested and brought back [from exile] to Leningrad. My children, four and eight years of age, were deposited at the entrance to my parents' apartment block and I was thrown into the NKVD jail on Voinovo Street."

The scene of her interrogation was a high-ceilinged room whose large window was covered by thick blinds. The man in charge of Voitlovskaia's interrogation was Raikhman. "He was twenty-seven or twenty-eight years old. I took a seat before him and my escort left. We looked at each other. He was shameless, smiling slyly. His eyes were shifty."[14]

> I was guilty of nothing. My interrogations were false and unceremonious casuistry, juggling with the facts and falsifications. . . . Whenever I began to resist, Raikhman began abusing me and swearing at the top of his lungs. Insults and threats would continue through the night. The gist of my answers was that I had played no part in counterrevolutionary activity and that neither myself nor Karpov had anything to do with counterrevolution, objectively or subjectively. Raikhman barked back acidly that he had materials that discredited Karpov and myself. I demanded that he show them to me. "Aha!" he would explode. "So you do not believe *us!* You do not believe *Soviet Justice, Soviet Power, the NKVD!* This means that covertly you took the counterrevolutionary road!" And so on and so forth.[15]

Indignantly, Voitlovskaia recounted interrogations that continued relentlessly for days. When the investigator left for the night or when he was distracted by other affairs, he locked her up in a "cage" (*dumalka*). There she was constantly watched by a guard who would not let her sleep. "From the adjacent rooms I used to hear the heartrending screams of men and women and the sound of windows breaking—my nerves were tortured." Even when she was returned to her cell, it would be for only half an hour or so. "Then I would be sent to the 'doghouse'" (*sobachnik*), an isolation box.[16] Eventually, Voitlovskaia signed her verdict: "Five years in the camps" (signing a verdict was tantamount to pleading guilty).[17]

Voitlovskaia's recollections help us to understand what raised suspicion against scholars: numerous arrests were made based on lists of the "untrustworthy" prepared by NKVD informers. Her memoirs also shed light on the methods used to extract confessions; although torture was not used widely in 1936, the day-to-day conditions in jail would have made resistance unthinkable for all but the strongest among the accused. The prisoner's sense of isolation comes across palpably. Informers—sometimes one's closest friends—helped the NKVD to "unravel" the tissue of human relations in the Leningrad scholarly community.

The position of the NKVD interrogator is also clarified: he was omnipotent in one sense and weak in another. Raikhman was under heavy pressure to squeeze out as many quick convictions as possible. Survivors recalled that interrogators were "driven" and that they "had to drive others or be broken themselves."[18] NKVD employees were warned time and again that dragging their feet "would lead to criminal charges against them."[19] Any interrogator who accepted that the accused was innocent immediately took the victim's place.[20] One of them recalled his constant fear of being "taken into the cellar" (*spushchen v podval*)—a euphemism for execution.[21]

The letters of appeal that Voitlovskaia wrote from jail were her main recourse; such letters served as channels for grievances during the late 1930s.[22] Once a month the inmates of Leningrad's jails received a pencil and a piece of paper so that they could pour their hearts out.[23] The accusers and the accused shared the assumption that some form of dialogue would continue between the two ends of the Stalinist penal system. Some prisoners, Voitlovskaia recalled, "wrote one petition after another like maniacs or madmen, expending all of their energy on this. Of course, petitions were addressed directly to Stalin the omniscient, who was expected to figure it all out immediately and establish justice."[24]

The later the appeal, the larger the distance between its author and the language of the NKVD. Voitlovskaia, for example, described her interrogations of 1936 as an outright war. She vilified the investigator, took pride in her refusal to break off communications with her Trotskyist husband after his arrest and exile, and confessed nothing she did not want to confess. The account she offered of how the investigator reinterpreted her testimony according to a preconceived scheme is worth additional attention. By conjuring up an illusory counterrevolutionary underground, Raikhman was applying, she wrote, "moral pressure." It seems, however, that despite their bitter clash, some aspects of the Communist worldview were shared by both sides: Voitlovskaia's reference to her denouncers' "double-dealing" comes to mind, as does her description of her husband as a "conscientious revolutionary"; the use of such terms amounts to complicity in the official language.

Earlier accounts announce the complicity of their authors in NKVD reasoning much more strongly. Ambivalence toward his tormentors is evident, for example, in the letter Shatskin addressed to Stalin on 22 October 1936.

> This is how I was interrogated. The chief investigator presented to me a four-page confession of involvement in terrorism. When I refused to sign, he threatened to shoot me either without a trial or after a formal hearing by the Military Collegium that would take place right there, in the investigator's office, and would last fifteen minutes. "During the trial," he told me, "you will be permitted to respond only with 'yes' and 'no.'" . . . On two occasions I was kept up all night—"until you sign." During one nocturnal interrogation that lasted fifteen hours, the interrogator suddenly began barking commands: "Stand up! Glasses off!" Flailing his fists before my face he ordered: "Pick up the pen!' Sign!"

Although Shatskin offered corroboration of Voitlovskaia's descriptions of brutal interrogations, he was interested not in denouncing the system that generated this brutality but only in the ways in which it was applied to him. "It is not my intention to protest what was done to me according to some abstract humanistic principles," he assured Stalin. "I only want to say that such methods can encourage false testimony. . . . While I do not question the legality of airing suspicions about my actions and while I understand that the investigation cannot rely on my words alone, I insist that the information received must be checked objectively and that I must be provided with the opportunity to disprove false testimony."[25]

A number of the appeals made by the Leningrad scholars convicted as members of the so-called Russian Nationalist Party (uncovered in 1933) illustrate some of the dialogical aspects of the NKVD interrogations. By exploiting those assumptions the accused and the state shared, interrogators were able to extract astonishing admissions without relying on too much bloody, bone-snapping pressure.

My first example is Gleb Bonch-Osmolovskii, an instructor at Leningrad Academy of Sciences, who had embraced the Bolshevik regime at a young age. Arrested on 29 November 1933, he was convicted as a counterrevolutionary and bundled off to a labor camp, an experience that would bring him into the nationalist camp later in his life. But upon his release in 1936, Bonch-Osmolovskii still portrayed himself as an individual committed to revolutionary values and requested permission to return to Leningrad so that he could contribute to socialist construction. By adding to his petition a document entitled "Description of My Investigation," he hoped to persuade Ezhov that he had never been a true enemy of Soviet power.

Foreshadowing some of Voitlovskaia's themes, the letter opened with a brief complaint about the use of solitary confinement, "deprivation of food, of reading materials, of recreation," and so on. The crux of Bonch-Osmolovskii's narrative, however, is a tale of disappointment, the story of the hopes a loyal Soviet citizen for a spiritual rapport with his investigator. Having been disappointed in 1934, Bonch-Osmolovskii was now hoping for happiness. This scholar wrote his "Description" on the assumption that the relationship between the citizen and NKVD should be reciprocal.

Most upsetting to Bonch-Osmolovskii was the failure to treat his interrogation as a comradely inquiry into the essence of his case:

> While I always placed complete trust in the investigation, the interrogator treated me as a proven enemy from the very beginning. . . . He consistently tried to give the impression that my situation was hopeless. Categorical refusals to sign the "declaration" of guilt he composed on my behalf led to such comments as "You are undoing yourself with your obstinacy!" "Your personal conviction that you are innocent is quixotic!" . . . The investigator claimed that my colleagues had impugned me and that as an unrepentant and incorrigible enemy I was looking at the prospect of at least five years in the camps. . . . Gradually, dropping a phrase here and a phrase there, he planted an argument that I assembled in my mind: "Fine, let us assume that you are falsely accused. . . . Do you really think that we want to convict you at all costs? It is not as if we were paid by the head, you know! On the contrary, we are fully aware that your accomplishments make you a very precious scholar. But we cannot sneak into your soul, can we? We conduct our investigations as we do because it is the only means we have at our disposal."[26]

The interrogator and the accused could debate which side possessed more structural advantages during the interrogation. In training young investigators, Shein, the chief interrogator at the Soviet procuracy, offered the following advice: "Remember that an interrogation is a contest in which the accused has a head start: he alone knows the truth for certain. . . . You can only make vague guesses as to where the truth lies, hoping to get it out of him." The accused, of course, strongly disagreed. Voitlovskaia described the investigation as an "unequal game in which the interrogators have marked all the cards."[27] Bonch-Osmolovskii's account shows that the interrogator had considerable power of his own by virtue of his position as the official bearer of the revolutionary truth. "The Party and all of Soviet society stand behind this investigation!" he said to the accused. "No one would believe you!" The interrogator may have had difficulties in penetrating the thoughts of the accused, but in offering a judgment he never hesitated and never erred. As Bonch-Osmolovskii's interrogator said to him, "You have to trust us completely. We, of the interrogation, will find out who you really are."[28]

The interrogator was deftly exposing the flaws in Bonch-Osmolovskii's armor: "By leaving your fate entirely in our hands and signing the confession, you will prove that you have complete trust in the organs of the proletarian dictatorship." Because of his assumption that the accused was driven by the same ideals as the NKVD, he repeated that only by accepting that truth lay not with the accused but with the organs of the Soviet state would Bonch-Osmolovskii have a chance of personal growth. "'Our investigation has an educational role,' the interrogator used to tell me," Bonch-Osmolovskii recalled. "'Every human being makes mistakes he later wants to set right. By signing the declaration you will free yourself psychologically from the various impediments to the unremitting revolutionary self-criticism you need.'"[29]

Finally "I decided that I had no right to distrust the investigator," Bonch-Osmolovskii wrote to Ezhov. "Of course, had I been a real enemy, I would not have believed his assurances that under the present conditions his methods were expedient." Having accepted that the interrogator spoke for the entire Soviet order, he wrote his first confession, employing the "strong revolutionary language" his interrogator advocated.[30]

A poignant dialogue can be made out between two voices within Bonch-Osmolovskii's soul. His original voice, still somewhat incredulous, was conversing with the voice of the interrogator, which grew more fully internalized with time:

> I must confess that the ensuing period of harsh self-criticism—I condemned my past and all of my mistakes—deepened my realization that I had to accept and trust the methods of the investigation. At times, however, I felt that those doubts that I experienced regarding the incessant switching between the "dialectical" and the "formalistic" modes of thinking . . . reflected my insecurities regarding the correct interpretation of the course of the investigation. This inner conflict threatened to drive me insane. . . . I was deprived of any critical perspective on what was happening.

As he came close to giving in to doubts about his hermeneutical competence, the book of his soul became quite illegible to him.[31] His interrogator gained the upper hand, and Bonch-Osmolovskii moved ever nearer to casting off his former self. He was invited to sign a second confession, then a third, "each listing more crimes than the previous one." There was no going back: "I believed that once embarked on a certain path, I should follow it to the end, that refusing to sign more declarations wouldn't make any sense, since the difference between the various accounts was insignificant compared to the difference between the first declaration and reality, so I signed them all."

In spite of the stark differences between comradely trials and NKVD investigations, Bonch-Osmolovskii expected interrogations to retain their familiar hermeneutical features. When this did not happen, he grew confused. "From time to time the interrogator said to me, 'You do not understand the political importance of what we do.' Since I couldn't grasp the meaning and the aim of the case as a whole, I somehow came to believe that the whole thing was an exercise in evaluating me and not an inquiry into a crime. At no point during the investigation were concrete crimes ever attributed to me." Functionally, the NKVD did not distinguish between hermeneutical court and criminal court, between thought crimes and actual crimes; Bonch-Osmolovskii could not help noticing the resultant ambiguities.[32]

Though "the investigator took advantage of his position," Bonch-Osmolovskii did not lose faith in the Communist cause. If his hopes that the newly appointed head of the NKVD would sympathize with his tempered appeal appear delusional given what we know today about Ezhov, in 1936 such hopes had not yet been exploded by wholesale repression. The letter ended with an emotional declaration: "Even today I can say that you will not easily find a scholar more sincerely dedicated to the revolution than I. Why was it necessary, under such circumstances, to accuse me . . . of crimes I did not commit and brand me with article 58 [counterrevolution] before exiling me from the world? I cannot understand or accept this. Still, I believe that the revolution is just and purposeful, a belief that helps me to endure everything."

Even as he insisted on his innocence, Bonch-Osmolovskii sought to understand his interrogator. The appeal never suggests an investigative process tainted by enmity; the victim shows himself willing to pay an extremely high price to break through. With failure came the feeling that he had "lost his ideological compass forever."[33]

Voitlovskaia also testified to "the complexity of the psychology of the investigation and of the accused himself."[34] She admitted that she had often been "drawn to the investigator, especially in the beginning. The accused thinks that the interrogator can help him establish the truth [*istina*], find justice [*pravda*]."[35] After all, she was being "interrogated by Soviet power. The accusations came from a government we saw as no different from ourselves—we even fetishized it to a certain extent."[36]

By recasting their NKVD interrogations in terms of a yearning for dialogue, Bonch-Osmolovskii and Voitlovskaia suggest a way of reading them against the hermeneutical framework of dialogue. When Bukharin wrote to Stalin from jail on the night of 15 April 1937, he expressed a similar desire: "Koba! I've meant to write for the past few nights, because now I feel you so close to me." And later in the letter: "My situation here is so contradictory: I take every Cheka warden as one of my own, and he sees me as a criminal."[37] Zinoviev's 1935 letter to Gorky is even more suggestive:

Think for a moment, I beg you, what it means to me to sit in a Soviet jail. Imagine this in concrete terms. . . . You can endure anything if you think you're face to face with the representatives of a different class. . . . But if the reverse is true, if you feel guilty all around (Guilty before whom? Before the Party in whose ranks one spent thirty-three years!), if you feel that you're confronted by the representatives of the working class, if in the gaze of each Red Army guard you read the reprimand of your beloved country, if every book, every newspaper, every line, every word—in short, if everything reminds you of your great guilt, what is there to keep you going, how can you survive?[38]

The following piece of advice confided by one prisoner to another in the Butyrskaia jail makes sense in such a context: "'If you want to end your moral suffering [*nravstvennye muki*], stop regarding your interrogators as your comrades. Unless you give up this attitude, you are doomed to a terrible life and a difficult death. . . . Treat them as your enemies and you will feel much better.'"[39] While the accused bitterly condemned their interrogators' methods, their language denied them critical distance from these would-be representatives of the revolutionary idea.

One might object that my approach elides the historical circumstances in which such appeals were written: what sort of discursive alternatives existed in a landscape dominated by Ezhov, Zakovskii, or Zhdanov? But what I examine here are the discursive representations of the self, not real people. It might well be that in different circumstances, Bonch-Osmolovskii and Zinoviev would have sounded different. Yet, it is very significant that the language of their negotiation with authorities engaged the self, called for speech that invoked the individual, his tribulations and doubts.

To win the approval of his OGPU-NKVD interrogators, the accused had to translate his old worldview into the new Soviet language of universal conspiracy. Soon after his arrest in 1933, Gidulianov, a professor of law in Moscow, was persuaded to confess that he had belonged to the "Nationalist Center." He testified that the group advanced the principle of "soviets without Communists" and was ready to seize Moscow if the German army occupied Russia. Gidulianov named as his associates Chaplygin (the director of the Central Aerodynamic Institute), Luzin (a professor of mathematics at Moscow State University), and Florenskii (a famous physicist who doubled as a priest); the first was the alleged chairman of the center, the second was its foreign minister, and the third was its ideologue. In the letter he sent to the procurator's office from his exile in Kazakhstan (the year was 1934 or 1935), Gidulianov emphasized that it was the switch from physical pressure to persuasion that led him to conjure up this phantasmagorical organization. "As long as it was a matter of coercion, I did not budge. Then the OGPU tried another method. I was treated gently and kindly, and I was transferred to a different cell and given better food." Shupeiko, the plenipotentiary of the Moscow OGPU, "told me that I was a victim [*zhertva*], . . . and that I should believe no one but him. He was my judge, my investigator, my accuser, and my defender. Shupeiko also said he would release me and allow me to return to my research if I unburdened myself and threw myself on the mercy of the OGPU. To do this I had to confess to being a member of a counterrevolutionary organization."

The investigator explained to the accused that "it was assumed that the graver his self-incrimination, the more heartfelt and sincere his confession and remorse." To prove that he could be saved, Gidulianov had to write himself into the counterrevolutionary order. His cell mate, an agronomist named Kolechits, "explained to me what he called 'the OGPU's Aesopian language' . . . and instructed me in what I was supposed to say." Having translated the OGPU language into something familiar, Gidulianov was finally able to produce the right kind of narrative. As a legal historian, he recognized in his investigation "a process of purification resembling what in the Middle Ages was called *purgato vulgaris*, and later *purgato canonica*." The *purgato canonica* was a procedure of the canonical law in which the investigator did not have to prove the guilt of the accused, but the accused had to prove his innocence through actions that would put them beyond suspicion—in its modern form, that meant confessing everything. "Having lulled myself to sleep with such learned historical parallels, . . . I succumbed to provocations. Since I believed the arguments about needing to disarm myself, and because I wished to please the OGPU, I begun 'straining myself.' The more they demanded that I prove my remorse, the more I maligned myself." His judge and defender, Shupeiko, used to summon Gidulianov to his office and, "through guiding questions and tips, prod me in the direction he chose." Once back in his cell, the accused had time to mull over what he had been told about the dread activities of the Nationalist Center. The fruit of this intellectual labor was "what Shupeiko himself called 'a literary creation,' which I described in writing as the 'essential' [*sushchaia*] and 'honest' [*istinnaia*] truth." Eventually Gidulianov wrote everything his interrogator wanted. "Handing myself fully to the power of the OGPU, I became the stage director and the tragic actor in the trial of the nationalists who were transformed at the OGPU's whim into national fascists."[40]

Making use of the right to participate in his own interrogation, Gidulianov tried to assist the interrogator with the evaluation of his character. Such a situation derived from the Stalinist notion of the self as something that could be articulated only at the nexus of the individual and the party collective. Prisoners interrupted the interrogator or dispatched an urgent letter to authorities whenever the investigation took what seemed to them a wrong turn, so that they might insert a personal insight that might get things back onto the right track—after all, from their perspective, they knew the most intimate movements of their soul. At the same time, they accepted the view of the investigating team that it might have known its prisoners' real worth best.

An officer named Fel'dman pledged his very self against the slim hope that the NKVD would forgive him. On 31 May 1937 he pleaded before his investigator, Ushakov: "I wrote the beginning and the end of my confession in keeping with how I see things. . . . Tell me yourself [what to put in the middle]—it's easy enough to rewrite stuff." The interrogator could no doubt provide the recipe for a better version of Fel'dman's self. On a different occasion, he begged the same Ushakov: "Pass on to Ezhov . . . that I am ready to speak anywhere and to anyone, and I'll tell everything I know about the military conspiracy. . . . At the very first interrogation you saw, quite correctly, that Fel'dman is not an entrenched, irredeemable enemy [*zakorenelyi, neispravimyi vrag*], but an individual who will repay your efforts [*chelovek nad koim stoit porabotat'*]. If this sort of effort is made, he will repent and help the investigation."[41] Referring to himself in the third person, Fel'dman turned his self into something objective that the NKVD could observe, evaluate, and help him reconstruct.

However indispensable his effort at full confession and reform, Fel'dman could not form a correct view of himself without outside help; the NKVD had to provide him with a model for his self-construction. The ideal of liberalism— an autonomous and self-sufficient self—was a sin in the Stalinist universe. Speaking about himself in the third person, Fel'dman turned his self into something objective, lying, as it were, outside himself for both him and the NKVD to observe and evaluate.

It is the brunt of the above examples that throughout the interrogations of the mid-1930s it was difficult to drive a wedge between the language of the accuser and the language of the accused. And it was next to impossible to escape the official frame of reference: Even when they persevered in the argument that they were innocent, Communist prisoners could not conceive of justifying themselves by anything but party values. Life outside the party was more frightening than death. Bukharin expressed this feeling well when he stated in court: "For three months I refused to say anything. Then I began testifying. Why? Because there was nothing to die for if one died unrepentant."[42] Weissberg made a similar point: "I can clearly remember the mental process which preceded my collapse. I wanted to compromise with the examiner, but I found it difficult to overcome the habit of long years during which I had regarded my personal integrity as ranking over everything else in the world. I was despairingly searching for some psychological justification of my weakness, and [my interrogator] offered it in the idea that I was subordinating myself to party discipline."[43]

A confession could also be construed as a moment of awakening, a conversion, the adoption of the proper, dialectical view of oneself. Anyone who challenged the verdict of the party, the state, and the conscious working class by clinging to claims of innocence had to be self-centered, egotistic, and narrow-minded. In 1939 the famous Soviet writer Isaak Babel' described to Beriia how his interrogators had helped him regain his sense of self and overcome his writer's block: "Due to a terrible separation from the people, my creative fountain dried up. My attempts to extricate myself from captivity, from blind, self-infatuated isolation, were pathetic and ineffective. Liberation came in jail. During the months of imprisonment I thought through more and understood more than I had in my entire life up to that time. . . . I saw clearly the corruption and decadence of my largely Trotskyist environment. . . . Overwhelmed by regret and a longing to wash myself clean, I told the interrogators everything about my crimes." Babel' did his best to embed his personal experience in a Communist master narrative. His search for redemption involved him in an aesthetic project, a search for self-transformation through self-expression. His task was dual: to write a good social-realist novel describing the enemy and to incarnate the novel's themes in his NKVD confession. Babel' begged Beriia to "allow me at least to set down the plan of my book in a belletristic form. This will be a book about a typical descent leading to crimes against the socialist country. . . . I recently realized that what people need to read is a merciless literary self-revelation [*samorazoblachenie*]." What was Babel' talking about, his novel or his confession? "I never did finish my novel," he noted, "which turned into the protocols of a juridical investigation."[44]

According to the admissions of the victims, most of the confessions were obtained through "persuasion" (*ugovor*) and not physical pressure.[45] The NKVD frequently appealed to the conscience of their prisoners and asked them to sacrifice themselves for the sake of the revolution. The investigator told the Moscow Communist Geleish in 1938, "I know that everything written in the protocol is a pure fable. Still, you must accept the charges. The international situation demands that."[46] And this is how the interrogator of the Trotskyist Sergei Mrachkovskii described his tactics: "I brought Mrachkovskii to the point where he began to weep. I wept with him when we arrived at the conclusion that all was lost, that there was nothing left in the way of hope or faith, that the only thing to do was to make a desperate effort to forestall a future uprising of the discontented masses. For this the government must have public confessions by opposition leaders."[47] Having returned after eight years in Kolyma, a certain Muralov (no connection to the executed Trotskyist) apologized in a letter to Stalin: "I proved susceptible to . . . the investigator who told me, 'If you love the Party, you must sign this investigation protocol,' and 'Our country needs such admissions these days.'"[48] Even the hardened Moscow informer code-named Snowflake agreed in 1938 to plead guilty to imaginary crimes so that a dangerous spy network could be unmasked. "Blindly believing the investigator, seeing in him a representative of the NKVD, I fell into his trap."[49]

Berger, rubbing shoulders with many political prisoners in the Arctic North in the late 1930s and 1940s, described two fundamental ways in which Old Bolsheviks responded to torment. Arrested in late 1936 or early 1937 as a "Trotskyist wrecker," X, a prominent Soviet engineer, understood that the NKVD operated on Central Committee instructions and that by opposing his investigators, he would violate party authority. "So X signed a confession which, in his own words, 'did not contain a single word of truth.' Returning to his prison cell, he stated enthusiastically: 'Dying, I will know I sacrificed myself for Stalin and the motherland.'"[50] Opting for the opposite approach, Rubinov, arrested in 1937, believed that his theoretical mind was superior to the Central Committee's. "'The intraparty struggle could not have had a different outcome,'" he claimed. "'The Russian proletariat cannot build a just society all alone.'" And yet Rubinov insisted that despite his suffering, "he remains a Marxist"; he too did not have a different language to anchor his political thinking in.[51]

Whether blaming themselves, as did the majority, or blaming the party—the option chosen by only the most steadfast of the Trotskyists—such prisoners remained locked within the framework of Communist martyrology. Willingly playing the role of a scapegoat, they sacrificed themselves for the revolution. Whether this was a gesture of oppositionist steadfastness or the hedonism of self-abasement for the proletariat's sake, they died as heroes.

Milan Kundera captures the specific predicament of the Communist interrogatees with a comparison between Dostoevsky and Kafka. Raskolnikov "cannot bear the weight of his guilt, and to find peace he consents to this punishment of his own free will." Here the offense seeks the punishment. In Kafka the logic is reversed. "The person punished does not know the reason for the punishment. The absurdity of the punishment is so unbearable that to find peace the accused needs to find a justification for his penalty: the punishment seeks the offense. . . . The 'autoculpabilization' machine goes into motion."[52]

Notes

1. The research for this chapter was financed by the Israeli Science Foundation, grant number 496–09. For general studies of the Moscow show trials, see Nicolas Werth, *Les procès de Moscou, 1936–1938* (Paris: Editions complexe, 1987); William Chase, "Stalin as Producer: The Moscow Show Trials and the Construction of Moral Threats," in *Stalin: A New History*, ed. *Sarah Davies* and *James Harris* (Cambridge: Cambridge University Press, 2006), 226–48.

2. Stephen Kotkin, *Magnetic Mountain: Stalinism as a Civilization* (Berkeley: University of California Press, 1995), 333–35.

3. Isaac Deutsher and David King, *The Great Purges* (Oxford: Oxford University Press, 1984); J. Arch Getty and Oleg V. Naumov, *The Road to Terror: Stalin and the Self-Destruction of the Bolsheviks, 1932–1939* (New Haven: Yale University Press, 1999).

4. A. V. Afanas'ev, *Oni ne molchali* (Moscow: Politizdat, 1991), 369.

5. Oleg Mozokhin, *Pravo na repressii: Vnesudebnye polnomochiia organov gosudarstvennoi bezopasnosti (1918–1953)* (Moscow: Kuchkovo Pole, 2006), 218.

6. Iu. S. Kukushkina, ed., *Rezhim lichnoi vlasti Stalina. K istorii formirovaniia* (Moscow: Izd. Moskovskogo Universiteta, 1989), 88.

7. "Prosti menia Koba: Neizvestnoe pis'mo N. Bukharina," *Istochnik*, no. 11 (1993); "'U menia odna Nadezhda na Tebia.' Poslednie pis'ma N. I. Bukharina I. V. Stalinu, 1935–1937," *Istoricheskii arkhiv*, no. 3 (2001).

8. James T. Siegel, *Naming the Witch* (Stanford, CA: Stanford University Press, 2006), 215–16.

9. Slavoj Žižek, *The Sublime Object of Ideology* (London: Verso, 1989), 125–127.

10. Andrzej Walicki, *Marxism and the Leap to the Kingdom of Freedom: The Rise and Fall of the Communist Utopia* (Stanford, CA: Stanford University Press, 1995), 463.

11. Joseph Stalin, *O nedostatkakh partiinoi raboty i merakh likvidatsii: Trotskistkikh i inykh dvurushnikov* (Moscow: OGIZ, gos. Izd. Politicheskoi literatury, 1937), 10–20.

12. *Voprosy istorii*, nos. 4–5 (1992): 25–26, 33.

13. Here "confession" is a translation of "priznanie" (admission of a crime) and not of the religious "ispoved'," and it therefore encompasses an element of interpretation. Still, the Russian term is used in the context of discussing intentions and motives, not just facts. The religious sense could be invoked as a metaphor. Thus the arrested playwright Meirkhol'd ended his letter to Molotov with the following words: "Here is my confession [*ispoved'*]. Following custom, I make it possible a second before my death. I was never a spy, never participated in any of the Trotskyist organizations (together with the Party I cursed the Judas Trotsky!), and never conducted any counterrevolutionary activity." Boris Sopel'niak, *Smert' v rassrochku* (Moscow: Geia, 1998), 254.

14. Voitlovskaia, "Po sledam sud'by moego pokoleniia " (unpublished manuscript, ca. 1990), 66.

15. A. Voitlovskaia, "Sud nad sledovatelem," in *Zven'ia*, vyp.1 (Moscow: Progress, 1991), 403–7; Voitlovskaia, "Po sledam," 77; emphasis in the original.

16. *Back in Time: My Life, My Fate, My Epoch; The Memoirs of Nadezhda A. Joffe*, translated from the Russian by F. Choate (Oak Park: Labor Publications, 1995), 97.

17. Voitlovskaia, "Sud nad sledovatelem."

18. Alex Weissberg, *Conspiracy of Silence* (London: Hamilton, 1952), 231.

19. Iu. N. Bogdanov, *Strogo sekretno: 30 let v OGPU-NKVD-MVD* (Moscow: Veche, 2002), 123.

20. O. F. Suvenirov, *Tragediia RKKA, 1937–1938* (Moscow: Terra, 1998), 152.

21. *Kniga pamiati zhertv politicheskikh repressii Ul'ianovskoi oblasti*, vol. 1 (Moscow: Institut eksperimental'noi sotsiologii, 1997), 896.

22. Every citizen in the camp had the right to petition the government. L. I. Gvozdikova, *Stalinskie lageria na territorii kuzbassa (30–40e gg.)* (Kemerovo: Kemerovskii gos. universitet, 1994), 60.

23. *Leningradskii martirolog* (St. Petersburg: Rossiiskaia natsional'naia biblioteka, 1995–), 3:569.

24. Voitlovskaia, "Po sledam," 93.

25. A. N. Iakovleva, ed., *Reabilitatsiia: Politicheskie protsessy 30kh–50kh godov* (Moscow: Izd. Politicheskoi literatury, 1991), 182.

26. L. Shein, *Nastol'naia kniga sledovatelia* (Moscow, 1949), 11.

27. Voitlovskaia, "Po sledam," 66–67.

28. F. D. Ashnin and V. M. Alpatov, *"Delo Slavistov": 30-e gody* (Moscow: Nasledie, 1994), 64–65.

29. Ibid.

30. When the theater director Vsevolod Meirkhol'd sent an appeal to Molotov, his letter sounded like something out of Dostoevsky. He cited psychological pressure in explaining why he had confessed to Trotskyism:

> When the interrogators supplemented their physical pressure with the so-called psychological attack, I was possessed by such a monstrous fear that the very roots of my being were exposed. . . . My nerves turned out to be close to the surface of my body, my skin soft and sensitive as if I were a newborn, my eyes ready to shed limitless tears (the result of intolerable physical and moral pain). . . . When people are afraid, they reveal their true selves. Fright [*ispug*] opens a hole in one's habits, and this hole reveals one's true nature [*natura*].

Meirkhol'd admitted to having "completely lost self-control: . . . I sank into a deep depression brought on by a recurrent thought: 'I seem to deserve it!'" As he became convinced of his own guilt, he found experts ready to help him build the case against himself: "My self split into two parts: one half searched for my 'crime' while the other half . . . invented one. The investigator applied his skill and experience to help me compose [the crimes]; ours was a close collaboration. When my imagination exhausted itself, the investigators teamed up . . . to bake protocols. Sometimes three or four different versions were prepared." This soon reduced him to a wreck.

> I couldn't eat a thing and for four months I couldn't sleep, so between hunger and insomnia, along with nightly heart palpitations and hysterical fits of uncontrollable sobbing and febrile shaking, I looked ten years older; the worried investigators began feeding and treating me. This helped my body, but my nerves remained wretched, my consciousness darkened [*zatumanneno*] and dulled [*pritupleno*]. I realized that the sword of Damocles was hanging above my head: the investigator kept insisting, threatening, "If you do not write something"—did he mean invent something?—"we will hit beat you again. Only your head and your right arm will remain intact and the rest will be turned into a formless, bloody, shredded piece of meat." So I signed everything. (*Sovetskaia kul'tura*, 16 February 1989)

31. Prisoners engaged in constant self-interrogation. Polynov, a member of the Academy of Science arrested in May 1937 on charges of terrorism, was tormented by the question of the real reason for his arrest. "I went through everything I was doing recently in my mind, looked for inadvertent [*nevol'nye*] mistakes, tried to recall all my conversations, meetings, activities . . . but could think of no fault." *Tragicheskie sud'by: Repressirovannye uchenye Akademii nauk SSSR* (Moscow: Nauka, 1995), 82.

32. The interrogator of Pavel Florenskii made this point very explicit: "We cannot follow the czarist government that punished only crimes committed. . . . We must preempt crimes, only then we will be safe!" V. Shentalinskii, *Raby svobody. V literaturnykh arkhivakh KGB* (Moscow: Parus, 1995), 162.

33. Ashnin and Alpatov, *"Delo Slavistov,"* 67–68.

34. Voitlovskaia, "Po sledam," 64.

35. Ibid., 67.

36. Ibid., 71.

37. Quoted in V. Sokolov, *Narkomy strakha. Iagoda, Ezhov, Beriia, Abakumov* (Moscow: AST Press, 2001), 81–82.

38. Maksim Gorkii, *Neizdannaia perepiska S. Bogdanovym, Leninym, Stalinym, Zinov'evym, Kamenevym, Korolenko* (Moscow: Nasledie, 1998), 208–13.

39. "Nepridumannoe," *Iunost'*, no. 5 (1988), nos. 1–2 (1989); Iu. Stetsovskii, *Istoriia sovetskikh repressii* (St. Petersburg: Glasnost', 1997), 1:168.

40. Shentalinskii, *Raby svobody*, 152–55.

41. Suvenirov, *Tragediia*, 204.

42. *Report of Court Proceedings in the Case of the Anti-Soviet "Bloc of Rights and Trotskyites"* (Moscow: People's Commissariat of Justice of the U.S.S.R., 1938), 777–78.

43. Weissberg, *Conspiracy of Silence*, 208.

44. Shentalinskii, *Raby svobody*, 38, 69–70. Other writers also applied their talents to writing confessions. Meerkhol'd's testimony extended over 31 pages; Kol'tsov wrote 31 pages of testimony, then added another 40 pages, then 17 more. B. Sopel'niak, *Smert' v rassrochku* (Moscow: Geia, 1998), 152, 249.

45. A. Vatlin, *Terror raionnogo mashtaba* (Moscow: ROSSPEN, 2004), 50.

46. Ibid., 42.

47. W. Krivitskii, *I Was Stalin's Agent* (London: London Right Book Club, 1940), 219–25.

48. Vatlin, *Terror raionnogo mashtaba*, 164.

49. Ibid., 133.

50. Y. Berger-Barzilai, *Ha-tragediia shel ha mahapekha ha sovietit* [The Tragedy of the Soviet Revolution] (Tel Aviv: Am Oved, 1968), 160.

51. Ibid., 167.

52. Milan Kundera, *The Art of the Novel*, trans. Linda Asher (New York: Grove Press, 1986), 102–3.

10.

ADITYA NIGAM

The Heterotopias of Dalit Politics: Becoming-Subject and the Consumption Utopia

MOST MODERN radical social and political imaginaries have been historically framed by a utopian search for a place outside the domain of the commodity and commodification.[1] The corrupting influence of capitalist consumption, the naked "cash nexus," as Marx called it, has spurred the radical imagination for a very long time, and the more commodity relations envelop us, the stronger the desire to escape into a place that is nowhere, or at least not-yet. "Utopia," then, is equally "uchronia"—a time that does not exist but will undoubtedly come. The politics of the oppressed—especially as articulated in the intellectual domain—has thus often been a search for a pure space outside the profanity of capitalist commodity relations. This is as true of most modern social imaginaries like Marxism and anarchism as it is of imaginaries inspired by religious eschatological visions. In this sense, Dalit politics, I believe, is about the here and now; it is what one may term *an existential politics of place* that seeks to transform *this* place in *this* time. I will explain later why I call this antiutopian politics heterotopic.

Dalit politics is not merely a politics of the here and now but also, unlike most other modern radical movements, would seem to celebrate what one might call the new consumption utopia. Many of the intellectual articulations by the Dalit intelligentsia have drawn heavily from Marxism, especially from the 1970s onward, and even today much of the intellectual discourse is framed by extant Marxist and left-wing critiques of globalization. The argument is familiar: globalization and the entry of foreign private capital will destroy and is destroying the public sector, and this will affect the Dalits most, as it will render them jobless. This fear arises from the fact that in the last six decades, given the high levels of discrimination against and exclusion of Dalits, their only hope has been vested in public employment, where due to policies of affirmative action, avenues continue to be open to them. However, two points need to be remembered in this context. First, this is primarily an intellectual current and not really reflected in mass politics. Politically, right from Ambedkar's time, the emphasis has been on the here and now, on a refusal to defer important questions of power and representation to any distant future. Second, in the last few years, fresh thinking on some of these issues has taken place and voices have emerged, one of which I will discuss at length, which have rapidly become a cult. These are, it seems to me, the voices of the future.

In what follows, I discuss media representations of Mayawati, the powerful former Dalit chief minister of Uttar Pradesh and leader of the Bahujan Samaj Party (BSP) who has led the political upsurge of Dalits in northern India in recent decades. I will then attempt, with the help of a contemporary Dalit short story, to explore the mode of becoming-subject of the Dalits and connect it with Mayawati's representation in public discourse.

Scene 1: The "Opulent Leader of the Outcastes"

"*For the Oppressed, Covered in Diamonds*—Govt Plays Host at Mayawati Birthday Bash," ran the headline in a front-page story of a leading English daily in India several years ago.[2] The reference here is to Mayawati, who was then (in 2003) the chief minister of the northern Indian state of Uttar Pradesh,[3] and who happens to have been the first Dalit woman chief minister. The report continued: "Uttar Pradesh chief minister Mayawati today celebrated her 47th birthday in style at a grand function on the La Martiniere grounds here, brushing aside accusations of using the occasion to 'mint' money." The report went on to say that the "Lucknow bash began with Mayawati, dressed in a pink salwar suit, cutting the cake and distributing colour TVs—sponsored by Bharat Petroleum—to women heads of 47 Ambedkar villages." It did not forget to add that "*she wore a diamond necklace, diamond-studded earrings and bracelets that had diamond coating over gold.*" Another news Web site ran this report: "Mayawati, who was laden with diamond jewellery, celebrated her 47th birthday in such style that it would have put many tycoons to shame."[4] Further: "A 51 kg cake, 100,000 laddoos, 60 quintals of marigold flowers and 5000 bouquets were among the few highlights of the day." The report also said that the forty-by-sixty-foot stage was reminiscent of the Hindi blockbuster film *Mughal-e-Azam*. Apparently, the architect of the stage, Janardhan (a BSP activist himself), confirmed this: "Yes, we have tried to copy the sets shown in a sequence from the legendary film when heroine Madhubala dances."[5]

Now consider this story in the *New York Times*, which appeared a few months after this report. It was titled "An Opulent and Pugnacious Champion of India's Outcasts." It began: "She arrived by helicopter and spoke for an hour and a half beneath an air-conditioned canopy."[6] The correspondent, Amy Waldman, had obviously been quick to pick up on what was probably the most discussed feature about Mayawati among middle-class Indians—her "opulence" and ostentatious display of wealth. Waldman's report went on: "Her critics charge that she is cut-throat and corrupt in the pursuit of power, and that she lavishes more money on ostentatious displays of status than on serving the poor she claims to represent." As evidence, Waldman cited Ram

Sharan Das, the president of Samajwadi (socialist) Party, her main rival in the state, as saying that "if a woman claims to be the champion of the Dalits after wearing a 30-million rupee necklace, there can't be any bigger lie than that." Waldman concluded: *"Draped with diamonds, she contrasted sharply with the understated homespun style that most politicians deliberately adopt."*

I have just cited from three news reports at random, but these could be said to represent the more general sense of disquiet, in fact, *agitation*, felt by the "sophisticated" and "cultured" middle-class public, an agitation that routinely finds expression in the ways in which Mayawati is talked about and reported in the media.

The contrast of Mayawati's style with what Waldman called "the understated homespun style" adopted by the political class in India could not be sharper. As is well known, since the advent of Gandhi on the political scene in the early 1920s, there has been a strong emphasis on spinning and wearing *khadi*—a coarse homespun cloth, usually white. Gandhi returned from his sojourn from England and South Africa, shed his Western attire, and donned the loincloth, thus effecting a shift to a different semiotic register as he sought to take on the task of welding together the nation that was waiting to be born. This shift was undertaken as an act of affiliation with the large and poverty-stricken masses of Indians. In doing this and in evolving the code of dressing in homespun, coarse khadi, Gandhi was also establishing a connection with the idea of *swadeshi*, which followed the partition of Bengal in 1905 and provided the ammunition for the major nationalist struggle for reunification. Swadeshi, which literally means "of one's own country," was the idea that became a point of mass mobilization against British-manufactured cloth. The struggle of Indian nationalism was closely meshed in this period with the struggle against the domination of cloth from the textile manufacturers of Manchester and Lancashire. It was in this context that nationalist singers of that time such as Mukunda Das sang: *"Ma-er deoya mota kapor mathaye tule ne re bhai/ deen dukhini ma ar je mo-der, er beshi aar shaddhyo naain"* (Treat this coarse cloth given by our mother with respect, dear brother, for this is all that this poor and forlorn mother of ours can afford).

In a recent essay Dipesh Chakrabarty has suggested that if the most common uniform for the politician has been, from before the time of independence, white khadi, this has something to do with its symbolism "as intended in official/nationalist discourse"; the white khadi, he writes, "stands for the Hindu idea of purity (lack of blemish, pollution), its coarseness symbolizes an identification both with simplicity and poverty."[7] Citing from a study by Susan Bean, Chakrabarty asserts that Gandhi's own gloss on "khadi" (in 1921) mobilized all of these meanings with an added one: "I consider the renunciation [of foreign cloth] to be also necessary as a sign of mourning, and a bare head and a bare body is such a sign in my part of the country."[8]

For the nationalists, the matter then came to acquire a highly emotive charge where the poverty of the large masses of Indian people came to be represented in the poverty and helplessness of "Mother India," and wearing the mill-spun cloth from Britain represented sacrilege—feeding into the drain of national wealth into the coffers of the British exploiters. There is, of course, a seeming irony in this, insofar as Dr. B. R. Ambedkar, a representative of the Dalits, the poorest and most oppressed section of Indian society, whom all Dalits will swear by (and who was Gandhi's contemporary), always preferred his Western-style suit to khadi. Ambedkar has now emerged in Dalit conscious-ness not merely as one of the great political leaders of the community but also iconized as a godly father figure. Neither in Dalit iconizations of Ambedkar nor in official representations of him as a national leader does he figure any-where in anything but a Western suit and with a book—the constitution of India, whose drafting committee he headed—under his arm.

This image of Ambedkar stands in sharp contrast to those of other leaders of the nationalist struggle—Gandhi in his loincloth, Nehru in *sherwani* and *chooridar*, and Maulana Azad in an *achkan* or *sherwani*. Kancha Ilaiah, for instance, invokes this Westernized image of Ambedkar in order to underline that the ordinary Dalit—or Dalit culture in general—does not place any spe-cial value on any indigenist notion of "authenticity." So he asserts that "unlike Gandhi and Nehru, Ambedkar wore a suit throughout his life without facing any problems from his community," whereas "Gandhi had to struggle a lot to de-westernize himself."[9]

Lest we begin to think that this representation is uniformly and uncritically extolled in the same way by all Dalits, let me also state that there is an element of the tragic here that might point to one of the deeper conflicts within the movement. I cite a slightly long passage from Anand Teltumbde, a leading intellectual who represents the left wing of the movement:

> The first attempt to iconize Ambedkar, and considerably successfully so, as the later times proved, is apparent in this early *post-Ambedkar* episode. That was the icon of the saheb—the epitaph [*sic*] used for an Englishman but later used as an honorific for natives who were educated, westernized and placed in bureaucratic authority. It denoted someone far above the masses, one who was endowed with authority and power. It was the icon of the sav-iour. It projected the leader as the saviour incarnate who would liberate them from their bondage and lead them to prosperity. All that the masses had to do was to stand solidly behind him. . . . This particular icon dis-tanced the Dalit leadership from the masses in every way, in terms of physi-cal attributes like appearance, clothes, language and life-style. It promoted blind and servile notions. The leaders were to be treated as their quasi-monarch (a la *Bhim Raja*).[10]

Teltumbde goes on to argue that this "saheb" syndrome, to the extent that it represented middle-class aspirations, "helped petty bourgeois-ize the entire Dalit movement." Teltumbde's reflections are important for us, not simply because they present an important critical counterposition from within the movement, but also because in making this critique they point to what is the dominant tendency at least among the emerging elite/middle-class sections of the movement. In Teltumbde's view, after Ambedkar's death, the leadership of the movement fell into the hands of Dadasaheb Gaikwad, a close associate and "trusted lieutenant" of Ambedkar since the days of the famous Mahad struggle. Gaikwad led, according to him, a militant struggle for land in Maharshtra involving large masses of Dalits. But, writes Teltumbde, "while the movement caught the fancy of the Dalit masses, the rest of the Dalit leadership thought otherwise." Gaikwad was "a rustic in the common man's Dhoti-Kurta attire, and not embellished with university degrees." He was thus "unacceptable to these people." Teltumbde criticizes this section of the Dalit leadership, who claimed they "fitted into the Ambedkarian mould (as they conceived it)" better than Gaikwad because, as he puts it, "this mould was based on middle class cultural norms that Ambedkar displayed in his attire and general demeanour."[11] Teltumbde reads in Ambedkar's own self-presentation "a counter to Gandhi's belaboured austerity" and "a representation of modernity as against Gandhi's anti-modern views."[12] In Teltumbde's reading, this specific contextual countermove by Ambedkar, when generalized into an overall valorization of the Westernized image by the post-Ambedkar leadership, is deeply problematic and has conveyed the wrong impression about the movement, and it has even fostered self-defeating tendencies within it—for instance, those that led to the rejection of Gaikwad.

Modernity is certainly an issue here, and the conflation of the modern with the Western is quite widespread among all classes through the late-nineteenth and twentieth centuries. At one level, this is what Teltumbde is trying to disaggregate by bringing in the rustic counterfigure of Gaikwad in his *dhoti-kurta*—a perfect counter, one could imagine, to Gandhi. Gandhi's investment of a very specific meaning in the act of wearing khadi—the dual signification of the Hindu idea of purity and the existence of British rule as something to be mourned—gives us further clues as to why this move is shunned by Dalits such as Mayawati even today. In the Hindu idea of purity, Dalit existence is the embodiment of pollution. Dalits are untouchable precisely because they exist to undertake all the polluting work of upper-caste society so that the upper caste may retain its "purity." Further, to the Dalits, foreign rule appears as the harbinger of liberation and is therefore to be celebrated, not mourned. Mayawati's "ostentatiousness" and her sartorial preferences can in fact be read as her symbolic countermove that mocks Gandhi's attempt at representing poverty and mourning through the semiotic transformation of his body. If

Gandhi the *baniya* (a trader caste) had to display the poverty and suffering he never actually experienced, here was Mayawati, a representative of the really poor and oppressed, by her very appearance ridiculing that attempt much like Ambedkar's Western suit did. It is tempting, therefore, to read the Dalit rejection of the Brahmanical power being allegorically performed here on the stage of *Mughal-e-Azam*, recalling Madhubala in the role of Anarkali, the defiant slave girl dancing for her love and mocking the power of Akbar, the great Mughal emperor.

At this level, at least as a first approximation, it is possible to see why there might be such a reaction to the renunciatory moves of the nationalists. What made matters worse, right from the days of the nationalist struggle, was Gandhi's defense of the caste system—what is known as *varnashrama dharma*. He had, after all, openly declared on numerous occasions that he was only against the practice of untouchability; the hierarchy of the caste order was not something Gandhi wanted to disturb. Mayawati, unlike Ambedkar, is an entirely homespun Dalit, without the benefit of the latter's education in the United States and his deliberately more modulated and cultivated speech and appearance. Mayawati arises from a different world—at once much more ruthless and degrading. Her style is therefore marked by a certain performative excess: the apparent crudity and aggressiveness of her language that are galling to her critics. This performative excess, we may note, is not a peculiar characteristic of Mayawati's personal style alone; it is evident in much of Dalit speech and literature as well as in other forms of writing. That, however, is not our immediate concern, but for the present let me note that if this is what arouses the strongest feelings of hatred among the upper castes or the twice-born (*dwijas*), it is precisely what endears her to her people and provides them inspiration. Even the reports mentioned earlier that describe Mayawati in such negative ways concede that the turnout at the rally was impressive and that people "had started pouring in from the morning, braving dense fog and bone-chilling winds."[13] One of them also mentions the many ballads sung in praise of Mayawati during the program.[14]

Waldman's report, for instance, cites one of the BSP supporters as saying that "she and her party have empowered the poor people." More significantly, it also cites Nirmala, one of the many admiring young Dalit women, who says: "Mayawati gives inspiration that anything can be achieved." I emphasize the word "anything" here and will return to it in a moment, for I believe that this "anything" is not just anything; it also refers to something very specific. Nirmala's is not an isolated instance. The overpowering impact that the image of Mayawati—confidently and aggressively dealing with upper-caste men—can have on young women like Nirmala is yet to be fathomed. Waldman probably sensed that something more was going on here when she noted in her report: "*In putting on an imperial show of power, she has touched something deep* [emphasis added]." To try to unravel this "something deep," I will refer to a fictional representation of Dalit life and, for the moment, leave Mayawati's story here.

Scene 2: The Dystopian Space of the *Paracheri*

Let us try to understand some of the questions above with the help of a Dalit short story. This story, "Reet" (Custom), is by an important Hindi writer and journalist, Mohandas Naimishray.[15] It is set in a village called Kisanpura and begins with what could be one of the most familiar descriptions of the spatial layout of a Dalit settlement:

> On the north of Kisanpura village, at some distance from the village, a colony of Mehtars with some makeshift houses of Chamars, right next to them.[16] The atmosphere permeated with a stench and alongside, the gurgling sound of earthen *hookahs*. Piles of garbage spread out here and there and innumerable diseases "swimming around" in the pool of dirty water that has collected nearby. Some pigs rolling around in the muck. Half-naked children playing in the open space, their space—but cut off from the rest of the village. Completely isolated, like an island in the sea.

As Naimishray puts it, an invisible *savarna rekha* (literally, a line of casteness) divides the village. Everything—the temple, the well, the pond, even the land—is marked by this line of difference, inhabited on one side by those who have the language of rights and power and on the other by those who have but duties.

This is the spatial layout of what is called the *paracheri* in Tamil—the living area of the pariahs (Dalits), situated on the outskirts of the village. I use this Tamil term to refer generally to Dalit settlements.[17] The pariahs/Dalits do not, strictly speaking, belong to the caste order—the *chaturvarna* of the four *varnas*. They are the fifth and therefore often referred to as the *panchamas*, or the outcastes. Hence their living space is relegated to the outer limits of the village, the access to which is also different in most cases. As is well known, the pariahs are not allowed to walk the roads used by the upper castes; they cannot drink water from the village wells or worship in the same temples.

The story goes on. Despite this chain of duty—or maybe *because* of it—every year people from this hellish part of the village escape to the city in search of a heaven. Who knows whether they ever find it? Some time ago, yet another such man disappeared from this hell. His name was Bulaki. His wife, Phulo, pined and cried for him day and night, for years. She was going on sixteen when Bulaki had married her and brought her home. She came dressed in colorful clothes from top to bottom, hands and feet tinted with henna. She also wore a little jewelry, which tinkled with each step she took.

The wedding pair had to cross two villages on the way and at one point had to announce who they were: "The sweepers of Kisanpura, my lord." Phulo's father had repeatedly warned her not to wear anything that made a sound and could thus attract attention. Had he not taught her over and over again the difference between the high and the lowly? Did she not know that all these things were forbidden for members of their caste?

Phulo did not listen. The old man's eyes darkened with fear as he bade his newly wed daughter farewell and prayed for her well-being. When Phulo left, she had only one regret: her man had not come to her on horseback because people of their caste were not allowed to sit on horses. On a couple of occasions in the past, the upper-caste people of the village had set their colony on fire because one of their grooms had dared to come on horseback.

The pigsty had been emptied and cleaned for her to spend her ceremonial first night with her husband. There she waited and waited, but Bulaki never came. However, other men did, and they forcibly took her away to the landlord's house, where he clawed and consumed her all night. Slowly it dawned on Phulo that this was not accidental. This was the custom.

But her man, her Bulaki, never returned, even after that disastrous night was over. Not for the next five years. In all that while, she never left the pigsty. She stayed there, thinking of her husband. People were convinced that she had gone mad. And then suddenly, one night, she heard his voice. He was calling out her name. She thought she was dreaming. The shouts grew louder and louder. She got up and looked out. There was Bulaki—on horseback. What is more, he had grown a mustache—which, too, was forbidden for "them"—and to top it all, he was carrying a double-barreled gun. She went up to him and jumped on the horse. For the first time, five years after their marriage, he held her and said, "Come, Phulo, we will not live here anymore," and they sped away. As they came out of the village, he pulled in the reins and the horse stopped. Behind them arose a great furor. Phulo looked back. The sky above the upper-caste village was red with flames. And as he sped off once again, Bulaki told Phulo, "No landlord will play with the respect of any woman of the village anymore."

The story is in many ways typical. However, I do not use it to simply narrate another instance of the everyday violence and oppression that mark Dalit life even today, nor of the resistance to it. Rather, I use it to reflect on the figure and trope of the paracheri as a particular kind of space and through it to delineate certain lines of *desire*.

The hellishness of the dystopic space of the paracheri is of course underlined by the series of prohibitions that its inhabitants have to observe. And the most obnoxious of these prohibitions have to do with the denial of access to even clean drinking water from the wells, so that often these inhabitants have to drink the same dirty water from the open ponds that animals drink from. But all this is too well known by now and appears even in non-Dalit fiction, as in the stories of Premchand, for instance. But it is not only acts involving the movement of untouchables into common spaces—thus carrying the threat of polluting the upper castes—that are prohibited for them. The "untouchability" of their caste is marked on their bodies; their very appearance is strictly policed—what they may wear and how they may look are the targets of violent control. Marking the bodies as untouchable is also not always enough; in many parts of the country, the untouchable was, until very recently, required to announce his/her appearance from a distance so that the upper caste could escape the polluting shadow of this impure body.

The paracheri is a dystopic, but certainly not an imaginary, space. It is a real place, located at the periphery of the village or the town, an exclusive space meant to house people who are to undertake what orthodox Brahmanical/ Hindu society considers polluting activities, so that "purity" may rigorously be maintained within the precincts of caste society.

In attempting to understand this space, it is useful to recall Foucault's reflections on a whole range of "other spaces" that he calls heterotopias. In the first place, heterotopias, writes Foucault, are real places, as opposed to utopias, which are "sites with no real place."[18] As is well known, Foucault's essay "Of Other Spaces" was excavated from some old lecture notes prepared by Foucault in 1967, incorporated in 1984 into an exhibition in Berlin, and published in English in *Diacritics* in 1986.[19] Foucault never really prepared the notes for publication, and therefore they do not have the character of a finished work. Precisely for that reason, however, they provide an opportunity to work on this extremely suggestive idea.

Foucault talks especially of two types of heterotopias. The first is in primitive societies, a particular form that he calls "*crisis heterotopias*" (italics in the original)—privileged, sacred, or forbidden places, reserved for individuals, who in the context of those particular societies are considered to be in a state of crisis: adolescents, menstruating women, pregnant women, the elderly, and so on. These places, writes Foucault, are now disappearing in contemporary Western societies and are being replaced by the second type, those he calls "*heterotopias of deviation.*" These places are for those whose behavior is considered deviant in relation to the norm and include rest homes, psychiatric hospitals, and prisons. There are two other kinds of spaces that Foucault discusses, although in passing, namely the heterotopias of "illusion" and those of "compensation"—those that either expose all other lived spaces as equally illusory or approximate some idea of perfection. Exemplifying the latter, writes Foucault, were the early Jesuit colonies established in South America, "marvelous, absolutely regulated colonies in which human perfection was effectively achieved." As an instance of the heterotopias of illusion, he mentions, in passing, "those famous brothels," about which we are given no further elaboration. The range of spaces that Foucault identifies under the rubric of heterotopias, then, are still in some way related to an unstated notion of utopia, a utopia propelled by a desire for some kind of normalcy or perfection—either by segregating the deviant or the crisis-ridden or by replicating some idea of perfection in some other place presumably uncontaminated by history (as in the case of the Jesuit colonies).

One of the features of heterotopias that Foucault enunciated is their "link . . . to slices in time," or what he also refers to as "heterochronies." Here he presents three kinds of heterotopias: first, those that embody a sort of absolute break with their traditional time, as, for instance, the cemetery. Second, those that embody "indefinitely accumulating time," for instance the museum and the library. Third, "those linked . . . to time in its flowing, transitory, precarious aspect, to time in the mode of the festival."

Given the immense diversity of the kinds of spaces that Foucault seeks to cover by deploying this term, it is somewhat intriguing that spaces like those produced by apartheid in South Africa, Jim Crow laws in the American South, and the concentration camp do not figure in Foucault's list. And yet, if the psychiatric hospital and the prison constitute heterotopias of one kind (segregating those whose behavior is considered deviant), surely it would not be stretching Foucault's sense of the term too much if we included within it these other spaces—in our case, the paracheri.

Edward Soja, in a fascinating discussion of bell hooks's writings, points to the idea of marginality in her spatial narratives of exclusion and struggle. Hooks writes: "As black Americans living in a small Kentucky town, the railroad tracks were a daily reminder of our marginality. Across those tracks were paved streets, stores we could not enter, restaurants we could not eat in, and people we could not look directly in the face. Across the tracks was a world we could work in as maids, as janitors, as prostitutes, as long as it was in a service capacity. We could enter that world but we could not live there. . . . There were laws to ensure our return."[20]

This description of the Kentucky settlement is similar to that of the paracheri— with one important difference. The paracheri is a nonmodern space whose boundaries are maintained and enforced through religious notions of purity and pollution, whereas in the American South or under apartheid these spaces were carved out and protected by modern law.

Unlike Foucault's heterotopias, however, none of these spaces segregates populations that are either crisis ridden or deviant. All of these spaces are reserved for those who are simply marked as different in order to produce a different kind of normality within the main body of society. Perhaps these could be designated as the *heterotopias of difference*. The paracheri is an exclusive space meant to house people who undertake what orthodox Brahmanical/ Hindu society considers polluting activities, so that "purity" may rigorously be maintained within the precincts of caste society.

By the middle of the nineteenth century, however, major transformations began to take place as new, modern colonial institutions came into existence.

The space of the city was rapidly transformed into a secular modern space, thrown open in principle to everybody, irrespective of caste or class. The prohibitions of the village and the paracheri were not quite possible to enforce in the city—a space also of anonymity, where the untouchable could now "pass." No longer was it possible to identify the untouchable body by simply looking at it, as Surajpal Chauhan recalls in his autobiography. There he describes how he and his wife had asked a zamindar for some water on a visit to the village during the summer vacation. The zamindar agreed, but when he discovered Chauhan's caste identity, he was enraged and began insulting them.

"Wear new clothes"—that was what Phulo had wanted in our story above, and not even every day, but to mark that special day of her wedding. "Wear new clothes and jewelry and dress up as a bride." But Phulo lived in the paracheri, unlike Surajpal Chauhan, who had found a place for himself in the city. However, the inhabitants of Phulo's paracheri had now heard of this other place—a utopia, at least for those who remained there. It was a place that beckoned, and every now and then some inhabitants, usually males to begin with, "disappeared" in search of that heaven. That is where Bulaki also disappeared. When he returned after five years, he was sporting a mustache, carrying a gun, and riding a horse. That was, after all, one regret that Phulo continued to have—that her groom did return on horseback. Coming back from the city, he fulfilled that desire—the city that had transformed Bulaki from a helpless Mehtar who could do nothing but run away, abandoning his wife to the wolves on the very first night of their wedding, into a confident man. This is the story of Bulaki's becoming-Dalit in the city.

It is also interesting to recall that in the prefatory comments to his reflections on heterotopias, written in the context of mid- to late-twentieth-century Europe, Foucault suggests that "contemporary space is perhaps still not desanctified," that many distinctions such as those between private and public space are "still nurtured by the hidden presence of the sacred."[21] It is this "hidden presence of the sacred" that in the context of our exploration of the becoming-subject of the Dalit assumes a certain critical import. If the paracheri was the place of virtual confinement of the untouchable castes almost until the middle of the nineteenth century, its peculiar transfiguration into yet another imaginary space in the modern age possibly underlies and provides the clue to many of the puzzles of contemporary India.

As modernity begins to reconstitute the spatial configuration of Indian society, carving out new and secularized public spaces in urban areas, the paracheri and all the lines of casteness that define it undergo a peculiar transformation. They become an imaginary boundary that a caste Hindu begins to carry with him or her, a boundary that is now dislocated from physical space. The paracheri as an imaginary space pervades the entire space of the nation. The hidden presence of the caste line structures every space that a caste Hindu walks into. Invisible to the secularized caste Hindu, it is a line that is always visible to the "untouchable," for s/he must always be careful not to transgress. Even the space of modern institutions and public places, where entry, at least in theory, is open to all, is structured by this invisible line. The molecular structure of the village is ceaselessly reproduced in the very institutions and spaces of modern society. This tale is endlessly repeated in all Dalit autobiographies and accounts. This invisible line of separation is what Ambedkar too had experienced—even in interactions with his upper-caste subordinates— after he came back to India with a doctorate from Columbia University and became an official in the princely state of Baroda (whose maharaja had sponsored Ambedkar's study in the United States). This is what Om Prakash Valmiki experienced repeatedly in apparently secular public spaces such as the train in his interactions with copassengers.[22]

It is in this space—the space of the dislocated and transfigured paracheri— that Mayawati confronts the mutated, upper-caste, and "cultured" city dweller, with her "30-million rupee diamond studded necklace." It is in this space that young Nirmala sees her—from her own very real paracheri—and tells Amy Waldman that Mayawati gives her the confidence that anything can be done. For Mayawati to appear thus is an act of defiance—and an act of becoming Dalit. And Waldman is right in discerning that "in this imperial display of power," "Mayawati has touched something deep."

Scene 3: The Dalit Capitalism Party: Becoming Dalit and the Consumption Utopia

On 23 December 2005, a party was organized to celebrate capitalism— capitalism in general, but especially what the organizers called Dalit capitalism. The party was held in a modest apartment in the eastern part of Delhi, across the River Yamuna. The organizer and host of the party was Chandra Bhan Prasad, a young and charismatic Dalit intellectual and journalist who emerged, within the previous few years, as almost a cult figure, known for his extremely provocative and unconventional political positions. The two-page invitation letter for the party began by recognizing that the idea might appear quite "socially incorrect," as "Dalits and Capital are a contradiction in terms." Parenthetically, we may note that this is how the Left views it, and even left-wing intellectuals sympathetic to the Dalit cause see the two as antithetical entities. So the invitation letter proceeded to add: "Like a remorseless despot, history mauled and molded us into the grave world of the untouched, un-heard and unspoken." It continued: "Frozen into the time frame of history . . . we now desire to defrost ourselves, and dissolve into the emancipatory world of Capitalism." It is interesting to note the intertextuality of the imagery of "dissolving into the emancipatory world of Capitalism" and of "defrost[ing] ourselves" here. For it recalls, in a not-so-hidden way, the well-known passage in the *Communist Manifesto* where Marx and Engels celebrate the advent of capitalism as the new revolutionary force that builds a world in its own image and cannot live without constantly revolutionizing the forces of production: "All that is solid melts into air; all that is holy is profaned." Prasad, a former leftist, was familiar with Marxian texts and drew quite often from them in elaborating his argument.[23] Thus the invitation letter continued: "Options are not many. Feudalism ought to be defeated, socialism stands self-defeated; Capitalism, which triggers industrialization and urbanization, remains the hope."[24] "Feudalism" here stands for everything pre- or nonmodern, especially the institution of caste and the Hindu religion that sustains it. This point again appears very often in Prasad's writings. However, the letter went on to say, "Indian Capitalism, like Islam, Christianity and Marxism," has got overwhelmingly "Indianized." In Prasad's language this means simply one thing: all these great ideologies have become incorporated into or been reframed by caste and the manifold ways in which caste hierarchy continues to live in modern Indian society. Capitalism too has become Brahmanical in India. Hence the solution: "A few Dalits as billionaires, a few hundred as multi-millionaires and a few thousand as millionaires would democratize and de-Indianize Capitalism. A few dozen Dalits as market speculators, a few Dalit owned corporations traded on stock-exchanges, a few Dalits with private Jets, and a few of them with Golf caps, would make democratic Capitalism loveable." So the brave new world of capitalism's consumption utopia is at hand. The dream world of the commodity with all its spectacular forms beckons.

The element of rhetorical excess, deliberately meant to shock, should not be missed here. After all, the party was being held in honor of a gentleman called Dr. K. P. Singh, who was hardly the embodiment of the features that Prasad described. In that invitation, Dr. Singh was characterized as somebody who was born in the Aligarh District, who took his master's degree from Jawaharlal Nehru University and a doctorate from the University of Wisconsin, and who now taught at the University of Washington, Seattle. Clearly Singh was an intellectual rather than a capitalist. But Singh—or KPS, as the invitation referred to him—shared Prasad's Dalit capitalism agenda and was one of the important ideologues of this new agenda and the chief organizer of the Dalit International Conference in Vancouver in 2003. This conference was held in the wake of the landmark Bhopal conference, which, in a sense, conferred a much wider legitimacy to Prasad's agenda and supported it at the international level.

So, what *is* the agenda of Dalit capitalism? In a way the genesis of this idea is linked with the emergence of Chandra Bhan Prasad as one of the most significant critical voices within the Dalit movement.

The onset of the 1990s saw India rapidly dismantle the Nehruvian import-substituting industrialization model and fall in line with the neoliberal "Washington consensus." Partial trade liberalization, privatization, and deregulation within had already been under way through the 1980s. But only in 1991, when India went for a second IMF loan, did it undertake the whole series of measures that would lead to the eventual dismantling of the public-sector enterprises—including many that have been known to be quite profitable. Now, as it happens, the heroic fight Ambedkar put up during the nationalist struggle, to ensure what he called "safeguards" for Dalits, led to the adoption of a policy of reservations (that is, affirmative action), crucial to which was the reservation of 22.5% of all government jobs for Dalits and the adivasis, or the "tribal" people. With the state in retreat and the rapid dismantling of the public sector under way, the first response of the Dalit intelligentsia was to join the left-wing campaign "against globalization."[25] Most Dalit intellectuals, as I have indicated, share in some sort of a left-wing, Marxist understanding of the world, even though they are deeply suspicious of the existing Communist parties, which they see as blind to the problems of caste oppression at best and complicit with the exclusion of the Dalits at worst. Dalit intellectuals spent the initial years of the neoliberal regime in thus mobilizing for "defending the public sector" and "opposing globalization." This was clearly a lost battle from the very beginning, as it is patently clear that nowhere in the world has it been possible to keep up such an extent of governmental intervention in the economy under the new conditions.

This was the context in which Prasad began articulating a different position—and a different vision. His logic was twofold. First, if it is true that Dalits cannot really defend their gains by rolling back the attack on the public sector; so rather than waste their time and energy in doing so, they must stake a similar claim in the private sector. Why must the private capitalist/corporate sector be exempt from its responsibility as equal opportunity employers? Here Prasad turned to the experience of the United States and its diversity program, in which even private corporations have to take affirmative action with regard to people of color. As he put it: "Another pet-theme of Dalit movements is opposing globalization and indulging in US-bashing. To me, globalization is a global phenomenon. Instead of wasting resources, time and talent in trying to stop the unstoppable, Dalits should seek their share in it."[26] From this arose the demand for what is now called "reservations in the private sector" and whose moral force is largely accepted across the political spectrum. In the course of raising this demand and the massive resistance put up to it by the Indian corporate sector, the critique of "Indian capitalism" too began to be elaborated by Prasad and a now growing community of intellectuals sharing this position. And here comes the second aspect of Prasad's argument. It was not enough for Dalits to be always the proletarians in industries that others owned. They had to become owners of property. They had to share in industry, trade, and commerce. "Democratization of capital" was how Prasad put it in a newspaper column.[27]

In early April 1999, Prasad was offered a column in an English-language daily, *The Pioneer*, published in New Delhi, and with that he became the first Dalit columnist and journalist—at least in the world of English journalism.

By this time, he was already emerging as an important countervoice, challenging many of the old articles of faith both within the Dalit movement and among the secular and left-wing political forces in India. With the column, modestly named "Dalit Diary," Prasad's voice started emerging with a certain regularity in the public sphere. It also began gaining him new adherents as well as new enemies. His columns were translated into and published in other Indian languages, such as Telugu and Kannada. From this point on Prasad began to articulate his new vision and position in a more systematic way. Soon a leading Hindi daily, *Rashtriya Sahara*, invited him to run a column that eventually turned out to be hugely successful. Prasad reiterated his point, with equal vehemence, against those Dalits—mostly of leftist inclination—who felt he was misleading ordinary Dalits into the path of hedonism. And so he emphasized that "the desire for a good education, a good job, good houses, decent bank deposits, insurance etc are fundamental in everybody."[28] Prasad, in fact, positioned himself against those Dalit leaders who thought that conversion to Buddhism, à la Ambedkar, was the right way to emancipation. This, he asserted, is only a matter of a counterspirituality to Hinduism, but the most important questions facing the Dalits were social, economic, and political: "In any society, the most fundamental conflicts are for control over resources, over power and for the good life."[29]

It is in pursuit of these aims that Prasad posited, much to the chagrin of his detractors, the United States as the exemplar. There is an air of the utopian in his representation of contemporary American society, and it certainly overlooks the long decades of struggle against racism that have made the recognition of diversity a value. In fact, he borrowed the expression "democratization of capital" from a paper on one of the U.S. government Web sites.[30] His columns, therefore, continually drew comparisons between the Indian media establishment and the United States, between the Indian academy and the United States, and between Indian corporations and U.S. corporations. In what many might see as an aspect of his perverse sense, he deliberately celebrated corporations such as IBM and Microsoft and welcomed the advent of foreign capital in India. And yet, it would be wrong to read this as simply evidence of his perversity. The argument is simple. It is much easier for Dalits to negotiate with foreign capitalists, unshackled as they are from the ideology of caste, which is clearly not possible with their Indian counterparts. What Prasad does is to set American corporations and American civil society against their Indian counterparts and underline the uncomfortable fact that the starkest forms of exclusion and discrimination continue in India—except within the sphere of state institutions, where, largely due to Ambedkar's role in constitution making, some guarantees and safeguards exist. So when he asks "Could IBM have achieved its preeminent standing in the IT sector by compromising on 'merit' and competitiveness?" he is addressing the Indian industrialists who have been opposing the idea of reservations in the private sector by arguing that caste-based reservations compromise on "merit."

Intellectuals such as Anand Teltumbde, among many others, would still argue that globalization is an unmitigated disaster, especially for the Dalits and the poorest, and hence to be resisted in every possible way.[31] Some others, like Kancha Ilaiah, initially responded in much the same way.[32] Marking his disagreements with scholars such as Gail Omvedt and V. T. Rajshekhar, editor of the periodical *Dalit Voice*, Ilaiah had in fact underlined how potters, toddy tappers, and shrimp cultivators were being displaced from their jobs and that is why in Andhra Pradesh they were raising slogans like "Down with tooth-paste, up with neemstick" (neem branches are traditionally used for cleaning teeth), "Down with Coca Cola, up with coconut water," and so on.[33] This was in 1997. However, very soon things began changing; in fact, arguments like the ones Prasad made started gaining wide acceptance, and even intellectuals such as Ilaiah began modulating their position. Ilaiah still believed that eco-nomically, globalization would be disastrous for the Dalits but argued that "cultural globalization" was to be welcomed. "The recent globalization pro-cess has re-opened channels of cultural integration of the productive mass culture with the global culture," he argued. Whereas "for a Brahmin scholar, for example, western culture came through the negation of his own inward-looking culture," for a Dalit Bahujan who learns English and adopts Western culture, this presents no problem. "When Ambedkar went to New York for education, he did not have to make promises to his parents or relatives, of preserving his food culture like Gandhi did," he added.[34] Such shifts in posi-tion should be seen as a manifestation of a larger set of processes and rethink-ing within the movement at large, though Prasad remains, in a crucial sense, its harbinger and its most forthright advocate.

This new vision eventually found its fulfillment in the Bhopal conference held in January 2002 (Bhopal is the capital of the northern state of Madhya Pradesh). Hosted by the Congress government under the chief ministership of Digvijay Singh, this huge conference was held inside the Vidhan Sabha (state legislative assembly) Building and brought together a wide cross section of Dalit intellectuals and activists. Thus was born one of the most significant programmatic interventions within the Dalit movement in its post-Ambedkar phase. As the *Bhopal Document*—the concept paper of the conference—put it, the effort sought to liberate Dalit imagination from the grip of the "job-reservation" framework that had dominated the movement so far. It explicitly stated that the movement now sought land redistribution and the democrati-zation of capital.[35] In practical terms, this meant not simply a demand for "reservations in the private sector" but, more important, a need to give a push to Dalit businesses. As Prasad put it in the course of his speech at the confer-ence, the almost total exclusion of Dalits from various spaces such as the media and the academy underlined the need for the Dalits to have their own newspapers, for example. And this was impossible given the scale of invest-ment and advertisement revenues that the newspapers required, unless the community had its own entrepreneurs.

The fact that the Bhopal conference was attended by intellectuals and activists from almost all political currents in the Dalit movement and was endorsed
by them gave the new vision and the program spelled out in the *Bhopal Declaration* unprecedented legitimacy. This position, in its different variations, is
fast becoming the common sense among a cross section of leaders, spokespersons, and intellectuals. One might, for instance, consider the fact that in October 2005, leaders of the All India Confederation of SC/ST Organizations
and the Dalit Freedom Network, in the persons of Udit Raj, a fiery emerging
mass leader in northern India, Joseph De Souza, Indira Athawale, and Kancha
Ilaiah, deposed before the U.S. congressional Committee on International
Relations (Subcommittee on Global Human Rights) regarding the question of
reservations in the private corporate sector. In fact, the news of the depositions
reportedly brought forth a sharp criticism from the historian and analyst Ram-
chandra Guha, to which Udit Raj responded in print. If the burden of Guha's
criticism was that this was an unpatriotic act and that the matter could be
taken up in political forums within the country, Raj's rejoinder was not unexpected either. Raj underlined that it was never because of the goodwill of the
nation or the nationalists that the Dalits got any concessions. They had obtained a separate electorate thanks to the British prime minister Ramsay Mac-
donald in 1932 (which had to be replaced by reservations due to Gandhi's
obduracy). It was only "after millennia" that British rule gave Dalits reservations in politics and government services.

In another piece written around the same time, Raj went on to argue, almost in the same language as Prasad's, that thanks to the diversity program
followed in the United States, there were now "75 Black CEOs on major
US companies," where there were none not very long ago.[36] He then continued: "In the US Billionaire Club, a few Blacks have found a place. Oprah
Winfrey became America's first black female billionaire, according to Forbes
magazine. . . . TV programmes show increasing participation of Blacks in
sports, music films etc."[37] Raj rounds off his rejoinder to Guha by asserting
that "if anyone is unpatriotic, it is the casteists and the business houses who
are resisting reservations, and not the leaders who testified before the US
House Committee." He reiterated Ilaiah's argument: "People like Guha welcome economic globalization but not cultural globalization, which is essential to having a liberal approach towards Dalit problems." However, a close
reading of these positions makes it clear that the dividing line between the
economic and the cultural is very thin. Cultural globalization is intended to
open the way for Dalits' entry into different sectors of the economy and thus
lead to the creation of a Dalit bourgeoisie. It is, at one level, a way of staking a
claim in the capital and other productive resources of the economy; at another level, however, it is a way of moving beyond the "normal" terms in
which Dalits are represented—terms in which even radical/liberal, secular,
and upper-caste elite can deal: pain, oppression, poverty, and violence on the

one hand and anger and resistance on the other. Recall the invitation letter for the Dalit capitalism party: "A few dozen Dalits as market speculators, a few Dalit owned corporations traded on stock-exchanges, a few Dalits with private Jets, and a few of them with Golf caps, would make democratic Capitalism loveable."

Power, Resistance, and Subjectivity

If one follows the logic of these arguments carefully, one can see clear attempts to displace the problem of Dalit emancipation from the temporality of the utopian "not-yet" and focus it on the here and now. These attempts continue to draw from Marxism the insight that Dalit emancipation is to be located primarily in the material domain of power, of control over resources and institutions; yet they reject the idea that this can be done by the Dalits' merging their identity within some larger class identity and waiting for that collectivity to take power. On the contrary, the entire attempt is to bring the question back into the domain of the present and to address it as a specific question of the Dalits alone.

In a sense then, the emergence of this new agenda is the emergence of the Dalit—a becoming-Dalit, if one might play with an expression from Gilles Deleuze. At one level, the expression "becoming-Dalit" should be taken to refer to the fact that it represents a move away from the majority. This is true in at least two senses. First, it posits itself against a certain Marxist or more generally revolutionary imaginary that seeks liberation through some collective and imaginatively majority action. The formation of such a collective is usually predicated upon the subordination of the part to the whole, which also means the dissolution of the specificity of the identity in question. There was an important phase, symbolized, for instance, in the activities of the Dalit Panthers in Maharashtra in the early 1970s, when this imaginary was quite powerful. So, for example, the "Dalit Panthers Manifesto," issued in 1973, took its direct inspiration from a combination of the prevailing Maoist ethos and language and the Black Panther movement in the United States. Thus it stated: "Due to the hideous plot of American imperialism, the *Third Dalit World, that is the oppressed nations, and Dalit people* are suffering."[38] In exact correspondence with this amazingly elastic notion of the "Third Dalit World," it defined the Dalits thus: "Members of Scheduled Castes and Tribes, neo-Buddhists, the working people, the landless and poor peasants, women and all those who are being exploited politically, economically and in the name of religion."[39] In keeping with the spirit of the times, it asserted that "the struggle for the emancipation of the Dalits needs a complete revolution. Partial change is impossible." And if this was true of the Dalit Panther movement, it was equally true of Dalit intellectuals such as Chandra Bhan Prasad, Kancha

Ilaiah, and Udit Raj, all of whom shared an active leftist past. Once upon a time, they saw their liberation in this revolutionary imaginary of the collectivity of the "majority of the oppressed." And yet, despite this deep connection to the revolutionary imaginary, there was a pervading sense of not really being part of the Left. I suspect the same sense is captured to some extent, in a very different context, by Stuart Hall in the context of the formation of the New Left in Britain. In the words of David Morley and Kuan-Hsing Chen, "In Hall's account of this story, a key role in the formation of the New Left was played by various (then student) colonial intellectuals, who came from outside Britain, and who were connected to, but never part of the dominant institutions of the British Left."[40]

This failure to connect with the dominant institutions of the Indian Left did not lead, in the case of the Dalit movement, to some other kind of Left. It was really a short-lived moment in the Dalit movement of trying to affiliatively connect with the larger revolutionary Marxist Left project. Earlier, during the nationalist struggle, Ambedkar had steadfastly refused to see Dalits as a part of any larger collectivity, be it the nation or the proletariat in the abstract. He was clear that any such move would mean the dissolution of Dalit identity within that of the larger entity. In fact, he always thought of the Communists of his time as "a bunch of Brahmin boys," the implication being that there was really nothing at stake in their radicalism.[41]

This brings me to the second, more specifically Deleuzian, sense, where the majority is not necessarily a numerical majority but constitutes the norm and where the minor or minority, therefore, represents a move away from the dominant norm. Below the state, writes Deleuze, "are becomings that can't be controlled, minorities constantly coming to life and standing up to it."[42] Offering a temporal rendering of the idea of nomads, Deleuze explains that "if we have been so interested in nomads, *it's because they're a becoming and aren't part of history*; they're excluded from it but *they transmute and reappear in different, unexpected forms* in the lines of flight of some social field."[43] The idea of a minority for Deleuze is the emergence of something new — against the norm that is the majority. It also means going against assigned history in a certain sense.

Deleuze distinguishes between what he calls "becoming" and "history" by invoking Nietzsche, for whom "the way things happen," "the events themselves," are different from the way history grasps them. "What history grasps in an event is the way it is actualized in particular circumstances; the event's becoming is beyond the scope of history."[44] Thus, writes Deleuze, "history amounts only to the set of preconditions, however recent, that one leaves behind in order to 'become,' that is, *to create something new*."[45]

Foucault too elaborates this Nietzschean idea of the genealogy as that which seeks to "cultivate the details and accidents that accompany every beginning" and posits it as "the union of erudite knowledge and local memories which allows us to establish a historical knowledge of struggles and to make use of this knowledge tactically today."[46] Seen thus, "becoming" is a way in which "subjectivation" takes place—the subject emerges, leaping outside assigned history, calling forth local memories and forming new historical knowledges. Such becoming-Dalit has then to do with the emergence of a different self from the other earlier ones, embedded in some notion of a majority (nation, oppressed people, working class, and so on).

In this section, I suggest that there might be some deeper connections between this process of becoming Dalit and the emergence of what Jean Baudrillard calls consumer society. I suggest that this connection can be seen to exist at two levels.

The first level has to do more specifically with the historical conjuncture of 1990s India. This is a period of the rapid collapse of the Nehruvian, state-led import-substituting industrialization strategy. This strategy, as we know, relied on curtailing current consumption and using forced savings for purposes of capital formation. It also required the production of a citizen who felt a sense of responsibility toward the nation and was prepared to forgo or defer her current desires. The Nehruvian state, therefore, valorized the figure of the "producer-patriot."[47] Even though this was a state project, it should be understood as part of a wider intellectual-political frame that determined or modulated most other kinds of political articulations, by prioritizing the continuing tasks of anti-imperialism in the immediate aftermath of decolonization. At the level of political culture, this Zeitgeist, as it were, demanded the subordination of individual self-interest to the cause of the larger national good. The onset of the 1990s and the "retreat of the state" that followed the crisis of this model brought about a profound cultural transformation in the political and everyday sense.[48] At one level, this retreat meant the abandonment of the state-led project of self-reliance, and at another, it opened up international trade (dismantling the restrictions of the earlier era). The rapid integration of the Indian economy into the global, the entry of global food and entertainment chains, the availability, very soon, of all kinds of consumer goods—all these now went with the calling-into-being of a different figure—that of the consumer. Deferral of current desire for some distant national good was no longer exalted; what we saw instead was the desiring consumer being called forth by the state as well as private corporations and the advertisement industry to spur the growth of the economy by simply consuming. A different ethos was put in place.[49]

It is of some significance that the Nehruvian period, which was marked politically by the hegemony of secular-nationalist discourse, was facing another challenge at this juncture. It was being challenged by what I have called the insurrection of little selves—the different articulations of identity that had been relegated to the realm of the unspeakable in the heyday of secular nationalism. The continuing exclusions and oppressions of the past could no longer be articulated within its framework.[50] Among these was the emerging Dalit movement. Its coalescence alongside the crisis of the Nehruvian project, at a time when the defense of the public sector was no longer a feasible option, provides, as we have seen, one line of connection with the new consumption utopia toward which all citizens were now being hailed by the state and private capital alike. We have also seen, through our examination of the figure of Mayawati and the paracheri, how the lines of consumption connect with a specific mode of protest in the transfigured public spaces, endlessly structured by the continuing but invisible presence of the caste line.

Jean Baudrillard cites Dr. Ernest Dichter, director of the Institute for Motivational Research and presumably a strategist and theorist of the advertisement world, as saying that "one of the fundamental problems of prosperity is to sanction and to justify its enjoyment, to convince people that making their life enjoyable is moral, and not immoral."[51] Baudrillard sees this as the process whereby "advertising takes over the moral responsibility of all of society and replaces a puritan morality with a hedonistic morality of pure satisfaction."[52] Zygmunt Bauman describes this cultural transition thus: "If the savings book was the epitome of modern life, the credit card is the paradigm of the postmodern one."[53] It is into this world that the former citizens of Nehruvian India open out. For the Dalits, however, the problem of morality is irrelevant: consumption is already a terrain of contestation and struggle—and a terrain of performing the self.

At another level, the connection of becoming-Dalit to the consumption utopia is more fundamental if one were to go by Baudrillard's rendering of the "object/advertising system" as "a system of signification," *a code of social standing*. At this level, Baudrillard posits the code as leveling in a significant sense. He argues that "the code is a form of socialization, *the total secularization of the signs of recognition*: it is therefore involved in the—at least formal—emancipation of social relations. . . . The system of social standing, at least, has the advantage of *rendering obsolete the rituals of caste and class* and generally all preceding . . . criteria of social discrimination."[54] One might lament, writes Baudrillard, the passing away of many other systems and their supplanting by this universal code, but "in a world where millions of strangers cross each other daily in the streets, the code of 'social standing' fulfills an essential function, while it satisfies the vital need of people to be always informed about one another."[55] Far from celebrating consumerist desire as emancipatory in any way, Baudrillard actually mourns it, but his general point about the fact that this desire arises in the field of this new universal code of "secularization of the signs of recognition" is crucially relevant for our understanding of the ways in which becoming-Dalit connects with this consumption utopia. In Baudrillard's dismal world, "in an important sense, individuals are no longer citizens, eager to maximize their civil rights, nor proletarians, anticipating the onset of communism. They are rather consumers, and hence the prey of objects as defined by the code."[56] At this point our story departs from the path Baudrillard charted out, for in it the highly contested terrain of consumption becomes one more theater of fashioning the self. If the eventual dystopia of consumer society that Baudrillard subsequently takes us toward is in some sense the end of the road for him, one can say that in all probability this is not where our story ends.

Heterotopia II

We can now return to our first scene— the public rally in the La Martiniere College grounds, Lucknow, to celebrate Mayawati's birthday. As we return to that scene, let us remind ourselves of the third kind of heterotopia/heterochrony that Foucault talks about—"linked to time in its flowing, transitory, precarious aspect, to time in the mode of the festival."

The stage, we may recall, mimics the sets of *Mughal-e-Azam*. Apart from the 51- kilogram cake and 100,000 laddus, there are 60 quintals of marigold flowers and 5,000 bouquets decorating the venue. The occasion is certainly Mayawati's birthday, but it is being observed as *swabhiman divas* (self-respect day).[57] Arches are set up in different parts of the city, on the roads leading to the venue.[58] Songs and ballads are being performed by various groups of folk artists and balladeers. According to one of the reports, one of the balladeers sang, "Ek hi tamanna, apne hathon ab Lal Quile par jhanda phehrao" (We have only one wish, that you unfurl the flag at the Red Fort), and in the words of the report, this refrain "sums up the feelings of her supporters who want to see her on the centre-stage of national politics."[59] The second event, covered by the *New York Times* correspondent a few months later, also presented "an imperial show of power." Waldman, the correspondent, remarks that many Dalits who came to this imperial show of power "had the thin frames and fraying finery of the rural poor." "But for a day they owned Lucknow, once defined by the extravagance of the Muslim nawabs."[60] The city had shut down because of the rally: "there were blue flags (the party flag) and blue elephants (the party symbol) and blue graffiti warning 'anti-Dalits' not to tangle with Ms Mayawati, whose image was everywhere."[61] Waldman continues: "Rural Dalits marveled at the grand memorial she has built to Dr Ambedkar on 28 acres [of land] here." She quotes a former police chief, Sri Ram Arun, a Dalit himself, as saying, "These are the places where downtrodden people can come and say, 'this is our symbol.'"[62]

The space of a BSP rally is clearly a place of celebration, of festival, abounding in symbols. But more than that, it marks the invasion of public space by the people of the paracheri—those who have lived in confinement for centuries. And this aspect of "invasion" is as much present in a political rally organized by the BSP as it is in the huge public celebrations of Ambedkar's birthday—popularly known as Ambedkar Jayanti.[63] To get a sense of the significance of this immense semiotic transformation of the meaning of space, one need only look at the way this event has become another mode and theater of the fashioning of the self. Owen Lynch's studies of the Ambedkar Jayanti celebrations in Agra (a district of the state of Uttar Pradesh) over the years are revealing in this respect. Ambedkar Jayanti celebrations began in Agra in 1957, initiated mainly by some Jatav youth of a Dalit locality called the Kaji Para.[64] Initially it was "almost exclusively *of* and *for* Jatavs."[65] Increasingly other Dalit *jatis* started joining the celebrations. It was celebrated "as a day of rest, feasting, games, political speeches and other festivities, culminating in a seven-hour parade which marches from Kaji Para, past the Jama Masjid, through several upper caste localities and Hing ki Mandi market up to the Collectorate and back again." Sarah Beth compares this to the Chuharmal mela held in Dalit localities in certain parts of Bihar, where there was no participation of non-Dalit caste groups.[66] However, more than participation by others, what is relevant from our point of view is that it did not involve any transgression, held as it was within the locality. I have suggested earlier that in the modern era the paracheri became an invisible imaginative line of casteness that went everywhere the upper castes went and lived. It is in that context that we must see the Dalit parade entering upper-caste localities and practically taking over the streets for the entire day. So, Lynch writes, "the parade was bitterly contested and participation in it was often dangerous. . . . In reaction from the roofs of upper caste homes in those neighbourhoods, stones and insults were apt to be thrown at the statue [of Ambedkar]."[67] In this connection, Beth narrates the conflict around the event in 1978: On the night of 14 April (Ambedkar's birthday), the parade for the Ambedkar mela (fair) made its way through the streets of Agra, as it had done every year. However, when bricks and stones were thrown at the parade, the Jatavs retaliated, and in the ensuing violence, a house and several small shops were damaged. The next day the upper castes marched to the police station shouting slogans such as "Change the parade route," "Death to Ambedkar." In response, members of the Jatav community "staged a peaceful protest and again marched through the streets of the upper caste localities. . . . Again stones were thrown on the marchers and the police made a lathi charge to dispel the protest." The conflict continued until 3 May, when the army was called in to end the violence. Thereafter, the state and national governments stepped in, many imprisoned Jatav leaders were released, and April 14 was declared a public holiday in Uttar Pradesh.[68]

   Two kinds of spatial practices are registered here in these descriptions. One, there is the attempt to take over public spaces, like the area around the parliament and the India Gate in Delhi—the part studied by Sarah Beth in her study of the Ambedkar mela in Delhi. Here the congregation is at a central place where people from different parts of the city and neighboring states converge and transform the area into a veritable fairground. This is also the kind that marks the BSP rally. The other is that of the Ambedkar Jayanti procession that originates from the Kaji Para and moves into the localities and streets of the upper castes. Note that these are technically public spaces, and anybody should be able to enter them. In the normal, everyday flow of life, many Dalits do enter these spaces, as these are no longer possible to guard on the strength of the upper-caste population alone. Urban anonymity provides the individual Dalit the possibility of entering these spaces. Yet, the entrance of the Dalit parade, marked very clearly as a procession of Dalits, can create nothing short of a crisis for the upper-caste inhabitants of these localities.

I suspect that these spaces—marked by the flow of time in its transitory, precarious aspect, in the mode of the festival— are places of carnivalesque freedom. These heterotopias of the festival or the carnival, involving a moment of a semiotic transfiguration of space, occupy a place of significant importance in the antiutopian politics of the contemporary Dalit movement.

Notes

1. I thank my colleagues, participants at the Davis Center's weekly seminars, for their thoughtful comments and suggestions. My thanks also to Gyan Prakash, the director of the center in the winter semester of 2006, and Nivedita Menon, who commented at different stages of writing this chapter. The word "dalit'" in the chapter title, meaning simply "oppressed" or more literally "ground down," is the term of self-description adopted by the new political community of the "former" untouchable castes in India. I put the word "former" within quotes because the abolition of untouchability remains a purely legal fact (more correctly a legal fiction).

2. Yogesh Vajpeyi, "For the Oppressed, Covered in Diamonds—Govt Plays Host at Mayawati Birthday Bash," *Telegraph*, 16 January 2003, front page; emphasis added.

3. In May 2007 Mayawati returned to power as chief minister, following an unprecedented performance by the BSP in the elections.

4. Sharat Pradhan, "Mayawati Spends Crores to Fulfil Her Birthday Dream," 15 January 2003, http://search1.rediff.com/dirsrch/default.asp?src=web&MT=Mayawati%20spends%20crores (accessed 15 January 2010).

5. Ibid.

6. Amy Waldman, "An Opulent and Pugnacious Champion of India's Outcasts," *New York Times*, 4 May 2003; emphasis added.

7. Dipesh Chakrabarty, "Clothing the Political Man: A Reading of the Use of Khadi/White in Indian Public Life," *Postcolonial Studies* 4, no. 1 (2001): 27–38.

8. Cited ibid., 27–28.

9. Kancha Ilaiah, "Cultural Globalisation," *The Hindu*, 22 February 2003, http://www.thehindu.com/2003/02/22/stories/2003022200621000.htm (accessed 5 January 2010).

10. Anand Teltumbde (1997), "'Ambedkar' in and for the Post-Ambedkar Dalit Movement"; http://www.angelfire.com/ak/ambedkar/BRanand1.html (accessed 5 January 2010). Bhim is the shortened form of Ambedkar's name, Bhimrao.

11. Ibid.

12. Ibid. In fact Teltumbde then goes on to launch a scathing attack on these middle-class Dalit leaders, who, he writes, could only "project themselves as better clones of Ambedkar," who wore their shirts and trousers, were "suited and booted [a deliberately sarcastic and funny Indian way of referring to such a mimetic taste], had university degrees and could command better sophistry than Gaikwad." In this view, Gaikwad and his ilk could be only activists and not leaders, writes Teltumbde.

13. Vajpeyi, "For the Oppressed."

14. Pradhan, "Mayawati Spends Crores."

15. Mohandas Naimishray, *Awazein* (Delhi: Samata Prakashan, 1998), 105–10.

16. Mehtars are a caste of sweepers, and the Chamars are leather workers. However, the words "sweepers" and "leather workers" are deceptively benign. The Mehtars have been traditionally forced to carry night soil and do the most demeaning of jobs for the village, and the Chamars scavenge dead animals under filthy and degrading conditions.

17. The settlements are generally known by different names in different areas— often even within the same linguistic region. I have therefore chosen this term as a more general one.

18. Michel Foucault, "Of Other Spaces (1967), Heterotopias," 2, http://foucault. info/documents/heteroTopia/foucault.heteroTopia.en.html (accessed 15 March 2006). All references here are to this text.

19. For further details, see Edward W. Soja, *Thirdspace—Journeys to Los Angeles and Other Real-and-Imagined Places* (Cambridge, MA: Blackwell Publishing, 2004), 154.

20. Cited ibid., 99–100.

21. Foucault, "Of Other Spaces."

22. See Om Prakash Valmiki's autobiography, *Joothan: A Dalit's Life*, trans. Arun Prabha Mukherjee (Calcutta: Samya, 2003).

23. See, for instance, Chandra Bhan Prasad, *Dalit Diary, 1999–2003: Reflections on Apartheid in India* (Chennai: Navayana Publishing, 2004) (henceforth, *Dalit Diary*), 11, where he cites the following from the *Communist Manifesto*: "The bourgeoisie, wherever it has got the upper hand, has put an end to all feudal, patriarchal, idyllic relations."

24. All the citations are from the two-page invitation for the party issued by Chandra Bhan Prasad.

25. In public discourse "globalization" functions as a stand-in for a whole range of negative features such as privatization, trade liberalization, and opening up for foreign capital.

26. *Dalit Diary*, xix.

27. Ibid., 104–6.

28. Chandra Bhan Prasad, *Sahara Salah—Samasyaein Daliton ki, Bhag-1* (Delhi: Dalit Multimedia Network, 2004), 8.

29. Ibid.

30. See *Dalit Diary*, 105.

31. See, for instance, Anand Teltumbde, "Globalization and the Dalits," http:// www.ambedkar.org/research/GLOBALISATIONANDTHEDALITS.pdf (accessed 5 January 2010).

32. "The State of Dalit Mobilization: An Interview with Kancha Ilaiah," *Ghadar* 1, no. 2, (26 November 1997), http://www.proxsa.org/resources/ghadar/v1n2/ilaiah.html (accessed 5 January 2010).

33. Ibid.

34. Ilaiah, "Cultural Globalisation."

35. See the *Bhopal Document*, Government of Madhya Pradesh, 2002. Also see Aditya Nigam, "In Search of a Bourgeoisie: Dalit Politics Enters a New Phase," *Economic and Political Weekly*, 30 March 2002.

36. Udit Raj, "United States Asked to Uplift Dalits" (2005), http://www.nepaldalit info.20m.com/news/USAsked.htm (accessed 15 March 2006).

37. Ibid.

38. See "Dalit Panthers Manifesto, Bombay 1973," in *Untouchable! Voices of the Dalit Liberation Movement*, ed. Barbara Joshi (London: Zed Books and Minority Rights Group, 1986), 145; emphasis added.

39. Ibid.

40. David Morley and Kuan-Hsing Chen, eds., introduction to *Stuart Hall: Critical Dialogues in Cultural Studies* (London: Routledge, 2005), 11.

41. Ambedkar used this expression for the Communists of Bombay in an interview given to Selig Harrison, cited in Eleanor Zelliot's *From Untouchable to Dalit: Essays on the Ambedkar Movement* (New Delhi: Manohar, 1996), 142.

42. Gilles Deleuze, *Negotiations* (New York: Columbia University Press, 1995), 152.

43. Ibid., 153; emphasis added.

44. Ibid., 170.

45. Ibid., 171; emphasis added.

46. Michel Foucault, "A Lecture (1976)," in *Art in Theory, 1900–2000: An Anthology of Changing Ideas*, ed. Charles Harrison and Paul Wood (Malden, MA: Blackwell Publishing, 2003), 991.

47. Satish Deshpande, *Contemporary India: A Sociological View* (New Delhi: Viking, 2003). See especially the chapter "Nation as Imagined Economy," 63, 69–71.

48. I have elaborated this argument at length elsewhere and am paraphrasing and summarizing it here. For a more detailed statement, see Aditya Nigam, "Imagining the Global Nation: Time and Hegemony," *Economic and Political Weekly* 39, no. 1 (3–9 January 2004).

49. The expressions "called-into-being," or "calling forth," should be read here as constituting what Louis Althusser termed "interpellation" (which I see as a way of becoming-subject), where it is not simply the "hailing" by the policeman (or the figure of the state) that is important but equally the moment of self-recognition by the individual.

50. For a detailed elaboration of this argument, see Aditya Nigam, *The Insurrection of Little Selves: The Crisis of Secular-Nationalism in India* (Delhi: Oxford University Press, 2006).

51. Jean Baudrillard, *Selected Writings*, ed. Mark Poster (Stanford: Stanford University Press, 2001), 15–16.

52. Ibid., 16.

53. Zygmunt Bauman, *Life in Fragments: Essays in Postmodern Morality* (Oxford: Blackwell, 1995), 5.

54. Baudrillard, *Selected Writings*, 22–23; emphasis added.

55. Ibid., 23.

56. Poster, introduction to Baudrillard's *Selected Writings*, 7.

57. Pradhan, "Mayawati Spends Crores."

58. Vajpeyi, "For the Oppressed."

59. Ibid.

60. Waldman, "Opulent and Pugnacious Champion."

61. Ibid.

62. Ibid.

63. For a study of Ambedkar Jayanti celebrations, see Sarah Beth, "Taking to the Streets: Dalit *Mela* and the Public Performance of Dalit Cultural Identity," *Contemporary South Asia* 14, no. 4 (December 2005): 397–410.

64. Jatavs are one of the many caste groups (*jatis*) that constitute the Dalits. All references to Lynch's study are cited in Beth, "Taking to the Streets."

65. Ibid., 4.

66. Ibid.

67. Ibid., 6. I am not sure, though, that the stones were hurled at Ambedkar's statues alone and not on the processionists.

68. Ibid., 6–7.

Contributors

Michael D. Gordin is Professor of History at Princeton University, with an emphasis on the history of science and Russian history. He is the author of *A Well-Ordered Thing: Dmitrii Mendeleev and the Shadow of the Periodic Table* (2004), *Five Days in August: How World War II Became a Nuclear War* (2007), and *Red Cloud at Dawn: Truman, Stalin, and the End of the Atomic Monopoly* (2009). He is currently working on two book projects: a history of "scientific languages" and a history of the modern category of "pseudoscience" in postwar America.

Gyan Prakash is Dayton-Stockton Professor of History at Princeton and served as the director of Shelby Cullom Davis Center for Historical Studies during 2003–2008. He is the author of *Bonded Histories: Genealogies of Labor Servitude in Colonial India* (1990) and *Another Reason: Science and the Imagination of Modern India* (1999). He has also edited several volumes of essays, including *After Colonialism: Imperial Histories and Postcolonial Displacements* (1995). His current research interest centers on urban history, and his book *Mumbai Fables* will be published in 2010.

Helen Tilley teaches in the Department of History, Classics and Archaeology, Birkbeck College, University of London, and is the author of *Africa as a Living Laboratory: Empire, Development, and the Problem of Scientific Knowledge* (forthcoming). She has also written articles and chapters on the history of ecology, eugenics, agriculture, and epidemiology in tropical Africa and is co-editor of *Ordering Africa: Anthropology, European Imperialism and the Politics of Knowledge* (2007). Her current project explores the interplay between law and medicine during the era of decolonization in sub-Saharan Africa (circa 1940 to 1980).

Dipesh Chakrabarty is the Lawrence A. Kimpton Distinguished Service Professor in History at the University of Chicago. He is a founding member of the editorial collective of *Subaltern Studies*, a co-editor of *Critical Inquiry*, a founding editor of *Postcolonial Studies*, and a contributing editor to *Public Culture*. His publications include *Rethinking Working-Class History: Bengal, 1890–1940* (1989); *Provincializing Europe: Postcolonial Thought and Historical Difference* (2000); and *Habitations of Modernity: Essays in the Wake of Subaltern Studies* (2000). Currently, he is completing *Presentism and the Predicament of Postcolonial History* and *The Climate of History: Four Theses*.

278 CONTRIBUTORS

Igal Halfin is Professor of History at Tel Aviv University and was appointed as Fellow of the Shelby Cullom Davis Center for Historical Studies, Princeton University, during 2005–2006. He is the author of *From Darkness to Light: Class, Consciousness, and Salvation in Revolutionary Russia* (2000); *Language and Revolution: The Making of Modern Political Identities* (2002); *Terror in My Soul: Communist Autobiographies on Trial* (2003); *Intimate Enemies: Demonizing the Bolshevik Opposition, 1918–1928* (2007); and *Stalinist Confessions: Messianism and Terror at the Leningrad Communist University* (2009).

Fredric Jameson is William A. Lane Professor of Comparative Literature and Romance Studies, Duke University, and has previously taught at Harvard, Yale, and the University of California. He has authored more than nineteen books, including *Marxism and Form* (1971); *The Prison-House of Language* (1972); and *Postmodernism, or The Cultural Logic of Late Capitalism* (1990). His recent publications include *Valences of the Dialectic* (2008), *Capital in Its Time and Space* (2008), *The Modernist Papers* (2007), and *Archaelogies of the Future* (2005).

John Krige is Kranzberg Professor and Director of Graduate Studies in the School of History, Technology, and Society of the Georgia Institute of Technology. During 2006–2007, he was appointed as Fellow of the Shelby Cullom Davis Center for Historical Studies, Princeton University. He is a historian of science and technology, specializing in the postwar reconstruction of Europe. He is the author of *Science, Revolution, and Discontinuity* (1978) and was a member of a multinational team that wrote a three-volume history of CERN (the European Organization for Nuclear Research), and the leader of the project that produced a two-volume history of the European Space Agency. His latest book is *American Hegemony and the Postwar Reconstruction of Science in Europe* (2006).

Timothy Mitchell is Professor in the Department of Middle East Languages and Cultures, Columbia University, and previously taught at New York University. He is the author of *Colonising Egypt* (1991) and *Rule of Experts: Egypt, Techno-Politics, Modernity* (2002). His current research brings together the fields of science and technology studies and postcolonial theory in a project on carbon democracy, which examines the history of fossil fuels and the possibilities for democratic politics that were expanded or closed down in the construction of modern energy networks.

Aditya Nigam is Fellow at the Centre for the Study of Developing Societies, Delhi, and was a Fellow at the Shelby Cullom Davis Center for Historical Studies, Princeton University, in 2006–2007. He is the author of *The Insurrection of Little Selves: Crisis of Secular-Nationalism in India* (2006) and the coauthor of *Power and Contestation: India since 1989* (2007). His forthcoming *After Utopia: Modernity and Socialism in the Postcolony* is in press. He is a political scientist by training, and his current research focuses on the contemporary experience of capitalism and globalization in the postcolonial context.

David Pinder is Reader in the Department of Geography, Queen Mary College, University of London, and was a Fellow at the Shelby Cullom Davis Center for Historical Studies, Princeton University, during the autumn of 2006. His research interests lie in developing critical understandings of modern cities and the ways in which their geographies are imagined, lived, and contested. He is the author of *Visions of the City: Utopianism, Power and Politics in Twentieth-Century Urbanism* (2005) and the co-editor of *Cultural Geography in Practice* (2003).

Marci Shore is Assistant Professor of History, Yale University, where she teaches European cultural and intellectual history. She is the author of *Caviar and Ashes: A Warsaw Generation's Life and Death in Marxism, 1918–1968* (2006) and the translator of Michal Glowinski's Holocaust memoir *The Black Seasons* (2005). Currently she is at work on two studies: "The Self Laid Bare," an examination of the central European encounters occasioned by phenomenology and structuralism in the first decades of the twentieth century, and "The Taste of Ashes," an account of eastern Europe's grappling with its memories of totalitarianism at that century's end.

Jennifer Wenzel is Associate Professor of English, University of Michigan, and was a Fellow at the Shelby Cullom Davis Center for Historical Studies, Princeton University, in 2006–2007. She is the author of *Bulletproof: Afterlives of Anticolonial Prophecy in South Africa and Beyond* (2009) and a number of scholarly articles. Her research interests lie in African and South Asian literatures in English, literatures of Third World liberation, and postcolonial theory.

Luise White is Professor of History at the University of Florida, Gainesville, and was Fellow at the Shelby Cullom Davis Center for Historical Studies, Princeton University, in 2006–2007. She is the author of *The Comforts of Home: Prostitution in Colonial Nairobi* (1990), *Speaking with Vampires: Rumor and History in Colonial Africa* (2000), and *The Assassination of Herbert Chitepo: Texts and Politics in Zimbabwe* (2003). She is the co-editor of *African Words, African Voices: Critical Practices in Oral History* (2001) and *The State of Sovereignty: Territories, Laws, Populations* (2008). Her current project is twofold, a book on the history of Zimbabwe's war of liberation and another on Rhodesia's renegade independence.

Index

Abraham, Itty, 175n88
Acheson, Dean, 113–14n44
advertising, and moral responsibility, 270
aestheticism, 38
Afflicted Powers (Boal et al.), 138
Afrikaners, 98
alienation, 37; "culture critiques" of, 36
All India Confederation of SC/ST Organizations, 266
All That Is Solid Melts into Air (Berman), 206–7
Althusser, Louis, 275n49
Ama-Xhosa: Life and Customs (J. Soga), 57–58
Ambedkar, B. R., 253, 255, 261, 263, 265, 268, 274n12; celebrations of his birthday (Ambed-kar Jayanti), 271–72, 276n67; as a represen-tative of modernity, 254; spatial practices within the Ambedkar Jayanti, 272–73
ambiguity, 35, 36, 39
American Red Cross, 72n87
anarchism, 24, 27, 250
Anderson, Benedict, 108
Anderson, Warwick, 101
Anglo-American Petroleum Agreement, 130
Anglo-Iranian Oil Company, 133
Angola, 102, 107
anima, 6–9, 13–14, 16n16
Annan, Kofi, 169
Apollinaire, Guillaume, 187, 188
Aragon, Louis, 190
Aramco, 144n54; efforts of to suppress labor organizing in Saudi Arabia, 128
Archaeologies of the Future (Jameson), 23, 25
architecture, 205, 209; open architecture, 11; "postmodern," 225n26; postwar, 228
Arendt, Hannah, 37
Argonne National Laboratory, 159
Aristotle, 37
artifice, 9–12, 13–14, 62, 64; of human consciousness, 10; utopian artifice, 11, 12
Ashworth, Adam, 72n88
Aspanfut (association of "Panfuturists"), 188
Astor, David, 113n35
Athawale, Indira, 266

atom, the: attempts to detach meaning of from military usage only, 157–58; promotion of the peaceful atom, 161, 162, 167, 168–69; utopian potential of, 152, 169n6
atomic energy, 10; and the education of desire, 152–53, 154, 158, 162, 168. *See also* atomic energy, Geneva conference con-cerning the peaceful uses of
atomic energy, Geneva conference concern-ing the peaceful uses of, 151–52, 155–56; political motivations of the U.S. reactor display, 158; technical information pro-vided by the United States concerning its reactor display, 158–59; U.S. exhibition of swimming pool-type research reactor at, 156–57, 163–64, 168;
Atomic Energy Commission (AEC), 154, 156, 167–68; bilateral agreements of, 164–66; educational programs of, 159–60; library of, 158–59; responsibilities of, 155
Atomic Energy Research Establishment (Great Britain), 166
atomic radiation: Cerenkov radiation, 157, 172n36; hazards of, 157
Atoms for Peace, 152–53, 154, 168–69; association of with imperialism, 161; and the distribution and control of atomic tech-nology, 162–67; Eisenhower's moti-vations in proposing, 155; Eisenhower's proposal for, 154–55; as an exercise in "consensual hegemony," 161–62, 173–74n67; promise and promotion of, 154–62; as a "psychological warfare" propaganda program, 160–61; traveling exhibits concerning, 161
Attali, Jacques, 24
Attwell, David, 72n94
Augustine, 39
Australia, 101
automobiles, 207; and city planning, 215; and oil consumption, 125; threatening of streets by, 216
avant-garde, European, 11, 176–77; interna-tionalism of, 184–88, 191; Polish futurists, 186. *See also* Dada/Dadaism